W9-CHI-747

THE CULTURAL LIMITS OF REVOLUTIONARY POLITICS

CHANGE AND CONTINUITY IN SOCIALIST CZECHOSLOVAKIA

DAVID W. PAUL

EAST EUROPEAN QUARTERLY, BOULDER
DISTRIBUTED BY COLUMBIA UNIVERSITY PRESS
NEW YORK

1979

EAST EUROPEAN MONOGRAPHS, NO. XLVIII

David W. Paul is Assistant Professor of Political Science
at the University of Washington

EAST EUROPEAN MONOGRAPHS

The *East European Monographs* comprise scholarly books on the history and civilization of Eastern Europe. They are published by the *East European Quarterly* in the belief that these studies contribute substantially to the knowledge of the area and serve to stimulate scholarship and research.

20. *Hungary between Wilson and Lenin: The Hungarian Revolution of 1918–1919 and the Big Three.* By Peter Pastor. 1976.

21. *The Crises of France's East-Central European Diplomacy, 1933–1938.* By Anthony J. Komjathy. 1976.

22. *Polish Politics and National Reform, 1775–1788.* By Daniel Stone. 1976.

23. *The Habsburg Empire in World War I.* Robert A. Kann, Bela K. Kiraly, and Paula S. Fichtner, eds. 1977.

24. *The Slovenes and Yugoslavism, 1890–1914.* By Carole Rogel. 1977.

25. *German-Hungarian Relations and the Swabian Problem.* By Thomas Spira. 1977.

26. *The Metamorphosis of a Social Class in Hungary During the Reign of Young Franz Joseph.* By Peter I. Hidas. 1977.

27. *Tax Reform in Eighteenth Century Lombardy.* By Daniel M. Klang. 1977.

28. *Tradition versus Revolution: Russia and the Balkans in 1917.* By Robert H. Johnston. 1977.

29. *Winter into Spring: The Czechoslovak Press and the Reform Movement 1963–1968.* By Frank L. Kaplan. 1977.

30. *The Catholic Church and the Soviet Government, 1939–1949.* By Dennis J. Dunn. 1977.

31. *The Hungarian Labor Service System, 1939–1945.* By Randolph L. Braham. 1977.

32. *Consciousness and History: Nationalist Critics of Greek Society 1897–1914.* By Gerasimos Augustinos. 1977.

33. *Emigration in Polish Social and Political Thought, 1870–1914.* By Benjamin P. Murdzek. 1977.

34. *Serbian Poetry and Milutin Bojic.* By Mihailo Dordevic. 1977.

35. *The Baranya Dispute: Diplomacy in the Vortex of Ideologies, 1918–1921.* By Leslie C. Tihany. 1978.

36. *The United States in Prague, 1945–1948.* By Walter Ullmann. 1978.

37. *Rush to the Alps: The Evolution of Vacationing in Switzerland.* By Paul P. Bernard. 1978.

38. *Transportation in Eastern Europe: Empirical Findings.* By Bogdan Mieczkowski. 1978.

39. *The Polish Underground State: A Guide to the Underground, 1939–1945.* By Stefan Korbonski. 1978.

40. *The Hungarian Revolution of 1956 in Retrospect.* Edited by Bela K. Kiraly and Paul Jonas. 1978.

41. *Boleslaw Limanowski (1835–1935): A Study in Socialism and Nationalism.* By Kazimiera Janina Cottam. 1978.

42. *The Lingering Shadow of Nazism: The Austrian Independent Party Movement Since 1945.* By Max E. Riedlsperger. 1978.

43. *The Catholic Church, Dissent and Nationality in Soviet Lithuania.* By V. Stanley Vardys. 1978.

44. *The Development of Parliamentary Government in Serbia.* By Alex N. Dragnich. 1978.

45. *Divide and Conquer: German Efforts to Conclude a Separate Peace, 1914–1918.* By L. L. Farrar, Jr. 1978.
46. *The Prague Slav Congress of 1848.* By Lawrence D. Orton. 1978.
47. *The Nobility and the Making of the Hussite Revolution.* By John M. Klassen. 1978.
48. *The Cultural Limits of Revolutionary Politics: Change and Continuity in Socialist Czechoslovakia.* By David W. Paul. 1979.

Contents

Author's Preface

When I was a graduate student, I was advised to choose my dissertation topic carefully because it would be with me for a long time even after the dissertation itself was finished. This has proved to be correct; the present book is the result of five years' sporadic efforts and countless revisions since that moment when I defended my doctoral dissertation. In many respects the book hardly resembles that earlier product from which it developed, but the germ of the idea running through it has been fairly consistent. Though the project has not been without its share of frustrations, I have never regretted the choice of topic that I made so long ago; and while one inevitably feels great relief at finishing a long-term project, one also feels the kind of ambivalent joy that attends a farewell party for an old friend who is moving away to assume a better job.

Many people have contributed to the development of the ideas in this book. To all of them I owe my deepest gratitude, but I first wish to acknowledge the patience and encouragement of those who advised me in the early stages of my work, at a time when my own ideas were vague and not well formulated. These include Robert C. Tucker, Cyril E. Black, Stephen F. Cohen, and Zdeněk David. Special thanks are due also to the following people who have read the manuscript for this book, in whole or in part, at one or another stage of completion, and offered their candid advice: H. Gordon Skilling, Vladimír V. Kusín, Archie H. Brown, John S. Reshetar, Jr., Jan F. Triska, Peter A. Toma, Peter F. Sugar, W. Lance Bennett, Richard E. Flathman, and Daniel S. Lev.

Others from whom I have gained valuable insights include Paul R. Brass, A. J. Liehm, Wolf Oschlies, Vilém Prečan, and Yeshayahu Jelínek. I am grateful to William Zimmerman and David D. Finley for permission to cite unpublished works referred to in Chapter Four. Typing and various forms of technical assistance were cheerfully provided by Mary Ingram, Gail Wells, Mary Pierce, LaVerna Cole, Marge Gustafson, and Barbara O'Halloran. Mrs. Margery D. Lang contributed to the editing of the penultimate manuscript draft and also offered some much-appreciated moral support. I am thankful to David E. Albright and Sandra Borycki for having facilitated communication about the manuscript while I was out of the country.

I also wish to express my appreciation for financial support from the following institutions: the Graduate School Research Fund and the Institute for Comparative and Foreign Area Studies (both of the University of Washington), Princeton University, the American Council of Learned Societies, and the National Science Foundation.

Finally, I wish to acknowledge the stimulation provided by my students, on whom I tested some of the ideas that have gone into this book, and the immeasurable support of my wife Nancy, who not only read the final manuscript draft with a critical eye but, even more important, offered much-needed comfort and encouragement through numerous twists and turns in the history of the manuscript.

It is customary for the author to assume sole responsibility for errors and shortcomings in his work. With so much good advice from so many wise people, I might be tempted to eschew such a statement were it not for the fact that I did not in every instance follow the advice I was given. Therefore, any mistakes of fact or judgment must, alas, be considered my responsibility entirely.

Introduction: Theory and Purpose

Revolutionary societies often *seem* to be changing more than they actually are. Old systems of rule can be abandoned and replaced by new ones. Economic structures can be reorganized, and even the nature of class relations can be transformed. Still, under the surface of these outward changes — important though they are — there generally are limits to the scope of possible change. Not everything can be changed; at least, not everything can be changed quickly. And perhaps some things can be changed for the moment but not permanently. Within every society there are underlying forces working to resist, retard, or condition the process of change. It may therefore appear that an entire society is caught up in the sweep of a revolution, but in fact the appearance of total change may be covering over resistant forces that are dormant rather than dead. Later, when the fury of the revolutionary moment has subsided, these forces then rise up and assert their influence on social and political development. These forces may be as tangible as former rulers or déclassé social groupings, but they may also be very intangible. It is on such intangible social forces that this study attempts to focus, specifically those deriving from Czechoslovakia's political culture.

The central argument presented here and throughout can be stated rather simply. The success of the Communist revolution in Czechoslovakia has been severely limited by the resistance of factors that are firmly embedded in the political culture. Of course, it cannot be denied that there has been very significant change. The old system of rule was discarded and replaced by a system with totalitarian pretensions. The economy was reorganized, brought under the aegis of central command planning institutions, restructured to pursue the Stalinist demand for heavy industry at the cost of all other goods, and integrated within the new socialist international system of trade. Peasants were herded onto collective farms against their will, and factory workers — the nominal source of political authority — were subjected to vigorous re-education programs aimed at grooming them for a leadership role which they still have yet to be given. Many other aspects of life, from educational curricula to leisure-time activities, were indeed transformed, some of them irreversibly. Others, however, were changed only temporarily or superficially, and in moments when the Communists have relaxed their control over society — such as in 1968 — the old patterns have come percolating to the surface.

Communist ruling groups have consistently articulated the goals toward which they wish to lead their societies — goals first outlined by Marx and Engels and later refined by Lenin, Stalin, Mao, and others. Setting goals and achieving them are, of course, two separate things. When the means of attaining social goals necessarily include fundamental upheavals of traditional norms, the purposes of the ruling group present a challenge that is difficult indeed. Ruling Communist parties have always been aware that they faced strenuous opposition from bourgeois and other nonproletarian forces; such is the nature of reality as hypothesized in Lenin's view of the dictatorship of the proletariat.[1] However, Communist rulers have often underestimated and misinterpreted the resilience of traditional impulses even among the working class. Overcoming these impulses and instilling a total acceptance of the new order on the part of the citizenry are crucial to the success of the revolution. If the pull of traditional forces remains strong at the base of society — that is, among the working masses — then the revolutionary changes promulgated within the macrosocial structure are not accurate measures of society's revolutionary development.

Many of the important political changes in Eastern Europe following Stalin's death caught Western political scientists without an adequate explanation. This was true of the Polish and Hungarian revolts, the assertion of a vigorous diplomatic initiative by Romania's leaders, and the reforms in Czechoslovakia. Under the influence of the totalitarian model of analysis, the scholars of the fifties and early sixties were temporarily distracted from the factors that stimulated and conditioned the course of destalinization — factors such as variations in social structures, levels of economic development, and patterns of national and local history. Instead, the scholars of the totalitarianism school focused on the outer, immediate political realities that developed as the product of the regimes' attempts to obliterate the national cultures in favor of a supposedly international class-oriented culture.

One cannot justifiably fault these earlier scholars. We are, in fact, deeply indebted to them for their pioneering work in informing us of the nature of the Stalinist system.[2] Moreover, it is not this author's contention that political science must be precise to the point of predicting specific events; if we cannot expect seismologists to give us the date of the next San Francisco earthquake, we cannot expect ourselves to predict human behavior — certainly a phenomenon of greater capriciousness than geological forces — with perfect accuracy. On the other hand, it does not seem unreasonable to suggest that some of the post-Stalin changes might have been foreseen, or at least more easily retrodicted, given a theoretical framework that allowed room for the impact of cultural and historical factors upon the politics of East European communism.

The proposition that intangible forces derived from the national culture exert a special impact upon political development is, of course, not at all new. In various forms the idea has appeared in classical treatments of political theory and history; Tocqueville's *Democracy in America* is an example. It is only since the mid-1950s, however, that systematic references to cultural aspects of politics have been developed. The seminal work of Almond, Verba, and Pye on noncommunist political cultures has by the force of its argument captured the attention of scholars in the field of Communist studies.[3] Communist societies are logical objects of political culture studies, for the problem of understanding the nature of the revolutionary task leads us directly to the party's role as a culture-transforming agent.[4]

Interestingly, the earliest use of the term "political culture" in western writing appeared in Beatrice and Sidney Webb's *Soviet Communism*. The Webbs used the term to refer to information and education related to politics, disseminated through schools and the mass media. The Communist party, as the Webbs explained, felt critically responsible for expounding to the masses the meaning of official policies and programs, as well as instructing them in the proper attitudes toward political activity.[5] This reference to political culture was not far removed from the meaning of the term as it appears in later literature, although the Webbs used it in a more restricted sense.

This brings us to the question of what political culture is and why it is important. Defining the term is not without its difficulties, and the application of the concept to empirical study is still more complicated.

The Theory

Political culture refers to the configuration of values, symbols, and attitudinal and behavioral patterns underlying the politics of a society. This complex of factors can, for the moment, be conceived as a set of intervening variables influencing the behavior of individuals or groups between the time of a political stimulus and the actual response to that stimulus.[6] On the level of the individual, the psycho-social response pattern can be described in the following terms. Whenever a political event occurs or a political fact is revealed, the individual must first interpret that event or fact through his own psychological processes in order to understand it in his own terms, evaluate its significance, and weigh alternative responses to it. Obviously, these processes are most often unconscious and frequently consummated within a very short span of time, but they nonetheless represent a crucial step in the formation of behavior patterns.[7]

Paramount to the mediatory process influencing behavior as a response to outside stimuli is the phenomenon known as apperception, or the interpretation of reality in relation to past experience.[8] Apperception involves the integration of one's previous knowledge and experience into one's understanding of present reality. It is precisely at this point that culture affects behavior, for previous knowledge and experience are directly related to culture. What one knows and experiences are part of one's culture, and the particular way in which one interprets present-day reality is derived in large part from one's cultural environment. Apperception, then, is the process by which an individual translates the knowledge and impulses he derives from his culture into an orientation toward contemporary reality. It is *because of his culture* that he perceives a stimulus as significant or insignificant, and it is at least partly because of his culture that he then chooses (or is driven) to respond in a given way.

As an illustration, consider the case of a man who meets a close friend, also a man, on the street. Both men are likely to be happy at meeting each other; they will exchange a greeting and perhaps some trivial pleasantries, and then proceed on to other things, separately or together. From a cultural standpoint, the manner in which they greet each other is most interesting. If the men are from a Mediterranean culture — Italian or South Slavic, for example — they are likely to express their joy at seeing each other very openly and uninhibitedly, embracing and kissing each other on the cheeks. They do this because they have perceived the initial stimulus (meeting on the street) as a happy and significant event, and they are accustomed by the practices of their culture to responding to such situations with unrestrained emotion.

If the men are Americans or Englishmen, on the other hand, they will exhibit considerably more self-restraint under the same conditions. Their culture does not prescribe the kissing of cheeks; in fact, it rather discourages such a practice because of associations with homosexuality. The men perceive the stimulus as a happy and significant event, as did their counterparts from the Mediterranean culture, but they express their happiness in a far more subdued way, perhaps by smiling and shaking hands heartily while exchanging their verbal pleasantries. A greater display of emotion, such as cheek-kissing and embracing, is immediately excluded as a possible response, because the men have learned from their culture that they are to exhibit their feelings toward each other in a restrained manner.

Thus cultural patterns condition behavioral responses to stimuli, and different cultural patterns will tend to evoke different kinds of response to the same stimulus. So too, it is hypothesized, with regard to behavior that comes as a response to *political* stimuli. Voting habits, patterns of ideological alignment, and many other political activities are influenced by cultural factors inbred into the consciousness of a society's citizens and transmitted from generation to generation through the processes of political socialization. The failure of radical movements to attract nationally significant followings in the United States, for example, can be only partly explained by the extent of economic affluence, for radical movements had only a limited success during the Great Depression, a time when economic conditions seemed conducive to leftwing tendencies. It is simply the case that left-wing movements have failed to appear politically acceptable to the bulk of the American public. The latter prefer parties and candidates who stay within an ideological spectrum that is quite narrow in comparison to that of, say, France or Italy, and rather conservative in comparison to that of Denmark or Sweden.

To return to the individual once more, let us make a further point regarding culture as a source of the mediatory processes referred to above. Rather than an intervening variable, culture might better be understood as a *supervenient* variable, something that exists in the individual's social environment and acts upon the psychological process generating a specific impulse to behave in a particular way.[9] Culture comprises objects, ideas, beliefs, and customs with which the individual is familiar because they exist around him. His values are most likely drawn from those inherent in his culture. When he acts within a given social situation, he generally refers back to his culture for guidelines on what to do and how to think — in what manner to hold his fork, how to begin a business conversation, how to respond to a new tax law, whether to consider the government legitimate or not, whether to speak his mind openly or keep his thoughts to himself. To some extent the individual's behavior will be determined by his own idiosyncratic judgments, but these too will be strongly influenced by what he has learned from his culture about making such judgments: how wide is his range of choices, how much freedom does he really have to make his own decision, what right does he have to make an independent choice — and so on. In other words, culture works a rather strong effect upon the individual's psychological processes, conscious and unconscious, ultimately conditioning his behavior very significantly.[10]

It must be said, however, that culture, strictly speaking, does not "cause" one to behave in a certain way. Culture *conditions* behavior; it influences and guides, rather than dictates, a course of action. It will set certain limits on, or boundaries to, the range of alternative actions likely in a given situation. Cultural considerations may even be, in Kluckhohn's words, "the 'strategic factor'" prompting a person to act in this way rather than that.[11] But culture is not the sole determinant of behavior. It is one conditioning variable among others such as personality, health, weather, and time of day.[12]

The dynamics of social action do not end with the behavioral response, the specific act. Behavior can become an element in the further development of a culture — not behavior as an individual action, that is, but rather behavior in an aggregate sense. In the aggregate, individual acts become *patterns* of behavior. Over a period of time patterns tend to take on definite and rather predictable forms, and in so doing they become part and parcel of the culture itself. Indeed, cultural change is generally brought about through the accumulation of shifts and adjustments in the aggregate behavior patterns of a society.

Here we have, in theory, the connection between the factors comprising individual motivation (the "micro-level" of our analysis) and larger social forces. The defining characteristic of culture is, as Alfred G. Meyer has lucidly argued, "the *pattern* of actions, reactions, and interactions" within a community.[13] It is also the pattern of values and symbols found among the members of the community, as well as the pattern of citizens' feelings about those values and symbols.[14] Culture is a way of ordering reality into a system of objects imbued with subjective meaning.[15]

We are not primarily concerned with how cultural objects come to be so imbued with symbolic meaning, but rather with identifying the salient objects, understanding their significance, and deducing the patterns of further reality produced within the culture. At this point it is appropriate to examine the relationship between culture and political culture, for it is the latter that forms the central concept of this study.

Most previous works have rightly assumed that the political sphere of reality should not be viewed as autonomous from the general culture.[16] We might think of the political culture as a distinct and roughly definable part of the larger culture. However, the problem of defining in specific terms what of culture is "political" and what is not cannot be easily resolved. The boundary between the political and the nonpolitical in a culture is imprecise, fuzzy, and sometimes arbitrary. Something considered political by one person may not be to another. To the leaders of modern totalitarian states everything, or nearly everything, is construed as having political significance, whereas to the nineteenth-century American pioneer, politics was something that impinged upon one's life only exceptionally.[17]

If we view aspects of culture, for the moment, in terms of a political-nonpolitical continuum, we may be able to state some propositions about this problem, however tentatively. We might, then, divide cultural phenomena into three rough categories fitting along a continuum, as in the diagram below. Category A consists of beliefs, values, symbols, behavior patterns, and other cultural phenomena that are essentially nonpolitical. These might include, for example, folk dances, funeral customs, and beliefs about the origin of the human species. Category B consists of phenomena that may or may not be political, depending on the circumstances. Literary forms, for example, can be politically relevant or not; social satire generally is, but lyric poetry generally is not. Religious beliefs, likewise, may or may not have political significance. The same can be said of certain value-related personality traits (avarice, skepticism), symbols (a flag vs. the Flag), and behavior patterns (marching in parades). Finally there are, in category C, phenomena that are clearly political: beliefs *about* politics, values regarding authority, patterns of interaction between elites and nonelites, and others.

```
          |        |
    A     |    B   |    C
 _ _ _ _ _|_ _ _ _ _|_ _ _ _ _
          |        |
          |        |

  ←  nonpolitical          political  →
```

As already stressed, the boundary between the political and the non-political cannot always be precisely located. That is why category B is analytically useful. Depending on the political salience given to the phenomena in this category by the society or the individual, they may be perceived as either political or nonpolitical. In a laissez-faire society, most of them will probably not be perceived as politically salient. Religious beliefs are assumed not to interfere with political relationships (separation of church and state), public gatherings are not inherently political, and most literature will be considered politically neutral.

In a totalitarian society, on the other hand, phenomena in category B will generally be construed as politically salient — if not always by the public, at least by rulers. Any public gathering will be suspected of having a political meaning. Literature and art forms have an explicit propaganda value and therefore must conform to approved norms. Religious beliefs will either support or threaten the official ideology, and nearly all personality traits can be important to the purpose of the state ("Socialist Man"). In some cases the boundary between the political and the nonpolitical may be very obscure, as in Stalinist society. Even phenomena normally far removed from politics might be perceived to have a political impact, whether consciously or not. With the efforts to rewrite the histories of the East European nations, for example, many old folk customs, including songs and dances, became temporarily unfashionable because of their irrelevance to the building of socialism. Instead, the people were encouraged to create "modern" folk art which would utilize the folk idiom as a medium of eulogizing the workers' state, Stalin, and so on. Thus even category A is not always unambiguously nonpolitical.[18]

If the foregoing has not entirely defined the "political" in political culture, it has at least pointed out the difficulties in separating politics from other social activities. The framers of political consciousness in each society — rulers, party functionaries, theorists, journalists, and educators — will add their own judgments of political salience in everyday affairs. The very matter of what constitutes politics is, like the nature of a culture, dynamic and subject to change.

Revolutionary politics is directly concerned with such change. Revolutionary leaders are faced with guiding society along new paths, and it is here that the challenge of established patterns of thought and action must be confronted.

Continuity, Change, and Revolution

A political culture is normally acquired by the accumulation of many years' experiences and passed from one generation to another through a learning process, explicit or implicit. The process through which a political culture is learned is that complex of experiences, instruction, indoctrination, and passively acquired assumptions known as political socialization.[19] Each generation tends to fashion its politics from cultural patterns handed down from its parent generation. This tendency toward cultural (and political) inertia should not be construed as absolute, however. Unforeseen issues can arise, or old issues can take on a new complexion.[20] Attitudes change, and a new political generation may adapt, reject, or ignore some of the values and orientations of the parent generation. This is not easily done, for cultures are usually resistant to large-scale, sudden changes. Strain and cultural tension generally result under conditions of such change.

If a political culture is not static, then, it must be said that the inertial tendencies are very strong. Political cultures can be characterized as rather durable and resilient, and they can also be said to be labile to one degree or another; therefore they are capable of absorbing gradual changes without undoing the overall configuration of value and behavior patterns. Large-scale changes will tend to occur only under exceptional circumstances, usually of a revolutionary nature.

Revolutionary societies are, in fact, characterized by radical changes in the critical elements of the political culture. A revolution, in its essence, is a violent rupture of traditional norms and practices, invariably accompanied by severe stress and generally in the face of strong resistance from one quarter or another. To succeed, that is, to transform society and persist, a revolution must prevail over great obstacles, for the revolutionary process always involves an upheaval in values, institutions, and symbols that are deeply rooted.

Communist revolutions, whatever their particular historical or national forms, have had in common the goal of fundamental change in the values, orientations, and behavior patterns that dominate in the lives of the citizenry.[21] Lenin certainly had this in mind when he wrote in 1918 of the necessity to rid Soviet society of "all the habits and traditions of the bourgeoisie."[22] Stalin carried this task to an extreme, assuming that the radical transformation of Soviety society by means of the "revolution from above" would lead to the birth of a "new Soviet man." This new creature would be an individual enthusiastically committed to the goals of communism and unwaveringly obedient to the authority of the party.[23] The transformation of attitudes and habits at the very base of society has been an explicit aim of the Chinese and Cuban revolutions as well.[24] Nor should Eastern Europe be an exception. Each regime has propagated its image of the emerging "new man," and although the tactics of pursuing this goal have varied, none has abandoned the idea entirely. To have a radically new society, one must have qualitatively different citizens. Communist revolutionary policies, from Lenin to Brezhnev and from Peking to Havana, have sought to construct the "new man" with attitudes and habits of behavior that are thoroughly consistent with the ends of the revolution.

Neither Marx nor Lenin actually used anything quite equivalent to the term *political culture,* and indeed both might have argued that any interpretation of culture as something with a dynamic of its own was mistaken. Culture, to Marx, was a part of the social superstructure, an organic outgrowth of the objective class realities in the societal base. As such, culture did not determine behavior but was, rather, only the product of behavior.[25] In practice, however, things turned out differently. Lenin quickly learned this, and his government's efforts at eliminating bourgeois habits amounted to a tacit reversal of Marx's idea that behavior could not be substantially conditioned by subjective forces. With the ethic of the "new man" and the party's efforts to intervene openly in the process of behavioral determination, the Marxist notion was abandoned.

The student of political culture in Communist-ruled societies is thus faced with the crucial question: how has the revolution fared? That is, to what extent have society and the individuals within it actually been metamorphosed as a result of the socialist revolution? Given the revolutionary goal of transforming the political culture, to what extent has the revolution wrought its intended effect? The task of the scholar is to determine the general nature of the prerevolutionary political culture and then to ascertain how, if at all, it has changed.

This is precisely the point in theory at which two seemingly separate notions of political culture converge. The first, predominant in the works of Almond, Pye, and Verba, sees the crucial problem to be the linkage between micro- and macropolitical factors, that is, the relationship between individual motivation and the broader pattern of historical continuity and change.[26] The second, emphasized by Tucker and Meyer, stresses the problem of accounting for change and development within a society as a whole.[27] In fact, both sets of problems are important, for a society's political culture is described by the patterns of beliefs and actions of its members. This is not to say that the political culture is merely the sum of individual and group patterns, but neither can it be conceived as something disembodied from the individual propensities that exist on the microlevel.[28] Thus political culture refers to both the relationship between micro- and macropolitical patterning and the broader questions of historical continuity and change.

The Aims of the Present Study

The larger part of the focus in the following chapters will of empirical necessity be on the subject of continuity and change in the Czechoslovak revolution. For reasons that are well known to students of Communist societies, it is simply impossible to assemble sufficient data on the nature of individual motivation to test such theoretical constructs as the Parsonian social-action model implied above.[29] Although we cannot pretend that the whole of the theory outlined here can be proved beyond the shadow of a doubt, we must nonetheless begin somewhere. The propositions offered in the foregoing discussion, therefore, will be assumed to underlie the dynamic processes that make up the political culture. To the extent it is possible, we shall try to establish the existence of attitudinal and behavioral patterns at the base of Czechoslovak society that contribute to the overall configuration of such patterns in the society as a whole. The latter will serve as independent variables that help to explain the performance of the political system in fulfilling the revolutionary task of transforming society in the image of the elite ideology.[30]

It will be further assumed that the Czechoslovak revolution alluded to above is an ongoing process, begun in 1948 and continuing (in intent, at least) indefinitely. It is to be distinguished from the Communists' political takeover of February 1948, the latter more accurately described simply as a takeover or a *coup d'état*. Thus the revolution will include not just the seizure of government but the entire, long-range task of altering the attitudes and behavior of society.

Three issues form the central concern of the following chapters. The first has to do with the nature of the Czechoslovak political culture as such — the values, beliefs, and attitudinal and behavioral patterns that have evolved from the past to have an important effect on political reality in the present. The second is the issue of revolutionary change, or more specifically, the problem of inertial forces in a society confronting the purposes of an elite dedicated to the successful realization of Communist ideals. The third is tied up with the question of political dependency: the conflict between indigenous patterns of political culture and the norms derived from an official ideology that has been critically influenced by Soviet communism.

The last-mentioned factor introduces a variable not accounted for in previous theoretical discussions of political culture, and it obviously complicates the subject. Czechoslovakia's political culture is not just the product of the interplay between revolution and tradition, or between micro- and macropolitical patterns, but also the result of a complex interplay between all these indigenous variables and the influence of strong international forces. This is not to suggest something unique about Czechoslovakia; Czechoslovakia is, to use James N. Rosenau's term, a penetrated political system — indeed, a system penetrated to a very high degree and throughout a wide range of issues.[31] Czechoslovakia's lesson might therefore shed some light on the general questions of dependency and penetration in the theory of national-international linkage.[32]

*   *   *

Before concluding this introduction, the author wishes to say a few words about his sources. At the risk of being accused of eclecticism, I have assembled a variety of rather disparate types of data drawn from a diversity of sources. Among these are interpretations of Czech and Slovak politics, social organization, and national characters by governmental leaders past and present, opposition leaders, novelists, theorists, counterculture spokesmen, social scientists, and random personal acquaintances who either live now or have lived in the Czechoslovak Socialist Republic. I have made a particular effort to weigh different interpretations against each other and, whenever these have seemed irreconcilable, I have tried to admit the problem. Where attitudinal data are available I have referred to them, but my primary concern has been with assembling data of a generally "softer" nature — more befitting a study of culture.[33]

Where I have had recourse to "harder" data on social stratification and other matters, certain problems well known to Communist-area specialists have arisen. The data are not always consistent, and the range of available data is generally narrower than what one can readily find in Western societies. Specifically with regard to social stratification (discussed in chapter five), it is unhappily the case that the most recent data are already more than ten years old as of the time of this writing; sociology in Czechoslovakia became discredited along with the politics of the sixties, and no serious work has been done in the field since 1969.

Finally, it must be admitted that the author's intuition always plays a role in the analysis of such ultimately unprovable enterprises as the present study. I have been told by people of reasonably sound judgment that my intuition is not bad, but it is to be hoped that I have not relied on it unduly.

* PART I *
- IMAGES AND REALITIES -

One characteristic by which a political culture can be described is the extent to which there exists a consensus among rulers and ruled about the nature of political reality and the saliency of political symbols. The evidence presented in the following four chapters suggests that the Communist leadership has simply been unable to project itself as the bearer of society's greatest traditions and the articulator of its fondest aspirations. In their effort to create popular symbols around the theme of the working class and its revolutionary development, the Communists have disassociated themselves from much of Czechoslovakia's past without having effectively substituted any compelling symbols around which public support can be rallied in the present. The reform government in 1968 seemed to be on the verge of resolving this dilemma just when it was forced out of power and replaced by a government that was once again insensitive to popular symbols.

A large part of the Communists' problem stems from the fact that, ultimately, they themselves are not entirely free to act in their country's best interests. Instead, they are ideologically and politically bound to a rather narrow framework of action that falls within the parameters of behavior considered by their allies to be acceptable. The fact that policy is constrained by the whims of more powerful outsiders gives the Czechoslovak political culture an air of humility and further serves to separate the public from the leadership. Throughout history, confrontations with foreign powers have generally resulted in humiliation for the Czechs and Slovaks, and the current situation thus reminds them of earlier periods in their history of national subservience.

A resulting atmosphere of political alienation has pervaded Czechoslovak society and rendered the attempts of the Communists to transform public attitudes fruitless. As discussed in chapter one, the regime in the 1970s found itself caught between its desire to persuade the public of socialism's rosy millennium and its realization that serious problems existed. Even comparisons of the present (as good, pros-

perous, and democratic) with the past (as bad, unjust, and exploitative) failed to persuade, for the regime's efforts to reinterpret history
have not discredited the more favorable images of the past — both the
more distant, bourgeois past and the more recent past of the 1968
reforms. (This is discussed in chapter two.)

The contradictory images of society as a whole, past and present, are
to some extent mirrored in the contradictory traditions of the ruling
party. Chapters three and four explore the complex backgrounds of
communism in Czechoslovakia. It is argued that the ruling elite
emerged from a political subculture with strong roots in Czechoslovak
society, but it came to power as a result of extraordinary political
conditions and began its period of rule with an extremely weak social
base. These circumstances, coupled with a threatening international
situation, thrust the Czechoslovak Communists into the lap of the
Soviet Union, and they quickly became dependent on the USSR not
only for military protection but for guidance on the most specific
questions of ideology and policy.

It is further argued that the Stalinist form which the Czechoslovak
revolution subsequently assumed was by no means preordained by the
inherent character of Czechoslovak communism; rather, the policies
and practices that ensued from Communist rule reflected Stalin's
interference in Prague's political processes. Thus was resolved a longstanding ambivalence in Czechoslovak communism between the
extremist path of class conflict and the more moderate approaches to
revolutionary change. Stalin's efforts at establishing political control
cast the USSR in the role of an imperial center, effectively ruling
Czechoslovakia indirectly through the subordinate Czechoslovak
Communists. The latter became a sort of colonial elite dependent on
the imperial center, and their resulting image as representatives of the
foreigner has tended to discredit them among their subjects as much as
has their insensitivity to public opinion. Since the fall of the popular
Dubček regime, the elite has been even more strongly and negatively
associated with the rule of the foreigner than before.

The leadership, of course, does not see itself in this light and insists
that Czechoslovakia is a sovereign workers' state. The party considers
itself the embodiment of social ideals and the center of the public's true
hopes and aspirations. Its policies, proclamations, and rituals are
designed to attract the working masses and win over public opinion.

Let us turn now to a detailed look at the images and the realities that
emerge from this contradictory situation.

I

The Theory of the "New Man" and the Reality of Czechoslovak Society

Every politically organized society has some set of values and ideals that provide a framework of normative cohesiveness for the polity. Along with these values and ideals often comes the development of myths attached to the political institutions and leaders, as well as a body of ritualized behavior presumed to reflect the underlying value system. In Czechoslovakia, as in socialist countries generally, the values, ideals, myths, and rituals spring from the revolutionary ideology of Marxism-Leninism. Based on the belief that society is undergoing a long-term process of transformation toward something entirely new and infinitely superior to all previous social orders, the ideology lays down a set of guidelines for the attitudinal and behavioral patterns of citizens. Progress toward the ultimate end of a Communist order depends on the progressive evolution of citizens' social and political personalities. The "new men" who finally emerge from this evolutionary process are the working people, who have matured in their revolutionary consciousness and come to form the backbone of the Communist order.

Although the imagery of the "new man" does not appear overtly in every Communist-ruled society at all times, something similar to this prototype can always be found. School children are taught certain moral precepts, and adults are expected to display certain behavioral traits, that give evidence of their class consciousness and dedication to the political cause. In Czechoslovakia, the imagery as propagated by the polity is quite overt, the prescribed ritualism quite straightforward, and the political myths quite bold. The gap between the theoretical ideals and the reality of social life, however, is very wide, and to compare the two is to draw a picture of great incoherence in the relationship between rulers and citizens. Although it can be said that ideal and reality rarely come together in any society, the degree to which they diverge in Czechoslovakia is so considerable as to warrant our particular attention from the beginning of this study.

To approach this problem properly, it is necessary to trace briefly the development of the "new man" theory in Marxist-Leninist thought, then to look at its specific manifestation in the official imagery of Czechoslovakia, and finally to compare that imagery with some evidence concerning real-life attitudes and behavior patterns.

The "New Man" in Marxist-Leninist Thought

A basic assumption in the Marxist-Leninist ideology is that the broad masses of working-class society must and will share a conscious dedication to the socialist purpose. Marx had predicted that socialist revolutions would come about as a result of changes already well-advanced in the collective mentality of the proletariat, the driving force that would overthrow the capitalist order and begin to build a new society. The revolution would be set in motion when the workers identified the source of their misery and alienation as the capitalist system itself and therefore purposely acted to bring about the demise of the existing order. To Marx, the revolution could succeed only when the workers themselves were conscious of their historical destiny and reasonably well aware of their ultimate purpose.

Lenin did not completely share Marx's optimism about the revolutionary awareness of the working class as a whole but instead emphasized the key role of a party-vanguard. Marx had written of the vanguard, of course, but in his paradigm the vanguard was a rather vaguely defined segment of the working class, distinctive for its superior perception of social reality. According to Marx the vanguard would lead the workers and determine the appropriate moment for revolutionary action, but that moment would be easily recognized by the working masses, of whom the vanguard was an integral part. To Lenin, the vanguard came to be embodied in the party, a full-time professional political group as described in *What Is to Be Done?* Lenin felt it unwise to rely on the impulses of the workers themselves, for the attractions of trade unionism, economism, and piecemeal material gains might dissuade them from their ultimate purpose of revolution. Going a step farther in 1917, Lenin argued that the revolution could be fomented on the basis of social support that was at best momentary and dubious. The time was ripe, he contended in *State and Revolution,* because Russia was in an uproar, social unrest was extremely widespread, and the existing government could not satisfy the needs of the day. His argument persuaded just enough of the Bolsheviks' inner circle, and power was seized in the name of the soviets.

But the society as a whole was not prepared for socialism. A bloody and protracted civil war ensued, and the Bolsheviks' policies of war communism only tended to inflame the divisions further. The forces opposing the revolution were beaten down slowly and at great expense. Toward the end of the civil war, the Bolsheviks found themselves faced with economic disaster and peasant revolts. Shaken by the attempted insurrection on the part of once loyal partisans at Kronstadt, the party beat a hasty tactical retreat. The result was the NEP, a series of policies aimed (in large part) at slowing down the pace of revolution and allowing time for society to develop a truly collectivist mentality in the context of gradual change. This was by no means a retreat in terms of the ultimate goals of socialism; rather, it was a period of adjustment, experimentation, and planned socialization programs meant to guide the masses more gently into the future.[1]

The problem of remolding societal values was not overcome during the lifetime of NEP, and when the moderate tactics of NEP gave way to the extremist strategies of the Stalin era, the demands on the Soviet people reached epic proportions. The countless peasants populating the USSR's countryside were forced onto collective farms by means of unparalleled brutality. Industrial workers were driven, many of them beyond their physical and mental endurance, to produce impossible quantities of goods. Families were torn asunder by the impact of mass occupational migration and deportation to labor camps. Needless to say, this all came at enormous social and psychic cost to the entire population.[2] And all bore witness to the fact that Soviet society simply was not ready to embrace the goals and methods that the revolution had by this time taken on. Far from exemplifying the will of the proletariat, the Russian Revolution had wrought a new oppression for the working man.

Given the population's resistance to the Stalin Revolution, the need for a thoroughgoing campaign of political education was obvious. The socialist man foreseen by Marx did not exist in the Soviet Union, so an ideal-type had to be devised. A model character-type was developed, based on political myth and psychological wishful thinking. The myth derived in large part from Lenin's image of the true Bolshevik; the wishful thinking grew out of the so-called psychological revolution, dating from the mid 1930s.

Lenin's model of the ideal Bolshevik was a person who professes unfailing loyalty to the party and exercises strict self-discipline in carrying out the party's work. He is willing to utilize any means — including, if necessary, self-sacrifice — to accomplish the party's ends, and he allows himself no personal loyalties other than those in common service to the party.[3]

Under Stalin, this image was transposed onto the official model of the ideal citizen, the "new man" whom the regime now sought to create universally. The "new man" was expected to internalize the norms of the regime and strive enthusiastically for socialism. He was portrayed as the embodiment of patriotism, party-mindedness (*partiinost'*), vigilance, collective-mindedness, modesty, self-discipline, optimism, and hatred for the enemy.[4]

During Stalin's lengthy tenure in power the question of individual autonomy was raised as a psychological debate, and the official interpretation of this changed radically at two points. The dominant tendency in Soviet psychology during the 1920s had assumed that a person's behavior could be attributed in large part to his social environment. Therefore, it was possible to excuse some transgressions because of external conditions over which the individual had virtually no control. In 1936 this view was discarded, and the individual was assumed to be fully responsible for his own aberrant behavior. The explanation for this change was the claim that the Soviet Union had now entered socialism, a historic step announced by the new constitution. Entering socialism meant the end of "bourgeois" influences in society and the universality of the collective mentality. If there were remnants of bourgeois mentality still floating around in the minds of certain individuals, their eradication could not come through any efforts at tampering with the social environment. Rather, they must be eliminated through *training*, that is, through all the processes that we know as political socialization: schooling, family upbringing, and so on. This was the major thrust of the first Stalinist revolution in psychology.[5]

The second revolution began in 1949, reversing the direction of the first and pushing Soviet psychology toward new extremes of reflexology and what Tucker has called "transformism."[6] Pavlovianism was revived and given an honored place in behavioral science, and a new system of assumptions about the role of the human being within his environment pervaded the field. It was now asserted that, far from being a relatively autonomous creature capable of determining his own behavior, the individual was the product of his social environment and could be molded to an almost infinite degree by the conditions in that environment. One of the conditions of the environment was language, and Stalin's growing interest in the uses of linguistic symbolism in his later years led him to infer that language played a crucial role in the conditioning processes of society. A second vital factor was the economic system — a "discovery" which, of course, was by no means novel in itself. Stalin reasoned that these environmental variables were themselves governed by "objective scientific laws" that were discernible by socially conscious men.[7]

This had obvious implications for the role of the state in fostering the desired attitudes among its citizens. By understanding the laws governing the social sciences, especially economics and linguistics, rulers could manipulate the critical environmental conditions determining behavior. In short, something approximating the ideal "new man" could be purposively created.

The reversals in Stalin's view of behavioral causality illustrate an important tension in the ambivalent legacy of Marxist thought on the question of human autonomy. To this day the theory and practice of Soviet communism have failed to resolve the question. Strenuous attempts are constantly made to mold personality through socialization processes that are closely guided by the state, reflecting the assumption that the training of the individual is important despite the existence of the proper social environment.[8] Thus we can infer a partial return to the theory that the individual does exercise some control over his own behavior and must be taught how to conduct himself.

Other Communist regimes have been similarly faced with the task of socializing their citizens into the norms of the revolution.[9] All Communist elites have therefore had to deal with values and behavior patterns that do not conform to the ideal of the "new man." The influence of the past has been an obstinate foe, demanding strong countervailing efforts.

The "New Man" in Czechoslovakia

The Communist regimes of Eastern Europe have borrowed heavily from the Soviet "new man" model in formulating their images of the ideal citizen. In Czechoslovakia, as in the USSR, the model citizen is one who fervently believes in the myths of the Marxist-Leninist ideological system and accepts the party as the unerring interpreter of that gospel. He freely chooses socialism over capitalism and does not resent the imperfections of the transitional present, for he knows that the future will be glorious. To this end he participates in the task of building socialism with the greatest enthusiasm.[10]

The "new man" model is, of course, more symbolic than actual. No man or woman is perfect, and the Communists would undoubtedly be pleased with partial success and a gradual momentum toward the ideal. Just as the Christian model of a sinless life is a symbol and a guideline for believers, the "new man" is exemplary and symbolic for Marxist-Leninist believers. Children are educated on the virtues of socialism, and the regime attempts to develop collectivist habits among them beginning at an early age. Textbooks and readers not only instruct the children in grammar and history, but they also drive home lessons of a directly ideological nature.[11] Education thus serves a dual function, as it does in all organized societies.[12]

There is an important difference between education in most Communist societies and that in liberal democratic countries. The ideological content in Czechoslovak education, for example, is far more uniform, pervasive, and overt than it is in American education. This is not to say that American education is free from ideological influences; surely there are few Americans who have gone through elementary school without having been exposed to considerable amounts of political indoctrination into the "American way," whether boldly or subtly. By the time an American reaches university-level education, however, some of the simple myths of elementary school days begin to break down in the more critical and pluralistic atmosphere of higher education.

In Czechoslovakia, higher education does not for the most part provide this contrast with elementary education. Higher education is meant to continue the civic training begun at earlier ages while preparing students for productive vocations. Both admissions policy and substantive instruction are aimed at channeling the universities' efforts into the social task. Admission is often contingent upon proper attitudes as evidenced in youth league participation or some other criteria. In the university curriculum, Marxism-Leninism occupies a central position, and all students must study the teachings of Marx and Lenin at one time or another. Marxism-Leninism plays a part in adult education, too, as a means of continuing socialization of the population even among adults.[13] There have been times when the system of controls loosened up and a certain degree of pluralism crept into the educational process, such as the early and middle 1960s. These were times of general crisis for the regime, however, and the breakdown in educational controls coincided with the gradual deterioration of the political authority structure as a whole.[14] After 1968 the government reasserted a stringent control over higher education, beginning with a purge in the university system and continuing with vigilant efforts to exclude ideologically unacceptable materials from the curricula.[15]

Young people's organizations form the second important instrument of political socialization. These, too, have undergone shake-ups in both institutional structure and purpose, centering around the 1968 "Prague Spring." At that time the old Czechoslovak Union of Youth (ČSM) disintegrated, while the leaders of the Pioneer Organization openly invited competition from the newly revived Boy Scouts. The spontaneous emergence of officially uncontrolled organizations clearly indicated the failure of the original institutions to capture the imagination and loyalty of the younger generation. Nevertheless, the post-1969 regime has once again brought about the consolidation of youth groups into centrally controlled structures. The Pioneers are the sole organization for children under fifteen years of age, while older youths and young adults are organized in a reincarnation of the former ČSM, now called the Socialist Union of Youth (*Socialistický svaz mládeže,* or SSM).[16]

The youth organizations are modeled after the pattern of their Soviet counterparts, the *Komsomol* and the Pioneers. As elsewhere among the socialist countries, membership is voluntary, but considerable pressure is exerted on young people to join. The pressure may be as indirect as peer-group tendencies to conform, or as overt as the threat of failed applications for university stipends or loans for non-members.[17] In the latter case, a student is not safe once he has been admitted to a university, for the youth organization committee plays a role in monitoring classroom activities, managing social functions, and approving renewals of financial aid.[18]

Like the schools, the youth organizations contribute to the ideological upbringing of children and young adults. Programs and meetings usually include a heavy dose of political propaganda. The leaders of local organizations tend to be politically orthodox, for being an SSM officer is frequently the first step toward becoming an adult functionary. There is a great deal of cynicism among the rank and file young toward the SSM and its "establishment," and the high membership roles do not seem to reflect the degree of members' commitment to the organizations' purposes.[19] It can probably be said that many (if not most) university students who belong to the SSM do so solely because of the personal advantages gained through membership — or the likely loss of these advantages from nonmembership.[20]

There are many additional instruments of political socialization. Radio and television, the press, books and libraries, theater and the cinema are all recognized by the party as important sources of social influence on the minds of young and old alike. All are scrutinized by the government so as to forestall harmful ideological messages and allow for the publication and circulation of positive propaganda. The state's efforts are not enough to prevent some "leakage" by way of foreign radio broadcasts, illegal and underground newspapers, and word-of-mouth communication, all of which has been very apparent since the early sixties. In fact, there are occasional signs that the party is aware of the failures of its ideological task, but it nonetheless persists in its efforts with fluctuating degrees of thoroughness.

In sum, Czechoslovakia's Communist leaders have endeavored to employ the instruments of political socialization for the purpose of bringing about thoroughgoing change in the political culture. To the degree that citizens willfully join mass organizations, accept the official ideology, and work at their daily tasks with the enthusiasm of true builders of socialism, the revolutionary purpose can be said to have been achieved and the "new man" created. The argument offered in the present study, however, suggests that the degree of success has been negligible. Czechoslovakia's history of political vicissitude notwithstanding, cultural change has been more gradual and the patterns of citizens' political orientations more stable than one might expect. In particular, the transformation of the citizenry to a society of workers sharing the normative social imagery of the leadership has not shown a great deal of progress from the point of view of those who purvey the official myths.

Two Views of the Workers' State

Czechoslovakia is blessed with many beautiful castles that enhance the country's picturesque landscape and recall an era of fantasy and romance. The castles seem strange, out of place in a twentieth-century socialist society. Most of the older castles are in ruins, perched atop high hills, majestic in their visual appearance and mystic in their symbolic connotation. They seem remote and unreal, yet they are in fact accessible by automobile or on foot; one can visit them, touch them, frolic in their ancient courtyards, envision the splendor that once was, and imagine oneself as a member of a great noble family in days of yore. They are marvelous places for a day's outing, places to escape from the humdrum of everyday life down below. One can enter an old castle and feel a part of a world different from one's own. From the castle one can look down upon the "real" world and see it from afar as something distant and objective. Indeed, from such a distance measurable not only in meters but in centuries as well, one can easily lose one's perspective on reality and unreality, and begin to wonder which world is real and which unreal.

A tourist brochure describing the thirteenth-century castle at Rabí, in southwestern Bohemia, guides us through the ruins and immerses us in the colorful history of the region. We marvel at the past events — the medieval gold rush that originally necessitated the construction of the fortress on this site; the heroism of the Hussite leader Jan Žižka, who lost his second eye in the process of capturing Rabí in 1421; the late-fifteenth-century local rule of Půta Švíhovský, notable for his cruelty as much as for his architectural additions to the castle. We are jolted back to reality, however, by the closing thought of the tourist brochure, reminding us that despite the glitter and romance of the castle, medieval life was harsh and unfulfilling in comparison with today's:

> Before our eyes, the excellent work of our ancient forefathers, slaving and exploited — the Gothic stone castle — merges with modern, free, lively work down below and all around us, the work of today's generation building the foundations of Communism.[21]

Thus are we drawn, in characteristic Marxist fashion, to remembering the past as prologue. Our fantasies about the idyllic nature of life long ago are shattered in the realization that for the vast majority of people their life was a struggle for the benefit of others more privileged. The castle above and the society down below are equally real, and moreover they are equally the product of the same toiling masses. The crucial difference is that the castle belongs to a time in the past, when the toiling masses created a world of beauty not for themselves but for their feudal lords, whereas today they are building their own world at their own behest and in service only to themselves.

As we descend from Rabí Castle once more into the contemporary world, we find ourselves wondering about this juxtaposition between the old world of oppression and the new world of freedom. Upon closer examination there are many respects in which the new world at the base of the castle hill is not much freer for the working man than was that of his oppressed forefathers. At least, there is evidence that the worker of the 1970s does not perceive his world as his own, does not enjoy the work that he does (supposedly) for his own benefit, and does not feel drawn to participate in the common task that the Communist party sees as the central component of the socialist order. Let us then take a closer look at Czechoslovak society, examining some aspects of the workers' state that may shed some light on the workers' political attitudes.

Any discussion of contemporary Czechoslovakia must start with a reference to the critical turning point of 1968, the year of the so-called "Prague Spring" and of an unparalleled convergence of Communist policies and popular sentiments.[22] The reforms of the Dubček era had promised a revolutionary change in the political atmosphere, and although the society as a whole was far from united in its perception of that change, the momentum of change itself was so compelling that at times it seemed as if the whole of the populace was caught up in the political movement. When the armies of the Warsaw Pact occupied Czechoslovakia, and particularly when the Prague leadership found itself forced to back away from the reform program, the atmosphere among the public turned from the jubilant activism of the Prague Spring to crushing disappointment, disillusionment, and ultimately a frustrated withdrawal from politics. When the reform leaders centered around Dubček were replaced by a more conservative and eventually reactionary leadership centering around Gustáv Husák, the public's political withdrawal became nearly complete; from a highpoint of voluntary public activism in 1968, political participation sank to the levels of activity and commitment characteristic of the Stalin era. For the majority of citizens, political participation became primarily a matter of performing the ritual partisan activities that were officially required if one wished to avoid public embarrassment and perhaps the loss of one's job.[23] For that special minority who were willing to compromise on matters of principle in order to achieve status in the post-1968 order, there were, of course, opportunities — but only if the persons involved were reasonably "untainted" by their roles in the events of 1968. For that even smaller minority who chose to stand by their principles, political activity was punishable by harassment, loss of profession, and in some cases imprisonment or exile. In time, one or more of these fates befell those who attempted to withstand the forces that replaced the reform leadership, those who circulated petitions and wrote open letters to the post-1968 leaders, those who attempted to communicate to the outside world the extent of their society's political regression, and those who authored and signed the document (much publicized in the West) known as Charter 77.

Ever since the reestablishment of authoritarian rule in 1969, the regime has been preoccupied with undoing the effects of the Prague Spring. The present rulers have consistently referred to the 1968 events as an attempted counterrevolution whose leaders brought Czecho-slovak socialism near the disaster point. In countless proclamations, broadcasts, and editorials the citizens have been reminded of those months when perfidious right-wing opportunists in league with foreign imperialist centers tried to bring about a revival of the capitalist order in Czechoslovakia. Despite the occasional distractions caused by petitioners, the official view is that the crisis has essentially passed. The workers have been returned to their rightful position of authority, as represented by the current leaders, and order has been restored. The suppression of the movement around Charter 77 in 1977 seemed to confirm, at least for the time being, that the Party has brought political life under its control. In the official view, the workers are thereby enabled to continue their efforts at establishing the material bases of welfare and security.

After 1969 the official watchwords were first "normalization" and later "consolidation." The former word prevailed in the policy discussions prior to the Fourteenth party congress in 1971; the situation in 1968–69 had supposedly been abnormal, counterrevolutionary, and strict measures had been taken to bring society back to its normal revolutionary course. After the Fourteenth congress, the "normalized" situation had to be consolidated, and the party began to search for positive directions and a renewed sense of purpose.

As positive achievements of the "consolidation" period, the party leaders sought to divert the public from direct political involvement and into a redoubled effort at raising the country's economic standards. There were some favorable results. By 1973, for example, the regime could point to a growth rate in industrial production of nearly 6 percent, in agricultural production of over 4 percent, in real income of over 6 percent, and in personal consumption of more than 5 percent.[24] In the first half of the five-year plan beginning in 1970, 215,000 new apartment units were constructed, and citizens' gross expenditures on consumer goods rose by eighteen billion *koruny* during the same time (1970–72).[25] In a report to the Economic Plenum of the Party Central Committee in November 1973, Federal Prime Minister Ľubomír Štrougal was quick to assert that these gains were due to the correct policy lines of the Party, the high degree of economic and political stability reached during the "consolidation" period, and the growing public confidence in the regime's policies.[26]

A great deal of attention has been paid to the increased production of consumer goods since 1970, for it seems that the leadership has decided to gamble on winning popular support by encouraging a higher material standard of living. As we have stressed earlier, public support is crucial to the progress of an ongoing revolution. The rulers want to believe that their policies are warmly received and that their leadership is accepted. Their frequent statements asserting a high level of public support are no doubt partly aimed at so convincing themselves.[27] There is much evidence, however, that they are not in fact satisfied with the level of their public support, for articles complaining about apparently widespread problems of moral and social indiscipline appear in the official press with surprising frequency.

Some of the most consistent sources of official grievance have been the shortcomings of the labor force — an ironic problem in a workers' state. In his report to the November 1973 plenum, Štrougal felt obliged to qualify his optimism about the state of the economy with a discouraging statement concerning the low level of labor productivity. Despite the fact that industrial machinery was in good order, the machinery was not being utilized to its fullest extent, and despite the overall improvements in gross economic statistics, progress was not as good as one might have expected.[28] Some improvement occurred toward the end of the 1971–75 Five-Year Plan; many targets were reached ahead of time, and officials boasted that the "basic" production goals were achieved. On the other hand, shortcomings were reported in the critical sectors of coal and chemical production and crude oil processing.[29]

As early as the Fourteenth party congress labor productivity was identified as the biggest cause of economic problems. The congress had charged all party, state, enterprise, and social organizations with the responsibility for improving productivity. Some improvement thereafter was jubilantly announced; labor productivity in primary industries rose between 1970–72 by an estimated 2.3 percent, and, in 1975 alone, industrial productivity rose by 6.1 percent over the 1974 level.[30] Still there continued much discussion about the need to increase labor productivity in all sectors of the economy, as Czechoslovak production persistently compared unfavorably to that in the industrialized capitalist countries and fell below that in East Germany and the Soviet Union. Official economists ruefully admitted in 1975 that in order to produce the same per-capita output of industrial goods as in the West, Czechoslovak industry required a work force 20–25 percent larger.[31]

It is perhaps unfair to place the blame for low productivity entirely on the workers, for obsolescent machinery and methods play an important role in the lagging economy. At the same time, however, officials have been well aware that some part of the problem is due to low worker morale. A *Rudé právo* editorialist in 1974 pointedly commented that "despite [improvements], it is simply obvious that we still have a long way to go in the utilization of work time. . . . In other words, not everybody has done what he should have done, not everyone approaches such serious tasks in a principled and responsible manner."[32]

The most important morale-related problems are absenteeism and indiscipline. The incidence of absenteeism from work climbed steadily between 1965 and 1970; on the average workday in 1970, 51 of every 1,000 workers were absent.[33] Prime Minister Štrougal once referred to this phenomenon as a "world rarity." Citing statistics showing daily work absence from illness alone to have been 47 of 1,000 during the first half of 1971, Štrougal added that an investigation had revealed that "at least 25 percent" of those absent workers were faking their illness.[34] Absenteeism seemed to decline somewhat since a 1969 law imposing the possibility of imprisonment for absenteeism without a genuine medical excuse, but the problem did not disappear. One statistic from Slovakia alone showed that unexcused absences accounted for the effective loss of 300,000 working days.[35]

More difficult to assess empirically, although equally detrimental to production, are manifestations of labor indiscipline such as workers' tending to personal matters during their worktime, prolonged breaks, unpunctuality, shortening the workday by arriving late and leaving early, and so on. In one machine-works factory, it was found that fully one-fourth of the 1,200 workers were allowed exceptions from the normal working time. In another factory 150 workers were allowed to leave work two hours before the end of their shifts, and yet because of low output the manager of the factory had frequently requested that his plant be assigned larger numbers of workers! Radio Prague reported in November 1974 that hundreds of thousands of workers regularly celebrate their birthdays, name-days, and other anniversaries — along with their friends and co-workers, of course — during work hours. In what may be the most outrageous example of all, it was estimated that overextended work breaks in one factory caused a loss of production in one year's time equivalent to that of 7,000 shifts![36]

Closely related to all these instances of indiscipline is the very widespread practice of taking time off work to attend to personal chores — having the family auto serviced, applying for new housing, shopping for groceries, and similar activities. A spokesman for the Labor and Social Welfare Ministry of the Czech Socialist Republic estimated that these activities cause the loss of 100 million working hours annually — or, in other terms, the worktime of 55,000 laborers.[37] In a certain sense, such a loss of worktime seems unavoidable because shops and agencies are open only during the regular workday; the estimates of lost time are nonetheless startling and remind one of Václav Havel's absurd play written in the sixties, *The Memorandum*.[38]

In 1972 a survey was conducted among foremen and workers in the East Slovakia Ironworks. The results of the survey showed that the plant's personnel were aware of serious deficiencies in their performance. To the question whether it was true that working time was used to only 70 or 80 percent of its capacity, one-third of the respondents agreed that it was true, one-half evaded the question, and only 14.6 percent said it was not true.[39]

Part of the problem lies with the supervisory personnel of some factories, who allow or perhaps even encourage workers to shirk their duties. Lax controls and generally slack discipline were two reasons cited, in the poll mentioned above, for the wastage of time.[40] Obviously, some of the blame must be placed on managers who tolerate tardiness, poor excuses for absences, and chiseling on coffee breaks. Indeed, management ranks have suffered considerably from the after-effects of political "normalization." Many talented members of managerial staffs throughout the country had been associated with the reforms of 1968 and the political activities of 1968–69, and of these a large number were removed or transferred from their positions.[41]

Important as management is, however, a workers' society cannot be built without the wholehearted participation of the workers themselves. The fact that absenteeism and indiscipline occur with such regularity indicates that many workers do not by any means share the regime's claim that it is they themselves who benefit from their best efforts. If, as Marx predicted, a true workers' society brings the end of alienated labor and the reintegration of the laborer with the product of his toil, and if therefore the workers come to participate freely and enthusiastically in the creative process, then it must follow that a high incidence of labor indiscipline and an apparent lack of enthusiasm for work in general are signs that the workers' society has not been realized.

Absenteeism, declining productivity, and other related industrial maladies are by no means unique to socialist societies. In the seventies, we have seen similar trends developing in the highly industrialized capitalist countries of the West — particularly Great Britain, France, and Italy, but also in the United States. The point to be made here is not that the ills of the workplace are a socialist phenomenon, but that they are perhaps endemic in modern industrial society and suggest a broader-scaled problem of incentive, reward, obligation, and belongingness among workers. It is important for us to note that, as a self-proclaimed workers' state, Czechoslovakia is not immune to these general problems. If it behooves us to moderate our judgment of Czechoslovakia's productivity, then we must also return to the argument that there is a serious incongruity between the values of the system and the realities of everyday life. If the difference between socialism and capitalism can be measured in part by the extent to which workers' alienation has been overcome, then it is difficult to see the progress in Czechoslovakia after thirty years of socialism.

This is what many workers seem to be saying through their actions. They do not live in a workers' society, despite the fact that the official mythology constantly boasts that they do; the workers are not their own masters, and they do not necessarily feel that they will benefit from hard work. Perhaps they even feel that, again contrary to the official myth, they themselves are only symbolically the ruling class and that, in reality, they are objects of manipulation in a political order which — like that of their feudal ancestors who built Rabí — is run by a relatively small group of privileged personages.

A Prague-based correspondent of the émigré periodical *Listy* has noted the low morale prevalent among his fellow citizens. Looking back in 1973 at the years that had elapsed since 1968–69, the correspondent characterized them as years of "regression, mediocrity, and stagnation." These conditions, he said, describe virtually every aspect of political, social, and cultural life and have an inevitably demoralizing effect upon the working population. The effect takes the form of "increasing political apathy, irresponsibility, humility, increasing incidence of neurosis, deformations of character. . ." and so on.[42] Workers are alienated, not only from the product of their toil but from the totality of the system in which they live. They have little confidence in their leaders; they see no evidence that their own autonomy and authority are increasing; and, although they do enjoy an improving standard of living, this one single benefit of the current system leads them to an unnatural introversion, a withdrawal from the meaninglessness of social life and a redirection of one's efforts toward material comforts for self and immediate family.[43]

It is not surprising that concomitant with the deterioration of public morale has come a serious increase in several social problems. Crime, for example, has been steadily on the rise. This has been true for a longer period of time than just the last few years, but there has been no significant abatement of the trend recently. Officials sometimes blame the rising crime statistics on foreigners, arguing that among the many visitors from the West there are numerous "pimps, black marketeers, and the like. . . ," but outsiders are not responsible for the bulk of the problem.[44]

Alcoholism is another social problem on the rise. Czechs have always been renowned for their beer-drinking, and in recent years Slovaks have begun to drink their share as well. Czechoslovakia competes with West Germany as the home of championship beer-drinkers. In 1973, the per-capita consumption of beer in Czechoslovakia was 145.2 litres; in the Czech lands alone 157.9 litres of beer were consumed for every man, woman, and child, while in Slovakia the statistic was 118.1 litres. (See Figure I.1.) Consumption of hard liquor is much higher in Slovakia than in the Czech lands; in 1973, the per-capita consumption of hard liquor in Slovakia was 11.5 litres, whereas in Czechoslovakia as a whole it was only 6.7. The statistic for Slovakia is particularly striking when compared with earlier consumption statistics: the 11.5 litres per capita consumed in 1973 contrasts with 3.7 litres in 1964 and 2.8 in 1936.[45] (See Figure I.2.) When computed in terms of pure alcohol consumed, Czechoslovakia finds itself the tenth-ranked country in the world, with 8.6 litres of alcohol consumed for every inhabitant in 1971. Between 1961 and 1971, expenditures on all

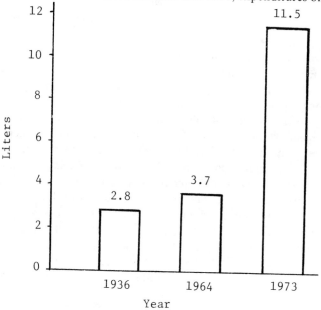

Figure I.1

Per Capita Consumption of Hard Liquor in Slovakia

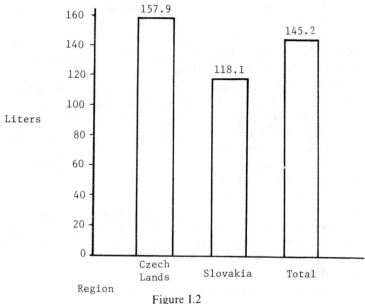

Figure I.2

Per Capita Consumption of Beer in Czechoslovakia, 1973

alcoholic beverages (including wine) increased from Kčs 7,850 million to Kčs 16,050 annually — more than double — throughout Czechoslovakia. The latter figure amounted to eight times the amount of money spent on nonalcoholic beverages.[46]

Statistics on alcohol consumption only begin to describe the social problem. That alcoholism is a serious matter can be further inferred from additional statistics. As of December 1971 there were more than 80,000 registered alcoholics in Czechoslovakia and, in addition, an estimated 200,000 nonregistered "heavy drinkers." At least 25 percent of all criminal offenses are committed under the influence of alcohol, and alcoholism figures in one-seventh of all divorce cases in the ČSSR. Moreover, an even sadder statistic shows that children of alcoholic parents account for 20 percent of all child psychiatric patients.[47] From time to time an official is heard to minimize the importance of such statistics,[48] but one nonetheless finds frequent references to the problem of alcoholism in the daily press.[49]

Drugs are generally not as great a problem as alcohol, but drug usage also seemed to be on the rise in the early seventies. In many cases, drug usage is blamed on foreign dope pushers and the Western hippie culture; most drug users in Czechoslovakia are members of the younger generation, many of whom "turn on" to other fads and fancies of decadent bourgeois culture as well. Newspaper articles warn them of the dangers to their health and reputation, and threaten the enforcement of stiff prison penalties for possession and use.[50]

Crime, alcoholism, and drugs are extreme varieties of response to one's social situation, and of course the bulk of the population is not driven to such extremes. Short of these overt social problems, nevertheless, there are many signs that public morale is low — that, in other words, the workers' society is not all it is supposed to be. Most citizens tend to react to the generally depressing state of Czechoslovak life in ways that show their dissatisfaction without engaging in outright socially deviant behavior. Not performing one's job duties well is one way of showing dissatisfaction. Not supporting and participating in the activities of official functions and mass organizations is another. To do the minimum amount of work acceptable by one's supervisors, to live one's daily life without a feeling of joy in service to society, to distrust and ridicule political and professional superiors, and to withdraw into personal and familial surroundings whenever possible — all these characteristics of today's Czech and Slovak workers testify to the persistent ineffectuality of party and state in persuading the masses and integrating them into the dynamic process of building socialism.[51]

One phenomenon typical of this withdrawal syndrome is the escape to holiday cottages in the countryside. Czechs have always enjoyed their weekends in the mountains, and an interesting feature of life under socialism has been the democratization of holiday cottages (*chaty,* or in the sometimes used Russian term, *dachi*). In the interwar years, such cottages were the privilege of those who could afford them, because building materials were relatively expensive. In recent years, however, more and more people have been able to afford *chaty;* many of the new cottages that have mushroomed in vacation regions have been built by the owners themselves — very frequently with building materials purloined from construction companies or bought on the black market.[52] In 1934, Prague residents owned a total of 3,000 holiday cottages; in 1974, they owned a total of 65,000 in Central Bohemia alone — with many others journeying greater distances to their cottages in Western Bohemia, South Moravia, or Slovakia. In 1967 there were 110,000 *chaty* in the Czech lands; by 1970 the total had reached 150,000 and continued to climb.[53]

The rapid increase in the numbers of holiday cottages has played havoc with the natural environment in recreational areas and caused some potential hygiene problems (potable drinking water, sewage and drainage). In June of 1974 the Czech government felt obliged to curb what was officially called "dacha mania" by ordering that no more than 25,000 building permits would be issued in the future. There was the additional possibility of acquiring some 33,000 vacant buildings in suitable vacation areas, many of these being farmhouses abandoned thirty years ago by Sudeten Germans forced to leave Czechoslovakia.[54] Once these possibilities are exhausted, the boom in dacha construction will be over, unless the Czech government can come up with a more tenable long-range policy. If it cannot, the effect will be to halt the proliferation of cottages, thus permanently foreclosing future dacha ownership for all who have not yet acquired one.

Aside from the government's concern for the environment, public hygiene, and thefts of building materials, the regime is undoubtedly disturbed by the ideological implications of "dacha mania." The rush to the countryside is indeed symptomatic of a frustration with life in the urban centers, with, as one observer has put it, the facts of daily existence in an oppressive and politicized world, ". . . the intrusive world of slogans, appeals, threats, promises. . ." so characteristic of the workers' society.[55] Ideologically speaking, dacha mania is reminiscent of certain petit-bourgeois traits that are officially considered unbecoming to socialist citizens — acquisitiveness, the urge to privacy, and escapism.

The holiday cottages provide the means for a temporary retreat from all the ugly realities of the workaday world. In those tiny huts with no telephones and often no electricity, outside society becomes remote and temporarily irrelevant. Like the bygone world of Rabí Castle, the workaday world is a place where the masses are involved in drudgery for somebody else's benefit. In the holiday cottage, on the other hand, one works for oneself and one's immediate family. One works hard, for life is simple and lacking in modern conveniences. Yet one works with pleasure, for once the wood is gathered and split, the fire built, the meal prepared, and other chores dispatched, one has a modest feeling of fulfillment, for one has done one's job and can now spend the leisure hours in the beauty and quietude of the countryside, unencumbered by the pressures of the distant urban world.

Resocialization?

The emergence of a dissident movement around the circulation of the so-called "Charter 77" in late 1976 disturbed the regime greatly.

Charter 77 was a formal protest written by political dissenters, many of whom had been in influential positions during the Prague Spring. The protest was signed by several hundred scholars, writers, churchmen, and deposed politicians who sought to gain public attention for the issue of human rights. The dissenters' manifesto chided the party and government for their violation of the International Covenant on Civil and Political Rights which grew out of the 1975 Helsinki Conference. Charter 77 called upon the regime to heed the provisions in the covenant for the guarantee of free expression, nondiscriminatory education policies, religious freedom, individual privacy, and the right to travel freely across the country's borders.[56] Such radical demands could not but stir the regime to action against the petitioners, and several of the most prominent perpetrators were arrested. Curiously, however, the authorities seemed to be caught in a position of uncertainty or disunity concerning the proper mode of response, and the immediate recriminatory actions taken were rather moderate.[57]

The events surrounding the circulation of Charter 77 reminded the authorities of the unpleasant experiences eight years earlier and highlighted the difficult, long-range task of political resocialization. The events of 1968–69 were so disruptive, in the party's official view, that the momentum of the ongoing revolution had been halted, the public was confused and led astray, and ideological development was pushed back to some earlier point of departure. Indeed, the process of ideological deterioration in Czechoslovakia can be traced back to a considerably earlier time than 1968, as Ján Riško has argued.[58] As early as 1958 rightwing forces began to surface, breaking the consistent pattern of positive ideological unity that had prevailed within the party since 1948. The rightwing forces fought for, and achieved, the possibility of speaking out, and in the course of the ensuing decade they wormed their way into the highest and most influential positions in society. From these vantage points they swayed the opinions of many unsuspecting people. The ideological disorientation caused by these rightwing deviants thus resulted in the widespread acceptance of subtle counterrevolutionary ideas masked behind the pseudosocialistic slogans and programs of the 1968 leaders.

Because of the disruption, ideological development in socialist Czechoslovakia regressed almost back to the starting point. Riško argues that the ideological confusion of the second socialist decade essentially negated the progress of the first. This explains the problems facing the leaders of the 1970s. In many cases, workers did not recover from the shattering of their illusory dreams in 1968, and the unmasking of the counterrevolutionary Dubček group led many to distrust all persons in authority. It may take some time to regain the workers' confidence in the party — but never mind that. At least the counter-revolution has been stopped, the right wing has been silenced, and the country is back on the forward road once again. In time the disillusion-ment of 1968–69 will fade, given the diligent efforts of party, state, and all social organizations. The task is clear; the masses must be re-educated: "This is once again the beginning of a process for moulding a socialist man, a conscientious builder of socialism, a man who is pure and firm."[59]

One characteristic of such pure, firm men is a strong dedication to the collective ethic of socialism. In this vein, statistics concerning thefts of socialist property serve as yet another cause for official dissatisfac-tion. These crimes are seen, ideologically, as more serious than thefts of personal property, because they reflect a certain amount of dis-respect for the collective ethic. It is therefore illuminating to examine the data available on thefts of socialist property, beginning with 1960, the year in which Czechoslovakia was officially proclaimed to have left the transitional stage of the people's democracy and entered into socialism.

Statistics on these crimes are not unambiguous, but it can accurately be said that the overall trend since 1960 has not been in the direction party leaders would like to see. Following a decline in the early 1960s, thefts of socialist property increased dramatically, reaching a peak in 1967, and then fell gradually back to levels similar to those of 1960–64 (see figure, below). It is not clear what caused the wild fluctuations in the crime statistics displayed in Figure I.3, but one possible explana-tion might be better, or more honest, reporting of such crimes between 1965 and 1969. If we assume for the present purpose that the 1965–69 data represent (for whatever reason) a deviation from the longer-term pattern, the overall trend was one of remarkable stability in the annual figures, as represented by line B of Figure I.3. Comparing five-year data from the first half of the seventies with those of a decade earlier suggests that in each case the trend was slightly downward, but the total incidence of the crimes was higher in the seventies than in 1960–64 (see Figure I.4).[60]

Statistics concerning the value of goods stolen are more difficult to find, but those available show cause for even greater alarm. In 1970, theft of socialist property amounted to the loss of goods valued at Kčs 120 million; in 1971 the total was Kčs 140 million, and in 1972 the figure shot up to Kčs 211.4 million. Additional scattered facts shed

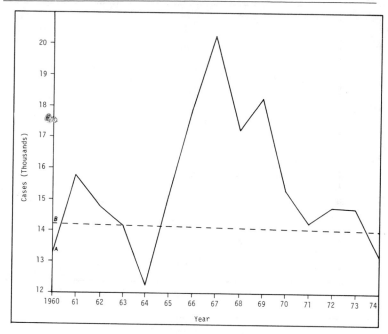

Figure I.3

Thefts of Socialist Property in ČSSR 1960–74 (Convictions)

Note: Solid line (A) simply follows the path of the data. Broken line (B) is the line of regression calculated to indicate overall trend of data, excluding 1965–69.

more light on the scope of the problem; according to one report, every third person prosecuted for crime in 1971 was prosecuted for theft of socialist property. Moreover, the available statistics reflect only *reported* crime. For numerous reasons — fear of being held responsible by one's superiors, fear of losing one's job, or just lack of concern — many workers and managers fail to report these thefts. It is estimated that the value of property stolen and not reported may exceed by several times that shown in the figures cited above.[61]

So serious is the theft of socialist property that the matter was discussed at length by the Federal Assembly in June of 1973, and leading judicial figures were called in to contribute to the deliberations. It was noted, with great concern, that many people seemed to have stern feelings about thefts of private property but showed a great deal of permissiveness toward thefts of socialist property.[62]

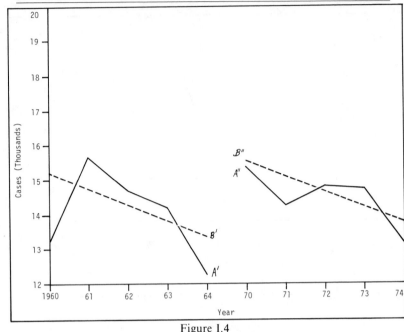

Figure I.4

Thefts of Socialist Property in the ČSSR, 1960–64 and 1970–74

Lines A' and A" trace the paths of the data. Lines B' and B" indicate five-year trends in data.

The statistics cited may seem small compared with crime in the industrialized parts of the capitalist world, but they are significant. The regime regards such crimes as an indication that not enough progress toward ideological purity has been made among the workers. Theft of socialist property is a "curse inherited from the past," a symptom of vestigial "bourgeois morality" based on the personal profit motive.[63] Many citizens seem to have the feeling that socialist property belongs to no one in particular, and therefore no one is hurt by the pilfering that goes on. The regime's concern is well-founded, for if these attitudes are indeed widespread they reflect a discouraging atmosphere of disdain for the fundamental purpose of collective enterprise. Stealing socialist property is robbing the public, and transgressing against society is tantamount to a rejection of the collective ideal. Those who condone or feel indifferent toward social transgressions are moral accomplices to the crimes, for they are expected, ideally, to watch diligently over the welfare of their fellow citizens.[64]

Public disdain for socialist property is symptomatic of the masses' disillusionment with the official system and its values. As at various times in the past, Czechs and Slovaks are living in a state of political alienation, cut off from their rulers by mutually incomprehensible views of the world. Yet no other political alternatives can be developed, for the possibility of discussing politics is severely limited; organizing is, of course, out of the question. The situation is one of serious moral disorientation: the official values hold no attraction for most citizens, but articulating an alternative value system is fraught with hazards — as the Charter 77 group discovered.

Some, perhaps, can find spiritual refuge in religion. In the churches one is offered an alternative set of ideals, and although the regime discourages churchgoing there is evidence that religious functions have attracted an increasingly larger number of followers in the seventies. Christenings, church marriages, and religious funerals have become more common than they were in the sixties, and religious instruction is being sought by more people. In 1966, only 22 percent of all church members in Czechoslovakia received religious instruction; according to a report published in 1972, in that year 34 percent of church members in the Czech lands, and 50 percent in Slovakia, were receiving instruction.[65] A reporter writing for *Tribuna* has suggested that religious functions were taking on the character of a "fashion" and ridiculed those young people who hurried away from the local magistrate's office following their legal marriage ceremony in order to be remarried in church.[66]

The evidence concerning religion, however, is not clear. Except in rural areas — particularly in Moravia and Slovakia — church attendance is generally rather low, and even among many of the staunchest professed Christians one perceives an ambivalence toward traditional religion. A survey conducted by the Institute of Sociology of the Slovak Academy of Sciences in the late 1960s indicated that 91.2 percent of the farmers interviewed (all Slovaks) considered themselves believers.[67] However, a later survey conducted among Slovak villagers showed that only 40 percent of the respondents believed the biblical version of the Creation, and only 3.7 percent in miracles.[68] These are, of course, only isolated surveys and cannot be taken as definitive evidence of the saliency of religious ideas. But they do indicate that there is some degree of uncertainty concerning the literal value system of the church among its adherents. Thus the church, an alternative source of moral guidance for only a part of the population, offers at best an ambiguous substitute for the Communist system of beliefs.

Party and government leaders are aware of the problem relating to citizens' attitudes. The frequency of articles dealing with aspects of political socialization indicates that a great deal of effort is currently going into the creation of the "new man." As always, the primary target of this effort is the younger generation. Among the youth is where the party expects to find its greatest receptiveness, for young minds are more easily influenced than older minds, and young hearts are more readily stirred to the support of revolutionary causes.

Here again the problem is not easily solved. Many of the regime's spokesmen have expressed their disappointment with some of the attitudes manifested by today's youth. An article in the Slovak party organ *Právda* reflected nostalgically upon the interwar period, when the universities were bastions of Communist strength, with as many as 25 percent of university students either actively registered as party members or sympathizing with the Communists. In the 1970s, the universities are not party strongholds. The article cites the Veterinary College in Košice, where only approximately six percent of the students are candidates for party membership, and adds that this figure might even be high compared to the party rolls at other advanced schools.[69]

Negative attitudes toward the regime and its objectives take on various forms among students. Several years ago the regime attempted to whip up enthusiasm for the visit of American black activist leader Angela Davis but afterward discovered some disquieting student reactions to Ms. Davis's talk of revolution.[70] At other times students have been overheard making slanderous comments to each other about the government, the Soviet Union, and the intellectual quality of their required courses in Marxism-Leninism. On the wall of Charles University's Clementinum someone once wrote, "Join the Communist party to prepare another 1968!"[71] A member of the Socialist Youth Union wrote a lengthy column in the pages of *Tribuna,* unburdening her frustration with the negative attitudes among her fellow members. She complained that within the very organization whose purpose was to foster healthy socialist ideas there was an ample number of "outright opponents of our policies, admirers of the West, and careerists." There were those who unflatteringly referred to the fraternal troops of the USSR as "Russkies" and those who used still stronger terms. Moreover, the writer complained that she often felt some considerable social pressure to conform to this prevailing cynicism.[72]

It is not only university students who show signs of youthful disillusionment. According to an article in *Rudé právo* in September 1972, the most important problem in the training of apprentices is their inadequate ideological preparation.[73] Young people simply have not been appropriately imbued with the correct view of their role in socialist society. Federal Deputy Prime Minister Matěj Lučan complained in a Radio Prague broadcast that young people were primarily oriented toward personal success and fortune, that they had incorrect political opinions, valued petit-bourgeois ideas, were prone to consumerism, admired the fashions of the capitalist world, and were too emotional.[74]

Still, the party has not given up on the youth. Speaking before a session of the party Central Committee, Václav Burian admitted that there were some disturbing trends among the younger generation but added that these were the exception rather than the rule:

> Some of our youth display tendencies to live from day to day, without any responsibility toward society, to live apolitically. But if we know how to utilize all of our possibilities for influencing the youth, then I believe that the overwhelming majority of young people will go along with us and become the noble heirs of those who fought, suffered, and often even died for a socialist society.[75]

Burian's comments reflect the prevailing official belief that the young can and must be brought to the support of the revolution. As a prominent educator put it, "Their moral qualities must be developed and ideological firmness furthered."[76]

The task is not an easy one. In the first place, there have been many problems with the quality of instructors entrusted with the responsibility of ideological training. The officials note the frequency of simplisticism in instructors' approaches, as well as a lack of attention to the connection between education and real life.[77] In the years after 1969, many teachers were found to have the wrong political attitudes. More than one-third of all teachers who had been party members were dropped from the party lists. As of November 19, 1970, large numbers of teachers were dismissed from positions in the Teachers' Trade Union — 42 percent from the union's Central Committee and Central Control Commission, 48.6 percent from regional committees of the union, 60 percent of the district committee chairmen and 43.8 percent of the members, 22.5 percent of basic committee chairmen and 15 percent of the members.[78] In subsequent years party education officials have seen their main task to be the consistent intensification of political-ideological work among university students and other members of the younger generation. To this end the universities have returned to control methods reminiscent of the 1950s: strict criteria of class origin and political outlook among students applying for admission, tight party supervision over teaching curricula, and diligent party control over student organizations.[79]

As it is in the universities, so it is in other aspects of public life. The party has shown an ever-vigilant concern with the message conveyed in the press, the mass media, films, and other vehicles of communication. Among the tasks outlined in the July 1973 Central Committee session were greater emphasis on purveying the Marxist-Leninist, internationalist outlook through the media and drawing the younger generation closer to the regime.[80]

Whether or not these efforts succeed in winning over the young remains to be seen. If past experience is a guide, it would seem that the efforts might very well prove futile. Limiting university admissions to children from working-class families was tried in the 1950s, and it was that very generation of students that became the most enthusiastic supporters of the reform movement in the 1960s. Strict control over youth organizations in the past has turned them into sterile, unchallenging institutions that defeated their own purpose by boring their members with meaningless rituals and an overdose of ideology. Those who rose to positions of leadership within these organizations were those most intent upon party careers, hence most prone to sycophancy, and their uncritical demeanor tended to hold the intellectual and cultural level of the organizations to a low point. If the regime's efforts are to succeed, the country's youth must be offered programs that stimulate and excite them. So far, no success can be seen.

The Rule of the Lie

Underlying the lack of public confidence is the regime's fundamental dishonesty.[81] Caught in the position of having to defend the Soviet protectorate, the regime has had to fabricate preposterous slanders about the alleged malefactors of 1968–69. Dubček's attempt to articulate a "socialism with a human face" now receives only scorn and derision in the official press.[82] All the major leaders of the reform period who were so popular in their day are now officially discredited. Alexander Dubček, Oldřich Černík, the late Josef Smrkovský and their colleagues registered astoundingly high popularity ratings in public opinion surveys conducted during 1968.[83] Similarly, the program of the post-January leadership received something akin to a popular mandate in numerous surveys conducted in diverse regions of

Czechoslovakia.[84] Today's regime in effect admits that the reform government was popular, and in slandering the Dubček group the present-day leaders are also slandering the public, who, the regime seems to be saying, were thoroughly duped.

The official version of the 1968 events has been elaborated many times; the regime has examined and reexamined the evidence, spinning explanations that varied somewhat at first but have now settled into a body of dogma. Josef Lenárt, an old Novotnýite who somehow survived all the battles of the sixties and has reemerged as a prominent member of the current ruling group, has compared the Czechoslovak reform movement with the Hungarian Revolt of 1956. Both, he says, aimed at overthrowing the socialist system and restoring capitalism; the difference was that the counterrevolutionaries in Czechoslovakia proceeded more slyly, camouflaging their intentions behind misleading socialist slogans, whereas the Hungarian counterrevolutionaries had fought openly. Deceit, chicanery, subversion of the party from within, and slander against the true nature of socialism were the weapons of the Czech and Slovak counterrevolutionaries. These perfidious traitors brought about a situation that, according to Lenárt, ". . . was moving toward a point at which an open clash between the antisocialist and socialist forces might have erupted in civil war. . . ."[85]

Of course, Czechs and Slovaks now have their fraternal allies to thank for having saved them from themselves. Lenárt explained that civil war was prevented at the last minute because "the revolutionary forces at home as well as our allies acted with great foresight. . . ."[86] Had it not been, in the words of a *Rudé právo* editorial, for the "timely international aid of our nearest socialist allies" in August 1968, Czechs and Slovaks might never have gotten back onto the right track.[87]

The current leadership indeed feels indebted to its allies for their role in restoring orthodox Communist rule in the ČSSR. Citizens are treated to frequent paeans of gratitude and obsequious proclamations of fealty to the Soviet Union. These appear more or less regularly in the press, especially at times when Soviet holidays are commemorated or on the anniversaries of important events in the establishment of the Czechoslovak-Soviet alliance.[88] A frequent slogan, now common among Czechoslovak officials on festive days, is "With the Soviet Union forever! With the Soviet Union and never any other way!"

As far as public attitudes toward the USSR are concerned, one need only recall the masses' immediate reactions to the invasion to understand public sentiment. Today the occupying troops are discreetly stationed away from population centers, and during their occasional forays into town they are, for the most part, ignored by the local inhabitants. Their presence is felt, of course, and citizens scoff at the promises made long ago to the effect that the troops would be removed as soon as the local political situation had "normalized." The situation is now quite normal, and General Secretary Brezhnev has expressed his satisfaction. Still the troops remain, a permanent reminder of Czechoslovakia's subservience to its "fraternal" partner.[89]

That the citizens do not realize their debt to their Soviet brothers is yet another theme of discouragement expressed in the official press. The regime is attempting to correct false impressions — again taking a long-term view of the possibilities for attitudinal change — by teaching schoolchildren of the wonderful benefits derived from their country's partnership with the USSR. A 1974 article in the *Teachers' News* recommended teaching children that the Soviet Union supplies Czechoslovakia with much-needed products such as machines, fuels, aluminum, cotton, grain, and butter. They should be taught arithmetic through the use of problems stated in terms of statistics from Soviet agricultural and industrial production. As always, they must be taught Russian language and literature, music and art. Finally, the meaning of the October Revolution and the role of the Red Army in liberating Czechoslovakia should be given central places in the teaching of history.[90]

Again it must be said that this is nothing new. It smacks of the heavy-handed distortions of Czech and Slovak pedagogy in the 1950s, when the national cultures took second place to that of the mother socialist country. Whether or not the historiographical distortions of that earlier era will be replicated remains to be seen definitively, but such are the implications of the *Teachers' News* article.

The biggest lie, of course, brings us back to the thought expressed several times earlier in this chapter. Despite all that the regime's spokesmen say, there is no convincing the public that Czechoslovakia is a workers' paradise. Workers are unhappy about the national humiliation inherent in the continuing cooperation, about the generally low quality of both political and industrial leadership, about their own inability to speak openly and freely, and about the utter lack of candor on the regime's part. They are frustrated with the severely limited possibilities of foreign travel, especially to the West. Because they are a generally rather sophisticated and well-read people, they are disappointed with the lack of intellectual leadership in their own country, and with the current low level of cultural life.

Politically, all remnants of the 1968 movements have been repressed. A total of 461,791 people lost their membership in the Communist party. Of these, 70,934 were pointedly expelled, and the remainder were simply dropped from the lists when their memberships came up for renewal. Some 11,000 of those expelled were people who emigrated and thereby automatically lost their membership. More recently, the party has taken a moderately conciliatory line toward those dropped from the lists who could not be identified (in official terms) with rightist or counterrevolutionary activities. According to KSČ Secretary Vasil Biľak, all who lost their membership had the right to appeal — but of those who did, as of September 1975, only one-fifth had been readmitted to the party.[91]

Needless to say, all those closely associated with the reform movements, both within and outside the party, have either gone into exile or sunk into obscurity. With them has gone the legitimacy of public discussion and the expression of dissent. When several dozen individuals were arrested late in 1971 for distributing leaflets advising citizens to show their dissatisfaction by abstaining in the November general elections, it became manifest that even this relatively modest form of open dissent would not be tolerated.[92] The activities of the Charter 77 group five years later brought a similar response. Political life in Czechoslovakia has become, as it was in the fifties, the carefully guarded province of an isolated elite purged for the most part of persons who dare to espouse fundamental changes in the system.

As for public political efficacy, there is little evidence to suggest that the workers in this workers' state have any real clout. Hard data, of course, are lacking, but an independent attitudinal survey conducted secretly by a correspondent of the émigré journal *Svědectví* in 1974 indicated a widespread feeling of political inefficacy; only 10 percent of the respondents — and, significantly, only 25 percent of party members polled — felt they had some influence on political affairs.[93]

The leadership of the seventies has justified the constraints on political participation by frequent allusions to the danger from the right. The danger, so it is argued, is evident in the emergence of the underground activities — the pamphleteers, the writers of open letters, the petitioners, and those who purvey information to foreign journalists for publication in the West. The fact that the hard core of the underground activists includes some of the central figures of 1968 confirms the regime's worst fears concerning the danger. The activists are political exiles within their own country, but the regime has continued to be wary of the influence these exiles might have upon the public.[94]

Intellectual and cultural life has suffered from a dual handicap. In the first place, there have been overt repression and renewal of tight censorship. Many talented people have either emigrated or found themselves denied the opportunity of publishing their works. A large number of scholars lost their positions in the universities and the academies.[95] They have, in addition, been barred from using the libraries and archival sources necessary for their research. Secondly, there has been what one observer calls "unofficial repression" — the atmosphere of moral and psychic stagnation that hovers over the activity of intellectuals who regret the departure of their former colleagues and fear that they too may lose their much-valued jobs if what they produce does not meet official approval. Such an atmosphere of intellectual uncertainty prevails not only among social scientists and humanists but equally among those engaged in the "hard" sciences.[96]

Few books, films, and plays have been produced since 1969 to compare with those that came out in such impressive quantities between 1963 and 1969. Some considerable excitement accompanied the publication in 1976 of Bohumil Hrabal's novel *The Haircut,* but as of this writing there is no evidence that Hrabal's noteworthy book marked the beginning of a broad cultural renascence.[97] Many of the names associated with the culture of the sixties — Škvorecký, Mňačko, Liehm, Němec, Kadár, Forman, and others — have emigrated. Most of those who remained behind, such as Milan Kundera, Václav Havel, and Pavel Kohout, have found it impossible to publish in their own country and have had to smuggle manuscripts abroad in order to reach audiences. The situation is extremely frustrating for these artists, whose foremost desire is to reach their own countrymen with their art and social commentary.[98] Meanwhile, the public taste generally runs to the classics and to those Western imports which either make it through the censor (such as *Airport*) or are smuggled in by returning tourists and foreign friends. Among the latter are the works of Alexander Solzhenitsyn, with whom many Czechs and Slovaks seem to feel a deep moral identity.[99]

The impression remains, then, that Czechoslovakia is a sort of prison. The "inmates" thrive at the behest of their leaders, who in turn look to the East for approval and guidance. The workers of the workers' state cannot speak their minds unless all those within earshot are deemed trustworthy. The diversions of their prisons are perhaps better than those available to most prisoners; they can retreat temporarily to the countryside, discreetly read a contraband book, or take a vacation on the Black Sea. They cannot, on the other hand, come and go freely — at least not to the West. The restrictions on travel to the capitalist countries have become increasingly tight in the seventies, and the average citizen cannot hope to leave the socialist world more often than once every three or four years. Even then, to travel with one's family is practically impossible. Citizens are therefore limited to the diversions available to them in their own part of the politically divided world.[100]

It cannot be said that all these hardships are totally without recompense. Workers in the Czechoslovakia of the 1970s live relatively well in a material sense. Their incomes have climbed steadily, and their buying power has increased markedly. In addition, there is the ever-present possibility of moonlighting in various ways for inflated black-market fees — especially for those engaged in service occupations, such as automobile mechanics and plumbers — and the occasional chance to steal things from the workplace, either to sell or to use for oneself. For those who are especially clever or especially virtuous in the eyes of today's authorities, life is not at all bad. Good workers who do their jobs in an exemplary manner — particularly those who are also loyal party members — are rewarded with adequate housing, good wages, and a better-than-average chance of foreign travel.[101]

Even for the average worker, the standard of living is quite tolerable. Food is relatively inexpensive, and there has been some measurable improvement in the distribution of food products. Automobile ownership has become possible for larger and larger numbers of citizens; in 1970, approximately one of every eighteen people owned cars, and it is expected that this will improve to one in fourteen by 1980.[102] Housing continues to be in short supply; although rents are very low, waiting lists are long, and only the privileged (or those able and willing to bribe the proper housing authorities) can move quickly to the head of the lists. Real wages have risen slowly but steadily, and increasing supplies of various consumer goods have made their way to the stores throughout the country.[103]

Antonín Liehm has referred to the current relationship between rulers and ruled as an arrangement governed by the "new social contract": the workers put up with politically repressive and culturally unsatisfying social conditions in return for a relatively comfortable living standard earned by a minimum of productive labor.[104] The cost of this arrangement is quite high on both sides. For the workers, it involves their continued subordination and acceptance of the party's political monopoly. For the regime, it involves subsidizing the consumer goods market to the tune of an estimated 30 percent or more of the national product.[105]

Even at that, the payoff is uncertain. The respondents to the survey mentioned above (page 45) show much ambivalence when asked to evaluate the prospects for their society and their families. To the question, "Do you think the situation will become more tolerable (within the time of your generation)?" 31 percent of the blue-collar respondents and only 18 percent of white-collar workers replied affirmatively.[106] When asked whether they thought any fundamental changes would take place in their society by the year 2000, 62 percent of white-collar workers and 74 percent of blue-collar workers responded negatively.[107] Again, these data must be read with the understanding that they were gathered under difficult conditions and may, therefore, not be very accurate, but they serve to strengthen the impression one has that the improved standard of living alone does not make Czechoslovakia, in the eyes of its citizens, a workers' state.

A final indicator of the present reality was offered directly and unabashedly by the regime itself at the time of the Fifteenth party congress in the summer of 1976. The security around the meetings and delegates was so tight that some older residents of the capital compared it to Hitler's ride from Prague to Vienna in March of 1939. Indeed, at least one citizen was overheard expressing the opinion that the security measures taken to protect the workers' representatives in 1976 were more extreme than those provided by the SS for the wartime rulers of a hostile Bohemia. "If the late Heydrich* had taken measures like those of Husák," the person said, "he would still be here today."[108]

Thus we might conclude that the reality of life in the Czechoslovakia of the seventies is something less than satisfactory, and the rosy picture that the Party would like the workers to have is far from universally accepted. One is tempted once again to reflect upon the confusing images of reality and fantasy, returning perhaps not to Rabí Castle but rather to that absurd castle depicted in the novel written by an illustrious earlier inhabitant of twentieth-century Bohemia, Franz Kafka.

Some Hypotheses

Rather than a society of active and enthusiastic builders of socialism, Czechoslovakia since 1969 is a society in which political

---

* Note — Reinhard Heydrich was Hitler's appointed governor (*Reichsprotektor*) of the Protectorate of Bohemia and Moravia in 1941–42. He was known for the severity of his rule, and he was assassinated in Prague in 1942.

cynicism is the general mood. Rather than a united society of workers well represented by a true party-vanguard, it is one in which the distance between party and workers is obvious and seemingly unbridgeable. The available evidence about social problems suggests that alienation runs quite deeply through the ranks of the workers, who bear scant resemblance to the normative model citizens of the Marxist-Leninist theoretical prototype.

An easy explanation of the current political situation is to point to the events that have taken place since 1968. Bluntly stated, the regime is a repressive one, sensitive about its unpopularity and fanatically distrustful of its subjects. The latter, by and large, have strong and very favorable memories of a day not so long ago when the political situation was much more to their liking. This refers not only to 1968, but also to the last years of the Novotný period, when through weakness and indecisiveness as much as anything else the regime had gradually relaxed its hold on social and cultural affairs. Indeed, many people who were not in agreement with the main tendencies of the Dubček months — and even some who were — recall the last Novotný years with nostalgia, for at that time the society was alive with intellectual and artistic experiments. Today the regime is fearful of ideas and refuses to allow — let alone encourage — intellectual innovation unless sensitive social questions are kept out of the discussion. The best writers of the sixties, moreover, are with few exceptions out of circulation in the Czechoslovakia of the seventies. Thus what seemed to many to be the saving grace of the Novotný era, the lively cultural life, is no longer present to cushion the impact of a repressive polity.

As far as the economic picture is concerned, here is an area of some greater promise for the average citizen. The "new social contract" has brought a new level of prosperity to the consumer. Whatever the level of public satisfaction that has resulted, however, must be weighed against the cynicism with which the new order is accepted. We have no direct empirical data by which to measure public acceptance of the current status quo, but the indirect evidence cited in the foregoing pages suggests that the dominant public mood is one that tolerates the political situation while remaining affectively distant from the regime and alienated from the official value system. The prevailing public cynicism makes a mockery of the Party's official mythology; Party slogans and official descriptions of the political reality seem rather empty in light of the public's attempt to withdraw from the revolution. The picture we see is one of outward ritualism — sloganeering, ideological training sessions, the resort to Party jargon in all aspects of public life — but an inner purposelessness. The secular faith that was meant to buttress the political system seems to have lost its compelling attractiveness and exists simply for lack of an alternative value system.

Behind this pervasive incongruity there lies a deeper and more complex element in the make-up of Czechoslovakia's political culture. The chasm separating the regime from the public is even more profound than the surface reality indicates. In the first place, the regime has effectively shattered all the hopes that had been inspired by the events of the Prague Spring. In so doing, the leaders have reintroduced a pattern of rule reminiscent of the ugly Stalinist years, less brutal than the earlier system but scarcely more tolerant of social diversity and no less protective of the elite's political monopoly. The Prague Spring had aroused the hope that the participatory democracy envisioned by Marx and Lenin might finally be in the making; the events following the intervention dashed that hope and reminded the Czechs and Slovaks of numerous earlier instances in their history when their national aspirations had been frustrated by more powerful neighbors.

The invasion of Czechoslovakia by her allies brought home a second poignant political reality, namely the country's inescapable dependency on the Soviet alliance system. No intelligent Czech or Slovak would have denied before 1968 that the Soviet Union exercised a powerful influence on Czechoslovakia's affairs, but the extent of that influence was frequently underestimated. The leaders of the reform government certainly misjudged Soviet intentions; the Dubček group consistently misunderstood the level of commitment the Soviet leaders felt to the maintenance of the East European status quo. The crushing military intervention left no doubt as to who is the ultimate legitimator of Czechoslovakia's political system; Czechoslovakia's allies, the USSR foremost among them, assume that role and stand ready to prevent any new departures that threaten to undermine the basic authoritarianism of the Communist system. The current regime is the offspring of the intervention, and its unpopularity is heightened by its association with the invaders of 1968.

The roots of the political incongruities, however, go back beyond 1968. Accurately speaking, they go back even beyond the era of Communist rule. It has been very characteristic of Czechoslovakia's Communist governments that they have been insensitive to the traditional political culture. Beginning in the early years of their rule, the Communists' dedication to revolutionary change has led them to deny many of the noble qualities of the national past. Revolutionary movements generally aim to redirect popular orientations away from old patterns of thinking and toward a new outlook, but the extent to which the past has been officially discredited in Czechoslovakia has been exceptional. Unlike some of the neighboring countries' recent successes in this respect, Czechoslovakia has failed to integrate its dominant historical symbols with the socialist view of history.[109] The result is a persisting incoherence in the society's collective self-image, as the regime seeks to create a new version of history in which the traditional national heroes — particularly those of the First Republic — are replaced by the less familiar heroes of the working-class movement.

In several critical respects, then, the Communists have generally failed to associate themselves in the public eye with compelling symbols. There is much evidence that popular views of history, handed down from the parent and grandparent generations, still pose a strong challenge to the party's attempts at re-creating a more revolutionary system of political symbols. The old images tend to live on in the collective mind of the public, encouraged by the party's inability to offer more persuasive substitutes.

It is not only old images and symbols that die slowly. Patterns of political orientations and certain conceptions of political reality also carry over from earlier generations. The Prague Spring brought out some of these older orientations that had been submerged beneath the surface of the Communist patterns between 1948 and 1968.

Two longstanding patterns that reemerged in 1968 were a view of politics as an arena of intense pluralistic activity and a strong sense of distinctiveness in the two national cultures, Czech and Slovak. The reform government tolerated, and even encouraged, the reemergence of these deeply rooted patterns in the political culture. It was for this reason that the reform government was so enthusiastically welcomed; the short-lived socialist experiment reawakened spontaneous political impulses that had lain dormant for twenty years. To invoke a well-worn cliché, the Prague Spring did not take place in a historical vacuum. Rather, it developed as a long-delayed reaction to the political austerity of the preceding twenty years, during which time the Party had manifestly violated certain profound national values. The process of reform, beginning with the intellectual renascence of the early sixties and culminating in the Prague Spring, led to a protracted self-examination on the part of both elites and masses. In the course of this many people discovered the true meaning of their past and sought to define their present and future in keeping with the spirit of that past. The abortive end of that hopeful process disturbed a movement of great significance, not only to Czechoslovakia but, more generally speaking, to the pursuit of the socialist purpose. The reforms had created an atmosphere in which the revolutionary ideas of communism were allowed to interact with national traditions that happened to be very receptive to both democracy and socialism. By abandoning the experiment of the Prague Spring and retreating into a mode of rule that had already proved ineffectual, the post-1969 leadership has brought upon itself a political situation that, in terms of pursuing the high ideals of Marx and Lenin, appears to be hopeless.

The following chapters seek to explore in greater detail the roots of the Communists' dilemma by examining the nature of political traditions in Czechoslovakia, the images these traditions have created in the public mind, and the position of the Communists vis à vis those images.

II

The Ambiguities of History

An eminent scholar once described Czechoslovakia's history as a tragic dialectic of triumph and disaster in which periods of political independence have alternated with periods of foreign domination. During times of independence, Czechs and Slovaks have made impressive achievements in the realization of national aspirations, political liberty, economic welfare, and cultural sophistication. During times of foreign domination, on the contrary, all or most of these accomplishments have tended to be minimized, reversed, or even (in some cases) negated.[1]

In the past three and one-half centuries the moments of political self-determination have been greatly outnumbered by the long periods of foreign domination. To a large extent, the political culture of Czechoslovakia has been conditioned by an environment of national insecurity and external pressures. Nonetheless, the relatively brief periods of genuine independence have left an equally strong mark on the political culture. Czechs and Slovaks take pride in their national achievements and greatly value the heritage of independence. Czechoslovakia, alone among the countries of East-Central Europe, has a background of democracy and progressivism during its historical periods of self-determination. This fact, many citizens feel, sets them apart from their socialist neighbors. It validates their claim to participation in the "Western" cultural tradition and provides them with relatively favorable, nostalgic memories of life as it was when they (or their forebears) were privileged to order their own affairs.

Czechs and Slovaks look upon their history with a mixture of pride and humility.[2] Some of the objects of national pride present themselves in an obvious way to the casual observer: Prague, the ancient capital of the prosperous Bohemian Kingdom and (for a while) of the Holy Roman Empire, preserved today as a gigantic, living museum; Bratislava, modern-day capital of Slovakia, for 173 years the seat of the Hungarian Kingdom; the Czech National Museum, its statuary hall including some of the "bourgeois" historical luminaries (e.g. Masaryk, Rieger) whose contributions to the national culture have been defamed or minimized in post-1948 textbooks; the unusual number of classic and antique automobiles from the 1920s and 1930s still to be found on the streets and highways, bespeaking the existence of a technologically sophisticated society long in advance of the socialist revolution; and in certain parts of the countryside, the persistence or re-emergence of local customs and mannerisms, now in competition with the pervading technological influences of the metropoles, but still reminding one of a past identity and a security that the present cannot match.

Pride in the past is often contradicted by a strong sense of humility, sometimes approaching self-abasement. For almost three hundred years the lands of the Bohemian Kingdom were merely provinces of the Habsburg Empire, and for more than a millennium the territory now known as Slovakia was just the northernmost outpost of the Hungarian Kingdom. When independence came following World War I, the ill-fated First Republic was created, ill-fated primarily because of an inhospitable international environment but replete with enough domestic problems to raise some doubts about its internal viability as well.[3] The downfall of the First Republic, the inglorious experience of wartime occupation and partition, and the frustration of attempts to devise a democratic socialist system within the postwar Soviet orbit all have left Czechs and Slovaks with a bitter taste and an ambivalence toward their recent history. The latest attempt at self-determination, in 1968, was ended by the intervention of Czechoslovakia's self-proclaimed allies. The residue of 1968, like that of earlier times, is a mixture of pride in the accomplishments of the short-lived Dubček era and frustration at yet another aborted experiment in democracy.

"Independence" and "subjection" are words that have a tone of relativity about them when applied to the Czechs and Slovaks. Few objective-minded persons would deny that both nations were subjects of Hitler's Germany from 1939 to 1945, despite the illusions of Slovakia's quisling rulers to the contrary, but other periods of modern history are not so clear-cut.[4] What would appear to be the "most independent" period of Czechoslovakia's history, that of the First Republic (1918–1938), was for many Slovaks a time of frustration. Slovak nationalists felt politically subjected by the rule of the Czech bourgeoisie and its Czechophile Slovak supporters.[5] Thus even the "most independent" and the "least independent" periods within the last 50 years are not, in retrospect, unambiguously independent and subject. Nonetheless, it is clear that we must discriminate between these two extremes by reminding ourselves that Interwar Czechoslovakia was indeed a self-ruled country that lost all realistic semblances of its independence in March of 1939, if not at the Munich Conference five months earlier.

Varying degrees of independence and subjectedness have character-ized the years since 1945. The Third Republic (1945–1948)[6] was what we might call semi-independent, a transitional system with its own domestic features but constrained in its foreign policy by the *de facto* suzerainty of the Soviet Union. The Gottwald-Novotný era (1948–1968) was a time of nominal independence but effective Soviet dominance. Both foreign and domestic policies were liable, immedi-ately or ultimately, to review and possible veto by the rulers in Moscow. By 1968 the immediacy of the Russian veto power had become submerged, but its ultimacy remained. The reformers, self-confident of their abilities and basking in a false sense of security, discovered too late that the ultimate arbiter of their policies even in that year of experimentation was the Soviet Politburo. From January to August, Czechs and Slovaks had felt free and acted freely, as if unaware that they were violating an unwritten code of membership in the Warsaw Treaty Organization. Czechoslovakia's leaders during this time acted *as if* they were independent, thus giving the brief period the very flavor of independence. Their rude awakening on August 21 brought home to them the finiteness of their autonomy, as the invading armies set about reincorporating Czechoslovakia into the Soviet sphere of domination.

Looking back over the sweep of the twentieth century, Czechs and Slovaks see a time of great turbulence. They have gone through two world wars, three radical changes in political and institutional struc-ture, eight presidents, countless changes of government, and the domination of four foreign powers.[7] The foreign controllers have exercised significantly differing patterns of authority over the Czechs and Slovaks, and each contributed something to Czechoslovakia's political culture.

By the end of the nineteenth century, Austria under Emperor Franz Joseph had become a relatively lenient oppressor. Internally, its politics were not liberal, but they were moderated by the *"Schlamperei"* of the awkward administrative system loosely presided over by the aging monarch. Austria's foreign policy was, on the one hand, tied to the interests of the rising German Empire and, on the other, con-founded by the complex Balkan problem. Under these circumstances the Czechs received rather mild treatment, especially in comparison to their later treatment at the hands of the Nazis. In contrast, the plight of the Slovaks was immeasurably worse. Hungary, for all intents and purposes, was independent of Austria in its internal authority structure. The semi-feudal institutions of Hungarian society were jealously controlled by the Magyar nobles, who were afraid of loosing the pent-up spirit of nationalism among the subject peoples.

The two systems did have something in common beyond the reign of the Habsburg monarch, however. Both systems militated against the ultimate aim of politically conscious Czechs and Slovaks; that is, both systems kept the subject nationalities from realizing their burning desire for self-determination. This was as true of the parliamentary system in Austrian territories as it was of the self-consciously repressive Hungarian order, for the Czechs in the Vienna *Reichsrat* found themselves persistently outflanked by other national groups.[8] To the Czechs this meant insufficient freedom for the development of their intrinsic egalitarianism and pluralism, as well as a lingering sense that their true national destiny was to have some degree of independence. This did not necessarily mean *total* independence, as a series of Czech politicians from Palacký to Masaryk had argued, but it did seem to require the removal of the class and nationality constraints impeding the political development of Bohemia and Moravia. For the Slovaks the matter was more purely one of national self-determination — indeed, it was a matter of cultural survival. They were being purposely denied the freedom to develop a Slovak political culture. In the end, for both Czechs and Slovaks the cause became that of independence from Austro-Hungarian rule.

Three important cultural patterns emerged from the Habsburg years. In the first place, both Czechs and Slovaks developed a strong awareness of their national identities. Beginning around the end of the eighteenth century and continuing into the twentieth, both nations came to "discover" themselves in relation to other national groups around them, at first in ways that had little political impact, but eventually in terms of a positive political identity. Secondly, the Czech lands began to industrialize in the mid-eighteenth century and underwent a further, more intensive, industrialization drive during the latter part of the nineteenth century. Although Slovakia was not to undergo a similar process until later, the effect in Bohemia and Moravia was the modernizing revolution which came to underlie the economic prosperity and political pluralism of the First Republic. Thirdly, the bureaucratic habits of the Austrians rubbed off onto the Czechs who were brought into the civil service. The development of bureaucratic government is, of course, not unique to Central Europe, but some distinctly Habsburg patterns of organization and attitude could be found in the bureaucracy of the First Czechoslovak Republic. These included both positive traits, such as the systematic processes of organization and operation, and negative traits such as excessive leniency and sloppiness (*Schlamperei*).

The years of the Second World War were a time of national humiliation, especially for the Czechs. To the Czechs, proud of their First Republic and disillusioned by its demise, the German occupation was a reminder of their pre-1918 captivity. They saw the West's capitulation at Munich as a sell-out, and the ensuing Nazi terror was worse than anything the Czechs had suffered since the Thirty Years' War. Although Czechoslovakia lost far less in material terms than any of the neighboring states, the losses in terms of political leadership, social coherence, and public morale were incalculable.[9] Many political leaders fled the country and spent the war years in exile. These included Beneš and most of his former cabinet, as well as a significant number of Communists (including Gottwald and Novotný). Of those who remained behind, the majority were imprisoned or executed. Of the homefront survivors, some became Nazi collaborators, while the rest fell into discord and inactivity.[10] Some resistance activities developed, and even a few highly placed officials (for example, onetime Prime Minister Eliáš, who was executed) were involved. Most resistance activities disintegrated in the wake of the civil terror visited upon the Czechs following the appointment of Reinhard Heydrich, Hitler's provincial satrap in the Protectorate of Bohemia and Moravia, in September of 1941.[11]

For the Czechs, then, the war years were doubly humiliating. Not only were they sold out by their allies and delivered into the hands of a merciless enemy, but once under the thumb of this enemy they submitted more or less passively to his superior force. With their leaders exiled, imprisoned, dead, or morally compromised, the masses lost their sense of purpose, and many of them joined the collaborating politicians by conforming to the dictates of a regime whose values were so alien to their own.

The Slovaks were deeply divided during the war. The Slovak Republic, established under German patronage following Hitler's occupation of the Czech lands, at the same time represented an attempt on the part of the far right to create an extreme nationalist state. The attempt failed even during the regime's existence, because the latter was neither independent nor totally united. Moreover, the domestic support that the regime initially generated under the leadership of Msgr. Jozef Tiso waned as the regime, in conformance with Hitler's directives, proved to be highly repressive and unresponsive to the public.[12] A determined resistance movement developed in the Slovak hinterlands. The abortive uprising of 1944 stirred up many previously passive citizens, thereby laying the psychological groundwork for Slovakia's liberation several months later.[13]

The Slovaks emerged from the war in relatively better physical shape than the Czechs did, but more sharply divided politically. Those who had supported the Tiso regime, for a brief while free from *Czech* dominance, tended to overlook the Nazis' constraints on their freedom and viewed the Slovak Republic as an interlude of national autonomy.[14] For many others, including the Communists, the Tiso state had been unbearably dictatorial. By 1945 the Slovak Republic collapsed, and its opponents were in ascendance.

The legacy of the Second World War is a complicated one. To some Czechs and Slovaks, the behavior of the French and British in 1938 suggested grounds for questioning not only the interwar alliances but the Western value systems which seemed to allow for the abandonment of one's weaker friends. This undoubtedly was an overwhelming factor in Beneš's decision to reach an agreement with the Soviet Union, and it probably also contributed to the postwar electoral strength of the Communists, who were known to be pro-Soviet and anti-West.[15] However, communism *per se* had never been a majoritarian tendency among Czechs and Slovaks. The experience of the First Republic seemed to indicate an overwhelming consensus behind progressive but nonrevolutionary social policies, and after the war a clear majority still chose not to vote for the Communist party. The country's disillusionment with the West, therefore, cannot be seen as a consensual turn to the East. It would be more accurate to describe the public consensus as one favoring a sort of moderate socialism, built around the ideal — often expressed by Beneš — of acting as a "bridge" between the political culture of the East and that of the West.[16]

It is not within the scope of this study to discuss the circumstances surrounding the Communists' assumption of power in 1948. This has been done elsewhere.[17] It is clear that Communist Czechoslovakia has not been independent. The client-state relationship cultivated by the USSR with the postwar regimes of Eastern Europe, like the nature of internal politics in each state, has varied slightly over the years. The general pattern, nonetheless, is one of a modern empire, based on a pseudo-theocratic legitimacy centering around Marxist-Leninist ideology (as interpreted by Moscow) and maintained by the threat or application of Soviet military force.[18] It is not always easy to determine the limits of Soviet tolerance, as the Czechs and Slovaks learned — too late — in 1968. East European leaders must constantly strive to maintain a conscious harmony between their own policies and the demands of the ideocratic Soviet Empire. Czechoslovakia's Communist period must be seen as still another in the long chronicle of national subjugation, broken only temporarily by the "Prague Spring."

It is probably safe to say that the majority of Czechs and Slovaks had no idea of the extent to which the Communists would transform society once they achieved power, nor of the extent to which the yoke of Stalin would be felt. Perhaps the Communists themselves did not know prior to 1948. They took power during a time of intensifying hostilities in the international spectrum. The sides were being drawn for the cold war, and the outlook for peace in Europe was not good. The Communists, now in power in Prague as well as the neighboring capitals of East-Central Europe, came under irresistible international pressure to integrate their state closely into the Cominform system. This was accomplished rapidly. In fact, the speed with which Czechoslovakia took on the outward aspects of a "satellite" state was almost blinding.

Again, this is not the place to repeat in detail what many others have said regarding the specific features of the Stalinist system. In summary, it was a system based on a bogus constitutionality with the Communist party as the practical arbiter of legitimacy and a tightly knit clique of insiders as the decision-makers of the Party. Other political groups were neutralized, their power restricted by statute and their leaders persecuted. The structure of the economy was modeled on the Soviet pattern and redirected toward producing capital goods geared to the input requirements of Soviet industry. Private enterprises vanished, voluntary organizations were dissolved or brought under rigid state control, and churches were forced into conformance with secular controls. The schools and all institutions of the mass media became compliant instruments of official propaganda. In intellectual life, Western influences were combatted and Western literature banned. All "bourgeois" influences, especially those of the First Republic and its great leaders, were similarly discredited. The judicial system, one of the First Republic's finest legacies, was politicized, and the courts were strictly controlled by the Party. Finally, the role of the security police was greatly expanded, and with the help of Soviet advisors a campaign of political terror was mounted in an attempt to cow the populace into uniformity and compliance.[19]

Probably the most demeaning aspect of the new system was the conscious derogation of national traditions, dismissed by the Stalinists as remnants of a "bourgeois" past. Centralistic rule from Prague was tightened up, despite promises made to the Slovaks at Košice in 1945 for some autonomy.[20] The touchy problem of the German minority, such a perennial source of conflict for many years and the ostensible cause of the First Republic's demise, was resolved simply and brutally after the war: all Germans were expelled with the exception of those who had been demonstrably anti-fascist.[21] The Magyar problem was somewhat more complicated, especially now that the Prague government did not wish to antagonize "fraternal" Hungary, by this time also under Communist rule. Resettlement of Czechoslovakia's Magyars had begun slowly in 1945, but only 12 to 15 percent of the Magyars had left when the decision was made to end this policy of expulsion in June of 1948.[22] Those who remained in Czechoslovakia once again were granted full citizenship, as they had before the war. But this was in a society now entering a period of extreme authoritarianism and Czech chauvinism. The regime not only infringed upon the civil rights of all its citizens but took special pains to deny the rights of non-Czech nationals.

The centralistic rule from Prague was a source of grievances on the part of Slovaks and Magyars, but the new rulers could hardly be called Czech *nationalists*. Indeed, the Stalinists fancied themselves to be dedicated *internationalists*. They sought to make society transcend its national traditions regardless of whether these were Czech, Slovak, or Magyar. In the emerging internationalist proletarian society, there would be no place for such vestiges of an earlier era. Because of this, the entire culture had to be reconstructed. Internationalism in practice was to translate into an attempt to "denationalize" society.

History, literature, and religion were obvious targets of the denationalization campaign. All were intimately tied in with national culture: the great heroes of the Czechs and Slovaks — Hus, Chelčický, Žižka, Comenius, Štúr, Kollár, Masaryk, and Hlinka — were deeply religious men whose personal ideals had an immeasurable impact on the development of "bourgeois" culture in Czechoslovakia. Moreover, the great literary figures of that earlier culture, including such writers as Čapek and Kafka, were widely admired in the capitalist West, and this naturally made their work unacceptable in the new society. A new literature had to be created according to the norms of socialist realism, and the forms characteristic of the past were discarded as unnecessary and even harmful.[23] History was rewritten and given an internationalist flavor, and the national heroes of the past were put into a new perspective. T. G. Masaryk, for example, now emerged from the text-books not as the "President-Liberator" that he had been to the previous generation of schoolchildren, but rather as a perfidious bourgeois alleged to have been once connected with a plot to assassi-nate Lenin.[24] In place of religion the people were offered the secular, materialist worldview of Marxism-Leninism, as interpreted by the international Communist hierarchy emanating from Moscow. Thus the new society had to be free from its past; the past was a burden and an impediment to the progressive development of Czechoslovakia.

This official view of the past came to be embodied in an entire system of new perspectives which had the effect of blaspheming many values long cherished by Czechs and Slovaks alike. Many of the Communists' policies were incongruent with the previous political culture, but this attempt at wholesale cultural revolution was quite possibly the least plausible. It was unrealistic because it was aimed at destroying values needlessly. No amount of hyperbolic rationalization could persuade Czechs and Slovaks that the past was as despicable as the Stalinists said it was, and no amount of internationalist cheerleading could erase the strong national self-perceptions of people who recognized the poignancy of their ancestors' long struggles for liberation. Further-more, even if socialism by this time represented a majoritarian sym-pathy among citizens — as electoral statistics from 1946 seemed to indicate[25] — it did not necessarily follow that in order to have socialism every fond memory of the past had to be obliterated.

That this attempt at cultural revolution did not succeed can be seen in the eventual destalinization of culture, in Czechoslovakia as else-where in Eastern Europe. Socialist realism did not survive much beyond the death of Stalin, and the works of some temporarily dis-credited "bourgeois" writers returned to the book stores. During the sixties conscious attempts were made to resurrect the national cul-tures, both Czech and Slovak, and scholars even came to a cautious rehabilitation of Masaryk.[26]

The religious heritage remained a sensitive question. Hus and Žižka were now seen as pre-modern progressives in their own right, but religion as an active force in contemporary society continued to concern the regime, especially in the more heavily Roman Catholic regions of Moravia and Slovakia.[27] A number of sociological studies were made into the strength of religion, and these turned up differing results.[28] It was clear that Czechs and Slovaks were undergoing a secularizing process similar to that in other modern European societies, but the Party has not been able to turn this general tendency into a universal rejection of religious ethics in favor of those derived from Marxist-Leninist ideology.

1968 was a turning point in more ways than one. The short-lived reform period represented a break with the past every bit as dramatic as that of 1918. Although the Communist party never relinquished power for a minute, all the most distasteful characteristics of the political system were suddenly brought before public scrutiny, and many of them were abandoned. It is true that 1968 represented, in many aspects, the culmination of processes developing during the preceding six or eight years, but the tone of the "Dubček Era" was nonetheless qualitatively different. Press and media censorship, the unjust political incarcerations of the past, lack of communication between party and people, restriction of public assembly and expression, economic failures and inequities, official privileges, the economic and political status of Slovakia, lack of intraparty democracy, and above all the meaning of the past — all of these problems were brought out into the public view, acknowledged by the party, and forcefully attacked by an amazingly articulate and well-informed public.[29]

The openness of scholarly and journalistic inquiry that characterized the brief reform period has given way, once again, to an overall dogmatism and a rather narrow view of the national heritages. The atmosphere since 1968 is not so poisonous as that of Stalinism, but the "bourgeois" past is treated with skepticism and circumspection.

Two interesting Czech polls, one taken in October 1968 and one in 1946, shed some light on citizens' own views of their history.[30] Some revealing consistencies are evident in the two polls, and although these were just two isolated surveys, the consistencies between the two suggest that their similarities are more than coincidental. In both polls, T. G. Masaryk emerged as the greatest personality of Czech history — despite the attempts on the regime's part in the intervening years to cast the President-Liberator as a villain. In contrast, neither poll showed a large number of respondents naming Klement Gottwald, the "founding father" of Communist Czechoslovakia and the object of intermittent eulogy since his death in 1953. Instead, the 1946 list included Beneš, Gottwald's political enemy, and the 1968 list included Svoboda and Dubček, the two symbolic leaders of the reform program.

To a question asking respondents to name the most glorious periods of their nation's history, another illuminating set of consistencies appeared. In each survey, respondents named the Hussite period, the time of the national revivals (19th century), the reign of Charles IV (1346–1378), and the First Republic as four of the five most glorious periods; the fifth was the reign of the legendary St. Václav (named in the 1946 survey) and the January–August period of 1968 (named in the 1968 poll). Significantly, respondents in 1968 not only bypassed the Gottwald-Novotný years in this list but indeed placed the First Republic at the very top of their list! Moreover, to a further question asked in 1968 only, Czechs considered the Soviet occupation of 1968, together with the 1950s, to rank among the four most unfortunate periods of their national history — in competition with the Nazi occupation and the "darkness" following the defeat of the Bohemian Estates in 1620.

By way of comparison, a similar survey was conducted among Slovaks in October 1968 only. To the first question, concerning the most glorious periods of the Slovaks' history, respondents named the time of Ľudovít Štúr (19th century), the reform period of 1968, and the Slovak Uprising of 1944. To the second question, concerning the most unfortunate periods, the responses most frequently given were the time of the Slovak state (1939–1945), the centuries of Hungarian domination, and the 1950s.[31]

These polls, singular though they may seem to be in the absence of larger-scale, systematic attitudinal data, give at least a semblance of empirical force to an intuitive feeling shared by Czechs and Slovaks with whom this author has discussed the matters in question. The regime's efforts at discrediting the memories of the bourgeois past and eulogizing the socialist present simply have not convinced large numbers of citizens. The First Republic still looks good in retrospect, and although Slovaks might not share Czechs' enthusiasm for the "old days," they do agree that the 1950s were a miserable time. Thus the Communist regimes have, it seems, made little progress toward orienting citizens' perceptions of themselves along the lines prescribed by the party.

There may be one significant exception to this. There is evidence that the citizenry has come to accept the general goals of *socialism*. In 1968, when citizens were free to respond to the contrary, two separate surveys showed only five percent favoring a return to capitalism and almost all others preferring socialism.[32] However, this was in the context of an increasingly pluralistic ideological atmosphere. Ideas about what constituted socialism were diverging radically from the previously accepted party orthodoxy, and the masses were now aware of many specific formulas for pursuing socialism. Moreover, as we mentioned earlier, there had been something of a consensus behind socialism prior to 1948. While this consensus had apparently grown to a point approaching near-unanimity, it cannot be said that the socialist consensus developed during the years of Communist rule, let alone as a result of it.

There are, then, serious incongruities between the regime's view of the past and the public's. Granting the moderation of the regime's view during the 1960s, it must be said that the Communists' interpretation of history has always been a rather strange one. The leaders would like citizens to see the First Republic and its personalities as a time of capitalist exploitation and general unhappiness. The Czech public seems to reject this view, while Slovaks tend to view the First Republic as exploitative in a national, rather than class, sense. The regime would like its citizens to view the Communist-ruled period with warmth and enthusiasm. However, Czechs and Slovaks alike view it with distaste and consider the present a time of subjection and misery in comparison with nostalgic moments in their previous history.

In the following pages we shall explore more closely the nature of these incongruent interpretations of the past.

The Problem of the First Republic

Of all the periods in the kaleidoscopic history of the Czechs and Slovaks, the most controversial is that of the First Republic. As time moves on the First Republic fades more and more into the past, and memories of the interlude between the world wars grow increasingly indistinct. Those citizens who came of age in the twenties and thirties are now the grandparent generation. The parent generation of the late 1970s has reached maturity since the Second World War. For this group, the First Republic is an unclear image seen largely through the reflections of the preceding generation. For today's youth, the First Republic is no more than "history." The younger generation may view it as a proud or not-so-proud moment in their country's past, but it is removed from their own experience, distant, archaic. Their history texts attempt to portray that time as a bad time, whereas their grandparents may speak of the twenties and thirties as a golden age.

Czechoslovak society under the First Republic was not without its contradictions. It was an ethnic crazy quilt held together by a political system based on Czech libertarian values: parliamentary democracy, separation of church and state, and unitary (rather than federal) government. Non-Czechs were guaranteed a place in political decision-making by means of a complicated proportional representation system, but Czechs nonetheless consistently dominated the main positions of authority. The economy was capitalist, on the whole quite modern (with important exceptions in the rural regions of Slovakia and Ruthenia), and in general very efficient. Yet, despite the preponderance of private ownership and the lack of comprehensive central planning, the national product was distributed relatively evenly, and the overall standard of living was high. In the area of social policies, the First Republic's programs of unemployment compensation, retirement benefits, labor legislation, health and education in many respects surpassed those of the most progressive West European democracies. Moreover, Czech rule over other national groups was remarkably benign. In comparison to their own treatment for three centuries at the hands of the Habsburgs, it must be said that the Czechs as a ruling nation were relatively tolerant and generally more sensitive to the problems of other national groups than the Austrians had been.[33]

A system of proportional representation in the parliament encouraged the proliferation of political parties. Parties represented a very wide variety of political shadings from left to right, and there were in several cases separate parties, or wings of the larger parties, representing most of the major ethnic groups (Czechs, Slovaks, Germans, Magyars, Poles). No party ever achieved a majority in either of the two parliamentary chambers, and government coalitions were always formed around four, five, or as many as eight parties. An extra-constitutional, *ad hoc* committee operated behind the scenes to work out compromise policies among the parties in government. This informal institution — known as the *pětka,* or committee of five, because it originally consisted of the leaders of five parties — was the effective executive committee of the government coalition. Together with the cabinet, the *pětka* represented quite a narrow little clique of rulers, its membership shifting somewhat with the transitory coalition groupings but nevertheless maintaining a degree of continuity.

The functioning of this unwieldy system depended on the talents of the president. Masaryk, president for seventeen of the First Republic's twenty years, displayed a firm but benevolent style of leadership that won him the respect and even love of most people around him. He drew upon the counsel of a semiofficial brain trust of his own advisors, known collectively as the "castle group." As a politician, Masaryk showed a great deal of personal adeptness. Not a member of any political party himself after 1918, he negotiated with party leaders, mediated among them, initiated proposals of compromise, reasoned, and soothed passions. More than any other person or institution, Masaryk symbolized the First Republic. The latter was his creature, and his name is inseparable from that period of his country's history.[34]

Masaryk has been hailed by his admirers as a just and wise leader, the modern-day incarnation of Plato's philosopher-king. To his biographer Jan Herben, Masaryk personified all that was good and noble in the Czech nation, and indeed represented the culmination of the long national revival. He was deeply and widely loved. Herben wrote of him: "I do not know of any example from the lives of kings and princes, nor from the lives of presidents of republics, of anyone who had the love of his people as much as did T. G. Masaryk."[35] Táborský has expressed a similar judgment, although qualifying it by explaining that Masaryk's popularity did not extend to "a few ultra-nationalist elements, and the Communists in their first years. . . ."[36]

Masaryk did in fact have his political enemies on both the Marxist-Leninist left and the German and Slovak right. He took a very firm stand against the widespread strike of December 1920, and again in the spring of 1932 his government dealt rather severely with another strike among miners and agricultural workers.[37] The Communists campaigned against Masaryk at the time of the 1934 Presidential election, and their obstructionist actions in parliament and elsewhere provoked a warrant for the arrest of four of their leaders.[38] Despite considerable popularity at the polls, the Communists never entered a governmental coalition. They consistently viewed the regime as a tool of capitalism, and Masaryk as a master bourgeois politician who may have had his redeeming features but nevertheless stood opposed to the class interests of the proletariat.[39]

The ultra-nationalists among the Slovaks had somewhat more ambiguous feelings about Masaryk. They applauded his efforts at national independence during the wartime liberation movement and frequently invoked his writings in support of their own cause. This was particularly true of the separatists among them, who used many of Masaryk's arguments concerning national self-determination in defense of their secessionist position.[40] This was, of course, not a position that Masaryk himself supported. Masaryk considered Czechs and Slovaks as blood brothers, and he in no way intended his theses on nationalism as an argument for Slovak independence. Masaryk's consistent championship of the "Czechoslovak" national position thus alienated the most ardent Slovak nationalists, who saw themselves being unwillingly assimilated into a culture that was not Czechoslovak but exclusively Czech in nature.[41]

Notwithstanding the enemies Masaryk did have on the peripheries of First Republican society, he was immensely respected by his fellow countrymen, and his memory has lived on to this day. Even his political enemies had respect for the man known as the "President-Liberator" of Czechoslovakia. Testimony to this is a massive biography of Masaryk by the Marxist historian Zdeněk Nejedlý.[42] Indeed, during at least the first few years of the Czechoslovak Republic, the general goals and ideals of Masaryk were accepted by even the most leftwing party of the time, the Social Democrats, prior to the rift that gave birth to the Communist party. It was only upon the splitting of the left, in 1921, and the subsequent radicalization of part of the working class movement, that serious Marxist-Leninist criticism of Masaryk's policies developed.[43]

In fact, for a year or two following the Communist takeover of 1948, the regime continued to pay honor to the memory of the President-Liberator, and such notables as Gottwald and Zápotocký were seen visiting his gravesite in the village of Lány.[44] The Communists at this time took pains to portray Masaryk as a relatively progressive, if bourgeois, ruler whose leadership had served a positive function in the development of Czechoslovakia's pre-socialist history.

As Stalinist cultural patterns were imposed upon Czechoslovak society, however, the official memory of Masaryk grew bitter. During the early and mid-1950s, the press carried on a campaign of slander and vilification against Masaryk, now seen as an enemy of the working class. Under Soviet influence, the history textbooks portrayed the First Republic as a dictatorship of the capitalists and landlords.[45] The accomplishments of the bourgeois government in every area of politics and diplomacy now were consistently minimized. Czechoslovakia was portrayed as a pawn of the Western imperialistic powers from the moment of its inception to the time of its abandonment by its nefarious allies at Munich.[46]

Even the literature of the era, represented by internationally renowned figures such as Karel Čapek and Franz Kafka, was criticized as bourgeois and of little value — with the exception, of course, of Marxist works. Čapek and Kafka were only two among a number of bourgeois writers who were "unpersoned" during the early fifties and only later rehabilitated. A 1960 history treats the literature of the First Republic in some detail without once mentioning Kafka, while writing off much of the remarkable Czech cinema of the twenties and thirties as "kitschy sentimentalism and beer-hall humor" whose main purpose was "to distract the audience's attention from the burning economic, social, and political problems of the period."[47] The Communists insisted on placing an exaggerated emphasis on the "progressive" literary works of the interwar years. To be sure, there were some very worthwhile products of the literary left, whose numbers included the novelist Jaroslav Hašek and the poet Vítěslav Nezval. But the undue adulation bestowed on a gaggle of minor literati, simply because they were "progressive," reinforced the distorted view of the past as painted by post-1948 historians.

This conscious effort to demean the past had a demoralizing impact on society. Czechs and Slovaks were too sophisticated to accept the new historiography, and the gap between what they knew as the truth and what the regime offered them in place of truth was profoundly felt.[48] The rewriting of history amounted to an attack on the national heritage, bringing the Communists into direct conflict with all the facts, legends, and symbols representing the cultural legacy of the First Republic. Of all the revolutionary changes introduced by the Communists, this was undoubtedly one of the most unpopular and counterproductive. It involved tearing away the society's proud self-image and imposing a warped and grotesque reflection of the past, unrecognizable and unacceptable to all but those who perpetrated the new image. The Communists' view of the First Republic was not assimilated by the citizens; in fact, the regime's perseverance in arguing its unpopular line only served to emphasize the alien quality that characterized the new order in so many respects vis à vis the general public. In other words, the regime defeated its own purpose of cultural revolution by its unsubtle, frontal attacks on the memory of the "Bourgeois Republic."

Where Is the Past?

In his famous novel of the 1960s, *The Joke* (Žert), Milan Kundera traces the quest of a onetime party loyalist for purpose and meaning in his turbulent life. His quest takes him back to his boyhood home in a rural village, after having cut through the wasted intervening years of youthful politicking, a lengthy stint in a prison camp, disillusionment and aimlessness. Returning to the rural village, Kundera's hero finds a society in transition, propelled ineluctably forward by modernization but struggling to recreate from its past a beautiful pageant, a local festival harkening back to the days when legend was reality and life was celebrated in song and ceremony. The attempt to recreate the past does not come off as planned, and the ending is a poignant reminder that even though the old does not die easily, it cannot be made new again.[49]

In the 1960s Czechs and Slovaks often seemed to be obsessed with their past. In an environment of gradually relaxed political constraints on literature and the arts, a very special generation of talented spokesmen grew up. This was, more properly speaking, a group of men and women *between* generations, many of them born during the First Republic but having had little or no adult experience in the bourgeois state of Masaryk and Beneš. The artists were thus aware of the democratic experience of 1918–1938, whether through the stories of their parents or in their own somewhat dim recollections, but they were also in many ways products of the Second World War, the resistance, and the socialist revolution. Like Kundera, most of them wanted to believe in the ideals of the revolution but had difficulty expunging the memory of the previous state. In addition, most of the artists had some bitter personal experiences with the brutality of the Gottwald-Novotný government, and they suffered the same disillusionment felt by Kundera's hero.[50] Their themes frequently dealt with the contradiction between revolutionary ideal and reality, and the problem of reconciling confusing images of the past. Literary and cinematic works were filled with references to guilt, self-doubt, and a general searching for identity.[51]

The effort in 1968 to rehabilitate Masaryk and reassess the First Republic flowed directly from the spirit of literary experimentation in the earlier sixties. To complete any review of the past, the First Republic would have to have been seriously examined and fairly evaluated. Only then could Czechs and Slovaks truly feel they had reconstructed their cultural heritages and be comfortable with their own self-images. Although it represented only a twenty-year interlude in a long history, the First Republic — as the Czech survey cited above illustrated — was indeed one of the most significant experiences in the evolution of modern Czechoslovakia.

The checkered history of the Czechs and Slovaks throughout the many centuries prior to the present has always been a source of both pride and humility. There is cause for pride in the legacy of the advanced and prosperous late medieval Kingdom of Bohemia. For Slovaks, the glory of the past is more obscure, but it reaches back to a time earlier than that of the Bohemian Kingdom, a time enshrouded in myth, a period whose historical records are the subject of archeological controversy.[52] There is cause for humility, on the other hand, in the long years of subjugation at the hands of foreigners. Those years of subjugation are more numerous than those of glorious independence, and the self-images associated with foreign control are therefore very poignant.

There are a number of different strains running through Czechoslovak historiography, both Marxist and bourgeois.[53] Nonetheless, with regard to the periods before the First Republic, there is general agreement between the Communists and others on which facts and symbols are positive elements in the national heritages and which are negative. Chief among the positive elements are the legacy of Hus and the Hussites, as well as the hard-fought revival of the national cultures in the nineteenth century. Chief among the negative elements are the collapse of the Bohemian Kingdom in the seventeenth century and the centuries of "darkness" for both Czechs and Slovaks under foreign rule.

The fifteenth century in Bohemia was one of the great epochs of Czech history. It was a time of political turmoil and relatively little progress in the arts and letters, but it was also a time of great spiritual heroism. Jan Hus (1369?–1415), a prophet of Protestantism, became the Czechs' first martyr and a permanent national hero when he was executed as a heretic. His teachings, like those of Luther a century later, had a far-reaching impact on theology, philosophy, and politics in Central Europe. Hus's doctrines of religious purification and social justice caught on among the Czechs and also spilled over into Slovak regions, where the biblical language of the Czech Hussites became the Slovak literary language until the nineteenth century.[54] In Bohemia, the dominant religion from the fifteenth to the seventeenth century was Utraquism, a moderate Hussitism based on the dispensation of both species, bread and wine, in the service of communion. However, the legacy of two offshoots of Hussitism, the Táborites and the Brethren, has had a higher degree of significance than that of Utraquism in the modern political consciousness of the Czechs.

The Táborites, a radical sect composed mostly of lower-class citizens, founded a short-lived communal society in which they sought to recreate the spirit of the earliest Christian communities. Táborism did not outlast the Hussite Wars (1420–37), despite the brilliant leadership of the blind general Jan Žižka, but the legacy of the underdog Táborites became an integral part of the national heritage. Marxists and non-Marxists alike are proud of the fierce spirit of the Táborites. The Communists encourage the veneration of the revolutionary strain in the tradition of Hus and Žižka, seeing in it a precocious forerunner of modern socialism.[55] A recent textbook, for example, asserts that "after five centuries the Hussite revolutionary tradition is still an enduring component of Czech thought, the source of all the revolutionary and progressive traditions of our people."[56]

On the other hand, it would seem unwise to make too strong and direct a connection between Hussitism and Czechoslovak communism. Hus's thinking did indeed suggest a radical social doctrine celebrating the oppressed, but it should not be forgotten that Hus's fundamental premises were theological, nonmaterialistic, and humanistic. It is indeed the humanistic aspect of Hus's teachings that has had the most lasting impact on Czech intellectual history, and not his rather primitive social ideas.

Hus's humanism was continued and developed further by yet another heroic figure of the fifteenth century, Petr Chelčický (1390–1460). The founder of the movement known as the Brethren (*Jednota bratrská*), Chelčický has been called by a recent Marxist historian "the most original and daring spirit of medieval Bohemia."[57] Chelčický's doctrine of absolute nonviolence distinguished him radically from the Táborites, although the community that the Brethren endeavored to create was based on the same ideal of Christian communalism. The Brethren believed in equality absolutely, rejecting the authority of political rulers and indeed all secular authority.[58]

Masaryk, a devoted student of Bohemia's intellectual traditions, considered the Hussite legacy a central and enduring part of the Czech mentality, seeing in both Žižka and Chelčický elements of a permanent national character. To Masaryk, the spiritual "ancestor" of modern-day Czechs was some combination of Žižka, with his determined fortitude, and Chelčický, with his personal moderation.[59] He felt himself to be a direct descendant of this tradition and found in it a constant source of inspiration.[60]

Thus both Marxists and non-Marxists draw a line of continuity from the fifteenth-century prophets to twentieth-century political man. The specific meaning of the historical connection may be disputed, but there is general agreement that somehow, the ideas of that earlier time live on in the mentality of modern Czechs.

Perhaps the real link is nationalistic rather than philosophical. Kamil Krofta, a scholar of Beneš's generation, argued that the nation first acquired a strong sense of its own identity during the Hussite period. This precocious national identity proved to be quite durable, capable of surviving the darkness of the long national oppression and reemerging later as modern nationalism.[61] The Marxist Josef Macek agreed, pointing out that "Hussitism gave aid and comfort to the Czech nation in times of decline and oppression."[62] Thus we might look upon the Hussite tradition as an expression of national self-identity that has persisted through the ages, radical in the extent to which the tradition differentiates Czechs from other nations but otherwise discontinuous and by no means revolutionary in the modern and secular sense.

In contrast to the positive image of the Hussite heritage, the 300-year period of foreign domination presents a very negative image. The "darkness" into which the Czechs fell began with the decisive defeat of the Bohemian estates at the Battle of the White Mountain, near Prague, on November 8, 1620. The Bohemians had revolted against their own elected monarch, Ferdinand II Habsburg, and deposed him in 1618, thus calling upon themselves the military retaliation which began the Thirty Years' War. Unfortunately for Bohemia, the Protestant armies that were later to fight the Habsburgs and their allies to a virtual stand-off intervened too late to save the Bohemian cause. Soon after the White Mountain battle, Ferdinand acted to eliminate all political and religious opposition in the Bohemian Crownlands. A methodical extermination of the Protestant nobility was carried out, their lands confiscated and redistributed to Catholic loyalists, most of them brought in from Catholic lands to form a new, imported nobility. Protestantism was banned. Jesuit priests and missionaries, who themselves had been expelled by the rebels' provisional government in 1618, were returned to bring the long-lost Czech flock back into the Roman Catholic fold, and this they did quite effectively. Bohemia was totally crushed. Having no influential spokesmen for its national cause, it became a forgotten country by the time the Peace of Westphalia was signed (1648). Thereafter, Bohemia was only nominally a kingdom, in reality a province of the sprawling Habsburg domains.[63]

With the death of the Bohemian Kingdom, the thriving culture of the Czechs was extinguished, and the Czech nation joined their neighbors the Slovaks in the class of subject peoples.[64] It has been argued by Beneš and others that the period of mutual subjugation served to identify the Czechs with the Slovaks, but this argument would seem difficult to accept. It is true that the spread of Hussitism among the Slovaks, and the acceptance of the Králice Bible among the latter, encouraged the convergence of the Czech and Slovak literary languages. The Slovaks later abandoned the Czech literary language, the argument goes, only under the influence of peculiar circumstances surrounding the Slovak awakening in the mid-nineteenth century.[65]

There is some truth in this argument, but it does not tell the whole story. The circumstances of national oppression were in fact quite different for the two peoples. The Czechs were a cultured people by the time of their subjugation, with a proud past and a common sense of incipient national destiny. The Slovaks were a primitive ethnic group — in no way a nation, not even incipiently or inchoately — with a past that may have included imperial splendor, but at a time so distant that it is difficult to establish the fact. Bohemian society reached a high level of feudal advancement long before the White Mountain, including a flourishing literary and artistic culture.[66] The Slovak lands, on the contrary, were merely a territory with ill-defined boundaries, and Slovak society had little or no cohesion beyond the perimeters of village communities.

It is significant that the symbol of darkness is used by Czechs and Slovaks to describe their years of political and cultural humiliation. So severe was the foreign oppression that the national cultures were nearly lost forever. Only gradually did they re-emerge from the "darkness" of the seventeenth and eighteenth centuries as Czechs and Slovaks moved into the "light" of national consciousness.

To many Czechs, however, the years of darkness were not entirely devoid of meaning. Krofta, a widely read historian of the interwar period, used a symbol even stronger than darkness in the title of his study of Czech culture from the White Mountain to the time of Palacký, *The Immortal Nation*. Writing in the summer of 1939, following a new national humiliation wrought by the Nazi occupation, Krofta realized that another period of darkness — but not death — was beginning. In the preface to his book, Krofta appealed to his countrymen to recall the lesson of the earlier subjugation and not to lose hope. He assured his readers that, just as in the past, the nation would again emerge to control its own destiny:

> And then, perhaps, without remorse and without bitterness it [the Czech nation] will remember the White Mountain, recognizing that from the terrible hardships into which it was thrown there also ensued something good: The consciousness that the strength of a nation is not in its being numbered among the great powers of this world, but rather in a people that is educated, conscious, physically and morally healthy; it is in the art of self-rule and reliance on its own self and its own work, and in the ability not to lose its courage even in the worst of times, and in the faithful devotion to the great ideals of humanity. To the degree that the Czech nation never forgets, to that degree it has learned from the school of the three-hundred-year bondage which followed the White Mountain.[67]

Indeed, the nineteenth century had seen a slow but determined awakening on the part of not only the Czechs but the Slovaks as well. Here again, the development of the two peoples' histories served as much to separate them as to draw them together. The Czechs experienced a cultural renaissance that drew to an important degree from their perception of the national heritage as interpreted by men who were gifted cultural figures in their own right: Josef Dobrovský (1753–1829), Josef Jungmann (1773–1847), Karel Hynek Mácha (1810–1836), and the great historian František Palacký (1798–1876), among others. Despite the efforts of some Slovaks who were very much drawn to the Czech movement, the Slovak awakening diverged significantly.[68] The earliest efforts at codifying and developing the Slovak language had aimed at standardizing a western literary dialect rather near to Czech.[69] In the course of the national movement, however, Slovak linguistic development came to favor the spoken idiom of central and eastern dialects. Under the influence of Ľudovít Štúr (1815–1856), the Slovak cultural movement was thus guided away from its ties to Czech culture. This divergence was reinforced by the political division of the Empire in 1867. Under Hungarian rule, the beginnings of Slovak political consciousness took place separately from the progress of Czech politics in the Austrian half of the Empire.[70]

While the Czechs lived under gradually improving political conditions between 1867 and 1914, the Slovaks were subjected to more and more oppression by their Magyar rulers. Czechs were becoming better educated; many of them were profiting from the industrialization of Bohemia and Moravia by sharing in the new wealth of the region; Czech political parties functioned in the Austrian parliamentary system, and the franchise was broadened gradually to the eventual promulgation of universal male suffrage (in 1906); Czechs were admitted into the civil service; and the prerogatives of local rule were expanded during this half-century.[71] Relatively few Slovaks, on the other hand, had even the right to vote, because Hungary's franchise laws were drawn to favor the propertied classes. Neither universal suffrage nor the secret ballot, both standard in Austria after 1906, was the practice in Hungary, and because of the property requirements scarcely one-fourth of the adult male population received the right to vote by 1910.[72] Slovaks were for the most part excluded from the civil service, and stringent police measures kept organized political party activities at a minimum. Of the relatively small number of Slovak political activists and their somewhat more numerous supporters, many were arrested and subjected to frequent harassment.[73] Larger numbers of Slovaks remained isolated from the political system altogether, remote from modern life and only loosely in contact with other parts of the region. The education system, a vital factor in the politicization of the Czechs, was incapable of having a similar impact on the Slovaks; their schools were dominated by the Magyars, and in fact between 1875 and 1918 there were no Slovak-language schools above the elementary level.[74]

Despite the obstacles, political awareness spread among the Slovaks in the last two decades prior to independence. The process underwent several different phases and produced widely varying political movements. Of the groups that emerged, those of the "Czechoslovak" persuasion occupied the strategic position at the critical moment in 1918 and led the Slovaks into a union with the Czechs. The Slovaks entered this union at a considerable disadvantage. Their cultural background was recent and thin, and compared to the rich heritage of the Czechs, it was a source of sensitivity. Their political experience was hardly adequate preparation for entry into a modern democracy. By 1918, politics among the Slovaks was scarcely a generation old. Moreover, it was not the politics of gradual democratization, such as that which had characterized Czech society after 1867, but rather the politics of national suppression and hatred, of clerical rural politics and agrarian revolt on the one hand, and a minority intellectual Czechophile movement on the other. Politically aware Slovaks were alienated from Hungarian society, but they were fragmented and often had no clear vision of how they should express their political dissent.

In any event, both nations had made great strides in the century preceding independence, and the nineteenth century is indeed a proud era in their histories. Again, as in the case of the Hussites, both Marxists and non-Marxists can find a source of inspiration in the struggle of the nineteenth-century patriots. Czechs and Slovaks today are aware that their existence as modern nations should not be taken for granted. They know that other ethnic groups of Central Europe have either perished in the clash of that region's nations or been rendered insignificant; historical examples are the Avars and the Sorbs. A similar fate might have befallen the Czechs and Slovaks had it not been for a fortunate concurrence of political and intellectual circumstances in Europe as a whole — the Josephinian reforms, French Revolution, German romantic nationalism — and the emergence of dedicated cultural nationalists such as Dobrovský, Kollár, Štúr, and Palacký.

A few words must be said about Palacký. More than any other single historian, it was he who put together the spiritual framework of modern Czech nationalism. His view of the national history as a long struggle between pious, peaceloving, democratic Czechs and bellicose, aristocratic, authoritarian Germans has been disputed and modified by later historians, but his original contribution to the consciousness of his nation cannot be denied. His ten-volume *History of the Czech Nation,* which he ended with the election of the first Habsburg to the Bohemian throne (1526), was written with the express purpose of educating his fellow Czechs to their ancient heritage.[75] Hans Kohn has written of Palacký that he gave meaning to the Czechs' past, dignity to their self-identity, and courage for the task of the national renascence.[76] Every Czech historian since Palacký has had to build in one way or another on his work, and he, like Hus and Žižka, has come to occupy an honored position in the national pantheon.[77]

The national heritage has been a stickier problem for the Slovaks than for the Czechs. The Slovak awakening in its own way produced results every bit as remarkable as those achieved by the Czechs. The Slovaks, after all, started at a much lower level of social, economic, and cultural development. That they have not reached the level of the Czechs even today in no way detracts from the progress they have achieved. Nonetheless, the national heritage still presents a problem. The Slovaks have had something of an inferiority complex toward the Czechs ever since their political merger in 1918, and one of the primary reasons is the Slovaks' lack of a centuries-old cultural heritage comparable to that of the Czechs. The dissimilarity of the two nations' backgrounds has strongly affected their relationship to each other. It is this problem that will be explored in chapters six and seven.

1968: The Recent Past and the Distant Past

Nineteen sixty-eight was a time for Czechs and Slovaks to reevaluate their relations with each other as nations and to look inwardly at themselves: to ask themselves who they were, where they had been, where they should be going. Like the interwar period, 1968 was too short a time for them to answer all the important questions, but it was a time when they sought their own solutions according to their own values. They were "free" from the constraints of Soviet imperialism for a few months, just as they were free from more powerful neighbors for a relatively few years prior to 1938. At both times, national values (humanism, egalitarianism) joined a set of values largely international or external in origin. The humanism of Masaryk's national heritage had joined a libertarian, democratic tradition proudly adopted from the West to make the dominant political culture of the First Republic. Thirty years after the passing of the latter, Dubček's "socialism with a human face" was to be grafted onto a system of political values based on Marxism-Leninism. Both the First Republic and the 1968 system were unique experiments in their times: the First Republic was the only viable democratic and pluralistic state in Central Europe between the wars, and the 1968 program was an attempt to introduce a qualitatively different brand of socialism into Communist Eastern Europe.[78]

It should not be surprising, then, that Czechs and Slovaks made a renewed effort in 1968 to appraise their past — including the First Republic.[79] As with the reforms in political and social affairs, the time available for reinterpreting the First Republic was not sufficient to the task. Scholars and journalists could only begin to scrape the surface, and the long-awaited resurrection of the not-so-distant past has had to be postponed for a future generation of Czech and Slovak historians. Since 1969, the objective study of the interwar period is forbidden, just as it was between 1950 and 1968. During the brief months of freedom, however, the history books were reopened just enough to see some of the facts. In the spring and summer of 1968 it was possible to discuss the First Republic and its leaders, Masaryk, Beneš, *et al.,* as a positive part of the national heritage. That this was possible was a very important reason for the popularity of the Dubček government, for Czechs and Slovaks were aware of their past and proud to celebrate it once again.

Nineteen sixty-eight has now joined the interwar period as a part of the disputed legacy. The rulers of the seventies have been anxious to forget what happened toward the end of the sixties, but citizens are by and large unwilling to forget. The year of reform communism is remembered by most Czechs and Slovaks as a welcome break in the general oppressiveness of their post-1948 political life. The regime, on the contrary, would like its subjects to view the Dubček era as a time of deviation from the hallowed norms of socialism, a time when perfidious, anti-socialist forces from both within and outside Czechoslovakia attempted to deflect society from its rightful purposes. Like the First Republic, the Dubček interlude is thus a tacit bone of contention between rulers and ruled, symbolic of a serious contradiction between two disparate perceptions of the national past.

The Communist Tradition: From Subculture to Ruling Elite

Generally speaking, the patterns of rule developed by the Communists have closely resembled those of the Soviet Union. The rulers have thereby aimed to create what Barghoorn has called an "ideological-partisan, subject-participatory political culture."[1] The Communists' operating norms derive from a view of reality colored by the acceptance of Marxism-Leninism, not merely as a body of theory meant to aid in the interpretation of history, but as a set of dogmas predisposing its adherents to certain foregone conclusions about the nature of reality. There has arisen a more or less formal ideological system describing the party elite's view of reality and serving as a set of prescriptive guidelines for political action. These are subject to some fluctuation arising from domestic circumstances, but they are at the same time strongly influenced by Soviet ideologists. With the exception of 1968, the Communist party of Czechoslovakia (KSČ — Komunistická strana Československa) has tended to rule as an oligarchy, through a pyramidal power structure whose pinnacle, a rather tight circle of men, is supreme.[2]

The official view of reality begins with the Marxian premise that class conflict lies at the bottom of all social relations. Czechoslovakia is now a socialist state, but the fact that the class enemy has been overturned has not obviated the social conflict. In their day, Lenin and Stalin found it necessary to combat the persisting influence of the bourgeoisie well beyond the revolutionary takeover. Therefore, a central feature of the Soviet view of reality is that the road to communism is fraught with difficulties.[3] The dynamic processes of politics are caught up in the ongoing conflict between the forces of progress and the forces of reaction, thus giving the course of history a continuing tinge of conspiracy. Moreover, the forces opposing socialist progress will frequently disguise themselves or utilize unsuspecting party members in order to divert the path of the revolution. Trotsky, Bukharin, Djilas, Nagy, Dubček — all these names are linked with tendencies that are assumed to be contrary to the purposes of the revolution. The various tendencies are given standard names to distinguish them from one another — dogmatism, subjectivism, revisionism, sectarianism — but they are all symptoms of a continuing danger to the progressive forces in society.

Throughout the Marxist-Leninist world runs a further assumption that colors the leaders' view of reality, namely that the Soviet experience must be taken as the paramount working model of socialist political development.[4] This includes both actual and symbolic aspects of politics; that is, the Soviet model prescribes not only certain forms of organization and political behavior but also a system of political symbols presumed to be universally compelling among socialist citizens. In the center of this system stands Lenin as founding father, prophet, and demigod; his onetime symbolic coequal Stalin has, of course, fallen from pedestals both real and symbolic since 1956. On Lenin's one side is the Communist party — all Communist parties, but especially the CPSU — as the enlightened vanguard of the chosen class. On the other side is the socialist worker, who is both creator and recipient of the new order's bounties.

The ideology that further describes the norms of politics is, in Barghoorn's words, "today's version of the credo of a quasi-messianic political sect."[5] The Communists' attempts to unify society around a shared set of symbols described by this credo can be seen as a purposeful attempt to create a sort of communistic civil religion, the reference points of which are secular rather than sacred but no less compelling than those of the American civil religion.[6] The Communists look forward to the day when all members of the working class will respond to the symbolism by immersing themselves wholeheartedly in the purpose of building socialism.

When communism comes, society will be self-governing. In the meantime, careful guidance is needed lest the forces of reaction seriously deter progress toward the ultimate goal. The necessary norms of rule include a single-party monopoly over political affairs, for only the Communists are sufficiently enlightened to recognize the potential pitfalls. (In Czechoslovakia, the party is supplemented by the National Front, but the latter is dominated by the former.) According to the Soviet model, political opposition is not allowed, and the idea of pluralism in any form is looked upon with skepticism due to its association in the Communist mind with conflicting class interests.

Subject-participatory citizenship entails numerous demands upon the masses. They are expected to participate by voting, essentially a ritualized public ratification of candidates pre-chosen by the party or the front.[7] They are also expected to join officially sanctioned voluntary organizations, attend certain public functions such as plant meetings and rallies, work productively in their places of employment, and give the party occasional feedback concerning specific aspects of their position in the system. Political participation has an obligatory character to it, as well as a tendency to be highly formalized, unspontaneous, and rigorously controlled.

Variations in these patterns occur within the limits of ideology, the political self-interest of the national leadership, and the inteerests of the Soviet-led alliance system. The parameters of what is permissible have been explored by several reformist governments — Nagy's Hungary, Kádár's Hungary, Gomułka's Poland, Gierek's Poland, Dubček's Czechoslovakia. The foregoing is a familiar list of successful and unsuccessful efforts to introduce so-called "national communist" solutions to political, social, and economic problems. Those that have been successful in one degree or another have avoided transgressing the limits of ideology, elite self-interest, or Soviet constraint; those that have failed have done so by moving beyond the parameters imposed by the system of norms and rules described above.

It has already been suggested that these norms of Marxist-Leninist politics are in conflict with the traditional political culture of Czechoslovakia. One might well ask at this point how it was that the political system came to be so thoroughly dominated by patterns that clash with the prevailing social values. Again, the easy answer would be to say that the Soviet Union overran Czechoslovakia and forced its system onto the Czechs and Slovaks. The question is not as simple as it seems at first glance, however, for the Soviets did not move into Czechoslovakia as conquerors and rulers. Nor did they blatantly coerce the post-1948 leadership into the new patterns of political operation. Rather, the Soviets came to benefit from the rise of a political subculture within Czechoslovakia. This subculture — the KSČ — grew up from roots reaching back into the Austro-Hungarian Social Democratic tradition and nourished in the interwar period by the dual influence of the Communist International and the First Czechoslovak Republic. The Czechoslovak Communists came to power as the result of fortuitous circumstances, both domestic and international, that cast them in the role of a minoritarian government. Soviet support was an important factor in the Communists' rise, although not necessarily the critical factor in the acual power takeover. Thereafter, however, the Soviet influence became paramount as an unstable ruling group jockeyed to maintain power against not only the possibility of a bourgeois resurgence but also certain potential rival forces within the KSČ itself. The ruling group, like others in neighboring countries at the time, was thus inherently weak and quickly fell into a position of extreme dependency on the guiding wisdom of the Soviet Communists.

Under the strong and direct influence of the USSR, the Communists in Czechoslovakia released a strain of undemocratic tendencies that had developed in the political culture before 1948. In so doing, they also resolved a longstanding ambivalence in their own political orientations as between violent class conflict and more moderate approaches to social revolution. Both of these strains had coexisted within the party ever since it was founded, and neither of them can be said to have clearly predominated before 1948; it was the Soviet influence that tipped the balance thereafter.

The Subculture Thesis

The norms of rule that prevailed after 1948 dramatically contradicted the dominant values of the traditional political culture, but they nevertheless did have a precedent of sorts in previous authoritarian subcultures. The First Republic had nourished all sorts of political groups, and some of them were by no means democratic or libertarian. On both the left and the right wings of interwar politics, extremist parties espousing authoritarian ideas or evincing authoritarian tendencies operated within the legal framework of First-Republican constitutionalism. Thus the emergence of a homegrown autocracy after 1948 did not take place overnight, nor did it develop without a certain basis of social support. That support was weak in comparison to the support for more moderate political ideas, however, and any government that would have based its rule on the authoritarian sympathies of the voters would not have been stable. It was only with the backing of an outside force that such groups were able to rule for any length of time. This had been true of the wartime governments, and it proved to be the case again after 1948.

The outside hegemonial powers in Czechoslovakia's history, then, have had a wildly distorting effect on the development of the political culture. This leads to the following propositions. Some important features of Czechoslovakia's politics are especially pronounced during times of independence but become submerged or recessive in times of foreign domination. Chief among these features is a tendency toward libertarianism and constitutionalism. In the atmosphere generated by independent political development, pluralism has surfaced; the resulting society-wide spread of institutionalized political participation has drawn large numbers of citizens into public life according to their social status, religious or philosophical beliefs, and perceived personal or group interests.[8] In times of foreign domination, on the other hand, the patterns of rule have been strongly authoritarian or even totalitarian, hostile toward pluralistic tendencies, and repressive of civil liberties. This has been the case regardless of the specific form the foreign domination has taken — imperial rule, military occupation, or Soviet dependency.

In these simple terms, the critical variable determining the nature of politics in twentieth-century Czechoslovakia has been the degree of freedom from outside interference. The First Republic, in these terms, was the most free. This is not to say that foreign influence was absent; the First Republic depended on French military protection and West European trade. Western influence, however, stopped short of interference in internal politics, and the constitutional system that developed between the wars was therefore the product of organic political groupings and freely-adopted values.

With some qualification, this can be said of the postwar Third Republic as well. To be sure, by 1945 Czechoslovakia was under a Soviet protectorate; the Soviet protector was far more demanding in its expectations regarding the coordination of foreign policy than the French had been (*vide* the dispute over the Marshall Plan), and the Soviets moreover exerted a strong influence on domestic policy through the Czechoslovak Communists in the coalition government. Nonetheless, the political system in effect between 1945 and 1948 reflected a democratic, semipluralistic interplay of Czech and Slovak parties and interest groups. These groups managed to function up to the moment of the Communist takeover, despite Soviet pressures, and came to an end only after the triumph of the Communists.

Twenty years of politics dominated by Soviet patterns were interrupted by the return of a genuinely indigenous political order in 1968. For nearly eight months Czechoslovakia's leaders felt the illusion of independence, and their politics proceeded as if that independence were real. In the spirit of earlier moments of independence, the reform leaders encouraged strong tendencies in their society toward democracy, constitutionalism, and pluralism — quite in contrast to the preceding years of politics inspired by norms developed outside their own country.

It is, of course, no coincidence that much the opposite has prevailed under the influence of outside hegemonial powers, Nazi Germany and Soviet Russia alike. Notwithstanding the fundamental social and ideological differences between Nazism and Communism, both powers have been characterized by severely autocratic rule and a strong missionary purpose implicit in their official ideologies. Given these facts, it would seem consistent that the impact felt by weaker neighbors would be in a similar vein, even in a country with a democratic political culture.

In this light, it is significant that the outside powers who have dominated Czechoslovakia since 1938 have found willing collaborators among the natives. Neither Hitler nor Stalin chose to absorb Czechoslovakia into his own state's political boundaries, and both made maximal use of native administrators and politicians to further their own ends. The local collaborators cannot be adequately described simply as traitorous agents, but rather they emerged from specific authoritarian political subcultures in Czechoslovakia. These subcultures thus were breeding grounds for forces that eventually rose as elites favored by the hegemonial powers and entrusted with the rule over a society that took on many qualities of a colony. In the case of the German rule, the imperial nature of the hegemonial relationship was undisguised; in the case of the Soviet dependency since 1948, the relationship is more subtle and complicated, but the vehement official denials of an imperial order in Eastern Europe do not change the objective character of that relationship.

Empire and dependency will be taken up in the next chapter, but at this point a separate conceptual clarification is in order. This concerns several political concepts that will occur in the following discussion, beginning with the terms *authoritarian* and *libertarian*. Authoritarianism simply refers to a pattern of rule in which authority impinges to a great degree upon individual liberty. Whether this impingement be in the name of higher social goals (the building of socialism) or a matter of expediency (the maintenance of order) is of no concern to this definition; we are referring only to a pattern of actual governing, as well as to the frame of mind that sanctions such a pattern (that is, the "authoritarian personality" that values order over liberty).[9] Libertarianism denotes the opposite, namely the tendency to actualize policies favoring individual liberties over the authoritative restriction of civil liberties — tendencies, that is, toward freedom and away from centralized regimentation of society, individuals, and groups.[10] Neither authoritarianism nor libertarianism denotes an absolute condition, but rather, they are both meant to represent opposite directions on a continuum of political power relationships.

Totalitarianism, a much maligned and overused word, shall refer here to a pattern of rule — not a systemic model — based on the ideal, whether explicit or implicit, of total state control over all aspects of society. The idea of total control need not be attained (and, indeed, probably never has been, even in Stalinist Russia), but it is nevertheless a driving force impelling the rulers to seek the elimination of all possible sources of political and ideological competition. Stalinism is a Communist version of totalitarianism with its own peculiar system of political, economic, social, and ideological characteristics.[11]

The authoritarian subcultures that developed in Czechoslovakia before World War II included such disparate groups as the Communist party, the Slovak People's party, and the right wing of the Agrarian and National Democratic parties. Czechoslovak communism itself, like the larger political culture, developed a pronounced internal dichotomy reflecting an ambivalence between authoritarian and libertarian norms.[12] By 1948, the year of the Communist takeover, it was not altogether clear that Czechoslovak communism was an intrinsically "totalitarian" force analogous to Soviet communism. In fact, the history of the Communist party of Czechoslovakia (KSČ) suggests that the party was intermittently rather deficient in revolutionary fervor. Certainly, to large numbers of Czechs and Slovaks their country's Communist movement was not viewed as a deviant or alien phenomenon — as the impressive Communist vote in 1946 would indicate.[13]

Once in power, however, the leaders of the authoritarian subcultures were quick to adopt the ruling practices of their foreign sponsors. Given the support of the German Reich after 1938, the Czech and Slovak right slavishly imitated German patterns of authority and policy. It is true that the role of Hitler's Czech puppets was considerably less active in the promulgation of totalitarian rule than were the more autonomous Slovak leaders, but both Czech and Slovak wartime elites proved to be obedient instruments of the Reich. Similarly, given the support and encouragement of the new (Soviet) hegemonial power after 1948, the victorious Communists adopted policies reflecting the totalitarianism of Soviet rule.

Communism does not necessarily presuppose totalitarianism, as we now know from the examples of reformism in post-Stalin Eastern Europe. Nor did the Communist movement that developed in Czechoslovakia between 1921 and 1948 lead inevitably to a Stalinist party and, in power, to Stalinist policies born of an inner logic compelling Communists to become "totalitarians."[14] The reality of communism in interwar Czechoslovakia suggests a rather more complicated pattern.[15] The authoritarian-libertarian dichotomy inherent in communism, and the Bolshevik-Social Democratic conflict in the KSČ specifically, were serious contradictions that never quite resolved themselves prior to 1948. Indeed, twenty years after the Communist coup the contradictions were to reappear in the form of the Prague Spring deliberations. Both in the 1940s and again in 1968–69 the impact of Soviet hegemonial power was decisive in resolving the contradiction in favor of the authoritarian tendency, and ultimately in favor of the totalitarian extreme. That the contradiction would have been resolved in a similar direction without the constraints of Soviet imperialism cannot be demonstrated. Indeed, there is no conclusive evidence that any of the authoritarian subcultures in and of themselves represented the basis of an indigenous totalitarianism; the evidence suggests, on the contrary, that totalitarianism in Czechoslovakia has resulted when the authoritarian subcultures have come to power with the aid, and under the strong influence, of external powers.

1918–38: Political Culture and Subcultures

The dominant characteristics of the First Republican system of values were derived from the Czech experience rather than the Slovak.[16] Because of the numerical, economic, and educational advantages of the Czechs, they imbued the political system with their own Western, liberal values. These values represented the dominant pattern in the political culture, overlying differences of an ethnic, demographic, or class nature, and embodied in the constitutional and institutional superstructures of the First Republic.

The most important articulators of the dominant interwar political culture were Masaryk and Beneš. Both were sophisticated political thinkers and prolific writers whose works frequently dealt with the philosophical heritage of their nation. They argued that Czechoslovak democracy stemmed from that strain of religious humanism so central to Bohemia's intellectual history since the days of Hus, combined in the modern era with the secular rationalism that had entered Czech culture from the West.[17] Masaryk, a Protestant by conversion, saw in his religious heritage a source of spiritualism, rational and antidogmatic, that could be harnessed as a liberating force. Masaryk's ideal state was one guided by Christian principles but unwedded to institutional dogma. He fought for the constitutional separation of church and state, and against the determined opposition of Czech and Slovak Catholics, managed to secure a compromise in the early days of the republic: separation of church and state was not written into the constitution, but neither was the Roman Catholic Church made the official state church, as many Catholics had sought.[18]

Beneš, baptized as a Roman Catholic but a religious freethinker in his adult life, was also firmly convinced of the spiritual essence in Czech culture. The thrust of his nation's intellectual history, he argued, had been "the search for moral and philosophical truths" and the purpose of the nation "the realization of ideals of justice and humanity."[19] He saw Czech culture since the fifteenth century as an island of progressive evolution in a sea of Central European absolutism, reaching beyond the nearby German civilization to its spiritual kinship with Western Europe. Like the latter, Czech culture was based on humanism and individualism. It was a culture of modernity, democracy, and equality.[20]

Both Masaryk and Beneš considered themselves and their countrymen to be in the mainstream of rationalist thinking, and their views of politics reflected this. They insisted, for example, that the meaning of democracy was the freedom to discuss alternatives and to settle conflicts by the force of reason.[21] Masaryk felt that his entire political career was aimed at realizing what he considered the most important task of democracy: "to organize the authority of its elected leaders — not rulers — through the freedom and cooperation of all. . . ."[22] Masaryk never abandoned his faith in the ability of humans to reason their way through problems. Speaking on his eightieth birthday before the Federal Assembly, he reaffirmed this faith in reason, discussion, and compromise: "If there exist conflicts between theory and practice, . . . democracy is for me discussion, and therefore compromise."[23]

Reason, then, leads to discussion, and discussion to compromise. In the fragmented multi-party system of interwar Czechoslovakia, the art of compromise was the science of governing, and no one knew this better than Masaryk. His skillful hand at harmonizing conflicts undoubtedly prevented many partisan differences from blowing up into irreconcilable clashes. Masaryk, already an old man when he assumed the Presidency, was perhaps something of a father figure in that young political system, now exerting a firm but patient influence on the feuding adolescents in parliament, now withdrawing to the sidelines to let the partisan combatants work out their differences on their own. There was a remarkable tolerance about Masaryk; his faith in the goodness of his fellow man was unshakable, and his patience with the sometimes unwieldy machinery of the pluralistic system was almost boundless. To his critics who disparaged the middle course leading through compromise he replied forcefully:

> Democracy, say its opponents contemptuously, consists of perpetual compromise. Its partisans admit the impeachment and take it as a compliment. Compromise, not of principles but of practice, is necessary in political life as in all fields of human activity. . . . For the maintenance and development of democracy the thought and cooperation of all are needed; and, since none is infallible, democracy, conceived as tolerant cooperation, signifies the acceptance of what is good no matter from what quarter it may come.[24]

Beneš, too, considered compromise a virtue of democratic systems and one of the fundamental distinguishing features of democratic ideologies. He believed that all politics contain an element of conflict and struggle, but in democracies conflict is mitigated by the possibility of cooperation among the competing forces. In authoritarian systems there is no political recourse to struggling, Beneš asserted, whereas the dynamic of democratic progress results from "the synthesis of the elements of struggle and collaboration, on the solution of conflicts through reasonable and human means."[25]

The dominant Czech-liberal value system articulated by Masaryk and Beneš was accepted by a substantial number of politically conscious Slovaks. These Prague-oriented Slovaks — "Czechophiles" or "Czecho-Slovaks" as they are sometimes called — included such influential politicians of the First Republic as Milan Hodža, Vavro Šrobár, and Ivan Dérer. Generally representative of a small intellectual elite, the Czechophiles embraced the philosophy of Masaryk and sought to guide their Slovak countrymen according to the democratic and humanistic principles of the Czech political culture. Their following in Slovakia was not small, although neither was it a majority. Preferring cooperation to conflict and advocating the gradual overcoming of Slovakia's backwardness by means of political and cultural assimilation, the Czechophiles acclaimed the politics of reason, compromise, and patience.[26]

It has been mentioned earlier that the political system in practice tended to concentrate a great deal of extraconstitutional power within the innermost circles of the cabinet and "Castle" and, ultimately, upon the person of the president himself. Both Masaryk and Beneš wielded this power with discretion, but the actuality of central executive power mitigated the pluralism of the constitutional order. This high degree of centralized authority was reinforced by a tendency toward rather strict internal discipline within the individual political parties. Parties frequently enforced adherence on the part of their members to centrally determined policies, and parliamentary representatives risked losing their party's support in the next election if they deviated from the party's public stand on important issues.[27]

As one moved from the center of the political spectrum to the extremes of the right and the left, the rigidity of party discipline was accompanied by authoritarian ideologies. Some of the rightwing movements, such as the Juriga Catholic party and the Fascist party, were ephemeral and on the whole not very strong. Others, however, were consistently important. Of these the most viable were the Communists on the extreme left and the Slovak People's party on the right. The latter, a Catholic nationalist group, was intensely distrustful of the Czechs and had little sympathy for the rationalistic libertarianism of Masaryk and Beneš.

Two other sizable parties evinced illiberal tendencies. The National Democratic party, the direct descendants of the Young Czechs, inherited authoritarian characteristics from the pre-independence struggles against the Old Czechs and the Austro-Germans. Staunchly Czech-nationalist and conservative, the National Democrats played a powerful role in the formative months of the republic, but after 1920, and especially after 1929, they went into a decline concomitantly with the rise of fascist tendencies within their ranks. By 1935 they had allied with the Fascist party in the National Union. Two years later that alliance fell apart, but in any event the National Democrats had distinguished themselves in the 1930s by their aggressive nationalism, antisocialism, and opposition to the policies of Masaryk.[28]

While the political influence of the National Union was relatively small, that of another group on the Czechoslovak right, the Agrarian party, was very great. For the most part, the Agrarians were a centrist party whose leaders supported progressive social policies, but after the death of the party's dynamic leader Antonín Švehla in 1929, a part of the Agrarian movement drifted to the far right. In the mid-1930s a number of influential Agrarians advocated rapprochement with Germany as an alternative to Beneš's alliance system with France and the USSR, and during the Second World War some Agrarian politicians became active collaborators.[29]

The Slovak nationalists will be taken up in later chapters, but they too must be mentioned in the context of authoritarian subcultures. The great debate over the nationality of Slovaks, begun by their cultural pioneers in the nineteenth century, was tentatively and uncomfortably resolved after 1918 in favor of those who believed in the near-identity of Czech and Slovak ethnicity. That is, in the dominant political culture of the First Republic there was only one "Czechoslovak" nation.[30] In this sense the clericalist-authoritarian tendencies represented most vividly by the Slovak People's party set off yet another political grouping as apart from the liberal-humanitarian tradition of Masaryk, Beneš, and Hodža.[31] The Slovak nationalist-populist subculture was by no means without its own internal divisions and even conflicts, but the overall pattern of political values, symbols, and policy orientations of the Slovak right was distinctive and indeed representative of a major political subculture. It was from this subculture that the leadership of the wartime Slovak Republic, a puppet state of the Third Reich, came.[32]

The left, too, produced a political subculture. The Communist party of Czechoslovakia, founded in 1921 after a split in the Social Democratic party, persistently stayed on the peripheries of First Republican politics. The interwar KSČ was a strong opposition party with support among all the ethnic and national communities of the republic. Although the party, as we shall see, was never a serious revolutionary threat during these twenty years, its leaders consistently eschewed direct cooperation with the various governments. In this respect the KSČ differed radically from the other two socialist parties, the SDP and the National Socialists. Moreover, the Communists tended to see themselves — in accordance with Comintern self-images — as the only true representative of the working class and, hence, unique within Czechoslovak society.

To what degree the Communists were immune from the political culture influences generated by their society's historical development is, of course, debatable. To some extent the party's own background within the reformist tradition of Austrian social democracy continued to mitigate the romantic pull of "internationalist" (that is, Bolshevik) revolutionary tendencies. The result was a certain ambivalence in the party's revolutionary character, a subject to which we must now turn in order to understand the indigenous background of communism in Czechoslovakia.

The KSČ: An Ambivalent Revolutionary Tradition

It is, of course, wrong to view communism, either in theory or in practice, as a totally authoritarian and unswervingly revolutionary movement devoid of any significant libertarian impulses and inhospitable to reformist tendencies. All Communist regimes to date have maintained primarily authoritarian systems of rule, even those that have nominally passed beyond the dictatorship of the proletariat and into the socialist stage. It is nonetheless important to remember that varying degrees of anti-authoritarianism, and even libertarianism, have appeared in a number of Communist systems. In Russia during the NEP, for example, cultural diversity and social reform flourished for a brief time within a one-party political order. Yugoslavia has been the scene of an important Communist experiment in which social constraints have been relaxed — particularly in the late 1960s — and a partial market economy institutionalized. Even political opposition within a Marxist framework was tolerated for a number of years (although it now seems to be discouraged once again, for the most part). Nor have the winds of reform bypassed other socialist countries: Poland during the New Course of the mid-1950s and again in the 1970s, Hungary ever since the early sixties, and China during the "Hundred Flowers" campaign, not to mention Czechoslovakia in the sixties.

In the context of Marxist-Leninist systems, reformism has often implied a movement along the political continuum from "more authoritarian" toward "less authoritarian," for systems undergoing reform have usually begun with the Stalinist extreme. In some cases the movement along the continuum has progressed sufficiently to justify our speaking of a libertarian tendency, for serious questions have been raised about the impingement of state and party upon civil liberties. Examples can be noted in the Hungary of 1956, the Czechoslovakia of 1968, and intermittently in Poland and Yugoslavia.

Libertarian tendencies and reformism in communism do not come from a theoretical vacuum, but rather from certain strains of thought reaching back to Marx himself. Eliminating alienation, a theme first expounded in the *Economic and Philosophic Manuscripts,* is the basis of the ultimate in libertarian societies, for the revolution foreseen by Marx had as its purpose the liberation of the human individual from the authority that acted to separate him from his creative product and, hence, his true self.[33] This theme in Marx's thought was obscured for nearly a century until his early writings were first published, and as a result it did not enter Lenin's consideration. It was picked up, however, by the so-called neo-Marxist theorists in the 1950s and 1960s, most notably by the members of the Yugoslav *Praxis* group (Petrović, Marković, Stojanović and others), who focused on the profound creativity of man's essence when liberated from oppression and integrated as a conscious participant in socialist self-government.[34] In Poland, Leszek Kołakowski's search for a Marxist humanism led him to explore the nature of the individual as a cognitive, as well as a creative, being.[35] And in Czechoslovakia, Karel Kosík explored the idea that man as a cognitive and creative being is quite capable not only of understanding the complex, total system of reality, but also of shaping his own social reality and thereby transcending nature itself.[36] Kosík, like the other neo-Marxists, has drawn our attention to the fundamental question of the individual in society, the microcosmic basis of all Marxian thought.[37]

Central to most Communist reform movements in practice has been a belief in the goodness and reliability of the people, the kind of trust Marx had in the working class as the bearer of historical destiny. Certainly this was true of Czechoslovakia's leaders in 1968, for Dubček and his colleagues spent a great deal of effort informing the people of political developments, listening to public opinion, and restraining those in the party who would have preferred to stifle the spontaneity of the masses. It is also true, on the whole, of the Yugoslav leaders, who — although not without considerable ambivalence — have sought to translate Marxist theory into reality through the mechanisms of workers' self-management. Ironically, Milovan Djilas, since officially disgraced, was the first postwar East European Communist to articulate a sincere faith in the people and to link that faith with a critique of centralist authoritarianism. Djilas wrote in 1953 of the "normal people" [sic] in socialist society, who are by their very proletarian nature "good and honest, and socialists too" — and who therefore deserve to be left as free as possible from bureaucratic meddling, and to be given their due authority over their own affairs.[38]

It is not only mid-twentieth-century Marxists who have found in Marx a stimulus to reformist or libertarian tendencies. Some earlier Marxists did so as well: Bernstein, Kautsky, and Bukharin are the most obvious examples. Even Lenin, the quintessential revolutionary, turned his attention in his last years to the task of reforming the new Soviet system and broadening the basis of its authority structure. His last few essays — particularly "On Cooperation," "Our Revolution," and "Better Fewer, but Better" — revealed his concern with the growth of bureaucratic power, and surely the relaxed authoritarianism of the NEP administration was a precedent for liberalist experiments in later Communist systems.[39]

Reformism within nonruling Marxist parties had already begun during Marx's lifetime. In fact, part of the ambivalent legacy of Marx is that he himself, in his Inaugural Address of the First International (1864), laid out what Lichtheim has called the "Charter of Social Democracy."[40] In this speech Marx made reference to reformist achievements of the English working class, and he seemed to hint that real progress — perhaps even the capture of political power — could be accomplished by nonrevolutionary means.[41] In the last decades of the nineteenth century, the mainstream of the Marxist movement in Europe underwent a gradual turn to reformism and parliamentary politics, a process to which Tucker has referred as the "deradicalization of Marxist movements."[42] This development, naturally, reinforced and concretized the reformist impulse in Marxism. In Central and Western Europe this part of the ambivalent Marxian legacy persisted up to the present time, reflected in the Social Democratic parties and today's Communist parties, whereas in Russia the opposite tendency has prevailed.

The ambivalence of the Marxian legacy is entirely visible in the development of communism in Czechoslovakia, from Gottwald to Kosík and beyond. When communism began in Czechoslovakia, it did so in a quite common way, that is, as the result of a split in the Social Democratic party. The latter was a powerful organization, the strongest party during the first years of the new republic, with four decades' development in the sometimes fiery but, on the whole, moderate and reform-oriented Marxist traditions of the Austro-Hungarian Empire. The Czechoslovak SDP thus inherited from its pre-independence past a strong but essentially non-revolutionary tradition on the left wing of Czech and Slovak politics. In the years after 1918 the SDP's leadership participated fully in the new Czechoslovak government. In 1919 the Social Democrat Vlastimil Tusar became Czechoslovakia's second prime minister, and his colleague Rudolf Bechyně was a member of the original *pětka*. The role of the Social Democrats in these formative years was very important in the fashioning of the First Republic's progressive social and economic policies, and the SDP was generally viewed as a constructive constituent of the political system.[43]

Although there was some sympathy among the party rank and file for the Bolshevik Revolution in Russia, this did not translate, by and large, into a revolutionary feeling toward the Czechoslovak Republic. Czech and Slovak workers were too much caught up in the euphoria of their new independence to be concerned about class revolution, at least during the first few years after the war.

Nevertheless, a split quickly developed within the ranks of the SDP over the question of the party's attitude toward communism and, more specifically, its relationship to the Communist International. Under the leadership of Tusar and Bechyně, the right wing of the party very strenuously sought to avoid any direct association with communism and the International, in spite of strong pressures from Comintern officials to affiliate. The left, under the leadership of Bohumír Šmeral, convened a party congress in September 1920 against the wishes of the party's leadership and in the face of a boycott by about one-third of the delegates. The congress took no firm stand on the issues under contention, but by this time the rift had grown nearly irreparable. The left proceeded to set up an organizational structure of its own and started to publish a newspaper, Rudé právo. In the highly charged atmosphere of autumn 1920, strikes broke out in a number of regions as left and right jockeyed for power among the workers. The strikes and demonstrations culminated in a five-day period of unrest in December. The government was able to restore order with a minimum of violence, but the damage to the SDP was permanent.[44]

The left formed a youth movement, the ČSM, in the following February, and proclaimed the formal establishment of a Communist party in May 1921. It took a few more months for the new party's leaders, primarily Šmeral and Antonín Zápotocký, to consolidate the organization, but this task was largely completed by October of the same year.[45]

The fledgling KSČ (Komunistická strana Československa) was still something short of a perfect Comintern member. Shaking off its roots in the reformist tradition was not such an easy proposition, and the KSČ remained until 1929 a movement rather weak in revolutionary fervor — a point publicly made by Zinoviev in 1925.[46] It was, in addition, a mass party of a non-Bolshevik character, with over 93,000 members by 1925 and an electoral tally of 934,223 votes in the Assembly elections of that year.[47] Still, the attitude of the party toward the government was generally negative. While the Communists played the parliamentary game by its rules, they remained always in opposition, even after the 1925 elections had established them temporarily as the second-largest delegation in the National Assembly.[48]

The KSČ in the 1920s was not a serious threat to the stability of the

First Republic. The nearest the left had come to a revolution was in Kladno in 1920, where they staged a shortlived, *de facto* seizure of power in the midst of the SDP infighting. A year and a half earlier a similarly abortive insurrection had taken place in eastern Slovakia under rather dubious circumstances. Aided by the Red Army of Béla Kun's ephemeral Hungarian Soviet Republic, Magyar and Slovak workers had seized power and turned the rule in the region over to local and district soviets, with the major power center in Prešov. The insurrection was suppressed within four weeks' time.[49] The fact that neither this insurrection nor the localized revolts of 1920 spread very widely among the Czech and Slovak workers would seem to indicate the lack of enthusiasm for proletarian revolution. Faced with this reality, the KSČ reconciled itself to a role of parliamentary opposition.

A turning point for the party's leadership and ideology came at the Fifth Congress of the KSČ, February 18–23, 1929. For several years another conflict had been brewing, threatening to divide the left once again. The conflict culminated at the Fifth Congress with the triumph of a "Bolshevik" faction under the leadership of Klement Gottwald, the man who was destined to head the party until his death in 1953. Once in control, Gottwald immediately began to pursue what he himself called the "Bolshevization" of the KSČ, an unceasing process of molding the party in the image of the Soviet Communist party so that it could carry out a genuine socialist revolution.

During the ensuing decade, Gottwald created a new leadership corps, fanatically loyal to himself and to the USSR. The factory cell, modeled after the soviets, replaced the local party branch — a hold-over from the SD heritage — as the primary organizational unit. In policy, a radical platform was formulated by the Sixth Party Congress in 1931, during the Depression. It called for the expropriation of all large enterprises and banks, church properties, and landed estates; the collectivization of agriculture; the nationalization of all public services, and state control of mass media. Further, in an appeal to Slovaks, Magyars, and other disgruntled ethnic groups, the KSČ now branded the Czechoslovak Republic "a new edition of the Austro-Hungarian prison of nations."[50] At the conclusion of the Sixth Congress Gottwald summed up the revolutionary task of the party in this ringing call:

> We must go further along the path we have entered; we must travel this road more quickly and determinedly than before. We must utilize the objective circumstances that have made the lives of today's prole-

tarian masses a living hell and show them that capitalism means their death, and the only way out is communism. . . . In the past we have gone through hard times as a party, but now we look forward to a new and rapid rise. There are still many further difficulties confronting us, but with the help of the Comintern and under its leadership, united and with our ranks closed, and secure in the conviction that we have been called to save humanity, it will go on, as the French revolutionary song "Carmagnole" says: *Ça ira*. We will cut off the heads of the capitalists![51]

Despite Gottwald's rhetoric, the party in practice did not change much. It stirred up isolated strikes and organized modest demonstrations, but ideological cleavages persisted and workers did not embrace the new rhetoric *en masse*. Severely weakened by the purges that accompanied Bolshevization, the party's popular appeal fell sharply following the Fifth Congress. Its streamlined membership fell to a low of approximately 24,000 in April 1929 and climbed slowly upward thereafter, never again reaching its pre-1929 peak until after the Second World War. In the parliamentary elections of 1929 the Communist vote fell by almost twenty percent, to just over 753,000 ballots. By 1935 the KSČ had managed to recover about half the votes it had lost between 1925 and 1929 and registered nearly 850,000 ballots.[52] The party thus came more nearly to resemble the ideal Leninist organization, relatively small and disciplined, but at great cost. Communism now diverged from the mainstream of Czechoslovak politics more pronouncedly than before. The KSČ and its closest followers became a true political subculture within Czechoslovakia, consciously separated from the Social Democratic tradition which had been closely connected with the Czechoslovak mainstream for decades. The Communists saw their spiritual connections to be the link with the Moscow-based Comintern and the international working-class movement rather than the national traditions of Czechs and Slovaks.[53]

At this point, however, another complicating factor entered the picture. In November 1934 the KSČ again shifted its policy line dramatically, this time because of the recently signed Czechoslovak-Soviet mutual defense agreement and the Comintern's new emphasis on popular-front alliances in the face of the fascist threat in Europe. As late as May 1934 the Communists had voted against the reelection of President Masaryk in the National Assembly, but now they suddenly became oriented more positively toward the system and assumed a stance of staunch patriotism. The party supported the candidacy of Beneš upon Masaryk's retirement in 1935 and for a short time moved toward closer cooperation with the bourgeois government. Indeed, it seemed that the new mood of cooperation nearly got out of hand during the temporary exile of Gottwald. Gottwald and several other Communist leaders had fled the country for the USSR following a strong anti-government pamphlet and a series of incidents surrounding the final reelection of Masaryk, incidents that brought a warrant for their arrest. By February of 1936 it was possible for Gottwald to return to Prague, and when he did he found it necessary to reestablish control and issue a sharp criticism of recent KSČ policies for cooperating too much with the bourgeois state.[54]

The Communists now backed away from the regime once again, but they still maintained a patriotic stance. The defense of Czechoslovakia against fascism became of vital concern to them, and accordingly, they were outspoken in their warnings against the Nazi danger. This they continued even after the dismemberment of Czechoslovakia at Munich. In fact, the loudest protests voiced on behalf of the aggrieved country in the months following Munich were those of the Communists.[55]

The KSČ, then, was something less than a unified revolutionary vanguard during the thirties. After 1929 the party's official rhetoric heated up considerably in comparison to earlier years, but even during the height of the Bolshevization period the Communists' relatively moderate practices belied the intensity of their slogans. They were, in many respects, analogous to the German Social Democrats prior to the latter's participation in the government of the Second Reich. Interestingly, the more vehement the party's slogans, the less appeal among the voting public; Bolshevization in 1929 produced a sagging Communist electorate, whereas the more cooperative demeanor of the party in 1935 regained some of the support it had had during the still more moderate days of 1925.

With the exception of the 1925 elections, at no time did the Communists command the support of a plurality of the working class. By 1929 the Social Democratic party had surpassed the KSČ as the most popular political force among the workers, and by 1935 the SDP's supremacy among the proletariat was firm. Given the continuing attachment of the Social Democrats to the bourgeois regime, it seems a reasonable inference that the working class was hardly a revolutionary force in the First Republic.[56] When we consider the fact that many workers supported parties such as the National Socialists and the People's party, the proportion of noncommunist proletarian workers mounts even higher.[57] With such a frail basis of support for the socialist revolution, it is no wonder that the Communist party itself failed to generate a significant revolutionary program in practice and, instead, found itself torn between the ideal of revolution and the pragmatism of parliamentary politics.

Finally, it must be mentioned that at no time did the KSČ have within its ranks a single major theorist. Gottwald was a practitioner, and although his collected speeches and articles have come to fill fifteen volumes, they are the utterances of a politician rather than a philosopher. Not before Kosík and Sviták entered the scene in the 1950s did any important Marxist philosophers emerge, comparable to Lukács, Gramsci, Marcuse, or other twentieth-century counterparts abroad. Czechoslovak communism thus lacked a significant intellectual basis within its own society and had to depend on external sources for the articulation of a revolutionary *Weltanschauung*. This was a further factor in the weakness of the revolutionary tradition.

The legacy of interwar communism was one of an ongoing tension between idealistic radicalism and the realism of political feasibility. The struggle between party factions, unresolved in 1921 and only partly resolved in 1929, centered around the persistent contradiction between the Bolshevik-Comintern image and the Social Democratic heritage. The former was the ideal, the latter a sticky vestige from the Austro-Hungarian past. The combination gave the KSČ collectively an ambivalent orientation toward revolutionary politics. Apparently never quite sure of its revolutionary mission, the party eschewed the politics of parliamentary coalition but refrained also from the politics of subversion. The mass-party organization of the 1920s, a non-Leninist holdover from the SD tradition, was abandoned only after the intraparty power coup by the Gottwald ring in 1929; this, it must be added, came upon the forceful intervention of the Comintern in the deliberations of the KSČ.[58] Despite the changes in 1929 and the streamlined membership thereafter, the new leaders had only limited succeed in instilling their revolutionary fervor into the party as a whole, and even less success in revolutionizing the entire working class.

The Outside Influence

The pattern of Communist rule after 1948 could not have been predicted from the pre-World War II history of the party. Nor did it logically develop out of the events that took place during the war. Between 1939 and 1945 the party found itself divided between those members who remained in their homeland and those who fled the country. Furthermore, each of these two groups was divided as well. Those who stayed behind were divided into Czech and Slovak wings that were in fact organized as separate parties, just as the country was split up into two parts. In the occupied Czech lands, life was particularly difficult, and many Communists went to prison; those who managed to avoid being captured were leaderless and isolated, and some even turned to collaboration as a means of surviving. Some Slovak Communists went to prison, too, but a large number were able to join the resistance movement that grew up in the remote mountainous regions.

Of the Communists who went into exile, some went to the West and eventually made it safely to London. Others went east and found refuge in Moscow. They maintained communications with each other, but their contacts with the homeside Communists were obviously difficult and distant.

All of these groups underwent quite separate experiences during the years of the war, and once again, one would be hard pressed to have predicted the further development of the party on the basis of these disparate wartime experiences.[59] Indeed, the divisions inherent in the party's situation as of the war's end ultimately contributed to an internal conflict that culminated in the great purges of 1950-54. The effect of the conflict was to narrow the composition of the ruling group and to effectively consolidate power into the hands of a few men, centered around Gottwald, whose primary loyalties attached to the Moscow center.[60]

To return somewhat more concretely to the nature of Communist rule, it must be said that the Soviet influence was felt very soon after the KSČ's rise to power. The role of the security police was greatly increased, the communications media were reorganized and brought under Communist control, the judiciary was coopted into the service of the party, local institutions were absorbed into nationwide organizations, and centralized command structures were established which set out to duplicate the Soviet pattern of industrial and agricultural policies. Purge trials followed, beginning in 1950. There is evidence that throughout 1949 Gottwald and his colleagues had resisted bloc pressure to embark upon this intraparty fratricide, but the pressure eventually became irresistible.[61] For the time being, the purges did succeed in eliminating the potential sources of opposition within the party, but they did so at the cost of a greatly narrowed elite base that drove the now-truncated KSČ into even deeper dependency upon the CPSU. The role of the Soviet advisers in the political terror of the fifties was so strong that it gave perceptive Czechs and Slovaks cause to resent Soviet tactics for many years thereafter.[62]

The terror of the early fifties, during which the purges begun in the ranks of the party spread outward indiscriminately upon society as a whole, represented the lowest point of Czechoslovakia's postwar plunge into political dependency. It symptomized the greatest deviation from the previously dominant political culture, for it violated the longstanding traditions of reason, libertarianism, and humanism central to the Czech mentality. Moreover, the secular religion imposed upon society by the Communists clashed with the traditional religion of the Slovak political culture. The zealous attempt to convert Czechs and Slovaks alike to this new religion recalled the counterreformation in Bohemia more than three hundred years earlier and, curiously, gave Czechs and Slovaks common grounds for alienation from the Communist government.[63]

The road back from this time of national humiliation was long and tortuous. Ironically, Czechoslovakia, the only bloc member with a background of democracy and pluralism, was very slow to destalinize in comparison with Hungary and Poland. There are several interconnected reasons for this. The purges of the early fifties in Czechoslovakia were the most thoroughgoing of all East European purges, eliminating large numbers of potential and imagined challengers within the KSČ.[64] Those left in positions of authority were personally associated with the practices of these early years. Although Gottwald died in 1953, his eventual successor, Antonín Novotný, and all his entourage were connected with the terror — unlike Nagy, Kádár, and Gomułka. Fearful that any relaxation of social controls might lead to an examination of the recent past and to the discovery of skeletons in their own closets, Czechoslovakia's leaders chose a conservative path aimed at self-preservation. They adhered closely to their Soviet protectors, deviating if at all in the direction of dogmatism in political and ideological matters.

Thus the absorption of Czechoslovakia into the Soviet empire, together with all the far-reaching implications for domestic policy, served to renew the old split between the norms of the Communist subculture and those of the rest of society. Instead of winning over the hearts and minds of the populace, the Communists once again set themselves off from the national traditions of both Czech and Slovak. The resulting gap between elite and masses was to persist in the political culture of socialist Czechoslovakia, interrupted only temporarily by the reform interlude of 1968–69.

The Communist system of rule, in large part imported from the USSR, was as much an anomaly to Czech and Slovak political traditions as were the wartime regimes at their greatest moments of severity. The Germans had exploited the most authoritarian impulses in Czech and Slovak society, especially in Slovakia, where the Tiso regime embodied a distorted clerical-fascist tendency within the populist movement; similarly, the Soviets after 1948 exploited the most authoritarian strains within the KSČ to promote an analogously alien political system administered by men drawn from an indigenous political subculture. Just as it had required a Hitler to translate the vindictiveness of interwar Germany into the fury of the Third Reich, and just as it had taken a Stalin to twist Bolshevism into a psychopathic perversion of Marxism, so it required the influence of these foreign rulers to bring out and exaggerate the most extreme impulses in the political culture of Czechoslovakia.

The political changes introduced by the Communists seemed particularly radical because they were imposed upon society not by a conquering enemy (as in 1938–39) but by an indigenous party that had not been widely identified as a Stalinist party. The policies came as a shock to a population that had freely elected a Communist plurality in the parliamentary elections of 1946, for they came directly from the Soviet model rather than from any program developed by the KSČ on its own. Thus the new policies were made in Moscow but introduced by a willing domestic agent.

In the new international system that evolved in the postwar years, Czechoslovakia thus found itself drawn definitely into the Soviet camp of a divided Europe. Once in that camp, the norms of politics were authoritatively defined not by the logic of history and national precedent but by the far-reaching prescriptions of a new kind of imperial system centered in socialist Russia. The nature of this system is the subject of the next chapter.

IV

The Ruling Elite as Colonial Elite

In the first half-decade following the end of the Second World War, Czechoslovakia became an outpost of the new Soviet empire. This came about through a rather complex set of internal and external circumstances: the instability of postwar Czech and Slovak politics, the build-up of global tensions that culminated in the Cold War, and the heightened insecurity of the Soviet position in a repartitioned Europe. Important as the external circumstances were, the process of imperial absorption might not have been completed were it not for the unique political conditions within postwar Czechoslovakia that enabled the KSČ to come to the fore.

It is therefore appropriate that we now turn to a review of those circumstances, internal and external, in which the Communist political subculture gave birth to the postwar Czechoslovak political system. The first section of this chapter discusses this development within the framework of a rough Parsonian theory of social revolution. The second section examines the backgrounds of the new ruling group that emerged after the war, and the final section shifts our focus to the nature of the socialist international system of which Czechoslovakia has become an inseparable part.

The "Victorious" February and Its Repercussions

The Communists of Czechoslovakia celebrate the bloodless coup d'etat of February 1948 as the great revolutionary moment in their postwar history. Indeed, the events of the "victorious" February were such a moment; although it is inaccurate to call the Communists' takeover a revolution in the sense that we have been using the word, it was nonetheless the necessary first step in the chain of political events that developed into the Stalinist revolution.[1] In the course of these events, the Communists not only consolidated their political rule but led the country through a series of social and economic changes that forever transformed Czechoslovakia.

Talcott Parsons has outlined four conditions that generally combine to produce revolutionary change. The resulting paradigm can be very instructive in understanding the Communist ascent in Czechoslovakia. The four conditions are (1) a widespread alienation from the existing structures and values, (2) the availability of a subcultural group that is sufficiently well organized so as to act on behalf of an alternative set of structures and values, (3) an effective ideology incorporating widely accepted symbols, and (4) the existence of a fundamental instability within the ruling group.[2]

The war had interrupted Czechoslovakia's political development, and the attempts to reestablish the institutional order after 1945 were by no means simply a matter of continuing along the familiar interwar path. Political structures were in a state of flux, and the values of the First Republic were subjected to a critical reexamination. In the Czech lands political parties had been disbanded following the German occupation, and those whose members the Nazis considered most dangerous had been relentlessly persecuted. Those who had collaborated during the war were excluded from postwar politics. The Agrarian party as a whole was outlawed in retribution for some of its members' wartime indiscretions. The same fate befell the Catholic Unity party of Slovakia (the consolidated, renamed political front that had succeeded the HSL'S in 1939). There was a widespread desire for revenge against those on the right wing who had committed what were now commonly regarded as treasonous acts against Czechoslovakia. Although many people who were punished after 1945 for their membership in the former parties of the right were in fact loyal patriots, their exclusion from politics was not lamented by the larger part of at least the Czech population.[3] The political drift of the time was, as elsewhere in Europe, distinctly to the left — but with no clear collective sense of ultimate purpose. There was a general disillusionment with the exaggerated multi-party atmosphere of the past, as well as a feeling that something inherent in the First Republican system had led to the disaster of 1938–39. Thus there was widespread alienation from at least the structures of the past, and a sense of openness about the values of the present.

The Czechoslovak Communists, formerly a subcultural group on the outside of political power, suddenly found themselves in an unprecedented position as the strongest and best organized force in their country. The KSČ and its Slovak partner the KSS enjoyed some distinct advantages over their competition. In the first place, they now commanded the lion's share of the working-class vote, owing to the greatly weakened relative position of the Social Democrats and the National Socialists. The latter two parties had suffered greatly from wartime persecution and were tainted (in the minds of some) by their former association with the government that had so humiliatingly capitulated to the terms of Munich.[4] Neither was allowed to organize in Slovakia after 1945.[5] Although the Communists' political organization had been destroyed soon after the German entry into the protectorate, many of the party's leaders had managed to escape into exile and thereby avoided the executions and prison-camp deaths that took such a heavy toll of the Social Democratic leadership.[6] Moreover, the Communists were quick to take advantage of the national committees that sprang up during the last months of the war, encouraged by Beneš's government-in-exile. The committees' wide-ranging functions, reaffirmed in the Košice Program of April 1945, provided a convenient vehicle for the rebuilding of an organizational base.[7]

In the Czech lands the Communists were remembered for their strong stand against acceptance of the Munich Agreement, and in the leftward drift of public opinion apparent after 1945 their association with radical social reform put them abruptly into the political mainstream. The Communists championed merciless revenge against former traitors and war profiteers — a popular stand in the vindictive atmosphere of the time — and made themselves visible in the transfer of enemy territories, mostly German, into Czech hands. This gave them a high esteem, particularly in the countryside, where the evacuation of the minorities left sizable tracts of land open for new tenants. In the industrial centers the party made quick inroads into the trade-union movement, capitalizing on the lack of viable competition.[8] Thus the organizational structure of the party was relatively solid and provided the necessary infrastructural basis for a drive to power within the constitutional framework.

The weak point of this infrastructure was Slovakia. There, the organizational base was not nearly as strong as in the Czech lands. In Bohemia and Moravia, the KSČ had a mass appeal and a large membership active in party functions; in Slovakia, the KSS was small and patriarchically organized. In addition, the "liberation" of Slovakia was greeted with great ambivalence, in comparison with the jubilation with which Czechs received the end of the war. Many Slovaks had been associated with the Tiso regime, and many others had felt some pride in Slovak "independence." Now they were being "liberated" by a Soviet Army whose advance across Slovakia was accompanied by excesses of violence, rape, and looting. The bitter divisions of the wartime regime had been intensified by the National Uprising of autumn 1944, and the identification of the Communists with both the uprising and the Soviet Army gave the KSS a very mixed appeal.

Nor did the KSS succeed in endearing itself to the Slovak masses after liberation. There were sharp conflicts between the Communists and the Roman Catholic Church; Gustáv Husák, provisional Minister of the Interior in Slovakia, clashed openly with the Church and thus won for his party the distrust of a wide section of the predominantly Catholic population. Nor did the Communists capitalize on the redistribution of enemy properties. Unlike in the Czech lands, the Ministry of Agriculture in Slovakia was not under the leadership of the Communists. Therefore, the transfers of property that took place, both immediately after the war and in the wake of the land reform two years later, were done under the auspices of non-Communist administrators.

Notwithstanding the difficulties in Slovakia, the Communists were the strongest single party in the country as a whole. Even in Slovakia, Communist appeal was greater than it had ever been before 1938. Part of the reason for this was the party's active involvement in the uprising, with which one large portion of the public did sympathize, and part was simply the relative lack of alternative political forces. (For all practical purposes, Slovaks had only two choices in the 1946 elections: the Communists and the Democrats, the latter a new party which operated without an affiliate in the Czech lands). The Communists were obviously the gainers in the reduction of the opposition.

The party's ideology, a bit out of step with the mainstream political culture of the preceding decade, was now more acceptable to a wider portion of the public. The party's emphasis on equality had always been compatible with the value system of the Czech and Slovak "little man," and the postwar conjunction of equality and radical social reform struck a responsive note throughout society. Class conflict came to be identified, to some degree, with revenge against those who had profited from the wartime experience, and this theme, too, attracted much support. Socialism, as Vladimir Kusin has argued, was always a favorable term to the majority of Czechs and Slovaks, and in 1945 the Communists appeared to be the paramount heirs of Czechoslovakia's socialist tradition.[9] The idea of a unitary socialist movement had gained some headway among Czechs in the early days of the wartime resistance, and later in the Slovak resistance, so despite the differences of tradition and temperament there was a rather strong pull toward the cohesion of the left.[10] Even among the very religious socialism had many followers, and a good number of Christian socialists saw the Communist party as the secular hope of the future utopia that was to be based on love, equality, and self-denying communalism.[11]

A factor that further helped to bridge the gap between the former outcast role of the KSČ and its latter-day public acceptance was the parliamentary politics now practiced by the party in the framework of a fundamentally unstable government. Gottwald steered the party along a gradualist course, gaining a plurality of the popular vote in the 1946 elections to the National Assembly and maneuvering adroitly within the framework of the provisional system. The outlines of the party's new strategy were explained in a closed speech by Gottwald to KSČ functionaries on July 9, 1945. The party would cooperate in the National Front system and gain control of critical ministries and agencies — the army, internal security, information, education, labor. The national committees would be used to solidify the local support base, and voluntary organizations would be coordinated on a national scale. The Communists would play an important role in the confiscation and redistribution of enemy properties. In short, all the tactics already mentioned (above) as instrumental to the party's drive for power were presaged by Gottwald in this speech.[12]

Although the Communists appeared to be just another party in the 1945-48 coalition, it is clear from Gottwald's closed speech that their participation in the coalition was meant to be temporary and that total power was in fact the ultimate goal. Interestingly, the Soviet Army did not play the crucial role in this drive that it had played elsewhere in Eastern Europe. The Red Army aided the KSČ in local organizational work after its entry into Czechoslovakia, and Soviet officers were instrumental in the reorganization of the country's armed forces. However, the most important factors in the ultimate Communist victory were domestic: the weakness and fissiparousness of the opposition and the tireless organizational work carried out on all levels of society by loyal Communist partisans. As in neighboring countries, party functionaries often overstepped the limits of legality in pursuing their ends; abuse of power, harassment, and even arbitrary executions were not unknown to Communist security police, and these practices undoubtedly contributed to the general timidity of the noncommunist population. All of these factors helped to ease the KSČ's way into power.

That Communist rule was inevitable is, of course, a retrodictive fallacy. Similarly, it is wrong to assume that the die was ineluctably cast in favor of the Communists in July 1947 (Stalin's intervention in the Marshall Plan affair), or in September of the same year (the first Cominform meeting), or November (the defeat of the Social Democratic left and the threat of Communist isolation within the National Front).[13] There is no point in speculating how or at what point the noncommunist politicians might have acted to prevent the "victorious" February (1948), nor is there any firm evidence of the lengths to which Stalin was prepared to go to add Czechoslovakia to his growing East European empire in the case that the KSČ had failed to come to power by itself.[14] The facts are that the KSČ did seize power, it did so by extraconstitutional means within an ostensibly legal framework of action, it did so (for the most part) bloodlessly, and it acted with the support of a sizable part of the population — although at a time when that support seemed to be slipping.[15] There was no foreign-imposed pretender to the throne comparable to the Lublin Government in Poland, but on the other hand there was no heroic, violent overthrow of the old order as in Yugoslavia and Albania. The KSČ came to power in a revisionistic way, through the side door of the parliament, so to speak, largely on its own initiative and with the Soviet Army at a distance. Of course, there was regular communication between the Czechoslovak Communists and Stalin's representatives, but the role of the Soviets in the coup of 1948 might best be seen as advisory. The critical variable in the Communists' victory was the crisis in the domestic political order of Czechoslovakia in 1947–48. To be sure, the available evidence suggests that the domestic political circumstances saved Stalin the trouble of doing what he might have done himself (that is, send his army back in in order to support the KSČ's bid for power).[16] However, it did not happen that way, and it is speculative to insist that Stalin would certainly have intervened militarily.

The conditions outlined by Parsons for the ascent of a subcultural group to power were therefore met in the Czechoslovakia of 1945–48. We shall return to the subcultural theme presently, but first it is necessary to examine the international factors affecting postwar developments in Czechoslovakia.

There was never much doubt that, in liberating Czechoslovakia, the Soviet Union acted out of anything but disinterested magnanimity. The Czechs and Slovaks responsible for ruling the strife-torn country, Communists and noncommunists, realized this and sought to accommodate the security interests of the USSR by attaching their own security to that of the Soviets. Beneš had dreamed of a postwar Czechoslovakia that would represent a bridge between East and West. Czechoslovakia's dominant political culture placed it squarely in the mainstream of Western democratic and humanistic traditions, and Beneš imagined that this intellectual connection would be reestablished in the postwar Europe. At the same time, his people's Slavic

blood and geographical location gave Czechoslovakia and the Soviet
Union a "very strong community of interests [in] cultural, economic,
and political [matters]."[17] In addition, both had a powerful interest in
forming a solid front against any future German resurgence; the West,
Beneš had learned in the bitter lesson of 1938, was distant and un-
reliable, so his postwar alliance system had to be based on a firm link
with the USSR.[18]

Beneš's position became increasingly untenable in the circumstances
of increasing East-West polarization. In 1947 Stalin intervened in
Czechoslovakia's foreign relations by pressuring the Beneš government to reject membership in the Organization for European Economic Recovery (and, with it, American aid through the Marshall
Plan). Upon the establishment of Communist rule in 1948, Stalin
chose to exert a strong influence on domestic policy as well. Because of
the intensifying cold war, Stalin felt an urgency to tighten the reins of
the Cominform in order to maintain the strategic *glacis* to the west of
the USSR.[19] The Tito heresy, arising in the winter of 1947–48, was an
ominous precedent suggesting that an independent People's Democracy could threaten to upset the unstable power configuration in
Europe. It was apparent that even a Communist state could undermine
Soviet military security, and so in order to prevent the rise of additional Titos, Stalin tightened his authority in Eastern Europe and
acted through the Cominform to standardize policy and processes
throughout the bloc.[20] To challenge Stalin's will at this point, therefore, would not only have endangered the Soviet support that stood
behind the rather shaky domestic position of the KSČ, but might have
brought on a military intervention. There is no strong evidence that
Czechoslovakia's leaders were inclined to go another route, but whatever their innermost preferences were, they were obliged to follow the
dictates of Moscow from this point on.

A Quantitative Profile of the Communist Subculture

The ruling group that emerged in the postwar years had made the
jump from the political periphery to the center of power in a short
timespan. This sudden transition suggests some empirical questions
about the nature of those people who were thrust into power after
1945: who were they? — where did they come from? — could one have
predicted their ultimate style of rule from any common experiences in
their past?

In his seminal study of communism in interwar Eastern Europe,

R. V. Burks has argued that the Communists tended to be something other than a working-class political party, both with regard to the nature of their leadership and with regard to their appeal among the electorate. Burks suggested, however, that this general, regional pattern did not fit Czechoslovakia quite as well as it did other countries. To be sure, communism's greatest appeal was among certain ethnic minorities (particularly Magyars and Jews), and the class composition of both party cadres and voting constituency was rather ambiguous. Nonetheless, communism in Czechoslovakia emerges from Burks's data as the closest thing to a workers' party that one could find in Eastern Europe. This was especially true of the party activists, of whom more than half were drawn from the industrial proletariat.[21]

More recently compiled data on the Communist leading cadres suggest that, among the party's elite, industrial workers also constituted a decided majority of those who rose to the top ranks of power and influence.[22] The data discussed in the following pages are drawn from 145 cases. Each case represents a Communist who (1) joined the KSČ (or the KSS) before April 1945 and (2) ultimately attained a level of intraparty rank, whether before or after 1945, of candidate member of the KSČ Central Committee or higher. The first criterion in my selection of cases was imposed in order to eliminate all those who became party members after the formal entry of the KSČ/KSS into the new governmental order as projected at Košice. The cases, therefore, represent people who joined the Communist movement while it was still a peripheral political force. The second criterion was imposed to limit the sampling to the most influential figures among the Communists. The cases probably do not represent *all* people who met both criteria of selection, but they do represent all those for whom workable data can be assembled. A sampling of 145 cases is by no means statistically impressive, especially given the fact that there are missing data for some of the variables analyzed in some of the cases. However, the sampling would seem to constitute a usable source of empirical information in light of the general dearth of knowledge we currently have about the subject.

The data tell us about more than just the class constituency of our sample, but let us start by looking at this important variable. Tables IV.1 and IV.2 display the available data concerning social class of the subjects' fathers and subjects' vocations.

The data on social class of subjects' fathers are vexingly sparse, but from those available we can discern a clear preponderance of working-class backgrounds (72 percent). If these data reflect the total distribution of social origins among the subcultural elite, the sample can truly be said to have been drawn from a primarily proletarian background, allowing for the relatively small numbers drawn from other social classes.

Table IV.1

Father's Social Class, as Identified in Communist Sources

Class	Frequency	Percent*
Intelligentsia	3	4.0%
Bourgeoisie	13	17.3%
Petty Bourgeoisie	2	2.7%
Proletariat	54	72.0%
Peasantry	3	4.0%
Total (N = 75)		100.0%

Missing Cases: 70

*Percentages adjusted to available data only.

Table IV.2

Subject's Primary Vocation, Other than Politics

Vocational Category	Frequency	Percent*
Professional [a]	39	36.1%
Managerial	2	1.9%
Industrial Worker	55	50.9%
Agricultural Worker	3	2.8%
Other [b]	9	8.3%
Total (N = 108)		100.0%

Missing Cases: 37

*Adjusted to available data only.

[a] includes law, medicine, teaching, and journalism other than short-term positions with Communist newspapers

[b] includes mostly craftsmen, tailors, and clerks

With regard to the vocations of the subjects themselves, the data are more nearly complete and show greater variation. Only slightly more than half were actually workers themselves, whereas nearly as many were employed in what were essentially middle-class occupations (professions, management, and those "other" categories of a petty-bourgeois character such as trades and crafts). The leaders themselves, therefore, seem to have been almost evenly divided between workers and other vocational groupings.

Cross-tabulating the two variables, we see that a substantial number of the subjects for whom data on both variables are available remained within the same general social-status group as their fathers (Table IV.3). 84.1 percent of the subjects who came from working-class families also became workers themselves, and 81.8 percent of those from bourgeois families entered the professions. The numbers of subjects from other social groups represented in the data are too small to be significant, but it is perhaps worth noting that of the two cross-tabulated subjects who came from the ranks of the intelligentsia, both entered the professions.

Table IV.3

Father's Social Class Cross-Tabulated with Subject's Vocation*

Father's Social Class	Subject's Vocation[a]				
	Agricultural Worker	Industrial Worker	Managerial	Professional	Total
Intelligentsia (N = 2)	---	---	---	100.0%	100.0
Bourgeoisie (N = 11)	9.1%	9.1%	---	81.8%	100.0
Petty Bourgeoisie (N = 2)	---	---	---	100.0%	100.0
Proletariat (N = 44)	---	84.1%	2.3%	13.6%	100.0
Peasantry (N = 2)	---	50.0%	---	50.0%	100.0

Total (N = 61)
Missing Cases: 84

* Percentages represent *row* pct., e.g., 84.1% of all subjects with working-class fathers became industrial workers themselves.
[a] "Other" is omitted here to eliminate ambiguity.

One further socio-economic variable included in the data set concerns the nature of the locality in which each subject was born. Table IV.4 shows that most of the subjects were born in localities where the primary economic activity was industry or a mixture of industry and agriculture. However, a substantial minority (38.3 percent) were born in mainly agricultural communities.

Table IV.4

Primary Economic Activity of Subject's Birthplace

Category	Frequency	Percent (adj.)
Industrial, Commercial	43	45.7%
Mixed	15	16.0%
Agricultural	36	38.3%
Total (N = 94)		100.0%

The members of the subcultural elite tended not to be a highly educated lot, although here again there were numerous exceptions. Nearly half went no farther than the completion of elementary school, but on the other hand more than one-third completed one form or another of post-secondary education. One-sixth of the subjects earned advanced university degrees (that is, post-graduate degrees). Table IV.5 breaks down the data for this variable.

Cross-tabulating subjects' education with vocations shows no great surprises. Most highly-educated subjects entered professions commensurate with their formal training, and most less-educated subjects became industrial laborers (Table IV.6). Thus status inconsistency, a phenomenon often cited by sociologists as a cause of political radicalism among certain social groups, would not appear to be a significant factor in the constituency of the Czechoslovak Communist subculture.[23]

Before moving on to a specific analysis of those persons who became rulers after 1945, two additional variables should be mentioned. These concern sex and ethnic identity. The data concerning sex are completely unambiguous; in our sample, 130 (89.7 percent) were men, and 15 (10.3 percent) were women. The data on ethnicity, however, are fraught with problems, mostly beyond the control of this author.[24] All we can say with any reasonable certainty is that most of the subjects were Czechs (perhaps two-thirds but probably fewer), no more than approximately one-fifth were Slovaks, and that Germans and Magyars each represented no more than about three percent of the total.[25] Male Czechs tended to predominate, therefore, but the actual ethnic proportions can only be guessed due to inaccuracies and ambiguities in the data.

Looking at the aggregate data concerning the political careers of these subjects, we see that fewer than one-fourth of them attained the rank of Central Committee or higher before 1945 (Table IV.7 and Graph IV.1). In fact, the median rank of the subjects (highest rank achieved) before 1945 was that of local, district, or regional official; the largest number of subjects held no official position at all but were simply Communist party members. This indicates a relative lack of political experience on the part of the sample as a whole, and when compared to the data on political rank between 1945 and 1948 the

Table IV.5

Subject's Formal Education

Level [a]	Frequency	Percent (adj.)
Elementary uncompleted	3	2.6%
Elementary, completed	52	44.8%
Middle school or gymnasium	19	16.4%
Commercial or teachers' institute	8	6.9%
University or poly-technical institute	15	12.9%
Post-graduate training	19	16.4%
Total (N = 116)		100.0%

Missing Cases: 29

[a] Highest level completed

Table IV.6

Subject's Vocation Cross-Tabulated with Formal Education*

Subject's Vocation [a]

Education (highest level)	Agricultural Worker	Industrial Worker	Managerial	Professional	Total
Elementary, uncompleted (N = 2)	---	100%	---	---	100.0
Elementary, completed (N = 44)	2.3%	95.5%	---	2.3%	100.1
Middle school or Gymnasium (N = 12)	8.3%	41.7%	---	50.0%	100.0
Commercial or Teachers' Inst. (N = 7)	---	14.3%	14.3%	71.4%	100.0
University or Polytechnic (N = 11)	---	18.2%	9.1%	72.7%	100.0
Post-Graduate (N = 16)	---	---	---	100.0%	100.0

Total (N = 92)   * Row pct.   [a] "Other" is omitted.
Missing Cases: 53

difference is startling. By February 1948, nearly half of the subjects had attained the rank of candidate member, KSČ/ÚV (*Ústřední výbor,* or Central Committee), and the overall median rank as I have coded the values falls just short of KSČ/ÚV (Table IV.8). Thus the rise of party leadership cadres was rapid indeed, indicating that the People's Republic was soon to be led by political newcomers.

Cross-tabulations of the data pertaining to political office 1945–48 with that of other variables give us more of a profile of the leading cadres who rose to power during this critical transitional period. Once again, the ethnic composition of leading cadres presents an analytical problem due to errors in the Pittsburgh coding, but one fact does emerge: of the 80 people who attained the status of Central Committee candidate or higher, apparently only four (5 percent) were Slovaks and

Table IV.7

Highest Political Rank of Subjects Before 1945

Rank	(code)	Frequency	Percent
Party member only	(1)	60	41.4%
Local, district, or reg. office	(2)	25	17.2%
Central Com., Slovak C.P.	(3)	3	2.1%
Higher position, Slovak C.P.	(4)	4	2.8%
National official, Mass organization	(5)	21	14.5%
Central Com., Czechoslovak C.P.	(6)	20	13.8%
Higher Position, party or state	(7)	12	8.3%

Total (N = 145)   100.1% *
Missing Cases: none

Mean = 3.062 σ = 2.243
Median = 2.000   Mode = 1.0

*Figures do not total 100 due to rounding.

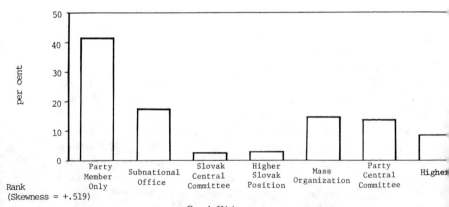

Graph IV.1
Highest Political Rank before 1945

Table IV.8

Highest Political Rank of Subjects
1945–1948

Rank	(code)	Frequency	Percent
Party member only	(1)	27	18.6%
Local, district, or reg. office	(2)	18	12.4%
Central Committee, Slovak C.P.	(3)	5	3.4%
Higher position, Slovakia	(4)	10	6.9%
National official, Mass organization	(5)	5	3.4%
Central Committee, Czechoslovak C.P.	(6)	57	39.3%
Higher position, party or state	(7)	23	15.9%
Total (N = 145) Missing Cases: none			99.9%*

Mean = 4.455 σ = 2.251
Median = 5.632   Mode = 6.0

*Figures do not total 100 due to rounding.

one (1.25 percent) was of Magyar identity (Viliam Široký). Sixty-eight (85 percent) were men and twelve (15 percent) women. Age-wise, those who occupied the two highest categories of political rank (KSČ/ÚV and above) were slightly older, as a group, than the total sample (class mean of 2.8 cf. 2.5 where 1 = under 30, 2 = 30–39, 3 = 40–49, and 4 = 50 and over). Table IV.9 and Graph IV.3 display the data concerning age groups of this sample. The data show that the sample as a whole was rather young, with just under one-half of the subjects under forty years of age, but that those aged forty and older tended to dominate the top political ranks.

Another matter that deserves our attention relative to the top ranks immediately after the war is what we might call the "Soviet connection" — direct, personal ties between the subjects and the USSR. These

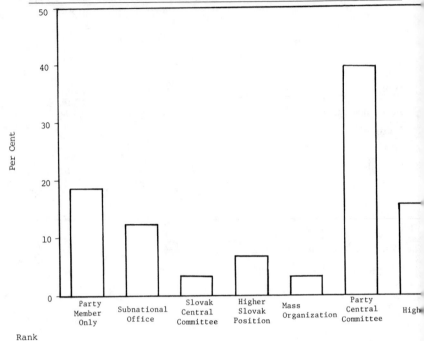

Rank
(Skewness = -.492)

Graph IV.2
Highest Political Rank 1945–48

Table IV.9

Age of Subject as of 1945*

Age Class	Total Sample (N = 145)	KSČ/ÚV ranks and higher, 1945–48 (N = 80)
Under 30	12.4%	6.2%
30–39	37.2%	32.5%
40–49	33.8%	36.2%
50 and over	16.6%	25.0%
	100.0%	99.9%[†]

*i.e., as of April 1945, when month of birth is known
[†] Figures do not add up to 100 because of rounding.

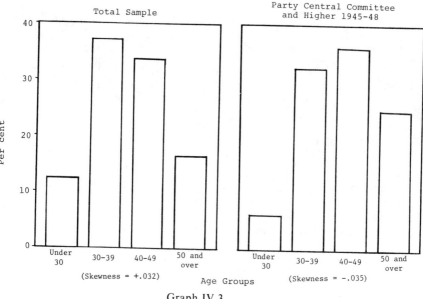

Graph IV.3
Age as of 1945

can be measured in terms of two variables, party training and wartime exile. In general, relatively few of our subjects received party training in the Soviet Union, as Table IV.10 shows, and therefore it would seem dubious to argue that this was a very significant factor in the make-up of the postwar Communist elite. The question of status during World War II is another matter, however, as Table IV.11 indicates.

These data indicate that the highest numbers of influential party members were incarcerated during the war, either in concentration camps or in prisoner-of-war camps. Those who fled to the USSR represented less than one-fifth of the total sample and only slightly more than one-fifth of those who entered the top two political ranks between 1945 and 1948. However, at the very pinnacle of power — the KSČ Presidium, Secretariat, and in the Ministries — those who had been in Moscow during the war became very important in Prague. In Slovakia, on the other hand, the situation was very different; only one Communist returned from the Soviet Union to occupy a position at the top of the KSS, whereas eleven of the fourteen top Slovak leaders accounted for in the Pittsburgh data had spent the war years fighting in the underground.

Table IV.10

Subjects' Party Training

	Total Sample (N = 145)	KSČ/ÚV and higher, 1945–48 (N = 80)
Training in USSR	21.4%	18.8%
Training in Czechoslovakia	2.8%	1.2%
None, or No Information	75.9%	80.0%
	100.1%[*]	100.0%

[*]Figures do not add up to 100 because of rounding.

Table IV.11

Political Status, World War II

Status[a]	Total Sample (N = 116)	Top 2 Ranks[b] (N = 61)	Highest Rank[c] (N = 18)
Exile in USSR	18.1%	21.3%	38.9%
Exile in USSR	18.1%	21.3%	38.9%
Incarcerated	41.4%	55.7%	38.9%
Active in Underground	31.0%	23.0%	22.2%
Other[d]	9.5%	---	---
	100.0%	100.0%	100.0%

[a] In cases where two statuses were present, e.g. both incarceration and exile, the one of longer duration is used.

[b] KSČ/ÚV and higher, 1945–48.

[c] KSČ Presidium, Secretariat, or governmental position of Ministerial rank.

[d] Includes exile in West and political inactivity at home.

In one further respect the profile of Communists at the very pinnacle of power after 1945 differs from that of the rest of the sample. Earlier it was mentioned that industrial workers made up the largest proportion of the subjects as aggregated according to vocation, and that professionals followed in second position (see Table IV.2, above). Above the rank of the KSČ/ÚV, that ranking is reversed; a clear majority of the top party and state officials represented in the sample were drawn from the professions (Table IV.12). It is interesting that those of relatively higher social standing in "civilian" life rose to the very top of the immediate postwar hierarchy, while at all other levels of authority the party more closely resembled a working-class political force. This situation persisted for some while after 1948 as well, as former professionals tended to predominate among the highest ranks of party and state (although not as decidedly so as prior to 1948).

Drawing an Aggregate Profile

The above discussion has been largely an exercise in laying out facts in an attempt to demonstrate both the diversity of the members of the Communist subculture and the points at which distinct patterns can begin to be seen. No theory is proposed to explain the patterns, but perhaps it would be useful now to look at the modes discernible in the

Table IV.12

Vocational Backgrounds of Top Communist Leaders, 1945–1948

Vocation	Top 2 Ranks [a] (N = 53)	Highest Rank [b] (N = 18)
Professional	43.4%	61.1%
Managerial	1.9%	0.0%
Industrial Worker	49.1%	38.9%
Agricultural Worker	5.7%	0.0%
	100.1% [c]	100.0%

[a] KSČ/ÚV and higher

[b] KSČ Presidium, Secretariat, or governmental position of Ministerial rank

[c] Figures do not total 100 because of rounding.

data. Modal statistics do not show the range of diversity in any given population of data, but they are useful for indicating a certain "average" case. Focusing on the modal member of the Communist subculture, therefore, will help us draw together the various data discussed in the preceding pages.

The modal profile that emerges indicates that the "typical" member of the Communist subculture was a Czech male approximately forty years of age (slightly older in the case of high-ranking politicians). He was an industrial laborer by vocation, from a working-class family in an industrial community. He managed to complete his elementary education but did not go substantially beyond that level. He entered the Communist party sometime before the Gottwald takeover of 1929 but received no special party education, either in the Soviet Union or in his own country. He quite likely spent some time in a prison camp during World War II, although if he was one of those people destined to enter the very highest political stations after 1945 he just as likely spent the war years in Moscow. He probably held no party office before 1945, but then he experienced a rapid rise to the level of Central Committee member or higher.

To go beyond this description is to do some minor violence to the strict empiricism thus far adhered to in this section. However, it might be added that the modal subject discussed above probably differed from other members of society in the strength of his political beliefs and his willingness to realize them by means that might have included tactics unacceptable to many of his noncommunist peers. Despite the relative moderation that distinguished Czechoslovak Communists from the more radical Comintern parties, the KSČ elite was rather consistently immoderate in its political program. Social revolution was the central purpose of the KSČ, and the party's leaders never made any pretense at disguising that aim.

It required an international upheaval for them to realize their central purpose. The war, the devastating social and political events of 1938–45, and the expansion of the defense perimeters of the USSR all played a role in the eventual triumph of the Communist political subculture. Of critical importance was the fact that the Communist subculture rose to power not just as one of any random political forces within Czechoslovakia but rather as a natural ally of the new hegemonial power in postwar Eastern Europe. By joining forces with the USSR, the KSČ ultimately made a major transition from the status of subcultural elite to that of a colonial elite.

The Nature of the Soviet Empire

Thus far I have used the term "empire" and several others associated with it without clarifying the meaning. I am referring to the system of authority relations regulating the international political, military, and ideological cohesion of the Soviet-East European network of alliances. I have chosen the terminology carefully, for despite the polemical usage to which the words "empire" and especially "imperialism" have fallen victim, none of the alternative terminologies — regional security system, hegemonial system, bloc, or commonwealth — is quite adequate to explain the pattern of relationship. Yet another alternative concept, that of dependency, gets us no further. Recently some scholars have begun an attempt to explain the Soviet-East European relationship in terms of dependency theory as derived primarily from studies of U.S.-Latin American interaction.[26] Although the comparison between dependency systems East and West is a promising new field of scholarship, it has been argued (persuasively, in this author's opinion) by Deutsch and Zimmerman that dependency theory essentially represents a modernized version of imperialism theory, leaning heavily on the Leninist school of interpretation.[27]

Empire and imperialism are in need of clear definition, given the modern and socialist context of our discussion. Most contemporary usages of the term involve reference either to obsolete political systems or to current systems of economic and political domination rooted in the outward expansion of capitalism.[28] "Imperialism" is frequently used as a polemical term, as in "Yankee imperialism," and therefore it is sometimes difficult to discuss the subject seriously and objectively. When used in reference to the Soviet Union, the word often serves to identify the user with a cold-war attitude that may detract from an attempt at objectivity. Notwithstanding these problems, it is this writer's opinion that imperialism is the most descriptive concept here, and it therefore behooves us to shed our ideological biases to the extent that it is possible and approach the problem objectively.[29]

Let us take as our point of departure a phenomenon that George Lichtheim has referred to as "post-capitalist imperialism." In his incisive essy on imperialism, Lichtheim has suggested that we may have discovered in the contemporary era the existence of capitalism without empire and empire without capitalism, but we have not yet moved on to a theory by which to account for this. Lichtheim himself has not volunteered for the task of developing such a grand theory.[30] It is not my purpose to take up the gauntlet on a comprehensive theoretical scale, but I do wish to suggest some aspects of the Soviet-East European relationship that can best be seen within the framework of an imperial reference point. Specifically, I wish to suggest that the structure of relations between the Soviet Union and the member states of the Warsaw Treaty Organization represents a modern variant of what S. N. Eisenstadt has chosen to call the historical bureaucratic empire.[31]

According to Eisenstadt's model, the historical bureaucratic empires — in which are included such chronologically and geographically disparate entities as the Babylonian, Byzantine, Ottoman, Russian, and Spanish American Empires — shared a number of general features. They were usually established during times of great unrest and social change, and the general pattern of territorial expansion was from a rather well-established imperial core outward across land or sea to peripheral, or colonial, regions. The imperialists generally came into conflict with the representatives of traditional authority in the peripheral regions and sought to establish a basis of local support within groups that had been alienated from the traditional sources of authority. To this end the imperial rulers devised instruments of political and administrative action through which they could maintain a basis of support, by offering rewards of a material or political nature to their local allies. Local citizens were coopted into positions of colonial authority, thereby creating new domestic elites who assumed a degree of administrative autonomy. Recruitment into the new elite had to be carried out on a basis other than traditional ascriptive values, in order to maintain the desired flow of authority from imperial center to colonial periphery; quite often, the most important criterion for elite recruitment was loyalty to the powers-that-be. Sometimes associated with that political loyalty was a concomitant loyalty to an official religion or some other set of doctrines held sacred by the imperial powers.[32]

Within the colonial territories there was a strong tendency toward centralized rule and the development of a professional bureaucracy with a wide range of administrative responsibilities. At the same time, political activities and roles among the elites tended not to take on a high degree of differentiation, and the level of political participation among the masses was quite low. Politics in general was largely separate from most other aspects of colonial society, and political goals tended to be articulated in terms that suggested a high degree of autonomy from the local cultures.[33]

With some updating, most of Eisenstadt's generalizations hold with regard to the Soviet-East European relationship during the past three decades. Although there was no serious thought given to the absorption of all East European lands into the Soviet Union, it is clear that Stalin and his successors have consistently seen these territories as an extension of the Soviet defense perimeters.[34] They were thus incorporated into the Soviet Union's strategic planning as a sphere of influence at a time when Europe was being redivided into two hostile camps, and throughout the years since the Soviets have not shunned violence (or the threat thereof) when necessary for the maintenance of the defense perimeters, as evidenced by the interventions in Hungary and Czechoslovakia. For reasons having to do with both convenience and ideological concerns — as well as a desire to minimize the objections of Western governments — Stalin and his successors found it advantageous to support the outward appearance of sovereignty for these states rather than to annex them.[35] The nature of this modern empire, therefore, has been one of indirect imperial authority and nominal state independence.

As far as Soviet interests were concerned, the Communists of Eastern Europe were ideally suited for the role of leadership. Not only did they come from groups that had long been allied with the USSR through the Comintern network, but within their respective societies they represented political subcultures whose members and leaders had been active opponents of the traditional authorities. In some countries the Communists were anointed to leadership by direct Soviet actions, whereas in others they came to power (with greater or lesser degree of Soviet help) because of domestic political circumstances. In all cases — Yugoslavia and Albania excepted — the Soviets came to dictate the general conditions relevant to ideology, policy, and personnel alike. Throughout the years the stringency of the hegemonial conditions has fluctuated from time to time, but the East European leaders have always had to be aware that their autonomy has limits and their policy decisions have to be made within those sometimes indistinct but always crucial boundaries of doctrinal legitimacy. Similarly, those who have held the mandate to rule have known that the mandate can be revoked if their loyalty falters.

The development of bureaucratic rule within Eastern Europe has been another point of commonality with the historical empires of Eisenstadt's model. The demands of modern technological society have dictated an increasing degree of specialization, and here the Soviet empire diverges somewhat from the historical model; nonetheless, there is a noticeable tendency toward the duplication of many administrative responsibilities, with party and state agencies or committees frequently involved in the same activities and a proliferation of interagency and intergroup checks within the bureaucratic systems.[36]

As in the historical systems, the level of direct and voluntary political participation on the part of the masses is rather low. The parties' efforts at mobilizing and organizing the citizenry notwithstanding, citizen politics has for the most part been distinguished by a lack of spontaneity, an unenthusiastic adherence to prescribed political rituals when unavoidable, and a tendency to apathetic withdrawal at other times.[37] Such withdrawal is not always easy, for unlike the historical systems, the political aspects of life in Eastern Europe overlap all, or nearly all, others.

Lichtheim has defined imperialism as "the relationship of a hegemonial state to peoples or nations under its control."[38] The objective nature of an empire is such that it can be said to exist "even when the imperial power is not constituted as such."[39] It might be added that an empire can be said to exist in spite of the imperial rulers' consistent and vehement denials of the relationship. The relationship itself need not come about as a result of conquest and overt territorial expansion, but rather it may be the result of diplomacy, treaty, or piecemeal economic dependency. "What counts," argues Lichtheim, "is the relationship of domination and subjection, which is the essence of every imperial regime."[40] Lichtheim's definition thus hinges on the absence of sovereignty on the part of the dominated people or nation, and on the concomitant ability of the imperial power to exert control over the other. It is a straightforward and simple conception of imperialism, unacceptable to some, but persuasively developed and placed within the long, historical context of empires from the dawn of civilization to modern times. It is therefore an appropriate working definition.[41]

Clearly, the critical question from the theoretical standpoint is *control.* Several recent studies of the Soviet-East European relationship have led to rather mixed conclusions about the USSR's ability to control all aspects of the relationship.[42] During the 1960s it occurred to some Western observers that the price paid by the Soviets for political stability in Eastern Europe was to allow the smaller states to become what Paul Marer has called a "net economic liability." According to Marer, the Soviet Union has been obliged to underwrite a certain minimum level of economic well-being in Eastern Europe to satisfy ever-rising consumer expectations and thereby help the local elites maintain peace and social order. In so doing, the USSR suffers in many instances from politically determined prices falling below world-market levels.[43] One might therefore be tempted to ask, "who is exploiting whom?" — that is, who gains and who loses from such a relationship, and what are the implications for judging whether or not this is an example of imperialism?

Marer is the first to admit that the data in this case are incomplete and should not lead to sensationalized conclusions. David D. Finley has argued that the two-way trade-offs in bloc economic relations do not negate the basic reality that, individually, the East European states are economically dependent on the USSR, but the reciprocal is not true.[44] Indeed, the mere fact of geographic size, as well as gross economic potential, would seem to dictate that the inherently weaker East European states are bound to come out second-best in any general economic comparison with the Soviet superpower.

When one looks at other aspects of the relationship, the evidence more clearly points to a Soviet domination. It would seem ludicrous to argue that, singly or together, the East European states are the military equals of the USSR. The same can be said of political and ideological strengths; the Czechs and Slovaks discovered in August of 1968 that all the dialectical logic they could muster in their own defense, and all the political support they had inspired within their own society, could not match the ultimate political argument of Soviet power.[45]

Again, historical evidence — particularly with reference to Hungary in 1956 and Czechoslovakia in 1968 — indicates that the Soviet leaders have both the capability and the will to use force as a means of control over Eastern Europe. The actions in Hungary and Czechoslovakia were meant not only to stabilize the region's defense perimeters but also to enforce the political and ideological limits of acceptable policy within the Soviet sphere of influence. It is therefore no exaggeration to speak of control, domination, and subjection — the essence, as Lichtheim has said, of imperial relationships.

In a more subjective vein, it is useful to speak of yet another characteristic of imperialism that bears relevance to Eastern Europe. That is the rather vague but nonetheless irksome attitude of superiority generally exhibited by imperialist leaders toward colonial subjects. Conversely, one might speak of a certain collective inferiority complex on the part of the colonial populace toward the imperialists. Certainly these phenomena can be seen in Soviet-East European relations. Soviet soldiers stationed in the allied countries are commonly viewed with a mixture of awe and contempt, but no one challenges their "might-makes-right" presence. Soviet academicians have been known to treat their East European colleagues at international scholarly conferences with unabashed condescension sometimes approaching scorn. Soviet tourists are frequently seen to move into East European resort districts and proceed to behave offensively toward their hosts. (This, of course, is not greatly different from the attitude and behavior of many American tourists in Western Europe or German tourists in Southern Europe, but it is no less a sign of imperialistic arrogance.)

In return, East Europeans are not immune to feeling that the Russians come from an inferior culture, are boorish, or deserve to be ignored and avoided. However, on the East European side such feelings are generally mixed with the deep humility that attends the knowledge of who ultimately controls whom. In this respect, as in others, the East Europeans' plight is the typical colonialists' lament.

The imperial mentality of the Soviet leaders seems to cast the East Europeans as peoples in need of political and ideological guidance. Here, the Czechs and Slovaks have apparently confirmed the imperial attitude. The Soviets seem to be saying that, left to themselves, the Czechs and Slovaks are likely to go off in some ideologically heterodox direction — thereby violating the secular religion (Marxism-Leninism) seen as a sort of legitimizing glue holding the empire together in a solemn bond. That was apparently what happened in 1968 before the momentum of the Czechoslovak heresy — the term is not inappropriate — could be brought under control. Again, this attitude is not new in the history of imperial systems; one has only to read certain accounts of the white man's *mission civilisatrice* in Asia and Africa as expressed by French and British spokesmen of the Victorian era. Just as the dark-skinned natives would never become "civilized" without European help, so too the Czechs and Slovaks might very well never reach communism without Soviet guidance.

It should not be incongruous, then, to see the East European system as a modern bureaucratic empire, reminiscent of Eisenstadt's historical bureaucratic empires in its basic authority patterns, although diverging from the historical model in ways directly related to the peculiarities of twentieth-century political reality. The empire cannot overtly be called an Empire, for the terminology of imperialism is reserved in Communist ideology for capitalist international relations. It is instead called a "camp" or some other such euphemism meant to disguise the relationship of domination and subjection. Nominally, proletarian internationalism is the normative description of the pattern, which is supposedly characterized by mutual, fraternal solicitude and "eternal friendship." The trappings of sovereignty are maintained by colonial elites, manifested in ways ranging from United Nations membership to the maintenance of national armies. It is true that decisions made within the context of the Warsaw Treaty Organization have become increasingly more multilateral in the past two decades, but it is clear that the Soviet Union holds the decisive vote on the most critical issues. In cases of conflicts perceived as a threat to the empire — such as the crisis of 1968 — only the USSR has the power to enforce its will if its leaders so decide.[46]

This having been said, one additional aspect of the East European empire needs to be mentioned. Here we are dealing with "pure" theory that cannot be empirically verified, but it is worth considering the long-range dynamic of what appears to be an increasing tendency toward the multilateralism alluded to in the preceding paragraph. Kent N. Brown has suggested that policymaking in Eastern Europe results from the formation of cross-national coalitions between certain factions in the smaller WTO countries and their supporters in Moscow.[47] To extend this theory further, it might be suggested that many broad patterns of policy are conditioned by the shared political-ideological assumptions of a cross-national elite composed of all the authoritative personalities of the Soviet empire. Adherence to a general code of "internationalist" political orientations is prerequisite to admittance into the imperial elite, and the maintenance of a reasonably stable and orthodox domestic social situation is necessary for continued membership. To put it another way, it is possible for East European elites to achieve considerable status and a substantial voice in the decision-making processes of the empire if they are willing to adopt the internationalist outlook and code of operations considered standard within the bloc.

One might very well be reminded at this point of the Austro-Hungarian Empire. It is wrong to carry historical comparisons too far, but if the East European empire of the late twentieth century is indeed moving in the direction suggested by the theory outlined above, it would seem to recall the multinational elite which ruled under the authority of the Habsburg monarch. To invoke the most tired of clichés, history does sometimes repeat itself — though usually only in quite general terms. The present author is by no means ready to predict the dissolution of the Soviet empire, as the Habsburg empire ultimately dissolved. Nor does the tendency toward multilateralism lessen the USSR's power advantage vis à vis the smaller allies. The relationship between the USSR and all other member states remains very asymmetrical, and the men in the Kremlin continue to hold in reserve the ever-present possibility of unilateral control over their weaker allies.

For the time being, Czechoslovakia represents the equivalent of a colony whose leaders have been co-opted into the imperial elite. The country's sovereignty has been surrendered to the empire, and its rulers operate within the constraints of ideological and political boundaries set largely by outsiders. The rulers themselves hold their positions at the sufferance of the empire's rulers; they must exhibit due fealty to Moscow or risk losing their mandate. The mandate itself, obviously, comes as much from the imperial center (Moscow) as it does from any domestic source. There is an official creed, Marxism-Leninism, to which the colonial elite must subscribe. The ultimate, unimpeachable authorities on the interpretation of the creed are the members of the Soviet Politburo. Together with the creed, the colonial elite communicates in a symbolic language the mastery of which serves to reinforce the ever-present gap between the colonial elite and the masses.[48]

This colonial elite, as we have seen, was and is drawn from a Communist political subculture native to Czechoslovakia but somewhat deviant from the dominant value systems of society. For some years prior to their rule the Communists labored to decrease the distance between their subculture and the dominant strain of Czechoslovak politics. By 1946 they had made remarkable headway in narrowing that gap, but once in power as the delegated bearers of a revolution whose form was to be determined by outsiders, the Communists fell under the decisive influence of those outsiders and, in effect, surrendered their country's sovereignty. When the reality of this imperial relationship was tested by an independent-minded Communist ruling group in 1968–69, brought into power by something akin to a revolt within the ranks of the party, the relationship ultimately proved incapable of redefinition. The attempt on the part of the reformers to rule their country according to independently conceived policies led to new realities derived in striking measure from the traditionally dominant political culture — a political culture incompatible with the imperial objectives of the Soviet Union.

Put another way, the leadership of the Prague Spring sought to reclaim Czechoslovakia's sovereignty and to find new methods of rule that would reflect the realities of their own society rather than the model prescribed by the Soviets. In so doing, the Czechs and Slovaks unleashed social forces that had been repressed since 1948 and thereby produced a situation of freedom and pluralism intolerable to their hard-line allies and imperial authorities. To the latter, the only recourse was to reimpose the imperial relationship and bring about the replacement of the unacceptable reform leaders with men who would not challenge the imperial orthodoxy.

* PART TWO *

- ENDURING PATTERNS IN THE POLITICAL CULTURE -

Czechs and Slovaks experienced major political transformations in 1918, 1938–39, and 1945–48. The reform rule of 1968–69 represented an attempt to introduce yet another major transformation, and the efforts of the post-reform leaders to counteract the effects of the Prague Spring have had their own disturbing effects on the course of political development. With so much fluctuation in the political system, it is hard to imagine that any permanent patterns could have taken root.

Nevertheless, there are some continuities that can be traced throughout the modern history of Czechoslovakia. Despite the cataclysmic changes in the political superstructure, devastating purges during the Second World War and the Stalin years, a secularizing and class-leveling social transformation, and a period of totalitarian rule that lasted well beyond the Stalinist era in other socialist countries, the Party has encountered persisting popular attitudes that reflect longer-running social patterns. Today's worker is not the socialist "new man"; instead, he is still in part a product of the prerevolutionary past, his beliefs and actions influenced not only by the Party's attempt to guide them but by deeper cultural forces as well. The four chapters in this section explore some of these longstanding cultural patterns.

It was the Prague Spring that brought these historical patterns into their most recent focus. The importance of the self-reflection that took place during the brief reform period was monumental. For years Czechs and Slovaks had been denied the possibility of national intro-spection, as their leaders not only separated themselves from the national traditions but spurned the whole notion of nationalism as a bourgeois distraction. In contrast, the leaders of the Prague Spring openly appealed to the best in the national traditions and encouraged citizens to support them in drawing out a new design for the future.

In the course of the reformers' search for new political forms, two old features of the political culture were uncovered: the deeply-rooted pluralism of society and the profound national distinctiveness of Czech and Slovak cultures. In chapter five we examine the first of these, tracing the development of pluralism through several phases. It is argued that the recurrence of pluralistic patterns reflects an underlying, society-wide proclivity to view politics quite naturally as an arena of diverging opinions and contested interests. Thus, even when the political rulers have not tolerated the institutionalization of pluralistic politics, there remains a cognitive aspect of pluralism in the orientations of the citizens. Czechs and Slovaks seem to share a feeling that everyone has his own opinion and should be afforded the means of expressing it. When given the chance to do so, they have rather consistently sought to organize their politics so as to reflect a diversity of viewpoints. The emergence of pluralistic tendencies in 1968 exemplified this and renewed a long, if broken, tradition.

Chapter six looks at the problem of national identity. Czechs and Slovaks emerge as two quite separate nations with their own specific cultures and traditions. Despite the intense efforts of intellectuals and political leaders to integrate the two peoples into a unified "Czechoslovak" identity during the first half of this century, the differences remained. Nationalism proved to be a very sensitive issue, particularly among Slovaks, and the long conflict over the identity of the Slovaks spawned a major political subculture of Slovak nationalists. Out of this subculture arose important political forces on the right (1900–45) and left (1924 to present); these are discussed in chapter seven.

Chapter eight looks at the tradition of political nonviolence among both Czechs and Slovaks, discussing several variants and also some contrary patterns. Within this context, a serious discussion of the peculiar subcultural phenomenon sometimes called "Švejkism" leads to the proposition that many members of Czech society find it most congenial to cope with political oppression by conforming and adopting a lighthearted attitude toward their own misfortunes. The fact remains, nonetheless, that the political history of Czechoslovakia is filled with tragedy. From among the many personal stories that have been involved in this tragic history, those of Edvard Beneš and Alexander Dubček are singled out as representative.

All of these historical patterns run counter to Communist norms in one respect or another. They reflect cultural traits that are apparently difficult to root out, and one must therefore surmise that they are in some way transmitted from one generation to the next through the informal processes of political socialization.

V

The Impulse to Pluralism*

The norms of the elite subculture, described in chapter three, conflict most acutely with the recurrent tendency to political pluralism in the broader body politic. At times manifested very overtly and at other times suppressed beneath a glaze of imposed mass conformity, pluralism in Czechoslovakia has been quashed by the most repressive governments, only to emerge again in another form before being suppressed once more. If the current regime will not tolerate the open expression of ideas contrary to its own, that does not diminish the underlying diversity of political outlooks among the citizenry. Patterns of social differentiation naturally give rise to diverging political orientations irrespective of the monolithic official value system. In the interest of survival, mass behavior is compliant and opposition movements exceptional. This has not been brought about by the acceptance and internalization of the regime's norms, but rather by the stifling of political alternatives and the imposition of ideological orthodoxy.

Recurrent tendencies toward pluralism highlight the Communists' failure to create a society of socialist men and women as conventionally defined. According to the official theory, pluralism is impossible in a socialist order. Objective class interests tend to unite the proletariat into an ideologically solidary whole. There may arise differences of opinion about specific tactical points, but if the practice of democratic centralism is followed, tactical differences will be resolved within the framework of Party discussions. Disagreements of a more longstanding nature are symptomatic of bourgeois democracies whose political systems are fundamentally incapable of resolving contradictions because of the unresolved class conflict within capitalist society. Because class conflicts by definition no longer exist in socialist society, there is no objective cause of ideological differentiation, nor of significant conflicts of interest among individuals or social groups. Pluralism, therefore, can arise only as a result of deviance from the fundamental solidarity of proletarian class interests.

Political pluralism can be defined in two ways, both of them useful

---

* *Note.* — Some of the material contained in this chapter appeared in my article, "The Repluralization of Czechoslovak Politics in the 1960s," *Slavic Review,* vol. 33 no. 4 (December 1974), pp. 721–40.

to our discussion in the following pages. In the first sense, pluralism has to do with the community's patterns of political behavior. A pluralistic society is one composed of identifiable, differentiated social groups that give rise to corresponding differentiations in the political behavior of citizens. Pluralism is not identical with social differentiation, but rather it includes such differentiation as a precondition to a diversity of political behavior patterns.

In the second sense, pluralism concerns the distribution of political power. A pluralistic society thus defined is one in which there are actively competing forces in the political system — parties or other organized groups capable of sharing in, or challenging, the established power structure. The multi-party democracies of continental Europe are the clearest examples, but they by no means represent the only type of system encompassed by this definition. The American two-party system is another example; the two major parties nearly monopolize electoral politics on the federal level, but they are sometimes challenged on state and local levels by so-called "third" parties or by independent candidates. Moreover, the major American parties themselves are umbrella structures composed of multifarious interests, competing within the parties' own organizations and responsive to pressure groups from the larger society. Still another type of pluralistic system consists of a single major party dominating electoral politics but subject to the influence of strong pressure groups competing for the attention of governmental leaders; the latter, in turn, achieve and maintain their power positions by balancing off the interests of the outside groups. India until recently offered an example of this type of pluralism.

Generally speaking, the pattern of multiparty political development tends to take place in the following way: Changes in the economic organization of society disturb the previous pattern of social grouping, thereby breaking down the substructure upon which the traditional political order is based. New groupings arise, based on the clustering of individuals into classes, strata, or other functional divisions in the society. Earlier divisions such as religion or ethnicity may persist, either causing a degree of fragmentation within the functionally organized groups or cutting across those new divisions — or both. Thus the new groupings may be based on functional orderings only (for example the Czechoslovak Small Traders' party), on functional categories subdivided by religious and/or ethnic groupings (the various national branches of the Austro-Hungarian Social Democratic party), or on nonfunctional bases entirely (European Christian Democratic parties). This is, however, getting ahead of the story.

As the society develops, the groups take on characteristics objectively different from each other, according to their place in the social order. They begin to develop specific group interests — industrial laborers become interested in working conditions, industrialists in securing a constant and minimally costly supply of workers and capital, small traders in the protection of their businesses against the competition of large-scale enterprises, religious groups in the preservation of holy days, ethnic groups in the protection of their languages and customs. Because of these objectively divergent interests, the groups are naturally set off from each other and begin to perceive themselves as interest groups. They then orient themselves to social and, ultimately, political reality in terms of their group self-perceptions. At this point the effect of political stimuli upon the members of a specific group will be to call forth a behavioral response conditioned by the perceived interests of self and group. In other words — to return to the paradigm of social action outlined in chapter one — group consciousness plays an important *mediatory* role, predisposing group members to perceive political events in terms of their self-interests and conditioning them to respond in terms of those self-interests. Because there are by this time a plurality of groups, the pattern will be one of diversity.

This is the nature of pluralism in the first sense mentioned above: differentiated social groupings give rise to corresponding differentiations in political behavior. In order for the development of pluralism in the second sense — pluralism in the distribution of political power — a further step must be taken. It is here that the salience of the political culture becomes obvious.

The social groupings and their individual members will inevitably be influenced by the society-wide system of values. That is, groups will tend to pursue their own specific interests which may or may not coincide with those of other groups, but when confronting choices of possible action they will also draw upon their past experiences as interpreted through the apperception process. As I have argued in the introductory chapter, one's culture will define the lessons learned from experience and thereby condition present and future responses to situations judged to be comparable. Interest-group action takes place within the overarching cultural context and cannot escape the influence of the latter. Thus the next step in the role of the interest groups will depend on members' (and especially leaders') evaluations of what is proper and feasible — proper in terms of the relevant value system, feasible in terms of the existing political conditions.

Pluralism in the distribution of political power, therefore, is a higher stage of political pluralism than the first-stage pluralism of group interests and behavior patterns. For interest groups to move from the lower to the higher stage, the political culture must be supportive of pluralistic action. Group constituencies must understand their role in politics as an active one and translate their activity into institutional forms.[1] Thus, organizations must be developed for the furtherance of group interests — parties, pressure groups, or other such organizations. For this to happen, citizens must believe it is their right to pursue their interests, hence the necessity of a supportive political value system. For them to be successful in organizing and aggregating, and for the resulting organizations to pursue their constituencies' interests in a realistic and meaningful way, the political conditions of the society must permit such activity. That is to say, the existing political regime must permit a modicum of freedom so that organization for the pursuit of political interests can take place.

During the last four decades of the nineteenth century, the growth of an increasingly modern, industrialized order in the Czech lands created new patterns of social differentiation according to occupational function. The new divisions combined with previous patterns based on nationality and (to a limited extent) religion. The resulting solidification of group interests gave rise to a multi-party political system of the continental European type. This was facilitated by the general trend toward democracy within the Austrian provinces, culminating in the franchise reforms of the 1890s and, finally, universal male suffrage by 1906. Among the Czechs, the trend toward democracy was particularly strong owing to the humanistic and egalitarian values of the national heritage; these were stressed by the leaders of the cultural revival in the nineteenth century and accepted by the majority of national politicians in the latter decades of Austrian rule. When, upon independence, Slovakia and Subcarpathian Ruthenia were added to the historic Bohemian Crownlands to create the Republic of Czechoslovakia, the tendency to pluralization was intensified with the addition of Slovak, Magyar, and Ruthene groups to those of the Czechs and Germans. The party system of the First Republic was thus an outgrowth of the social and political development in the Czech lands for half a century prior to independence.

During the time of the First Republic, the citizens of Czechoslovakia participated in a political system that encouraged the aggregation and articulation of the most diverse political views. In addition, a large number of clubs and special interest organizations existed, many of them serving as vehicles of political pressure or quasi-political activity. Anyone interested in politics could easily find a party or some other organization to speak for his needs — or if not, he could start his own. (A popular joke dating from the First Republic has it that whenever two Czechs get together they immediately form three political parties.)

The political system of the First Republic was shattered by the European conflagration of the thirties and forties, and the postwar revolution completed the destruction of the social order that had consistently developed between 1860 and 1938.[2] After 1945, new patterns of differentiation began to take shape in the society.[3] These developed because of the nature of postindustrial society in its specific Czechoslovak, socialist context — but they formed *in spite of* the nature of the political regime. The Communist leaders overlooked and underestimated the forces producing patterns of social differentiation, all the while energetically suppressing the outward manifestations of the latter. Because political authority was ubiquitous and Communist leaders extremely jealous of their power monopoly, the incipient social groups remained disaggregate and even inchoate during the fifties. They became clear only during the years immediately leading up to the Prague Spring. By 1967 it was evident that Czechoslovak society was in fact highly differentiated, and social groups conscious of their own specific identities were emerging under the surface of an outwardly homogenous sociopolitical order. In 1968 a reform-minded set of leaders took over the reins of power from within the Communist party. One of their reforms was, in effect, the abnegation of direct political coercion throughout the society. Immediately, the previously repressed social forces were released. Encouraged by numerous intellectuals who had already noticed the potential for social pluralization, groups now surfaced and began to organize as political actors, still rather disaggregate but tantalized by the possibility of influencing the decision-makers on all levels of government and party.

The Prague Spring was a transitional step in a movement toward a new socialist pluralism. The movement was unique in Communist-ruled countries. 1968 was only an early stage in this course of development, but it was of great importance, for it involved an attempt on the part of masses and leaders at identifying the nature of the political dynamic. The movement toward a pluralistic order was genuinely revolutionary in its implications, for although it was only beginning, it bespoke a potential threat to the very foundations of the established order. Yet in another sense it was nothing new, for the pluralization of the 1960s replicated in many respects a pattern well known in Czechoslovakia's earlier history.

Capitalism and Pluralism, 1860–1938

In the 1925 elections to the Federal Assembly, twenty-nine political parties were listed on the ballot.[4] This was the record for the First Republic, but that improbable number of parties serves to illustrate the extent to which pluralism in Czechoslovakia was manifested in an outward, and directly political, form. No fewer than twenty-three parties gained parliamentary representation at one time or another between 1918 and 1938, and there were in addition a number of smaller splinter parties, mostly of an ephemeral nature. Among the major *Staatsvolk* themselves, as many as twenty-one Czech, Slovak, and Czechoslovak parties appeared at least once. No party at any time controlled a majority in the National Assembly, and the closest any ever came to this was in 1920, when the Social Democrats (not yet divided into Communist and SD parties) captured 74 of the 300 seats.[5]

It was not only party politics that reflected Czechoslovak pluralism. For half a century Czech society had developed a strong tradition of interest- and pressure-group politics. During the late Habsburg period, voluntary organizations formed ostensibly for cultural, economic, and athletic purposes frequently took on political tones, engendering in their members a sense of national patriotism and political awareness. From the Sokol gymnastic clubs to the trade unions, and from choral societies to rural cooperatives, Czech society was characterized by a multiplicity of voluntary organizations. After 1918, the pattern caught on among Slovaks as well, although not to such a great extent.[6]

All in all, the system ensured an effective means of aggregating political interests. Of course, it had its problems. Governmental coalitions were formed of insecure, temporary alliances, and policy compromises were difficult to reach within these coalitions. The individual voter often came to feel removed from the decision-making process by the politics of the extraconstitutional *pětka*. Frequently the party and the policies for which a person voted would become lost in the governing process, for even if one's party "won" — that is, secured a role in the government coalition — the party's programs might have to be seriously compromised in the game of coalitionary politics.[7]

It is not my purpose to pass judgment on the First Republic, but rather to explain how it came to be what it was. For all its strengths and weaknesses, the First Republic was a highly pluralistic society. To understand the bases of that pluralism it is necessary to look back at the social transformation of the Bohemian Crownlands during the second half of the nineteenth century.

Admittedly, to look at the evolution of Czech society is to focus on only one of several strains leading into the development of the First Republic. To get a total picture, one would also need to trace the evolution of the Slovak, German, Magyar, Ruthene, and other ethnic communities. My concern, however, is with the political culture of Czechs and Slovaks. Because the pluralization of their society and politics began with the Czechs and, in many of its features, was carried over into Slovak society following independence, it is most revealing to examine the origins of pluralism in Bohemia and Moravia. We should keep in mind, however, that Slovakia developed quite differently prior to 1918 and that the later course of Slovak politics never led to the complete transfer of Czech patterns onto Slovak soil.[8]

The origins of Czech politics between 1860 and 1900 represented nothing unique in the European experience. Similar social conditions elsewhere grew out of the burgeoning industrial order, producing functional groupings with specific interests, and eventually political parties.[9] In the Bohemian Crownlands the situation was rendered particularly complex by the fact of Austrian rule over a numerically dominant Czech community. This community coexisted with a German community that was less populous, but economically and politically more powerful than the Czechs; the Germans were the favored nationality in the Crownlands, dependably *kaisertreu* and protective of the established order. Czechs were not strongly alienated from the Austrian political system, however. Among the politically conscious Czechs there was a feeling of ambivalence. The Austrian system set some limits to the Czechs' freedom of action, but within these limits there was the opportunity for social mobility, a gradually broadening electoral franchise, increasing degrees of self-government on the local level, and a growth in the number of Czechs entering the Austrian civil service. Most (if not all) of the major Czech politicians during this time favored not independence from Austria but autonomy within the Empire, on a model similar to that of Hungary.[10]

Czech society in the last half-century of Austrian rule was characterized by all the features of a modernizing capitalist order. Industry was building up steadily, and the basic industrial sector was marked by a consistent trend toward the concentration of capital. The Czech population was increasing rapidly, and there was a gradual but measurable migration from the villages to the industrial centers. There were particularly noticeable movements of population within the same district, increasing the size of the one already large city (Prague) and making major urban centers of a few previously smaller cities, such as Brno and Ostrava. In the countryside, the rising population rate —

produced by advances in medical technology and the simultaneous decline of the death rate and increase in the birthrate — led to problems of overpopulation. This contributed to the rural-urban immigration pattern and also produced a high rate of emigration, particularly to America. The pattern of economic development was very uneven, both as between different districts and regions of the Empire and within individual districts as well. For the people caught up in this swirl of economic and social change, there was a widespread feeling of confusion and insecurity, that all was provisional and nothing permanent.[11]

In most respects, the pattern of economic and social development in Czechoslovakia after 1918 proceeded further along these same general lines.[12] Slovakia was now brought into the stream of social progress, thus experiencing at least some of the spillover effects of Czech industrialization — although economic development there lagged considerably behind that in Bohemia and Moravia. Despite the general continuity, however, there were some changes in the social structure following independence. These resulted from the conscious social policies of the new government in the first few years immediately after the adoption of the 1920 constitution. The latter gave all citizens an equal vote and outlined an elaborate formula for the proportional representation of political parties in parliament. Together with other class-leveling legislation, such as the abolition of rank privileges for royalty and nobility and the extremely consequential land reform in the countryside, these measures had an immediate impact upon authority relations throughout the republic. In addition to the land reform, a series of further socio-economic laws were passed, establishing the eight-hour workday, providing for renters' protection, and instituting programs of social insurance.[13] All of these measures effectively democratized society, shifting the locus of power and influence away from the wealthy and formerly privileged toward the middle and working classes. The result was to the immediate advantage of the socialist and agrarian parties.

The First Republic was a modern state based on a society with a built-in dichotomy, primarily regional and national. On the one hand, interwar Czechoslovakia occupied seventh place in the world in the percentage of its population engaged in industrial production. In 1930, industrially employed persons accounted for 34.4 percent of the Republic's population. In this respect Czechoslovakia was more highly industrialized than France, Italy, or republican Austria. The proportion of the population employed in all of what we might call the

"modern" sectors — industry, trades, commerce, banking, and transportation — totaled 47.4 percent compared to 34.6 percent in agriculture, fishing and forestry. If we exclude the remote region of Subcarpathian Ruthenia from these figures, we find that for the same year
(1930) these percentages were 49.3 percent in the modern sectors and
33.0 percent in the rural.[14]

On the other hand, there was a great disparity between the
Bohemian Crownlands and the other regions. In Bohemia, for example, 56.9 percent were employed in the modern sectors and only 24.1
percent in the rural sectors; these statistics were almost the direct
reverse in Slovakia — 29.2 percent in the modern sectors, 56.8 percent
in the rural. In Ruthenia these proportions were even more starkly
drawn: 20.8 percent and 66.3 percent, respectively.[15] Taken separately,
Bohemia would have been the third most industrialized country in the
world, surpassing all continental states including Germany and Belgium; Ruthenia, on the other hand, represented one of the most
backward regions in all of Europe, and Slovakia was not very far
ahead.[16]

That these facts reflected a long, consistent trend can be readily seen
in the following statistics showing the evolution of occupational
groupings. (See Table 5.1 and Figure 5.1.)

It is interesting that, although Slovakia and Ruthenia did indeed lag
behind the other regions, they too experienced the trend toward
greater industrialization between 1900 and 1930.

At a closer glance, the division of society into industrial and
industry-related occupational groupings ("modern" sectors) and the
traditional rural groupings is misleading. It oversimplifies a rather

Table 5.1

Percentage of Working Population Employed in
(M) Modern and (R) Rural Sectors[17]

	1869		1900		1930	
Czechoslovakia	n.a.		M=40.51	R=45.97	M=47.40	R=34.64
Bohemia	M=33.97	R=50.73	M=48.59	R=35.68	M=56.87	R=24.06
Moravia	M=28.05	R=57.14	M=42.38	R=43.76	M=52.95	R=28.56
Silesia	M=33.41	R=51.80				
Slovakia	n.a.		M=22.64	R=66.27	M=29.24	R=56.82
Ruthenia	n.a.		M=15.12	R=75.06	M=20.85	R=66.29

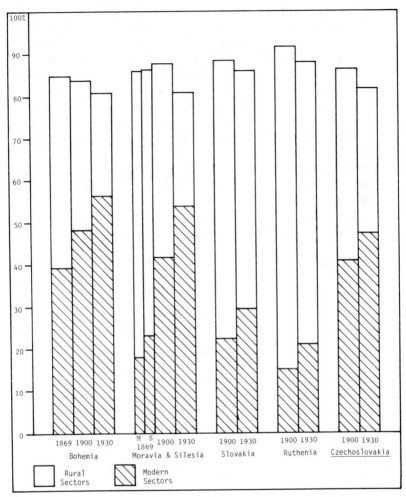

Figure 5.1

Percentage of Working Population Employed in Modern and Rural Sectors

more complicated social structure, given the fact that there were wide variations in the experiences of people working in different industrial situations. Between 1860 and 1940, large numbers of Czech and Slovak industrial workers were employed in small- and middle-scale enterprises. Thus, although the proportion of Bohemia's employed citizens engaged in industrial occupations in 1930 was 42 percent, only

approximately 25 percent were actually employed in large-scale factories characteristic of Western, assembly-line industry. If middle-
scale industrial enterprises are added to this tally, still only 34.2 percent
of the population worked in what would be familiar to the Westerner
as factories.[18] Fully 19 percent of Bohemia's gainfully employed
population were engaged in small-scale enterprises (*Kleingewerbe*),
either as artisans, proprietors, or their hirelings. Moreover, industrial
enterprises could be further broken down in terms of those engaged in
the production of "industrial" goods, strictly speaking, and those
connected with the agricultural sector (such as sugar refineries,
breweries and distilleries). In this latter breakdown we find that more
than 25 percent of Bohemia's population were associated with the
secondary production of agricultural products.[19]

The following table gives a breakdown of Bohemia's occupational
groupings in 1930, based on categories somewhat more enlightening
than the "modern-rural" dichotomy — but not including the category
of industries concerned with the production of agriculturally-related
products:

Table 5.2

Bohemia, 1930: Percentages of Population Engaged in
Occupations, by Categories[20]

Rural occupations, excluding handicrafts[a]		27.2
(including handicrafts)	(34.2)	
Industrially employed[b]		34.2
Small enterprises, including rural handicrafts		19.0
(excluding handicrafts)	(12.6)	
State and civil service		11.4
Clergymen and religious orders		.2
Independent professions		6.2
Other		1.8
		100.0

[a] farming, fishing, forestry
[b] large- and middle-scale industry

Breaking down the industrially-employed category further, we find the
following statistics:

Table 5.3

Bohemia, 1930: Percentages of Population Engaged in
Various Categories of Industry[21]

Large-scale industrial concerns	22.9
Large-scale trade, finance, and transportation[a]	2.2
Middle-scale industrial concerns[b]	7.3
Middle-scale trade, finance, and transportation	1.8
	34.2

[a] i.e., private transportation
[b] i.e., those employing more than approximately ten persons but not predominantly mechanized in character

The more detailed breakdown of occupational groupings given immediately above becomes very important in relation to perceived group interests and, ultimately, politics. This should be readily apparent upon further reflection. The large furniture manufacturer, as a social type, has nothing in common with the small, independent cabinetmaker. The former is the head of a large work force and concerns himself with detailed problems of wages, capital investment, gross market trends, the demands of organized labor, efficiencies on a mass scale, transport, and so on. The independent cabinetmaker, with perhaps one or two helpers, builds his own products himself, one at a time; like the big entrepreneur, he must be concerned with efficiency, the market, and perhaps wages, but all these considerations are an entirely different thing, much closer to home and less subject to conditions beyond the immediate control of the cabinetmaker. Likewise, the employees of the two enterprises differ significantly in the nature of their work. The worker in a large factory, for whom many of the characteristics described by Marx exist as realities — alienation from one's labor-product, atomized disciplined, isolation from one's colleagues, and so forth — has nothing in common with the worker in a small family shop, who is likely to work together with his peers and his boss in producing whole products with which they can identify and in which they take personal pride.[22]

As Marx pointed out, one's role in the productive process to a large extent determines one's role in society. The conditions in one's work-place influence one's life outside the workplace. The quality and tone of working conditions, then, ramify into people's outlooks, lifestyles, and perceptions of self-interest. The connection with political life is thus obvious: one's orientation to the political process will be crucially conditioned by the attitudes and perceptions of self- and group interest originating in the workplace.[23]

Marx did not account for the possibility that the productive process in the modern era can give rise to a rather complicated pattern of social differentiation with concomitantly complex ramifications upon politi-cal orientations. To Marx the dynamic of the modern era was the ever-increasing concentration of capital, and the ever-sharpening concen-tration of social forces into two contradictory groups, labor and capital. Marx assumed that these two polar forces would eventually subsume all politically relevant actors within the society, drawing them into one or the other hostile group according to their ownership or nonownership of the means of production.[24] The evidence for the Czech Crownlands between 1860 and 1940, as well as for Slovakia during the latter part of the same period, contradicts this. The pattern of social differentiation described above ramified directly into political life, producing an intricate but logical system of pluralistic politics centering around clearly discernible interest groups. The configuration of these groups was rendered all the more intricate by ethnic and religious factors representing additional determinants of political orientation. To understand this more fully it is necessary once again to backtrack chronologically and trace the development of political parties in Bohemia, Moravia, and Slovakia.

The first Czech political parties were formed in the 1860s, but they in fact had their backgrounds earlier in the progress of the national renascence. The cultural nationalism of the first half of the nineteenth century spawned a few small underground groups. These surfaced for the first time in the revolt of 1848, the Slavic Congress, and the Czech delegation to the abortive Kremsier (Kroměříž) Assembly of 1848–49.[25] Prior to that time, neither the circumstances of social develop-ment nor the relatively firm control exercised by the Vienna monarchy was conducive to the formation of a viable national political move-ment among the Czechs. Following the monarchy's recovery from the 1848 revolts — more serious in Hungary and Italy than in Bohemia — a decade of neo-absolutism under the government of Alexander Bach suppressed the movements of 1848, but the new constitutional system of 1861 induced anew the formation of national political groupings.

These now focused their efforts toward parliamentary politics and incremental gains in national and regional status within the Empire, foreswearing the ill-fated revolutionary impulses of the earlier generation.[26]

Modern Czech politics really began with the formation of the National party and the National liberal party following the adoption of the 1861 constitution. These parties later came to be known as the Old Czechs and the Young Czechs, respectively. Organizationally, they were unified until 1874, when they formally divided. The battle lines had been drawn a decade sooner, however, over the symbolic issue of support for the Polish uprising of 1863. (The Young Czechs were sympathetic, the Old Czechs were not.)[27] On all other issues the two parties occupied positions that scarcely diverged in any fundamental way. On the only major question of the period from 1861 until the 1880s — scope and nature of national rights within the Empire — the two groups had no important differences. Their basic stance was a version of the idea first elaborated by the historian František Palacký: Austria should be a federative state in which all the Danube nations would be equal and, to one degree or another, autonomous. The major difference between the Old Czechs and the Young Czechs grew not around their stands on the salient political issue of the day, but rather around the social groups that came to form the respective parties' constituencies. Simply put, the Old Czechs represented the very wealthiest strata of the Czech nation, namely the commercial and industrial bourgeoisie in the cities and the large landholders of the countryside. The main support for the Young Czechs, in contrast, came from the petit-bourgeoisie of the towns and the middle farmers in the villages; in addition, they gained some favor among the as yet unfranchised, but increasingly mobilized, workers of the industrial centers.[28]

This first political division, then, came on the basis of inchoate social interest groupings which expressed themselves in terms more of attitudinal differences than objectively definable issue orientations. The Old Czechs stood for the traditional privileged groups, in many respects including non-Czechs as well as Czechs — the rural lords and the industrial interests allied with them (the milling entrepreneurs, sugar refiners, brewers, and distillers) — plus their new allies at the very top stratum of the bourgeoisie (capitalists and financiers, especially those connected with the machine and energy industries). The New Czechs, on the other hand, gathered around themselves the rising social forces of the Bohemian Crownlands, primarily the urban and rural petit-bourgeois interests. These were attracted by the liberal and, in some cases, radical philosophical orientations of the Young Czechs, even though these orientations were expressed only in the latter's rhetoric.[29]

These two parties were thus formed at the very beginning of the monumental social revolution born of late-nineteenth-century industrialization. They formed without any distinct relationship to specific class interests, although the seeds of a class conflict were evident in the parties' differing constituencies. No such conflict ensued, however. The Old Czechs suffered a decline following the defeat of the Hohenwart Program, with which they had become identified and in which they had invested their political reputation. Their alliance with the nobility became a handicap in the increasingly more polarized nationality relations of the 1880s and 1890s, and their social support gradually drifted into the camp of the Young Czechs. In turn, the ongoing changes within Czech society coupled with the gradual liberalization of franchise laws to encourage the rise of organized interest groups, drawing some of the Young Czechs' own previous support base — particularly industrial workers and farmers, but eventually much of the petit-bourgeoisie as well — away from them and into new groupings more specifically representative of their own increasingly self-evident interests. By the mid-1890s the Young Czechs, curiously enough, were the most conservative party in the newly burgeoning political spectrum, representing Czech commercial, industrial, and financial interests centering around the great *Živnostenská banka* (Bank of Commerce) in Prague.[31]

Meanwhile, political parties were forming out of other social interest groupings. Primary among these were the Social Democrats and the Agrarians. The former had emerged from a democratic movement among workers identifiable as early as 1871, but the establishment of the SDP (as a branch of the Austrian SDP) did not occur formally until 1878. The Social Democrats' constituency was almost entirely based on the working class, particularly those who came to be organized in the powerful trade unions. Needless to say, the effective power of the SDP in parliamentary politics was greatly limited prior to the adoption of universal and equal male suffrage. After 1906, however, the SD's became a major political force. In the 1907 elections they drew a plurality of the vote among the Czechs, and in the First Republic the SDP was the largest party until its split in 1921, the second-largest during the 1930s. Even after the formation of the Communist party (KSČ), the Social Democrats remained the favorite party of trade-union leaders.[32]

The Agrarian party, too, was hampered by the electoral laws before 1906. Nonetheless it arose in the 1890s under the leadership of large landholders who were uneasy about the increasing dominance of financial interests within the Young Czech party. After 1906 the Agrarians, officially known as the Republican party of Farmers and Peasants, grew into a widely based party of small, middle, and great farmers. The party's outstanding leader Antonín Švehla cultivated this seemingly precarious alliance, and he built the Agrarians into the strongest and most consistent single political force in the First Republic. After his death the alliance weakened considerably, but the party nevertheless continued to occupy powerful positions in the government, including the prime ministry.[33]

Thus it is evident that social class in its simplest sense did not explain the configuration of political interests as perceived by the members of Czech society. The example of the Agrarian party illustrates the possibility of a political alliance cutting across rural class distinctions. That the alliance began to deteriorate during the 1930s was the result of three coincidental factors — the Depression, relatively weak leaders, and the seductive attraction on the part of the party's right wing to the idea of an alliance with the *Sudetendeutschpartei*.[34] For nearly three decades the Agrarian party had functioned as a non-class, or supra-class, rural political organization — and a very successful one at that.

The complex social basis of the party system was further illustrated by the emergence of still more groups. The socialist movement splintered into two, and later three, separate parties. The first to compete with the Social Democrats was the Czech Socialist party, founded in 1897 and renamed the National Socialist party in 1926. This party proclaimed the goals of the working class, the national traditions of humanism, and the kinship of Czech culture with the spirit of the Western Enlightenment. Some industrial workers identified with the National Socialists, but the party in fact, like the Agrarian party, extended across stratificational lines. The bulk of its constituency was drawn from the ranks of white-collar workers, civil servants, and the intelligentsia; most of its support among laborers came from skilled workers in small and middle-sized enterprises. This was the party of non-Marxist socialism, and as such it attracted many intellectual democrats; its founder was Václav Klofáč, a newspaper editor, and its most prominent member was the second president of the Republic, Edvard Beneš.[35]

The third socialist party to emerge was the Communist party, born of a split in the SDP in 1921. The Communists drew considerable support from industrial labor, although they were not as strong among the trade unions as were the Social Democrats. The Communists, moreover, attracted many supporters for reasons other than class affiliation. An "internationalist" party, the KSČ spoke for minority rights and thereby made inroads into the disgruntled ranks of the Magyar and Ruthene minorities, as well as among Jews. In addition, many radical Slovaks joined or voted for the KSČ; it is interesting that the Communists attracted most of the former Social Democrats and their supporters in Slovakia after 1921.[36] Thus the Communist party, the most outspokenly class-oriented of all the parties, was by no means the unchallenged representative of the proletariat, nor was it even based solely on working-class support.

Still another special-interest party was the Small Traders' party, representing independent retailers and craftsmen. Usually allied informally with the Agrarians, the Small Traders were the most important of the numerous minor parties. They experienced a significant growth between 1920 and 1938, reflecting the rise in numbers and political importance of their constituency. In the 1935 elections the Small Traders' party captured enough popular votes to put seventeen of its candidates into the National Assembly — as many seats as were captured by the National Democrats, the heirs to the Young Czech tradition.[37] Small businessmen had apparently become a political force as serious as the large corporate interests, at least in their ability to elect members of parliament.

One additional Czech party needs to be mentioned here. The People's party was a Catholic party, and as such it drew Catholic votes from various social strata. Prior to independence, its leaders had developed a reputation for being Habsburg loyalists. After 1918, therefore, the Czech populists had to overcome an image of toryism, in addition to another characteristic that was in public disfavor in the first years of the Republic: clericalism. The latter characteristic was never discarded by the populists, but they quickly overcame the handicap of the former by pledging themselves to the Republic. The party became a major force in First Republican politics thereafter, under the careful middle-of-the-road leadership of Msgr. Jan Šrámek.[38] The party was loosely allied with the Slovak populists until 1922 — hence its official name, the *Czechoslovak* People's party, which it retained even after the split with the Slovaks.

Needless to say, the preceding analysis has disregarded the history of German parties within the Crownlands. These are not properly the subject of my inquiry, and I hope therefore that it will suffice to acknowledge the existence of numerous German parties that arose from similar circumstances in the nineteenth century and continued to function as representatives of their national socioeconomic constituencies in interwar Czechoslovakia.[39]

More important to the subject at hand is the matter of Slovak political movements. The lively political life of the Bohemian Crownlands prior to independence carried over into Slovakia after 1918. This is not to deny the existence of Slovak political movements in the earlier period; however, before 1918 there were in Slovakia, as one observer has put it, "no political parties in the modern sense. . . ."[40] There were at least three separate movements by 1914 — the People's party, the National party, and a Slovak branch of the Social Democratic party — but none of them had achieved any consistent electoral success because of the restrictive political processes in Hungary.[41] Two of the three movements showed tendencies of class orientations; the Social Democrats appealed to the small stratum of industrial workers, and the People's party appealed (through its predominantly clericalist leadership) to peasants. The National party was made up of rather diverse strains with no cohesive characteristics other than nationalism.[42] These movements grew out of several waves of political thought among Slovaks around the turn of the century but failed to coalesce into consistently effective organizations by the time of the First World War.

Still, the early political movements are evidence that Slovaks, like Czechs, were beginning to see politics according to perceptions that might vary with the social circumstances and personal self-interest of the individual.[43] During the war, the movements fell upon hard times as Hungarian rule became particularly oppressive. When political forces regrouped in 1918 to join the Czechs in a proclamation of Czecho-Slovak unity and independence, the National party became the focus of Slovak activities. The leaders of this group — all men of the Hlasist, Czechoslovak persuasion — dominated the Slovak Club in the provisional National Assembly. At first this situation was moderately satisfactory, but soon divisions within the ranks led to the establishment (or, in some cases, reestablishment) of separate parties. The Slovak Populist party was reconstituted in December 1918 under the leadership of Father Andrej Hlinka, and within the next six months two more parties were formed, both branches of the socialist parties then existing in Czechoslovakia (SD's and Socialists).[44] The National party was then reorganized under the name Slovak National Republican Peasants' party (*Slovenská národná republikánska strana roľnícka*). This party joined the Czech party of the same name to form an Agrarian union that lasted throughout the First Republic.[45]

Slovak politics became pluralized to a degree that belied the relatively backward nature of Slovak society. As in the Czech lands, the patterns of political orientations were shown in the elections. The populists consistently attracted the most votes, but their total never approached a majority of the popular tally in Slovakia. Some distance behind the populists came the Agrarians, followed by the Communists, Social Democrats, and National Socialists in that order of popularity. Again as in the Czech lands, minor parties made a sporadic showing; at least two of these, the (Protestant) National party of Martin Rázus and the Juriga Catholic party, were specific to Slovakia. The specifically Slovak parties were based on a unique kind of appeal, that is, on their strident nationalism and the charismatic qualities of their leaders. The other parties, however, drew their support from the same social groupings associated with their Czech counterparts. Thus they reinforced the overall socio-political structure of the Republic.[46]

On the whole, politics in the First Republic was diversified and fraught with conflicts of interest, but yet it cannot be accurately characterized as riven by irreconcilable class conflicts. There was indeed a strong tendency toward identification with one's own particular social stratum, but this did not translate into the language of the class struggle.[47] The growing industrial proletariat of Slovakia was to some degree an exception to this generalization, as the strength of the Communist party there might indicate.[48] In general, however, the most bitter conflicts of the interwar period were not of a class, but rather of a national, nature: Slovaks against Czechs, Czechs against Germans, Magyars against Czechs and Slovaks. To the extent that there was a serious fissiparousness in the political system, it was due primarily to nationality problems.

The complicated division of society into specific subclass groupings served to dissipate the class tensions of each stratum, while at the same time preventing the strata from coalescing into forces that might have been capable of sparking a revolution or counterrevolution. The fact that much of the republic's industry was organized on a small scale and located in small towns minimized the working class's tendency to radicalism; the large numbers of workers who voted for the moderate socialist parties bore witness to this. Moreover, as we have seen, the bourgeoisie was by no means a unified social interest group. The disunity of proletarian and bourgeois forces thus kept them from polarizing ideologically against each other, and the additional force of the agrarian, Catholic, and nationality groups served further to disperse the locus of political conflict. The fact that many of the parties had overlapping social constituencies made for moderate fluctuations in their popularity from one election to the next and probably facilitated the formation of coalitions.[49] With the exception of the Communists and the extremist nationality groups, therefore, politics settled into the relatively nonconflictual mold of shifting coalitions, the various parties jockeying for position in a context of stable constituencies and gently fluctuating parliamentary representations.[50]

The democratic and nonrevolutionary tendencies in Czechoslovak politics can be attributed in part to the nature of political leadership between 1861 and 1938. The absence of an ascriptive elite caused the Czechs to turn elsewhere for leadership during their long cultural revival. As a national intelligentsia developed, this group became the source of leadership for the political task after 1861. The intelligentsia became an elite by virtue of their achieved status — a surrogate nobility admired and respected by the masses, who looked to their more learned brothers for guidance. The native intelligentsia were very close to the people; they were themselves of humble origins, and it was much more natural for the Czechs to identify with them than with the agents of traditional authority in Austria — nobility, clergy, and military elite — for the latter were, of course, alien. An unusual proportion of Czech political leaders between 1861 and 1938 were drawn from the intelligentsia, including Palacký, Rieger, Kramář, Masaryk, Beneš, and Klofáč.

The intelligentsia shared many basic ideals and values, but they diverged from each other in their political views. Most of them were either Protestants or religious skeptics who found in the humanistic national tradition a compatible outline of their own philosophical beliefs. Their veneration of the national traditions extended beyond the philosophical aspect; they were proud of their language, literature, history, folk songs and customs. They believed, moreover, in the worth of the little person — malý člověk — who for two centuries had been the only bearer of the national culture; the intelligentsia had grown up as little persons, and they maintained their faith in the creativity and moral righteousness of their countrymen. Once educated, they returned to their people, bringing to them the fruits of the educational process. They founded schools, theaters, newspapers, publishing houses, musical organizations, artistic, scientific, and professional associations, all of them created and nurtured and developed independently by the Czech nation, both before and after independence.

Because all of this was accomplished by the little person, and furthermore because for two centuries previously the little person had been
kept down by the traditional authorities, many Czechs developed a
strong tendency toward antiauthoritarianism.[51]

Lacking a vested interest in the old order of the pre-independence
period, Czech leaders developed their own ideas about how society
should be run. Some of them, like Kramář, believed that the fate of the
nation lay in the growth of a strong, capitalistic economy; others, such
as Klofáč and the prominent Social Democratic leader Dr. Soukup,
favored a socialistic system. At the moment of independence, some
wanted a constitutional monarchy, whereas most preferred a republic.
Among the socialists, some considered violent revolution a necessary
prerequisite to the establishment of a just order, but others believed in
the path of reformism. On many other specific policy issues the
nation's leaders formed diverging views. The differentiated social
structure of the Crownlands, of course, contributed to the diversification of political thinking while at the same time providing the social
bases for political movements receptive to the various ideas.

This is not the proper place to discuss the parallel developments in
Slovak political leadership; that will be taken up in the following
chapter. It is important to note here that Slovak political patterns
diverged from Czech, owing to the very different socio-political
realities coloring the two nations' history between 1867 and 1918.
Those Slovak intellectuals who fit the pattern of the Czechs as members of a surrogate elite were by and large not representative of the
Slovak masses. Nevertheless, it is true that several important Slovak
political leaders in the First Republic — including Milan Štefánik,
Vavro Šrobár, and Milan Hodža — arose as intellectuals much in the
same fashion as their Czech counterparts.

The pattern of political pluralism in Czechoslovakia's capitalist era,
then, is clear. Politics was based on a complex configuration of social
interest groupings arising from the development of a modern industrial society. The new social bases of political differentiation combined
with the traditional ethnic and religious patterns, resulting in an
intricate system of party politics. The diverging interests within society
found articulate spokesmen in the national intelligentsia, who led the
causes of the various groups and became the politicians of the First
Republic.[52]

Political pluralism was supported by an institutional structure that
encouraged group formation. Just as importantly, pluralism was supported by a value system that celebrated diversity of opinion and

rational discussion of political alternatives.[53] The result was the steady growth of a pluralistic political culture and the formation of a general Czech and Slovak consensus (though not without exceptions) about the nature of politics as an arena of competition among social interest groups. Thus from the reality of pluralist politics, the citizen could hardly escape being drawn into the frame of mind that accepted and indeed applauded the phenomenon.

The turbulent events of 1938–48 interrupted the course of social development, and the conscious reshaping of politics undertaken by the Communists changed society greatly. However, a thin thread continued to connect the social structure of the Communist era with the earlier political culture, and when socialist society developed its own structure of interest groups, a society that had long been accustomed to pluralistic politics began to evolve a new form of political pluralism.

Socialism and Social Structure

The unlimited pluralism of the capitalist era ended in Czechoslovakia in 1938. The Munich Agreement marked not just a temporary loss of sovereignty but the literal end of democracy in its capitalist form. The loss of the Sudetenland destroyed Czechoslovakia's economic independence. The so-called Second Republic was immediately converted to a German dependency as Czechoslovakia's other neighbors, Poland and Hungary, annexed Těšín and southern Slovakia.[54] Truncated, demoralized, and under a weakened leadership,[55] the state now came under attack by the Slovak separatists. The latter seized their opportunity and seceded from Czechoslovakia in March of 1939; two days later President Hácha acceded to new demands by Hitler that his country become a German protectorate, and German troops occupied Bohemia and Moravia. As the subsequent situation developed, politics became equivalent to violent social control, and opposition became resistance.[56]

The events of 1938–45 changed political attitudes significantly. In the first few months after Munich many Czechs beat their breasts and pondered whether their nation was worthy of independence. The Nazi occupation was even worse, an experience that divided both Czech and Slovak nations against themselves, leaving scars of bitterness and revanchism.

During the war many Czechs and Slovaks saw fit to rethink their political situation. The exiled leaders were determined to avoid the most egregious mistakes of the First Republic if and when they returned to power. They decided to eliminate the most obvious threat to stable rule, the troublesome minorities. In order to eradicate what they perceived as a second destabilizing condition — the fragmented multi-party system — they agreed to set up a national front, based on a genuine coalition of interest around a left-reformist program. This meant, in the first place, the nominal elimination of opposition parties as all political forces were joined together in support of a common purpose. In the second place, the strategy necessitated a reduced number of political parties and the exclusion of the political right. (Excluding the right also served the purpose of settling a score with those who had collaborated with the Nazis.) The parties that emerged after the war were the Communists, Social Democrats, National Socialists, Czech People's and a new Slovak group called the Democratic party.[57] All these policies were agreed upon in newly-liberated Košice shortly before the war's end and put into practice after liberation. The Košice Program, as it came to be known, in many respects fitted the stridently nationalistic and radical spirit of the times, when most Czechs and Slovaks sought an escape from the immediate past and the establishment of a new order that would be superior to the old.

The Third Republic (1945–48) was by no means the free and unfettered system that had developed before 1938, but it was still relatively pluralistic. The elaborate means of interest aggregation embodied in First-Republican party politics was lacking after 1945, but there was a modified multi-party system that allowed the voters an electoral choice. The political right was not directly represented in the Czech lands, but conservative voters had the alternative of voting for the centrist People's party. In Slovakia the attempt to eliminate the right did not succeed, as populist forces regrouped around the Democratic party. Thus a rather wide spectrum of political preferences could be accommodated within the new party system. Moreover, despite the steady infiltration of social organizations by the Communists, there still were many that could serve to channel one's political inclinations into activity.[59]

The system introduced by the Communists after the 1948 coup has been described in great detail by many previous scholars, and there is no need to do so here. It must be said, however, that that system was monolithic, that it was based on a one-party monopoly of political power and expression, and that this monolith was supported by an elaborate police network whose efficiency was surpassed only by its brutality.[60] Two minor political parties, the Socialist party and the People's party, continued to function in the Czech lands, but their enrollments were forcibly limited and their independence removed by the revamped National Front. The Social Democrats were simply absorbed by the Communist party following the coup. Thus party politics, even in its limited National-Front form, was brought to an end. In the process of imposing the new, alien system upon the Czech and Slovak public, the Communists beat down every overt manifestation of pluralism, leading one articulate Czech intellectual to liken the 1948–55 period to times of war.[61]

Institutions, modes of political action, and public behavior were transformed by Communist rule, but the new rulers were less successful in changing the underlying values and orientations of the masses, nor were they able to prevent the regrouping of society into socially differentiated strata. The events of the 1960s were to illustrate the gradual reemergence of some traditional patterns, but for more than a decade the Stalinist system continued to sustain itself.

The sixties were a momentous decade, but on the surface there was little change prior to the Prague Spring. The institutional structure of state and party remained basically as it had been in the fifties, and there were relatively few changes in the top leadership. Antonín Novotný, president and party chief, resisted pressures for economic and social reforms, and although reforms had been in the planning since 1956 (and especially 1962), little progress was made.[62] Nor did the party relinquish its monopoly over legitimate political activities. Censorship of the media continued, although there was a tendency to increasing laxness particularly regarding the publications of the self-censoring Writers' Union prior to autumn of 1967. Citizens were vaguely aware of these relaxation trends, but they still felt largely alienated from the system. The system seemed at all times to resist penetration from the outside, that is, the public.[63]

The system, an alien order immovable and yet self-maintaining, was superimposed upon a society which it did not fit. Just why it did not fit was not immediately clear. One might have expected some incongruity, given the democratic and pluralistic backgrounds of the republic, but it was only a handful of sociologists and political thinkers who had come to discern the true nature of the problem. For the public, the forces brewing under the surface were ascertained only upon the release of the political constraints on mass behavior. This occurred in 1968, when the social forces that had been repressed for twenty years came rushing to the fore.[64]

Various reformist tendencies had developed in the Communist party early in the decade, some of them reaching back into the late fifties.[65]

By 1967 the Novotný leadership found itself confronted by several incipient factions that suddenly emerged as competition within the party. These were unorganized and in some instances inchoate, but they were nonetheless in evidence by the middle of the year. There was a group that we might call a liberal-technocratic interest, consisting of economists, scientists, and others favoring greater investment in technology and more attention to market considerations in economic planning, including such personalities as Ota Šik, Evžen Löbl, and Radovan Richta. Another group clustering around issues of cultural freedom included the majority of writers and artists, concerned with the further relaxation of social and cultural constraints. Moreover, stirrings of disgruntlement among Slovaks were now being voiced in high places — by Dubček, for example. In addition, there were numerous prominent party members who fit into no identifiable groups but made known their dissent. These included Zdeněk Mlynář, legal scholar Michal Lakatoš, and some scattered leftwing Marxists with strong anti-bureaucratic and even anti-authoritarian sympathies. Novotný and his associates managed to hold power, maneuvering among these splintered but increasingly restive forces, until the end of 1967. At that time an *ad hoc* coalition formed at the top level of the party hierarchy and toppled the old regime, electing a new leadership and creating the momentum that led to the Prague Spring.

The course of governmental politics in 1968 showed considerable disunity about the methods of what was now called the "democratization" (*demokratisace*) of Czechoslovak society. The party came to share power with other institutions such as the National Assembly, the cabinet, and the trade unions. Because censorship had been largely abandoned, the political momentum inevitably spread to the masses. There the new atmosphere created by the party leaders met a society prepared for a renewal of political pluralism.[66] The party and government attempted to remain in the forefront of the reform movement, but events went beyond their capacity to control them.

Ivan Sviták has said that the spontaneous activities in the spring and summer of 1968 represented "several democratization movements . . . other than the one that operated under the leadership of the Communist party." These reflected a spectrum of ideological groupings "ranging from Maoists to veterans of the Czechoslovak Legion who had fought the Russians during World War I."[67] These are obviously extreme examples describing very minor groups, but Sviták's point is that many political orientations appeared in the moods of the public. It seemed that everybody became politicized. Soon spontaneous organizations cropped up to accommodate groupings clustered around mutual interests; some of these were old institutions that had long been moribund, while others were entirely new. Some were spur-of-the-moment organizations that dissipated almost as quickly as they had formed, while others attracted large followings and began gradually to take on definable structures. And everywhere public discussion of political issues took place — in the pubs, on the streets, in living rooms, on the trams, over the telephone, in the newspapers, and at the meetings of such groups as KAN.[68] By the middle of the summer, the possibility of a genuine multi-party system had become a matter of serious public discussion. The leadership continued to resist pressures in this direction, but it is doubtful that they could have resisted indefinitely without resorting to coercion, a most disagreeable prospect that ultimately became a reality at the hands of the August invaders.

Communications media, the intellectuals, and the youth played critical roles in the mass movement. The media were a catalyst of public activism, transmitting news of the government's deliberations and encouraging the masses to become involved. Reporters opened some sensitive topics that had been festering for a long time. Almost nothing was beyond the bounds of their inquiry — the political trials of the fifties, the mysterious death of Jan Masaryk in 1948, contemporary foreign policy, and candid interviews with public officials were all a part of the citizens' everyday reading and listening. Foreign journalists, astounded by the new atmosphere, declared that Czechoslovakia had the "freest press in the world," uncensored by the state and unbeholden to commercial sponsors.[69]

Intellectuals had figured prominently in the reform movement since as early as 1956, when the Second Congress of the Czechoslovak Writers' Union opened the door to a literary revival.[70] A number of discredited "bourgeois" writers, including Čapek and Kafka, were rehabilitated, and an increased variety of Western books were now translated and made available. Socialist realism virtually died, and writers began to experiment cautiously with new styles.[71] By 1967, the writers had made great strides and captured the attention of the wide public, who now enthusiastically read and celebrated the ever more exciting works of gifted literati such as Škvorecký, Kundera, Mňačko, Havel, Klíma, Vaculík, Liehm, Mucha, and Goldstücker.[72] Parallel developments in the cinematic arts made of Czechoslovakia an international wonder, as one after another film produced at Barrandov Studios won major awards. Back home, one spoke of the "Czechoslovak miracle" in filmmaking; the list of talented directors and script-writers who emerged in the sixties is long indeed — Forman, Menzel, Jasný, Němec, Passer, Chytilová, Škvorecký, Brynych, Kadár, Klos, Krumbachová, Schorm, and many others.[73]

In 1967 a revolt broke out within the Writers' Union, as the Union's Fourth Congress became the setting in which several prominent writers challenged the policies of the incumbent regime, openly calling for radical changes.[74] The regime struck back, suspending some of the outspoken writers from the party and placing the Writers' Union, along with its publications, under direct governmental supervision. This action effectively deprived the Union of its previous autonomy.[75] The regime's victory turned out to be only temporary, for the dissident intellectuals found support among the would-be party reformers. Ironically, Novotný's move against the writers in September 1967 backfired by giving these reformist forces a new issue to use against him.

Other intellectuals had been opening new doors, too. Philosophers and theorists such as Kosík, Sviták, Tondl, and Cvekl probed into the question of human existence in socialist society, often finding in their student audiences an enthusiastic reception. Historians began a reexamination of the past, striving to overcome the distortions of the fifties.[76]

Many of these intellectuals jumped to the forefront of the social movements in 1968. There were some who demurred, welcoming the chance to do their own work without interference from the politicians, but many others were drawn into political activism. They diverged somewhat from each other in their specific ideas, but all worked to promote the cause of intellectual freedom and to bring themselves together with the mass public in a common purpose.

Many university students joined the intellectuals in this purpose. Although apolitical attitudes had characterized the larger part of the student population during the earlier sixties, some had become politicized following the Strahov Hostel incident in the fall of 1967.[77] In 1968 larger numbers of students became politically active, many of them joining the mass movements that were springing up around the country. Some formed their own organizations as the old youth union, the ČSM, splintered into a dozen or so more specialized clubs. Later on, following the invasion, a prominent youth-movement leader was to make the curious dialectical argument that the pluralization of the youth movement actually served to unify it, for the "new political reality of socialist Czechoslovakia" demanded a plurality of young

people's organizations to answer the diverse needs of their generation.[78]

Adult organizations, too, were revitalized. The structure of the
central trade union (*Revoluční odborové hnutí*, or ROH) was
loosened, and many new personalities — some of them noncommunists — moved into positions of leadership. Old professional associations such as the lawyers' union, medical society, architects' union, and
others functioned once again. Unique new organizations arose, such as
KAN and Club 231, the latter an association of former political
prisoners convicted during the fifties under the notorious Law Number 231 (the so-called Law for the Defense of the Republic).[79] In short,
voluntary organizations sprang up everywhere. These were not yet
effective vehicles of political aggregation, but they were nonetheless
incipient political groups, binding their members together because of
mutual interests arising from their various positions in society.

To fully understand the pluralization of mass politics in 1968 it is
necessary to examine the structure of society that gave rise to these
groupings once the political constraints were removed. It is to the
subject of that social structure that we now turn once again.

The economic and social revolution following the Second World
War produced a superficial homogenization of Czech and Slovak
society. In economic terms society was leveled by the policies of the
postwar governments, especially the nationalization of industry, land
reform and collectivization, and a series of draconian monetary and
price reforms that wiped out personal savings and discriminated
savagely against the middle and upper strata. These trends were begun
by the National Front government and intensified after the 1948 coup.
In contrast to the Stalinist revolution in the USSR during the thirties,
where one of the costs of rapid industrialization was a partial reversal
of the previous decade's trend toward socio-economic leveling,
Czechoslovakia's Stalinist revolution continued the pattern toward
greater equalization. Wages and salaries became significantly less
differentiated, social security and public health insurance were made
universal, educational opportunities were expanded for many who
previously had little or no access to them, and the gap between the
economies of Slovkia and the Czech lands narrowed somewhat.[80]

Income distribution, then, is relatively egalitarian. This is not to say
that income distribution is perfectly equal, nor that there are no great
disparities. There are serious disparities between the sexes, and pen-
sioners' incomes tend to be very low. The average working woman's
income is only 66 percent that of the average working man, and the

average pensioner lives on the edge of subsistence.[81] In 1965 the lowest decile of wage-earning population earned only 2.9 percent of the total national income, while the highest decile earned 20.2 percent. These statistics, however, compare favorably with similar figures for Czechoslovakia in 1946 (1.7 percent and 26.2 percent, respectively), and dramatically so in comparison with analogous figures for recent years in France (0.5 percent and 36.8 percent) as well as West Germany (2.1 percent and 41.4 percent).[82]

Table 5.4

Percent of Total National Income

	ČSSR, 1966	Hungary 1962	Poland, 1965	Yugoslavia, 1964
Highest 1/5 of wage earners	30.5%	34.9%	35.6%	36.7%
Second 1/5	22.7	23.6	23.1	22.3
Third 1/5	19.3	18.1	18.0	17.7
Fourth 1/5	15.6	14.2	14.1	13.7
Lowest 1/5	11.9	9.2	9.2	9.6

Income disparities are not unique to Czechoslovakia. They are common throughout Eastern Europe. In overall terms, Czechoslovakia appears rather more egalitarian than her socialist neighbors. The above table, comparing three other industrialized socialist countries, shows this. (Note that the statistics have been adjusted to include only the most productive members of society — wage-earners exclusive of agricultural fieldworkers.)[83]

Despite the consistent tendency toward greater equalization of incomes, socialist Czechoslovakia is a stratified society, as a team of Czech and Slovak sociologists asserted in the sixties. Pavel Machonin and a collective under his leadership explored Czechoslovak society in depth and emerged with some exciting discoveries.[84] The previously existing class structure had indeed been eliminated by the postwar revolution. The removal of distinctions among proletariat, bourgeoisie, and peasantry meant at the same time the elimination of the class basis of pre-1938 pluralism. Moreover, the policies of the state after 1948 had nullified the churches' social importance, thereby secularizing politics and removing the religious basis of political dif-

ferentiation. Although temporarily quieted, national differences between Czech and Slovak remained, but the expulsion of the Germans
and the repression of the Magyars did away with the minority problem. Notwithstanding all these radical changes removing many of the
old divisions, Czechoslovak society once again developed a discernible
pattern of social differentiation, both horizontally and vertically.

Horizontally, social groupings emerged around a pattern of differentiation based on occupational and other spectra deriving from the
sophisticated socialist division of labor and its impact on personal
lifestyles. Differentiation in this horizontal sense thus revolves around
such factors as type and complexity of work performed, style of life
and leisure, geographic locale, ethnic identity, biological considerations (sex, age) and level of spiritual life.[85] It is clear that these factors
are quite different from those that characterized stratification in the
presocialist era, for under socialism the class distinctions between
capitalist and laborer, between industrialist and small merchant,
between assembly line worker and shop attendant, no longer exist.[86]
All gainfully employed citizens have become proletarian, nearly all
work either for the state or for the collective, and relatively few small-
scale enterprises of any sort remain in the wake of nationalization and
consolidation. Still there are factors differentiating groups within this
proletarian society. The Machonin team recognized these factors as
important determinants of the individual's sense of identity and
hypothesized, further, that the evolving social groups had objectively
different self-interests.[87]

Lest this sound rather un-Marxian, the sociologists were careful to
consult with some of the more important theorists of the sixties,
notably Jiří Cvekl. Cvekl explained that the new pattern of social
differentiation characterized socialism in its second, "post-niveliza-
tion" stage.[88] During the first stage, the broad aim of the socio-
economic revolution was leveling, or nivelization, in every sector. At
the same time that incomes and standards of living were being
equalized, there occurred a general leveling of talents and abilities
among individuals due to the lack of incentive for developing these
attributes and the tendency to associate *all* inequalities with the
capitalist past. As society moved into the second phase, this changed.
Once the revolutionary momentum was firmly established, individual
differences in talent and ability, skill and training, needs and interests
reemerged as socially positive forces. Cvekl explained that this does
not signal a return to capitalism or a weakening of the revolution, but
rather a return to "those general sociological precepts that are charac-

teristic of every civilized society." Thus the nivelization of society in the first phase was temporary, a step necessary for the eradication of the former privileged classes. Society could not continue in its nivelized stage, however, for the demands of continued economic and techno-logical progress necessitated a recognition of diverse talents.[89]

The organization of society in this second stage of socialism is there-fore based on the utilization of individual talents in their most produc-tive capacities. This in turn means that people with similar talents and abilities will tend to cluster together in one way or another; they will have gone through similar educational experiences, may have devel-oped similar leisure-time interests (reading as opposed to loitering in pubs), and may tend to live in similar neighborhoods. When other social factors are taken into consideration, these functional similarities among individuals will tend to distinguish them socially from others not sharing the same characteristics, giving rise to social groups (*společenské skupiny*) that are definable by all these features.[90] How-ever, no normative standards as yet describe this differentiation pattern; rather, the groups are merely defined by their objective characteristics. This, then, is the nature of horizontal differentiation, specifically defined by Machonin thus:

> By horizontal differentiation we understand a distinction of such specific concrete activities (functions), and of various groups . . . that are not mutually commensurate. [Such a distinction] excludes com-parison in terms of higher or lower values of certain levels of inequality.[91]

It is in Machonin's concept of *vertical* differentiation that we find the relevance of social stratification. Machonin has defined vertical differentiation — also called "social stratification," as he points out — as "the division of specific activities (functions), as well as various groups, insofar as they are mutually commensurate, that makes pos-sible a comparison in terms of higher or lower values and includes within it connotations of inequality."[92] In some respects the vertical pattern corresponds to the horizontal pattern, although the two are not totally commensurate. The critical factors producing vertical dif-ferentiation — the so-called status-forming variables — are com-plexity of work, lifestyle (especially as related to consumption and leisure-time activities), education and training, income and material standard of living, and participation in management (power).[93] Al-though the aforementioned are the most important determinants of one's status, Machonin adds that other factors will tend to condition or reinforce the effect of the status-forming variables. Age, for example, often conditions one's ability to perform certain occupational tasks — skilled labor is sometimes difficult for the elderly, power not easily attainable by the young — and therefore affect one's status ranking. Ethnicity often reflects a condition of one's cultural development; Machonin found that Czechs are more prone to the higher status groupings than are Slovaks. And regionalism will also have an impact; industrialized areas, and cities in particular, will offer greater opportunities for complicated jobs and a higher level of cultural life.[94]

Czechoslovak society, according to Machonin, is unquestionably a stratified society, and the massive 1969 volume is devoted to offering an empirical proof of the fact.[95] Social groups definable by objective characteristics were also definable in terms of the prestige they were accorded within the society.[96] That such distinct status rankings did exist in socialist society by no means discouraged the researchers; in fact they included social stratification as one of several defining characteristics of modern socialist societies.[97] Like their counterparts in other East European academies, the Czechs and Slovaks assumed that stratification was a temporary phenomenon destined to disappear as society progressed to the communist stage.[98] But for the time being, it is a fact of life and as such deserves scientific attention.

Interestingly, the sociologists relied to a heavy extent on Western modes of analysis in determining the configuration of vertical differentiation. Jaroslav Kapr, for example, used an index modeled after that of the American National Opinion Research Center to show the status ranking of occupational categories as seen by his respondents. In this ranking, Kapr found that the five most prestigious occupations were 1) minister (in the government), 2) director of industrial enterprise, 3) doctor of specialized medicine, 4) professor of higher education, and 5) president of a Regional National Committee (*Krajský národní výbor*). Ironically for a working-class society, the five occupations judged lowest in prestige all entailed menial labor; at the bottom of the scale was parking lot attendant, preceded (in ascending order) by unskilled laborer, tollgate attendant, member of a fieldwork team on a collective farm, and postal clerk.[99]

Machonin found a high incidence of correlation among three of the status-forming variables: complexity of work performed, lifestyle, and education. Taken together, these variables formed what he called a "cluster" of factors that tended, more than any other variable or variables, to determine social status.[100] Somewhat surprisingly, he found that income differentiation was the most independent variable, correlating the least to the others; some high-income persons were found to have low socio-cultural indices, and *vice versa*. This was illustrated, for example, by coal miners and hospital nurses. The former tended to earn very high incomes despite low levels of education, whereas the latter earned relatively low incomes despite their specialized training.[101] No single variable was found to be a dominant determinant of social prestige, not even that of political office.[102] Rather, no fewer than three correlating variables were considered necessary to identify a stratification dominant.[103]

Based on a correlation analysis of the variable clusters, Machonin and his colleagues produced a model of vertical differentiation that consisted of four clearly definable social strata and three inconsistent categories. They then ranked the four strata in descending order, from stratum "A" (highest on the cumulative scale) through "D" (lowest), noting the rough proportion of the population belonging in each, thus:

Stratum A (2.9–4.7 percent): persons with a high level of education (secondary and university) whose work is diverse and complicated, and who spend their leisure time in a highly cultured way. Members of this stratum play generally greater roles in management and tend to earn higher than average incomes.

Stratum B (7.1–12.9 percent): persons with secondary education whose work is mostly nonmanual and relatively complicated, but rather routine and repetitive; lifestyles reflect above-average cultural tastes. These persons participate in management to some degree and tend to earn slightly above-average incomes.

Stratum C (16–23.4 percent): persons with elementary education who perform mostly manual labor requiring apprenticeship or specialized training; lifestyles are average in quality. Participation in management is low, and incomes average.

Stratum D (20.6–28.4 percent): persons who do the simplest manual work and, in many cases, have not completed elementary school. Cultural level tends to be low, as does average income. No participation in management.

The inconsistent categories found by the researchers reflected groupings of people whose status-forming variables deviated in one or another way from the clustered patterns of the four major strata. Group I (5–8.9 percent) had low levels of education and lifestyles, did simple work and had practically no management responsibilities, but earned relatively high incomes. Group II (4.5–9.3 percent) were specialized or skilled laborers with generally low incomes. Group III (2.5–4.6 percent) had relatively low levels of education augmented by apprenticeship experience, little or no management responsibilities, above-average (and sometimes quite high) incomes, and a high cultural lifestyle. It is apparent that Group I is similar to Stratum D, but with a deviation in income patterns; Group II is like Stratum C but with a (lower) income deviation, and Group III is comparable also to Stratum C but with both an income deviation (higher) and a higher level of cultural lifestyle.[104]

Time and again Machonin and his colleagues remind us that the social patterns they have described are decidedly *noncapitalist.* There are no relics of private ownership and no vestigial class privileges associated with the former order.[105] Nor did the researchers uncover any hard evidence that a bureaucratic "new class" had formed; the bureaucracy was admittedly large, but it did not appear to be a separate stratum.[106] Social differentiation in Czechoslovakia was found to be subtle and gradual, and stratification "somewhat smaller" than in capitalist societies.[107] Nonetheless, it clearly existed.

What about the political implications of all this? Does a modern socialist society of this type give rise to pluralistic political interests and the development of politically competitive groups? The Machonin team approached these questions but stopped short of answering them. Lubomír Brokl, for example, offered a lengthy theoretical discussion of the role of politics *vis à vis* the social structure, including a discussion of the dichotomy between elites and masses. He even referred to the Communist party and how it functions in the system, but he stayed mostly in the realm of the abstract.[108] In Machonin's summary, moreover, the author noted a "sharp" differentiation in political affairs, but he explained that this could be only partly identified in the research, because the "power elite" (*sic*) did not represent a significant part of the data sample.[109] Machonin's explanation for this was that he and his colleagues were not centrally concerned with politics. He argued that "political-organizational stratification" is an autonomous vertical pattern, representing a paradigm that is actually and analytically separate from the "socio-cultural" schema that served as the focus of the 1969 volume.[110] Notwithstanding his apologia, one senses that the real reason the research team did not deal with the question is that it *could* not; the empirical research was carried out in 1967, when the power elite was still closed and jealous of its privacy. Presumably, the team must have been considering further studies in 1968 which would have led them into the political question directly, for in the completed volume there are occasional oblique references to the interconnection between socio-cultural and political-organizational stratification.[111]

Thus it was perhaps not so much the researchers' empirical fastidiousness, as it was the inaccessibility of data, that prevented their examination of the political aspect.

Socialist Pluralism

Political power in Communist Czechoslovakia is an exclusive province of the ruling elite. With respect to power, society is sharply divided into two main components according to access to, and share in, political authority. Regardless of one's occupation, level of education, income, or overall status ranking in the socio-cultural sense, an individual who is not a member of the political elite is distinctly apart from one who is, because the former has no influence whatsoever on the political decision-making process.[112] In pre-1968 (as in post-1968) Czechoslovakia we find a clear and omnipresent barrier dividing those who have power, actually and potentially, from those who do not. This barrier also divides the *many* from the *few*. The *many* are those outside the ranks of the elite — powerless, incapable of affecting the political system, relatively equal among themselves but relatively impoverished in comparison with those on the other side of the barrier. The *few* are the power elite: party leaders, bureaucrats, high-level military officers, trade union officials, police, economic planners, and managers. The elites live in their own world, removed from the masses, almost totally out of touch with them except to the extent that they can enforce demands upon them — and this usually through a chain of subordinates. (In some cases, even this kind of contact between the elites and the masses weakened during the gradual breakdown of the system in the sixties. Directives would sometimes get lost on the way down the governmental transmission belt, or they might be ignored here and there, or confused with apparently countermanding directives from competing agencies. The latter was a particularly common occurrence.)

As Machonin hinted, the political organization had been divorced from society's other patterns of differentiation. The most frustrating aspect of the political system, from the average citizen's point of view, was the almost total lack of communication upward through the ranks of the state bureaucracy, itself functioning as an effective filter through which any presumptuous demands from below could not pass to the top. The starkness of differentiation between rulers and ruled tended to outweigh the subtler patterns of socio-cultural differentiation, both horizontal and vertical. The connection between political and socio-cultural differentiation now becomes clear with the rise of social groups, for the latter — as Cvekl argued — inevitably come to have perceived, identifiable, stratum-specific interests.[113] However, the rigid bifurcation of society into elite and mass assured the supremacy of political over social considerations, and therefore the groupings that developed within mass society were unable to aggregate their specific interests and translate them into demands upon the state for policy outputs.

As mentioned earlier, one of the effects of the socio-economic revolution was to make nearly all individuals employees, directly or indirectly, of the state. When the state in such circumstances is characterized by a monopolistic rule, downward-flowing administrative command networks, and a hierarchical managerial elite, the ultimate effect is the re-creation of a class society. In Czechoslovakia, as in all totally nationalized and collectivized East European countries, proletarian mass society came to be exploited, in a very real way, by the party and managerial elites. Postwar Czechoslovakia became a class society in which a relatively small power elite assumed dominant control over a much larger mass. Thus, crudely put, the political stratification of socialist Czechoslovakia approximates the "new class" formulation of such Marxist critics as Djilas, Kuroń, and Modzelewski. That the "new class" in Czechoslovakia was not clearly recognizable in the research into socio-cultural stratification does not lessen the impact of its existence in the political structure of society.[114]

In short, the picture which emerges is that of a neo-class structure complete with superordinate exploiters jealous of their power and infected with a class-consciousness of their own, and a great mass of subordinate "exploitees" who have little or no chance of influencing the power structure or ever penetrating the inscrutable stratum of the privileged few.

The fact that mass society became restratified under socialism — and under the conditions of the bifurcated power structure, as well — intensified the potential for political conflict, because the central government could not satisfy the multiple interests of the various social groups without the benefit of open channels of communication. The more perceptive members of the non-elite strata became frustrated with their own political impotence, while the few leaders who did recognize the problem were too weak to effect any fundamental change in the political superstructure. It is true that the economic reforms before 1968 had a decentralizing impact on economic decision-making, but this in fact served to perpetuate, and even intensify, the vertical cleavage in society. A few more people entered the elite ranks as plant managers and technocrats, but the division between those who had influence and those who had none persisted.

Directives continued to flow downward through the media of the mass organizations, with no corresponding transmission of influence upward. The press was not yet in a position to speak for the incipient interest groups, save for the increasingly defiant and sometimes beleaguered organs of the Writers' Union.[115] Nor could the Communist party, riven with internal differences though it was, become an effective force for aggregating the interests of the various social groupings, for the party leaders continued to guard their power monopoly closely, and the predominant forces managed to keep their opponents isolated from each other. This situation, as we have already seen, lasted until late 1967.

In the meantime, a number of people independently of the Machonin collective had begun to probe into the matter of the political system and its relationship to social differentiation. Zdeněk Mlynář, a legal theorist and high-ranking party member who headed an Academy team to study possible modes of political reform, recognized the outlines of the problem and suggested a solution. Mlynář's concern with this subject had been evident ever since the publication of his important book, *State and Man* (*Stát a člověk*), in 1964. Mlynář attacked the problem from the angle of a Marxist scholar whose task was to clarify the rights and obligations of the individual in socialist society, as distinct from those of the state.[116] By 1966 Mlynář had hit upon the notion of interest groups, recognizing the objective differentiation within society and believing that the resulting groups had specialized interests which needed to be aggregated. He therefore proposed the establishment of regular, institutionalized channels for the functioning of interest groups, arguing that mass organizations should not be used only as transmission belts for directives sent downward: "The action must be reciprocal; there must be a flow of influence *from the people generally to the state (and to the party).*"[117]

Mlynář's argument was contained in an article discussing the problems involved in implementing economic reforms. This was a matter of great concern for many of the members of the elite during the sixties, for, as Radovan Richta argued, the perpetuation of obsolete authority relations and the constraints imposed on scientific inquiry had retarded Czechoslovakia's economic progress and relegated the country to a second- or third-rate industrial status. Richta's team of academicians had unearthed startling data demonstrating that the gap between the socialist and capitalist economies of the industrialized world was widening rather than diminishing.[118] This was in contradiction of the regime's self-conscious pronouncements that Czechoslovakia stood "at the threshold of the scientific-technological revolution." However, as Machonin put it, this was wishful thinking; Czechoslovakia stood "*before* the threshold . . . , and rather at a distance, moreover." Czechoslovakia, Machonin said, could no longer be considered a part of the "industrially mature" part of the world, and for reasons "known to all of us."[119] To Mlynář's way of thinking, economic reform was indissolubly linked to authority patterns, and once the question of authority patterns arose, the subject of interest groups came up as well.

Michal Lakatoš, a Slovak-born scholar of jurisprudence, agreed with Mlynář and took the argument one step further. In a series of articles written in a surprisingly radical tone, he advocated the formation of autonomous organizations whose sole function would be the aggregation and articulation of group interests. These must be *new* organizations, because most of those already in existence did not (and could not) serve this purpose.

Lakatoš rejected both the "new class" theory and the official "theory of conflictlessness" (*bezkonfliktnost*); he said that the latter errs by overestimating the commonality of interests within society, the former by exaggerating the intensity of conflict between groups. In a series of articles appearing in 1965–66, Lakatoš developed his own theory that the driving force of progress within society is the confrontation of divergent interests. Socialist ownership of the means of production had not brought about the end of divisions within society. On the contrary, it had created divisions anew among individuals and interest groups (*zaujmové skupiny*). Differences of interest and the potential for conflict, he argued, are natural in human relations: "Even a socialist society must consistently resolve its divisions by methods adequate to their character if a conflictual situation is to be avoided."[120] But because there were no available vehicles for the aggregation of interests, the individual at present is a "political unit isolated from his interest group." The only way to reconcile this problem of the atomized individual is to put him in direct touch with the proper institution and to allow that institution to function as a direct agent of its constituents' true interests, an organized go-between to link mass society with the party and state.[121]

Lakatoš suggested that interest groups could be formed along any of several possible lines, each including within it the possibility of subgroups: by relation to means of production (for example, groups for workers in a state sector, for collective-farm workers, for artisans, and so forth); according to the division of labor (industrial workers, farmers, physical versus mental work); according to ethnic identity, territorial interests, or male-female distinctions.[122] Finally, he argued that the new institutions must be subject to truly free elections lest they merely revert to the unrepresentative character of the mass organizations already proven to have failed.[123]

Lakatoš warned that if nothing were done, the worst features of the political system would be perpetuated. Specifically, his proposal to institutionalize interest groups was aimed at eliminating the "manipulation" that he saw in society. This manipulation, he said, can and does lead to the alienation (*odcudzenie*) of "a significant part of society." Lakatoš left no doubt as to the existence of widespread alienation in Czechoslovakia as he quoted the following powerful lines from a piece by J. Pražáková in a contemporary issue of the Slovak periodical *Literárne noviny:*

> ". . . it seems to me that something big, unseen, watches over me, a little person. . . . It is infallible, omnipresent. . . . It follows us at every step. In the streetcar, in the train, in the laundry, in the national committees, in the flat. And with the accuracy of a machine it detects our transgression, and all our obligations. If some calamity occurs, if it rains, again if it does not rain, during sickness, during vacation — nothing stops it. There is in it something great, inhuman, unnatural. Perhaps a modern-day titan, a hundred times bigger than the apple trees in the garden, devoid of human form, without a great, shining eye? A giant that does not defend me but lurks and follows me and demands that I fulfill my obligations — but has no obligations toward me? A giant that is blind and deaf to my appeals and my wishes? But there are no giants; this was made clear to me when I was little.
> Yet even so, I fear the giant. . . ."[124]

Frustration, alienation, even fear characterized the contemporary system. Perhaps the symptoms were of something more serious than just the atomization of individuals, but then again, perhaps they were not. Perhaps the solution to the problem was indeed in the creation of competent organizations that could advance the interests of their constituents — to whom they would be accountable — while breaking down the inhuman, self-serving, and self-protecting "thing" that ruled over everyone.

The fundamental issue thus raised by Mlynář and Lakatoš in 1965–66, and taken up by Šik and others as well, was the question of how to guarantee the expression of divergent interests and how to harmonize the divergencies to the advantage of social progress. That there were legitimate social forces working to make these interests real was amply demonstrated in the studies of the Machonin team, who documented the diversification of the social infrastructure. These scholars laid the indispensable groundwork for the events of 1968; the issue they raised permeated the politics of 1968 on all levels. As Vladimir Kusin has suggested, the secret to the real meaning of the Prague Spring was the revitalization of the political infrastructure — that is, society's reawakened groups.[125] Before 1968 the groups were more latent than actual, "quasi-groups" in the sociological sense, not totally conscious of their own existence and not precisely identifiable.[126] In 1968 they became aware of themselves as potentially autonomous parts of society, with separate and frequently conflicting, but not irreconcilable, interests. They were now changing from quasi-groups to genuine interest groups, and threatening to become what Dahrendorf has called "conflict groups."[127] They began to demand a share in the political structure, and many felt they were on their way to achieving it.

Whether or not all this would have led to the creation of a new party system in the absence of renewed repression is a matter of conjecture. Public opinion seemed to favor the notion, as was indicated in several opinion surveys beginning in March. In that month, respondents were asked to name one or two improvements they would favor in the political system; 28 percent mentioned opposition parties.[128] To a poll conducted in June, 81 percent of respondents favored a multi-party system. To a separate question in the same poll, 41 percent advocated the proposition that at least one noncommunist party be allowed to share the political stage in the spirit of cooperative, perhaps united-front, participation; 33 percent favored the addition of a party that would recognize the leading role of the Communists but operate independently.[129] In October, two months after the occupation, respondents were asked if the present system of single-slate, National Front elections was satisfactory. Only 34 percent of all respondents — and, surprisingly, only 47 percent of Communists polled — replied affirmatively. In another poll, 57 percent felt that the best way to guarantee the continuation of the 1968 reforms would be multi-party elections.[130]

As far as most Communist leaders were concerned, a multi-party system was out of the question. Barring the use of strong legal sanctions or even coercion, however, the party might not have been able to resist indefinitely the pressures for a multi-party system of some sort. There were new stirrings within the Czech Socialist and People's parties, both previously moribund, and although neither party was highly regarded among the wider public, both experienced a sudden growth in membership.[131] In addition, there were many individuals who wished to form new parties and contest the Communists' authority outside the framework of the National Front.

Polls indicated that the Communists would have been the likely winners of elections held in a hypothetical multi-party context, and this fact must have been of some comfort to the leaders.[132] Moreover, the leaders themselves showed up very well in the 1968 surveys, thus confirming the popularity they seemed to enjoy among the people.[133] The acid test of the party's authority, however, would have been the resurrection of the Social Democratic party. A number of former Social Democrats pleaded with Communist leaders privately on several occasions to let them restore their party. The Communists steadfastly refused, and the would-be SD restorationists accepted this for the time being, but pressures from the public might have changed this.[134]

Even among some Communists there was sympathy for the creation of a new party. Karel Kosík, then a member of the Central Committee, proposed two Communist parties — a traditional, "Bolshevik" one and a neo-Marxist, "humanist" party. Petr Pithart, a party member close to Dubček, was sympathetic to the idea of contested elections, and he may have favored the participation of noncommunist parties in one way or another.[135] Mlynář and Lakatoš advocated a revival of the National Front in something like its 1945–48 form, and both intensified their appeals for interest groups.[136]

The leaders, by and large, did feel that a diversity of political views should flourish, but most party officials insisted that this be accommodated within the one-party system. A new set of party statutes was drafted during the summer, and several interesting changes appeared. "Factions" were still forbidden, but allowance was made for something called "oponentura" — a non-Czech word, actually, by which the drafters presumably meant a sort of advocacy procedure with regard to policy proposals. The new statutes called for the protection of the rights of those holding minority positions on policy questions. In addition, there were a number of rules providing for the rotation of offices and prohibiting the concentration of power in the hands of one person, the latter by forbidding any individual to hold multiple offices. Thus the party leaders were sensitive to the question of pluralism and sought to account for it structurally.[137]

All of the foregoing adds up to what I have called elsewhere the "repluralization" of Czechoslovak society.[138] Before 1968 one could perceive only the dim outlines of social differentiation, not yet explicitly defined but real and tangible. In 1968 the underlying patterns began to get clearer; with the release of political constraints, groups appeared, sometimes haphazardly but in many cases clustering around strongly felt mutual interests. They were composed of people in search of means by which to express themselves and reintegrate themselves into the political structure. They had not yet found their proper niches, let alone the matter of contesting the established authority structure. Therefore, the pluralization process in a political sense had only begun by the time of the intervention. The eight months of reform rule were far too short a time for any stable patterns to solidify, and many persons were still seeking their proper group identity when the invasion called a halt to the pluralizing momentum.[139]

Thus the repluralization was still in a formative stage as of August. The mood of the public was rather volatile, and it was difficult to guess what directions it might take from one day to the next. The groups were nonetheless going about their business in a remarkably steady manner, for the most part careful not to upset the reform process being carried on at the level of the political authorities. If the Prague Spring was a revolution, it was a peaceful and deliberate one — in contrast to the anarchy that characterized the revolt in Hungary twelve years earlier. The 2,000 Words manifesto and the isolated anti-Soviet outbursts reported in July and August were somewhat aberrational. That they occurred, however, and particularly the fact that they went unpunished, signaled a radical change in the authority relations of the republic.

The threat to the party's authority was a real issue. In many respects political initiative had passed from the party to the new social groups. The masses were out in front of the party, constantly putting pressure on Dubček and his colleagues to move in one new direction or another. The groups and their spokesmen were openly challenging the Communists' hitherto exclusive right to formulate policy. What had started in January as a palace coup, and evolved by April into a controlled program of reform-from-above, had exploded into a democratic, or at least democratizing, mass movement which ultimately threatened the bases of the party's rule.

The events of the summer of 1968 had revealed the extent of pressures felt by the government in Prague. The government showed that it was either unable or unwilling to constrain the momentum of mass political movements. This more than anything else was what finally brought on the Warsaw Pact intervention, because the Russians and their hardline allies feared the implicit threat of the Czechoslovak groups to the stability of the Communist party's rule. Soviet Marxists have never shaken themselves loose from the utopian assumption that socialist society will be free of conflict and politically homogeneous. No doubt recalling the unhappy events of 1956 in Hungary, Czechoslovakia's allies reached a point in August 1968 when they felt that the unchecked pluralism of the Czechs and Slovaks was a serious, and possibly permanent, deviation from the socialist path. Not only did the interest groups challenge the party's monopoly of power, but they threatened to institutionalize what to the Soviets could only be seen as a "bourgeois" order, for only bourgeois orders were based on conflicting political interests. This was intolerable, given Czechoslovakia's strategic position within the Soviet security system, the cultural and intellectual ties many Czechs felt to the West, and (not to be underestimated) the possible "spillover" effects the Czechoslovak reforms would have on the neighboring masses of East Germany, Poland, and even the USSR.[140] Seen from this angle, the decision to intervene was not only rational but probably the only outcome that could have been expected.

In Summary

Early in this chapter the evolution of Czechoslovak pluralism between 1860 and 1938 was explored. Now we have seen how an analogous process had begun to take place in the mid-twentieth century under conditions quite different. The earlier pluralism had developed around national, religious, and class bases; of these, the last-mentioned was the latest to develop and the most revolutionary in its political impact. After 1945, class and religion as bases of social differentiation were nullified. The third pluralizing force, nationalism, was temporarily suppressed in a wave of Czech chauvinism (see next chapter). The earlier pluralism had developed in the circumstances of a gradually opening political system under Austrian rule and reached its high point in the libertarian atmosphere of the First Republic. The post-1945 pluralization began slowly in the wake of the revolutionary social upheaval, and haltingly under the heavy thumb of the totalitarian regime prior to 1961. Thereafter, however, the process had something in common with that of the earlier period — a gradual evolution of group formation and self-consciousness in the context of a loosening system of political controls. In 1968 the floodgates opened in a change of political context more sudden and startling than that of 1918. Only two decades (at most) after the beginning of the repluralization process, the new social groups burst forth, in many cases anomically but in others purposefully and in a disciplined way. Then, almost as suddenly as they had been released, the pluralizing social forces were once again contained and the momentum halted.

The readiness with which potential political forces returned after twenty years of repression, and the thoughtful, disciplined manner that characterized the process of group formation, suggested that 1968 was no historical anomaly. Unlike the Hungarians, Czechs and Slovaks had had an earlier experience with freedom and democracy, one that for the Czechs had developed over the course of nearly eighty years. The basis of the modern Czechoslovak political culture was formed during those years. The political culture was shaken and in many respects changed after 1938, but the depth to which the normative assumption of pluralistic politics had taken hold was revealed in the regrouping of political movements after 1945 and, especially, in 1968.

It is apparent, then, that pluralism is rather firmly embedded in the consciousness of Czechs and Slovaks. It is indeed normative in the sense that the citizens feel a need to identify with organizations that express their political orientations; the citizen feels it natural that individuals perceive politics in different ways, and he finds it similarly natural that the political system allow for these divergent perceptions by providing an adequate institutional framework for the aggregation of political interests.

During the Stalinist years and again since 1968, Soviet-imposed regimes have forcibly prohibited the organized expression of pluralism, thereby exposing a minority subculture of authoritarianism and antipluralism. The events of 1968 bore witness to the shallowness of this subculture, as first the pluralist *avant-garde* (the intellectuals) and then the masses quickly rejected the "unnatural" system of the previous twenty years.

The persistence of pluralistic political orientations had posed a thorny problem for the Communist leadership. The regime's utmost efforts at resocializing the masses in the 1950s obviously failed. There would seem to be a lesson here, but the regime has not learned it. Instead, the leaders of the post-1968 period have set out upon yet another attempt to create Socialist Man in his Stalinist image, voluntarily committed to a narrowly defined ideal and purposefully directed toward the good of the society rather than to his own individual or group interests. In the years since 1968, Czech and Slovak society has once more become artificially homogenized, its intrinsic pluralism constrained, as it could only be, by coercion.

Czech, Slovak, and Czechoslovak*

The problem of national identity has been implicit in much of the foregoing discussion. The clash between official views of reality and those of the public, conflicting interpretations of the past, perceptions of sovereignty or colonialism, and repressed pluralism all say something about the collective self-images of Czech and Slovak society. All lead us back to a question that has confounded scholars of many societies for a long time, the problem of national character. The subject is rendered particularly difficult because of a longstanding tendency to speak of "national character" as a catch-all, a residual notion used in random ways to explain things that one does not really wish to explain at all.

It is not our purpose here to attempt a systematic discussion of something so inherently unsystematic as national character. We are interested in the matter of national identity as it helps to explain a society's self-perceptions. By focusing on national identity rather than national character we do not mean to sidestep a complicated issue, but rather we hope to approach what should be considered a serious question in a way that sheds light on problems of political integration.

Sidney Verba has argued that national identity is a critical element in the make-up of a political culture: "It is the sense of identity with the nation that legitimates the activities of national elites and makes it possible for them to mobilize the commitment and support of their followers."[1] Lack of a positive sense of national identity as shared by rulers and ruled will generally undermine the rulers' efforts to integrate society. Other tasks will incur great obstacles — for example, economic mobilization, political socialization, and the maintenance of unity and discipline in times of crisis. A lack of identification between two groups in a society may lead to serious conflicts over the sharing of

---

* *Note.* — My ideas on the subject of nationalism have been strongly influenced by my colleagues associated with the University of Washington's Program in Comparative Studies of Ethnicity and Nationality. I have especially profited from a number of insights of the program's director, Paul R. Brass.

resources or the distribution of political power. In countries like Czechoslovakia, where more than one group can justifiably lay claim to national status, the task of political leadership becomes one of persuasively presenting itself as the legitimate executor for all important national constituencies.

It is only since the Second World War that Czechs and Slovaks have been officially acknowledged to be two separate nations. The prevailing assumption of the First Republican elite, disputed by important political subcultures, was that the two peoples were simply branches of one "Czechoslovak" nation. Because Czechs were numerically greater and socially more advanced, "Czechoslovakism" generally translated in practice into Czech dominance. The attempt to assimilate Slovaks into a primarily Czech culture ultimately failed, as a strong Slovak-nationalist movement evolved into a separatist party and, with the support of Hitler, seceded in 1939.

The "Czechoslovak" theory was rejected by the Stalinists, but in a way that produced an equally unsuccessful result in terms of political integration. While paying lip service to the separate traditions of Czechs and Slovaks, in practice the Communists treated both societies the same. In line with the Stalinist interpretation of proletarian internationalism, the national traditions of both peoples were rejected in favor of denationalization policies. Not only did this further obstruct the integration of Slovakia into the republic as a whole, but it resulted in the *dis*integration of the Czech political consensus as well, intensifying the ever-widening gap between rulers and ruled in both parts of the republic.

Slovak grievances against the Czechoslovak state had a longer history than Czech grievances, and perhaps for this reason the revival of the national question in the 1960s began in Slovakia.[2] Even before the rehabilitation of purged Slovak nationalists in 1963, the so-called "Slovak question" was opened; it reached a culmination — and generated a solution of sorts — in the federalization law of 1968. The "Czech question," on the other hand, was not awakened until the Prague Spring. During the few short months of reform rule, Czech intellectuals eagerly explored the meaning of Czech nationalism. Unlike the Slovaks, the Czechs found no solution to their identity problem in federalism; Czech intellectuals were after something bigger — nothing short of complete democracy, consistent, they argued, with their historical traditions. In the end, both groups found only frustration. The policies of the seventies have transgressed both national traditions. Although the federal solution partially satisfied

Slovak aspirations, by the mid-1970s the larger political tide had turned against those Slovak nationalists who had fought the hardest for federalism; the Czech democrats, of course, had fallen by the wayside much earlier.[3]

The problem of national identity goes back to the very formation of the republic, at a time when the political map of Europe was being radically redrawn. Czechoslovakia became one of numerous East European states carved out of the old regional empires on the basis of essentially Western notions of legitimacy, centering around the premise that the *nation* represents the ultimate source of legitimate rule.[4] Despite the efforts of Wilson and his peers to create a coherent system of nation-states in post-1918 Europe, the political boundaries of the twentieth century have not come to reflect the Wilsonian ideal of self-determination for every nation, neither in Europe nor elsewhere. The result, as we know, is a complex world of states with varied patterns of ethnic and national constituencies.[5]

There is probably no better example of the twentieth-century nationality problem than Czechoslovakia. This small country was established on two fragile premises: the historical unity of Bohemia, Moravia, and Silesia, on the one hand, and a dubious application of the nationality principle to Slovakia, on the other.[6] The historical unity of the Bohemian Crownlands, a fact that argued for political unity, was counterbalanced by the ethnic heterogeneity of the region. Slovakia, also ethnically mixed, became attached to the Bohemian lands on the grounds that its Slovak majority was closely related to the Czechs — enough so that the two largest ethnic groups in the new country, Czechs and Slovaks, could be considered a single nation comprising a large majority within the state's boundaries. Although most of the Slovak political elites accepted this reasoning, the cultural and historical differences between Czechs and Slovaks eventually proved to be a vexing problem indeed, and the ethnic heterogeneity of the Crownlands themselves utlimately became the cause of the First Republic's demise.

Despite the contradictions in the Czechoslovak national formula, the statesmen at the Paris Peace Conference in 1919 sanctioned the new creation. They did so partly for strategic reasons and partly because Czech and Slovak leaders presented them with a *fait accompli* in the form of their self-proclaimed Czechoslovak Republic (October 1918). Edvard Beneš, chief representative of the fledgling republic at the Paris talks, found much sympathy for his government's position. The wartime diplomatic efforts of Masaryk, Beneš, and Milan

Štefánik, together with the activities of the Czechoslovak Legions on behalf of the Allied cause, had predisposed the West favorably.[7] Beneš now persuaded the Western leaders that Czechoslovak unity was the proper solution to the question of national self-determination in the two regions. No doubt the Western statesmen who controlled the outcome of the peace talks found Beneš's argument especially persuasive in view of the smallness of the Czech population (approximately seven million) and the added population base represented by the Slovaks (approximately three million). One of the primary concerns of the peacemakers was to create viable states in East-Central Europe in order to contain any German military threat. A strong Czechoslovakia appeared to be crucial to this new regional order.

For related reasons, Beneš was unwilling to give up the predominantly German and Magyar districts within the desired borders. Both represented territories with a high degree of strategic importance. Moreover, the areas heavily populated by Germans held a symbolic value for Czechs as historically integral parts of the Bohemian Crownlands. As far as the predominantly Magyar territories were concerned, Beneš was unwilling to part with these because large numbers of Slovaks were intermixed with the Magyars. With all these arguments the statesmen in Paris concurred.

Because of all this ethnic diversity, the First Republic found itself constantly beset after 1919 by nationality and minority conflicts. The troublesome relationship between Czechs and Slovaks was only one aspect of a multifaceted ethnic problem. The *minorities* problem — that is, the problem concerning the Germans and Magyars — was of a different character from that of the *nationality* (Czech-Slovak) problem. Germans and Magyars living in Czechoslovakia had strong ties of kinship and culture with their co-nationals in irredentist neighboring countries. The irredenta gave the minorities conflict an international flavor, whereas the Czech-Slovak tension was in the nature of a domestic social problem, unrelated for the most part to conflicts in the international arena.

It is not my purpose to pursue the question of the minorities in any depth. This has been done elsewhere.[8] There is reason to believe that the First Republic might have been on the verge of resolving the most urgent problem, that of the German minority, had it not been for the rise of fanatical pan-Germanism and the agitation of the pro-Nazi *Sudetendeutschpartei* in the mid- and late 1930s. The so-called "activist" German parties in Czechoslovakia had come to the fore during the late twenties, but the advent of Konrad Henlein and his

Sudetendeutschpartei drew most of the following away from the "activists" after 1933.[9]

This is a moot point, however. The fact remains that the Sudeten German issue became the focal point of Hitler's campaign against Czechoslovakia. Whether or not the First Republic was strong enough to resolve its internal conflicts, it could not survive the international crisis threatening Europe in the thirties. At least, it could not survive without the support of its more powerful European allies. One can only speculate about the possibility of integrating the German minority into the First Republic if the course of events in Germany had taken another direction in the 1930s.

Additional minorities problems concerned the status of Poles, Magyars, and Ruthenes in the First Republic.[10] These groups lived in territories subject to persistent border disputes between Czechoslovakia and irredentist Poland and Hungary. This, of course, aggravated the First Republic's domestic problems by serving as an issue in Prague's relations with Warsaw and Budapest — never friendly for any lengthy time between the wars. Among these three ethnic minorities, the Magyars presented the greatest difficulty because of their large numbers and the persistently hostile attitude of the Hungarian government vis à vis Czechoslovakia. Serious though these minority conflicts were, however, none was as critical as the Sudeten German problem. Even the Magyars, who may have numbered nearly one million, were never the problem that the Germans were, due to the smaller population of the Magyars, their relatively high standard of living as compared to that of their co-nationals in Hungary, and the military weakness of the diplomatically isolated Hungarian state.[11]

The problem of the minorities faded into the background after the Second World War.[12] Most of the Sudeten Germans were eliminated through expulsion; by 1950 fewer than 5 percent of the German minority remained in Czechoslovakia. The Ruthenian problem was, for the most part, settled by Stalin; his annexation of Ruthenia in 1945 came over the protest of President Beneš, but it in fact removed from the Czechoslovak domain a territory hard to rule and thus eliminated a part of the minorities problem. There are still some Ruthenes (now generally called Carpatho-Ukrainians) in eastern Slovakia, but they represent a relatively small ethnic minority today. The Magyar and Polish questions were more complicated, and no real solution was found. Early postwar efforts at evacuating Magyars were abandoned in 1948 after the departure of only 12–15 percent of the total Magyar population. This coincided with the *rapprochement* between the "fraternal" governments in Prague and Budapest, now both under Communist domination.[13] As for the Polish minority, it had never numbered more than 110,000 and therefore represented a relatively minor domestic problem. With the new, Stalinist regional order in East-Central Europe, Warsaw, too, was obliged to mend fences with Prague, and any lingering tensions related to the disputed territories and peoples on Czechoslovakia's northern borders subsided.

In contrast to the minorities problem, the tensions between Czechs and Slovaks persisted. Throughout the interwar period, the political coexistence of the two peoples had proved to be far more difficult than the Republic's founding fathers had imagined. Czechs, numerically greater and politically dominant, had only gradually come to recognize the seriousness of the Slovak problem. The Slovaks themselves had been deeply divided over their sense of national destiny and their affective orientations toward the Prague government. Between 1945 and 1948, serious attempts to resolve the problem were made. The separation of Czech and Slovak lands had increased the differences between the two nations, while the courageous resistance of Slovaks in 1944 served to distinguish them and to validate their claim to national autonomy. Provisional arrangements for Slovak autonomy were made at the war's end, but the promises made at that time were gradually whittled down in subsequent years. Although the Communists were initially staunch defenders of Slovak rights, they eventually backed away from the issue. Once in power, the Communists in principle continued to acknowledge Czechs and Slovaks as separate and equal nations, but until the federal reform of 1968 the state remained unitary and centralized. Authority flowed from Prague into all of Czechoslovakia, bypassing the decentralized structures that had been set up immediately after the war.[14]

Both before and after the Second World War, then, Czech personalities and Czech ideas dominated political life. There were always a number of Slovaks who accepted the unitary idea, whether out of sincerity or political opportunism, but many others resented the centralism of the Prague governments both before 1938 and after 1945. Only during the Second World War, beginning with the short-lived federal system of the Second ("Czecho-Slovak") Republic and continuing on another level during the six years of the Slovak Republic, did Slovak nationalists realize a part of their dream for self-control.[15] Again after 1945 — and especially after 1948 — the Slovak nationalists' desires for autonomy were frustrated as Slovakia was reincorporated into a unitary Czechoslovak state.

Traditionally there have been two major schools of thought regarding the relationship between Czechs and Slovaks. Those whom we shall call *Czechoslovaks* (or, as sometimes used with specific reference to Slovaks, *Czechophiles*) have held that Czechs and Slovaks are branches of the same nation. The two branches, according to this argument, happened to have been politically separated for a thousand years, and the differences that developed as a result were of a relatively minor scope; Czech society was more advanced, more industrialized, and culturally more sophisticated, whereas Slovak society lagged behind in its socio-cultural development. The Czechoslovaks contended that the political reunification of the two peoples, who had originally been united and shared many similar features (including a remarkable closeness of language), would enable the two branches to fuse together once again and become as one stalk of the national tree. It was thus a matter of national integration, or reintegration, much as Western political scientists of the mid-twentieth century would acclaim. To speak of a Slovak national identity separate from that of the Czechoslovak "nation" did not make sense to the Czechoslovaks, and to perpetuate the accidental cleavage between the two branches by establishing separate political and administrative systems would be wrong.

The second school of thought on the subject is that of the *nationalists*. We are speaking here primarily of Slovak nationalists, although it is true that there have been Czech nationalists who have traditionally assumed the separateness of the two peoples. Because the political institutions were developed according to the Czech experience and under the influence of Czech values and symbols, the importance of Czech nationalism vis à vis Slovaks has — at least until recently — always been less problematic than that of Slovak nationalism vis à vis Czechs. Throughout the interwar period Czechs held the upper hand politically; their cultural values were hardly threatened by the Slovaks, their standard of living was higher, their sense of national self-identity was reasonably firm. This is not to deny the saliency of Czech nationalism vis à vis Germans, the historical enemy, or Russians, the latecomers on the scene of Central European conflict. Nor should we forget the genuine grievances felt by Czechs toward the Slovaks between 1938 and 1945, for the Slovak nationalists eased the way of the Germans to their wartime dominion over Czechoslovakia. During most of the Czechoslovak Republic's history, however, the more salient grievances have been those of the Slovak nationalists against the Czechs.

The Slovak nationalists have always considered the two peoples as separate nations. They admit that their languages are similar and that they probably stemmed from the same ancient ancestry. However, the long period of political separation from the tenth century on meant a corresponding separateness not only of social development but of national character as well. By the time of independence, Slovak society was still an overwhelmingly rural society. Although a few industrial centers had sprung up, none were very large; the modest metropolis known as Pozsony (Bratislava) was the largest — a city of only 78,223 inhabitants according to the 1910 census, and many of them Magyars, Jews, and Germans.[16] Pozsony/Bratislava was, moreover, nestled in the southwesternmost corner of the Slovak regions, remote from the vast majority of the Slovak population.[17]

Appropriately, the center of Slovak nationalism prior to independence was Turčiansky Svätý Martin, a town of some 3000 inhabitants situated in the Low Tatra Mountains of the central region. Here the Matica Slovenská (Slovak Foundation) was established, and here also several important national periodicals were published. Turčiansky Sv. Martin reflected the rural character of Slovak society, where simple ways of life and traditional modes of authority prevailed. Poverty was an everyday fact, and despite the beginnings of industrialization, the region lagged far behind the Czech lands. Illiteracy was relatively widespread, and the generally low educational level formed a vicious circle along with poverty. Religion, a spiritual refuge from the physical misery that surrounded the Slovak, was a dominant force in the community, centered around the village priest. The latter interpreted the scriptures, presided over the important traditional ceremonies, and commonly extended his authority into the realm of secular politics.

All this was in contrast to conditions in the Bohemian Crownlands. The Czechs lived in a thriving industrial society, the most productive region of the former Austro-Hungarian Empire.[18] Literacy was high and education well developed by the end of the nineteenth century. Because the main thrust of industrialization had taken place in the second half of the nineteenth century, personal and familial ties between rural and urban regions remained strong. Village and city (or town) thus developed to some degree together, for the organic links between the two guaranteed an ongoing, mutual exchange of experiences. As we have discussed in the preceding chapter, political orientations had diversified, and this pluralistic tendency characterized city and village alike.

The social differences between Czech and Slovak were underscored by differences in religious outlook. Czechs were proud of their tendency to religious skepticism, inherited from the Hussites and stressed by the national reawakeners of the nineteenth century. Most were Roman Catholics, but secular trends drifting in from the West, together with the self-conscious Protestantism of many leading intellectuals, contributed to a view of religion very different from that of most Slovaks. Catholicism itself took on something of a national character, relatively undogmatic and hospitable to modern theology. In the nineteenth and twentieth centuries, many educated Czechs broke away from Catholicism, usually under the influence of that dominant strain in the national historiography that equated Roman Catholicism with the Habsburg oppressor. Masaryk was himself such a convert-by-national-allegiance who adopted the faith of the Bohemian Brethren.

Regardless of whether they were Catholic or Protestant, it became typical of the "modernized" urban Czechs to maintain a conscious distinction between the sacred and the secular in their lives. This sacred-secular distinction was, of course, not characteristic of all Czechs, but it was sufficiently widespread to give the nation a reputation for heresy in a region of traditional religiosity. (No doubt a significant part of this reputation was the history of the Hussite movement.) Certainly, to many Slovaks the Czechs were a nation of heretics and profligates.[19]

With these divergent backgrounds, it should not be surprising that Czechoslovakism faced great difficulties from the moment of independence. The Czechoslovaks perceived their task as one of nation-building, integrating the Czechs and Slovaks into a unitary sense of national identity. The Czechoslovaks assumed that political unity would lead to national unity, and that the dissimilarities between the two peoples would eventually lose their political significance — if not disappear entirely. In the course of this development, Slovak society would take on the features of Czech society more and more, for the pattern of history in the modern era had brought the Czechs to an advanced state to which, it was further assumed, Slovaks should logically aspire.

The Persisting Czech Question

Kusin has remarked that the "favourite pastime" of the Czechs is their preoccupation with self-examination and soul-searching.[20] Indeed, it can perhaps be said that no other people has ever spent so much time and so many words on self-analysis — per capita, at least — as have the Czechs. A number of Czech scholars and politicians devoted great efforts to analyzing their own national character in the interwar period, and the theme recurred again in the 1960s, particularly during 1968. Earlier, the national awakeners of the nineteenth century, particularly Palacký and Masaryk, had delved into the collective psyche. The general findings of all these self-analysts show a remarkable degree of consistency, although not without some disagreements and unresolved ambivalences.[21]

Notwithstanding these ambivalences, shared by masses and intelligentsia alike, there emerges a vague sense of who and what the Czech nation is. It is a small nation geographically located at the crossroads of Europe, surrounded for the most part by larger nations and caught in an ageless confluence of different political, religious, and cultural currents. The Czechs have managed to survive amid the nearly constant threat of national destruction and the continuous temptation to assimilate into greater cultures. In their best moments, Czechs feel themselves associated with the noblest of human characteristics: democracy, humanitarianism, egalitarianism, spiritual firmness, and intellectual innovativeness. In their worst moments they recognize in themselves strong feelings of pathos and martyrdom; tendencies toward extremism and anarchy, or obversely, helpless passivity; self-righteousness and a proclivity to blame others for their woes; and even a capacity for great cruelty, coupled sometimes with a burning vengeance. (Compare, for a moment, the Hussites with their ethnic heirs of half a millennium later: the spiritual firmness of Hus and Chelčický, the martyrdom of Hus; the spirituality of Masaryk, the repeated humiliations of Czechoslovakia; the theological and social innovativeness of the fifteenth-century reformers, the eventual demise of Czech Protestantism; the political philosophy of Masaryk, Beneš's attempt to fuse democracy with socialism, the 1968 reformers' attempt to realize socialism with a human face, and the repeated frustration of these efforts; the gentleness of the Brethren, the ferocity of the Táborites; the rationalism of the First Republic, the coldblooded terror of the early fifties; and so on.) In addition, Czechs see in themselves a tendency toward iconoclasm and a degree of messianism.

These abstractions from the Czech character help to explain the vicissitudes of the national history. During good times — that is, times of national and cultural progress — the Czechs have exhibited some of the most high-minded traits and accomplished remarkable human achievements. The Hussite rebellion, a precocious religious revolt against the seemingly uncontestable power of Catholic Europe; the national revival, a courageous effort at rescuing the nation against what seemed to be enormous odds; the political experiments of 1918–38 and 1968–69, democratic oases in East-Central Europe — all these glorious moments attest to the existence of greatness in the small nation and confirm the optimism in Masaryk's image of his people.[22] Jiří Mahen saw the best qualities of his people to be intellectuality, idealism, organizational adeptness, and a capacity for greatness;[23] these too were evident in the highpoints of Czech history.

Even during the good times, however, things can get out of hand, as Pavel Tigrid has argued. The nation gets excited, nervous, even anarchic. The public is easily led into heights of exuberance and over-indulgence, threatening to undo through extremism the good that might be accomplished with the help of patience and self-discipline.[24] Self-discipline itself is a quality that an earlier writer, Josef Karásek, found lacking in Czechs.[25] Tigrid cites the exuberant mood of the nation in 1918–19, bordering on anarchy and nihilism as a result of the political jockeying immediately following upon independence.[26] He might also have cited the mood of the nation in 1945 and again in 1968. In 1919 the Czechs had the advantages of firm leadership in the founding fathers of the First Republic, and the exuberance came to be channeled into constructive, progressive action. In 1945 and thereafter firm leadership was available only among the ranks of those who sought to turn the nation's exuberance into a vehicle of political extremism, and the nation let itself be led into Stalinism. In 1968, the political leadership was neither firm enough nor unified enough to satisfy the imperial powers in Moscow, who demanded that the restless social forces be contained. As in 1948, the nation's exuberance was the cause of its downfall.

In all of these instances, the Czechs lived up to the tragic self-characterization drawn by Ferdinand Peroutka: "we flare up but then die down . . . we easily penetrate into the profound, but we do not stay there . . . we are characterized by incompleteness, a failure to think things through, and a tendency to hold back."[27] Historical circumstances have in large part determined this frustration complex, but it is not entirely correct to pin the blame on outsiders (as Czechs are often wont to do). Mahen, too, noted a lack of perseverence among his countrymen, as did his contemporary Emanuel Chalupný.[28] Still, one must not forget the geographical location of the Czech lands and the logicality of the historical dialectic.[29] As a journalist explained it in

1968, the lesson of Czech history is that internal and external reality are inseparable. The historical attempts to achieve greatness failed through a lack of understanding of either the internal or the external reality. The leaders prior to 1948 did not fully comprehend the international situation of their day — or if they did understand it, they were incapable of handling it correctly. The opposite was true of the post-1948 leaders: they did not comprehend domestic reality and could not govern according to the nation's true needs.[30] Of the 1968–69 leaders it can be said that they, like the generation before 1948, failed to grasp the nature of the threat from beyond Czechoslovakia's borders, and this, more than their problems with internal social groups, was the cause of their downfall.

When things are bad, Czechs are prone to humiliating extremes of defeatism and capable of great ignobility. Tigrid and Mahen both noted a dearth of courage and an overwhelming nonmilitancy.[31] Czechs are sometimes obsequious before dangerous adversaries, and they are frequently found gullible to promises given insincerely.[32] Their *humanita* and their general goodheartedness are relative qualities; they can give way to a searing cruelty — as Tigrid has put it, "a cruelty bordering on perverse brutality" — which can occur at times of victory as well as defeat.[33] Masaryk, too, was aware of this trait, exemplified in Žižka. When combined with the zealous pursuit of a goal assumed to be paramount, this cruelty can take the form of an "unbreakable stoutheartedness, horrible to a rival, horrible in its all-shattering victory, horrible because in the depths of the soul there burns a certain doubt and consciousness of guilt."[34]

It is very difficult to face up to guilt. Tigrid notes that with every national crisis in this century Czechs have been quick to point the finger of guilt at others, refusing to admit their own role in the tragedies of 1938–39, 1948, and 1968–69:

> . . . those guilty were the socialists, the communists, the agrarians, the fascists, Beneš, General Syrový, the army, Gottwald, the Jews, the intelligentsia, the workers, the English, the Russians, the French, the National Front, the National Socialists, the Social Democrats, Truman, Stalin, Zorin, again Beneš, Laušman, Helena Koželuhová, the People's Militia, the People's Democracy, the secret police, Slánský, Barák, Novotný, again the intelligentsia, Dubček, Smrkovský, Kriegel, Sviták, the radio, the television, *Literární noviny,* Matica Slovenská, Moscow, Brezhnev, the Soviet Marshals, Jodas, Štrougal, Husák — but only rarely *we.*[35]

Moreover, Czechs tend to pass very quickly into a state of despair when defeated. Visionaries and prophets they may be, but when their vision is frustrated and their prophecy denied they can sink into the depths of pessimism, gloom, and self-hatred.[36] They feel themselves to be, like Hus, the arbitrary victims of fate, destined to a collective martyrdom.[37]

These unbecoming features of the national character do indeed contrast with the *humanita* so prominent in the better traditions of the Czech nation.[38] Perhaps it is yet another feature of the national character that the extremes of the Czech psyche are reflected also in the way they appraise themselves: their virtues are magnificent, their faults despicable. They expect much of themselves, become enthused and even feverish when pursuing a goal, but come crashing down to the pits of self-abasement when unsuccessful. They have perceived their purpose as a righteous one, an exemplary one; they perceive their failure as a sign of unworthiness.

Indeed, the articulation of a Czech national purpose has been a long and arduous process. The national awakeners of the last century worked under the pressure of very great obstacles. Their success in re-creating the nation in a modern form was remarkable, for they labored against the pull of the robust German culture and within a political context that was only partially free. A century later, Communist reformers attempted to revive the national purpose in a similarly non-free context; the limitations on their freedom were clearly shown by the 1968 intervention. Thus the Czechs remain prisoners of their smallness and geographical location, both of which give them an abiding sense of insecurity.

To counter this insecurity Czechs have attempted to prove by one means or another that they *deserve* their nationhood and the sovereignty associated with it. During the drive for independence, Masaryk and Beneš, Wilsonians themselves, capitalized on the growing international sympathy for national self-determination. As Beneš argued a decade after independence, the national idea was the "direct offspring of democracy." Just as democracy guaranteed the rights and privileges of the human individual, so national sovereignty carried democracy one step further to make democratic principles applicable to entire nations. Beneš saw the nation as an organic whole, possessing rights of existence and liberty from control by other nations.[39]

Four decades later, at a time of national humiliation, the Marxist philosopher Karel Kosík reflected bitterly on the recent Soviet invasion of his homeland and expressed a belief in the nation similar to Beneš's:

> The Czech question is a conflict over the meaning of the existence of a political nation in Central Europe. The nation exists, renews itself, and secures iteslf in that conflict, in which the lofty is distinguished from the lowly, the noble from the humbled. Amid that conflict the nation exists in the persistent danger that it will fall to a lower, sub-servient, derivative position, either by its own doing or by that of others. The "Czech question," then, is a historical conflict over whether a political nation can be transformed into merely a popula-tion, whether a country can decline to the status of a province, whether democracy will yield before fascism and humanism before barbarism.[40]

In addition to their belief in the universal right of national self-determination, Czechs have sought to justify their existence by the virtues in their history and culture. Overlooking their negative charac-teristics, they have frequently emphasized their democracy, equality, and *humanita*. They have sought to persuade themselves and others that they are part of a long tradition of progressivism in intellectual and political affairs, extending from Charles IV to the present, punc-tuated by the great moments in their history. They are not unlike other nations in this urge to glorify themselves, but the perennial insecurity of their situation gives to their argument a tone of particular poignancy.

Four generations of scholars, bourgeois and socialist, have articu-lated what they perceive to be the special, precocious nature of Czech culture. Palacký and Masaryk believed that this special quality was derived from the skeptical but profoundly religious mentality of the Czechs. The highpoint, and the point of reference for subsequent generations, was the Hussite rebellion, from which the architects of the modern national consciousness drew their inspiration.[41] Zdeněk Nejedlý, an important Marxist historian of Beneš's generation, re-jected the centrality of religion but affirmed the positive strain running through Czech history. He argued that the national revival of the nine-teenth century was primarily a secular phenomenon, its humanistic and democratic inspiration deriving from the secular aspects of the Hussites. Hussitism was not only a religious movement but a social and national one as well, and Nejedlý stressed the latter two over the former. The heresy of the fifteenth century was therefore "the most thorough, the highest victory of the moral renaissance" in Europe, "a movement filled with a fresh force which gave origin to the lifeblood of the whole national life."[42]

Thus the Czech question goes beyond politics. Kosík saw it as a question of freedom versus constraint, but also a a never-ending quest for collective identity.[43] Masaryk saw something more transcendental in it:

> To me, the Czech question is a question about the fortunes of mankind; it is a question of consciousness. I believe with Kollár that the history of nations is not accidental, but rather that a definite plan of Providence is manifested in it. The task of historians and philosophers, therefore, as well as the task of every nation, is to comprehend that world plan, to become aware of their place in it, and to act, in all their work — including political work — according to that understanding, with a consciousness as complete and as clear as possible.[44]

From here it requires only one step more to perceive the Czech question as one with a messianistic lesson. The obverse of martyrdom is messianism. Inherent in messianism is some degree of arrogance. In their best moments Czechs have not been satisfied with mere pride in their own accomplishments, but rather, they have let themselves feel that they are above other nations. This trait, too, can be traced throughout Czech history, but it has been especially pronounced in the twentieth century. To Czechs, the First Republic was a model of parliamentary democracy. To Beneš, post-1945 Czechoslovakia would be a bridge between east and west, a hybrid system combining the best points of socialism and democracy. To the orthodox Communists, Czechoslovakia was the first of the Soviet Union's allies to enter the socialist phase of development (in 1960). To the reformers of 1968, they were the synthesizers of socialism, democracy, and humanism.[45] (It cannot have been merely coincidental that Dubček, a Slovak, called upon both Czechs and Slovaks to contribute to the building of "socialism with a human face." Dubček must have been conscious of the powerful appeal this slogan would have upon the Czechs, an unusually historically-minded people.)

It is important to understand the complex make-up of the Czechs' national self-perception in order to appreciate the basis of Czechoslovakism. The latter cannot be adequately explained by conventional theories of imperialism; there were economic motives underlying the Czechs' desire to unite with the Slovaks, but these were not primary. Likewise, there were political motives, but these were not purely self-serving. Czechs did not force Slovaks to join their political movement, and Slovakia was not held after 1918 at the point of bayonets. More-over, it is not enough to argue that Czech-Slovak unity came about as a result of the mutual advantages the elites of both peoples perceived in their merger. There were elements of both mutual benefit and imperial-ism, in a subtle and mostly benign way, but the question cannot be explained by these motives.

For Czechs, the tendency to messianism is an important explanatory link between the complex matter of Czech nationalism and the urge to unite with the Slovaks. The belief that there was something universally relevant and virtuous in their own experience compensated for the negative elements Czechs recognized in their national character, and the possibility of sharing their traditions with their nearest ethnic kinfolk helped in some measure to justify their long national martyr-dom. A small group of educated Slovaks came to accept the proposi-tion of Czech-Slovak unity, and Czechoslovakism was born. The Czechoslovaks seized upon linguistic similarities and the thinnest thread of historical interconnections between the two people, and on this basis they conceived the vision of a single nation upon which Czechoslovakia as a political entity was eventually founded. Accord-ing to the vision, the Slovaks would share in the virtues of the Czech culture and contribute in their own way to the building of a Czecho-slovak society.

The Younger Brother

The Czechoslovak argument was partly drawn from a number of historical precedents in which the Czech and Slovak cultures had con-verged or run parallel at various times — their common ancestry in the early Middle Ages, the education of Slovak scholars at Prague Uni-versity beginning in the fourteenth century, the spread of Hussitism into Slovak regions, and the assignment of Czech Jesuits as mission-aries to the Slovaks during the Counterreformation. Of these, the strongest influence was that of the Hussites, whose missionary activity and pamphleteering shaped the development of the Slovak written language for more than three centuries. In fact, when at the end of the eighteenth century Hussitism revived in the Czech lands, much of its inspiration flowed from Slovakia, where the Counterreformation had played a much smaller role and the Hussite literature had survived.[46]

These facts, however, cannot outweigh the long political separation of the two peoples. Although there was some commonality of develop-ment during the Absolutist periods of the eighteenth and nineteenth centuries, diverging economic and political circumstances in Austria and Hungary kept Czechs and Slovaks apart. Cultural intermingling was rare, and even the connections between Czech and Slovak Protestants served very little to unite them; in the first place, Protestantism was a minority religion among both peoples, and in the second place, the Czech Hussite revival was aimed at restoring the spirit of the fifteenth-century Brethren, whereas Protestantism among the Slovaks was more under the influence of the sixteenth-century Lutheran and Calvinist traditions.

More importantly, the development of Slovak cultural nationalism had taken a sharp turn away from the Czechs in the mid-nineteenth century. Earlier, a number of Slovak intellectuals had identified themselves with the Czech revival and sought to direct their own literature onto the same path. The most notable personalities of this school were Ján Kollár and Pavol Jozef Šafárik (Pavel Josef Šafařík, as he signed himself using the Czech orthography). With the codification of the Slovak language by the great scholar and national hero Ľudovít Štúr, however, Slovak cultural development took a separate path. Notwithstanding the efforts of his panslavist contemporaries to work within a larger framework, the step that Štúr took in the 1840s had a permanent effect on Slovak culture. Previously, Slovak literature had been written exclusively in Czech or in a dialect of Slovak hardly distinguishable from Czech; its impact was limited primarily to the educated ranks. Štúr's codification of the language brought literary Slovak into a far greater degree of congruence with the spoken idiom, thereby making it more easily understood and learned by the masses. At the same time, the Štúr reforms had the effect of further separating Slovaks from Czechs. Not until the end of the nineteenth century did intellectual trends among the two peoples converge once more, and by that time the linguistic separation was well established and the respective folk cultures permanently disjoined.[47]

By that time also the Austro-Hungarian Compromise of 1867 had reestablished political separateness. The Czechs belonged to Austria, and their political development (as we have already said) reflected the relatively benign, semi-tolerant authoritarianism of the constitutional monarchy. The Slovaks belonged to Hungary, and their politics were those of a brutally repressed minority striving for the privilege of national existence within a system in which constitutionalism meant only words on a piece of paper.

It was under these unpropitious circumstances that the first impetus toward Czech and Slovak political unity occurred. Slovak national politics, in the modern sense, really began in the 1890s with the first stirrings of dissident activity. Some of these stirrings grew out of a new literary movement centered around a group of educated Protestants who had studied in Prague. There they had come under the influence of the then Professor T. G. Masaryk, who was himself half Slovak.[48] Masaryk's humanistic philosophy and democratic political ideas stimulated his students to form a Czechoslovak Union (*Ceskoslovenská jednota*) in 1896. The union's members founded a periodical, *Hlas* (The Voice), from whose name this group and other like-minded Czechophile Slovaks came to be known as the Hlasists. Prominent among the members of this group were Jaroslav Vlček, a literary historian, and Vavro Šrobár, who was destined to follow a long and distinguished political career.

Among the Czech public there arose a wave of sympathetic feelings for the Slovaks at the turn of the century. Magazine articles and books began to appear with the purpose of acquainting Czechs with the little-known people to the east. Typical of this new literature was a book entitled *Slovakia,* published in 1901 by the Artistic Society of Prague. The book was expressly aimed at helping Czechs "to become better acquainted with their brothers to the east, who in these difficult times cannot through their own efforts spread the knowledge of their present, past, and hopes for a better future."[49] Pointed mention was made in several articles to the political and cultural repression under Hungarian rule, and the implication was clear that the Slovaks shared the Czechs' self-perceived condition of national frustration.[50] The book began with a lengthy, adulatory poem by Adolf Heyduk entitled "To Our Slovak Brothers" and ended with an equally warm offering by the Slovak national poet Pavol Országh-Hviezdoslav, "To Our Czech Brothers."

The most important single popularizer of Czech-Slovak unity among the Czechs was a schoolteacher named Karel Kálal. Kálal had become interested in Slovak culture through his boyhood encounters with a wandering tinker who shared with young Kálal stories about his native Slovakia. As Kálal grew older he began to travel to the east in order to pursue his curiosity firsthand. He published a number of articles in a popular Czech magazine, *Osvěta,* in which he painted an idyllic picture of the Slovaks as the "younger brothers" of the Czechs. Although in retrospect his highly idealized portrait of the Slovaks appears rather condescending, he genuinely admired them for their simplicity and goodheartedness. From Kálal's depictions of them, the Slovaks emerged as the Czechs' next of kin, less cultured and indeed very backward but pure and educable. They seemed very much like Czechs who had simply not undergone the latter's social and cultural development.[51]

Kálal came into contact with Masaryk because of their common interest in the Slovaks. He pointed out to Masaryk the potential political advantage in Czech-Slovak unity — that is, the strength of Czech political movements would be increased if the civic base were augmented by the addition of nearly three million Slovaks to their numbers.[52] Kálal may also have discussed with Masaryk the likely advantages of developing the economic resources of the Slovak lands; both Kálal and Masaryk favored Czech capital investment in Slovakia, and both saw joint economic ventures as a promising means to further Czech-Slovak unity. It would be inaccurate to interpret these ideas as the basis of a Czech economic imperialism, however, for the motives behind them were neither so cynical nor so singleminded.[53]

The Slovak intellectuals who adopted the Czechoslovak point of view were in no way traitors to their nation.[54] They saw the same advantages to unity that Masaryk and Kálal saw, trusted the Czechs, and admired the modernity of Czech society. They believed, as Kollár had, that neither Czechs nor Slovaks would ever realize their national aspirations alone.[55] Thus their duty to their nation, as they perceived it, was best fulfilled by their attempts to bring their countrymen together with the Czechs, politically and culturally.

The task was not so easy. Even taking a long view of social and cultural development, the gap between Czech and Slovak societies was enormous. Slovakia was not as primitive as the third world of the twentieth century, as Lipták has pointed out, but it was a decidedly backward (*zaostalý*) territory in comparison with Western and Central Europe.[56] The population was mostly rural, clustered in small villages dotting the rugged landscape. No national nobility existed, and only a small middle class had begun to form. Very few Slovaks had ever set foot beyond their immediate district or community, and as a result knowledge about the outside world was limited. It is a mark of the parochiality of the populace that when poverty drove large numbers of Slovaks to emigration around the turn of the century, some who landed in America and elsewhere were unaware of their specific national identity; they knew only that they were from a certain village in what was called Hungary, they were sternly ruled by people who spoke a different tongue, and they were very poor. Although most Czechs had superficial and highly romanticized notions about the Slovaks, it is safe to say that very, very few Slovaks had as much knowledge about the Czechs.

Like the Czechs, the Slovaks lacked a national nobility. In addition, the obstacles in the way of their developing a surrogate intellectual elite in the course of the national awakening were extreme. For centuries the only route to upward social mobility was through "Magyarization," that is, assimilation into Magyar culture. Relatively few Slovaks received higher education, and with the exception of some who managed to study abroad, the few who did found the pressures to assimilate irresistible. The Magyarones, as they were called, thus entered the mainstream of elite Hungarian society by leaving their national identity behind. From this position they were admitted to the ranks of the clergy, teachers, civil servants, attorneys, police, and so on. Far from being outcasts among their own people, they were admired and respected for their success in self-elevation, even though they themselves considered their kinfolk primitive, ignorant, and unworthy of social or political privileges.

The rise of a national leadership, therefore, appears all the more remarkable in light of this Magyarone tradition. The leaders of the Slovak awakening were obviously exceedingly dedicated to their cause.[57] Their long struggle during the nineteenth century represented something of a miracle, miraculous not only for its occurrence following nearly a millennium of national oppression but also for the difficulty involved in mobilizing the long-dormant nation for the eventual political task.

Reliable statistics are not plentiful, but a few social indicators are helpful in drawing a picture of Slovak society around the turn of the century.[58] In the first place, it is worth noting that Hungary as a whole was backward by West European standards, although progress in industrialization had just begun. According to Lipták, industrial growth in Hungary between 1900 and the beginning of World War I averaged 7.3 percent annually — the highest growth rate in Europe, with the probable exception of the Russian Empire. At the same time, however, Hungary's late start in economic development continued to be evident; with approximately 6.5 percent of Europe's population, Hungary produced only 1.5 percent of the continent's industrial goods. In per capita terms, industrial production both in Hungary generally and in Slovakia ranked in the bottom one-third of European lands, with Slovakia outproducing only Russia and the Balkan countries.[59]

Industry in Slovakia after 1900 began to grow up, along with that of Hungary in general, around a number of large, localized concerns. These included many factories that have continued to function as the core of late-twentieth century Slovak industry — textile works in

Žilina, Rajec, Čadca, and Trenčín; cotton mills in Ružomberok; cement works in Lietavská Lučka; and a rather diversified industrial center in Pozsony including oil refineries, electrotechnical works, machine factories, and other plants. In various parts of Slovakia there were sugar refineries, cabinetry factories, leatherworks, metalworks, a few machine factories, chemical enterprises, and so on.[60] Coal and iron ore were found in abundance, and mining had become important. However, the fact that considerable amounts of iron *ore* were exported indicates a relative scarcity of smelting facilities.[61] We might therefore conclude that Slovakia was approaching something of a "take-off" point but had not yet become economically modernized.[62] Large parts of the rural areas remained remote and only marginally affected by the modernizing process.

The educational sphere was the least developed. Few Slovaks received a substantial education, for in order to become schooled beyond the primary level during the decades prior to the world war, one had to attend Magyar-language schools. Three Slovak-language secondary schools had been opened in the 1860s, but these were closed under the regime of Prime Minister Kálmán Tisza in 1875 as a means of counteracting what Tisza saw as a panslavist threat.[63] In subsequent years even primary education became harder for Slovaks to obtain. As of 1869 there were nearly two thousand primary schools where instruction was given in the Slovak tongue; this number was systematically reduced, and by 1912 there were only approximately 240 remaining.[64] G. W. Prothero estimated that only "some 8 percent" of school-age Slovak children attended primary school in 1910.[65] It is small wonder, given the scarcity of schools in their own language. Relatively few Slovaks spoke Magyar.[66] True, those who did could often advance into secondary school and even (occasionally) move into institutes of higher education. Here again, statistics show that this was the province of a privileged few. In 1898, for example, only 89 Slovaks were enrolled in higher trade schools compared with 3,938 Magyars, only nine Slovaks in technical institutes (cf. 1,221 Magyars), and 63 Slovaks in universities.[67]

The dearth of educational opportunities ensured the perpetuation of unsophisticated attitudes, a low standard of living, and the lack of widespread knowledge about social and political matters. Contrasted with the educational system in the Czech lands, the difference is obvious. The schools, a vital factor in the political socialization of contemporary Czechs, could have no comparable effect upon the Slovaks.

In contrast to the already modern Czech society, then, Slovak society was just beginning to modernize. Better put, it was a society of differential modernization. For the most part Slovakia was composed of villages and rural hamlets joined together loosely by a common language and a shared history, populated by people who had (at most) a limited consciousness of national identity. In addition, however, there existed enclaves of modernization where industry had begun to develop, opportunities for social mobility were greater, and a mixture of ethnic groups ensured some exchange of experiences as well as a sharpening of national consciousness. The interchange between Slovak and Magyar in the mixed communities produced a small number of Slovaks who learned the Magyar language, went to school, and then either became estranged from their own ethnicity as *Magyarones* or turned their education to use for the Slovak national cause. We shall presently return to a discussion of the intelligentsia, but let us first take one more look at Slovak mass society.

In the villages, the age-old ritual of traditional life was punctuated by a primitive religious outlook. Roman Catholicism was very strong and lacked the modernist tendencies it had taken on among the Czechs. Rural Protestantism, too, often manifested a more dogmatic tendency than was present in the freethinking neo-Hussitism of Bohemia. The peasant accepted his religion with a mixture of superstition. If he was a Catholic (and chances were high that he was) he identified whatever nationalistic feelings he had as a Slovak with the Church. His village priest was a man of unquestioned authority whose ecclesiastical training outside the village lent him an air of omniscience among his uneducated flock. Indeed, the relationship of priest to villagers was aptly — and consciously — symbolized by the shepherd-flock metaphor. This was more than just a biblical reference, for the priest played a vital role in the entire complex of village life, conscientiously tending his flock. He was confessor, celebrant, counselor, teacher — and, very often, political spokesman. His flock followed him, trusted him because he knew what was best for them.

Within the flock, strict patriarchal authority over the family mirrored the authority of the priest over the village. The traditional extended family persisted as the basis of Slovak village society until late in the nation's history, breaking down concomitantly with the industrialization of the region.[68] That is to say, the extended family broke down gradually as occupational alternatives to agriculture drew men into the factories to escape the poverty of the overpopulated countryside. This process of social change, like that of industialization itself, began toward the end of the nineteenth century around the new industrial centers and spread outward very gradually, continuing for several decades into the twentieth century. To a significant extent patriarchal authority within the family has persisted strongly to this day, and the strength of the father's authority within families today contrasts with the relatively more egalitarian family patterns among Czechs.[69]

From these deeply ingrained microsocial patterns evolved parallel strains in the Slovak nationalist movement. Slovak nationalism sprang from the countryside. Its most important political vehicle for half a century, the Slovak People's party, was founded by a Roman Catholic priest, Andrej Hlinka. Many of its leading personalities were clerics, and its primary basis of support was among the Catholics of the rural regions. The head of the Slovak Republic (1939–45), the only nominally independent Slovak state since the Dark Ages, was a priest. The party's ideology, from its inception to its death, centered around the concept of a mystical union between church and nation. It was a highly authoritarian party, both in ideology and in organization; although not without its internal factions, the party commanded a fanatical loyalty from its members and supporters. Throughout its history, the Slovak People's party was considered synonymous with the name of its leader — Hlinka until his death in 1938, Tiso thereafter. In fact, even the name of the party came to reflect this absolute personal identification; in 1925 the party's name was changed to *Hlinka's* Slovak People's party (*Hlinková slovenská ľudová strana,* HSĽS).

In fact, Slovak political parties in general reflected the same personality syndrome. Throughout the First Republic the Slovak wing of the Agrarian party was commonly referred to as Hodža's party (after Milan Hodža), the Social Democrats were Dérer's party (after Ivan Dérer), and the Protestant National party was called the Rázus National party (after its leader Martin Rázus).[70] The heads of the respective parties understandably wielded enormous power as a result of their public prestige. As we have seen in chapter five, the tendency to intraparty discipline prevailed within Czech and Czechoslovak parties as well throughout the First Republic, but with the possible exceptions of Švehla (Agrarians), Gottwald (Communists), and Kramář (National Democrats), the personality syndrome was not as strong in the public eye as it was in Slovakia. Class, religion, and special interests were stronger points of identification among the Czech parties than were their individual leaders.

Not surprisingly, a major conflict developed within Slovak politics around the issue of nationalism versus Czechoslovakism. The conflict began shortly before the First World War and continued to dominate the national politics until 1938. The configuration of sides in the conflict reflected underlying divisions within the society. These divisions, in the first instance, grew out of diverging strains in the earlier cultural revival and, secondly, coalesced around new divisions in the Slovak political elite. In contrast to the cleric-politicians of the People's party, there emerged a small group of *intelligent*-politicians among the Czechoslovaks. The latter were generally members of the professional or middle strata, and they were often Protestants or atheists. Hodža and Dérer were lawyers, Vlček a historian, Šrobár and Pavol Blaho physicians. Emanuel Lehocký, the founder of the Slovak Social Democratic party, was trained as a tailor but became a newspaper editor. Milan Rastislav Štefánik, who was to join the Czechoslovak independence movement during the world war from his position in France, was an astronomer.

Intensifying the cleavage between Slovak nationalists and Czechophiles were their religious differences. Ecclesiastical jurisdiction over the Roman Catholic parishes had long been exercised from Hungary, and therefore the Slovak Catholic hierarchy had developed a strong allegiance to Budapest which was not matched by their more recent political attachment to Prague. Despite the fact that many of the clergy blamed the Hungarians for Slovakia's pre-war oppression, they tended to remain faithful to their ecclesiastical superiors, choosing thereby to separate their attitudes toward religious authority from their views of political authority.[71] Slovak Protestants, on the other hand, had no ambivalence about their dislike for Hungary and indeed had reasons to feel an allegiance to Prague: their religion had originally come to them through Czech Hussite missionaries, their Bible was the Czech Kralice Bible, and their clergy was largely educated in Bohemia. It is small wonder, therefore, that Slovak Protestants were more receptive to the Czechoslovak idea than were Slovak Catholics.[72]

It is an oversimplification to break down the Slovak political movement into only two strains. The Social Democrats were not identical with the members of the National party, many of whom were to transfer their loyalties after 1918 to the Agrarians; nor were Hodža and the people around him in every respect like those around Šrobár and the Hlasists. Furthermore, the Protestant nationalists occupied an anomalous position somewhat on the margins of the budding Slovak political activity, neither allied with the Hlinka populists nor sympathetic to Czechoslovakism.[73]

The Rázus group aside, it is nevertheless justifiable to view the primary division among Slovak politicians as one between the nationalists and the Czechoslovaks. The differences between Hodža and the Hlasists were not important enough to outweigh their natural alliance for the Czechoslovak cause, and the orientation of the Social Democrats on this question was similarly compatible with that of the Hlasists.[74] Indeed, in the very early years of Slovak political movements, all were more or less united in a common purpose. Prior to their secession and formation of an independent party in 1913, the Slovak populists formed a part of the Hungarian People's party, within which they worked to promote the national cause; in the 1906 elections, Hodža and Šrobár appeared on this party's list of candidates for parliament. The Social Democrat Dérer and the future Agrarian Milan Ivanka both wrote articles for the nationalist newspaper *Katolícke noviny* (Catholic News). This cooperation between Protestants and Catholics, Hlasists and nationalists, disintegrated following the notorious Csernova affair of October 27, 1907.[75] The imprisoned Hlinka underwent a serious reconsideration of his position and emerged with the conviction that the real enemies of Slovak nationalism were the Hlasists, Socialists, Protestants and freethinkers who had become more and more active during his stay in prison.[76] Thereafter Hlinka led his L'udáks (*l'udáci,* as the populists were called) into a long fight not just for national rights or independence but for an amalgam of ideological-cum-theocratic principles that would be central to *l'udáctvo* (populism) for the rest of its development.

Seen in a longer perspective, the temporary alliance of Catholic populists and not-so-Catholic Hlasists was a shaky one. The two movements came together because of the extreme difficulties inherent in Slovak politics at the turn of the century. They were probably predestined to separate, not only because of the differences in their current leaderships but also because of their longer historical roots. The Catholic populists sprang from the native soil; the priests who formed the core of their leadership came directly from peasant backgrounds, usually left their immediate district only long enough to receive their theological training, and returned to minister to a population that accepted them as its own flesh and blood. The Hlasists, on the other hand, stemmed from the tradition of Kollár and Šafárik, Protestants educated abroad. This was a tradition of clergymen and literati who, in contrast to the populist priests, admired the neighboring Czech society and adopted a cosmopolitan outlook parallel to that characterizing the Czech intelligentsia. With their belief in reason, progress, and democracy, the Hlasists found a readier audience among Slovak Protestants, although some Catholics of the middle and professional strata embraced them.[77]

It was from the latter movement that Slovak agrarianism emerged. The Slovak wing of the Agrarian party was formed after independence, but the basic precepts of Slovak agrarianism were articulated by Hodža before the world war. Hodža was instrumental in the "agrarianization" (his term) of the old National party; the latter had been threatened with extinction because of its increasing tendency to appear as a party of bankers and lawyers. The effort met with some success, and the agrarianized National party began to attract the support of peasants and small craftsmen as well as the professional strata. The party never managed, however, to shed its "Protestant" image and continued to be at its strongest wherever it was able to project itself as a party of "Evangelical populism."[78] This public image was inherited in the First Republic by the Agrarian party, the direct descendant of the prewar National party.

The foregoing discussion about the origins of Slovak politics in the pre-independence years must be qualified by the political circumstances prevailing in Hungary. Despite the lively activity of political groups, participation in actual decision-making and even in voting was a privilege that relatively few Slovaks enjoyed. Because of discriminatory election laws, only eight percent of all Slovaks voted in the 1901 parliamentary elections; in 1906, the year of widest Slovak participation, the proportion was 15 percent. The secret ballot, standard in the Austrian half of the Empire, was unknown in Hungary, and those who were allowed to vote did so in the knowledge that their ballots would very likely be subject to official scrutiny. Voters were commonly influenced by pressures on the part of the militia and sometimes the army. Corruption was ever-present; offices could be bought, and the chances of a poor candidate's being elected were consequently slight. Not surprisingly, few Slovaks were ever elected to the Hungarian parliament. In 1901 there were four Slovak delegates, in 1905 one, in 1906 seven, and in 1913 only three.[79]

This was in dramatic contrast to the well-developed parliamentary politics in the Czech lands, and it should have indicated that the prospects for a smooth political integration were doubtful. In fact the relative weakness of the Slovaks' political experience before independence was a critical factor in the political alignments of the First Republic.

On the other hand, the political activity between 1900 and 1914 had generated some effect on the Slovaks' political awareness. This could not be seen in electoral statistics, but one measure of the growing public consciousness was the number of readers reached by the press of the national political groups. The leading periodical was *Slovenský týždenník,* a weekly published in Budapest by the agrarian wing of the National party, with a circulation of more than 14,000. The populist paper *Ľudové noviny* reached a readership of 12,000. *Slovenské robotnícke noviny,* the newspaper of the Social Democratic party, together with its monthly magazine *Napred,* were read by 8,000 people, and the older organ of the National party, *Národnie noviny,* was read by 1,000.[80] Another measure is the large number of Slovaks arrested for political crimes — according to one observer, more than 500 between 1896 and 1908.[81] It is hard to tell exactly how "political" all the offenses were, but it serves to reason that the arrests had the effect of further politicizing those involved and many around them.

A further factor that undoubtedly played a role in the politicization of Slovaks was the First World War. For several decades the Hungarian rulers had systematically repressed the schools and the budding cultural institutions of the Slovaks. Now Slovaks were forced to fight in a war for their oppressors. Between 400,000 and 450,000 Slovak men fought in the Austro-Hungarian Army, while at home their families suffered intense economic hardship and official harassment. There were some revolts at the front, such as the mutiny of the 71st Regiment in June of 1918, and significant numbers of Slovaks joined the Czechoslovak Legions abroad. Strict military discipline prevented widespread disruptions at the front, and strong-armed measures taken by the militia forestalled any serious rebellion among the civilians.[82] The world war thus heightened Slovak nationalism, as the hardships visited upon the public increased and the repression became excessive.[83]

The war did not contribute to the nation's preparation for democracy. The Slovaks entered the union of 1918 politically divided along the lines outlined above, although by the time of independence all major political groups favored union with the Czechs. Even Hlinka joined in the momentous decision reached at Turčiansky sv. Martin on May 24, 1918, to pursue Czechoslovak union. This decision, made primarily by representatives of the National party, gave birth to a Slovak National Council comprising prominent politicians of all current persuasions. On October 30, 1918, this body proclaimed Slovakia's independence from Hungary and approved union with Prague.[84] The harmony among the political groups proved to be short-lived, and within a year after independence the prewar division had reappeared.

In fact, the developments that took place in the decade preceding the First World War were to determine the configuration of political forces in Slovakia until 1948. The division between nationalists and Czechoslovaks ran through the middle of Slovak politics, while the Social Democrats diverged from the Agrarians and former Hlasists on strictly ideological matters. The division of the Social Democrats into SDs and Communists completed the picture of major political forces. Thereafter, the basic pattern of social forces and their attachment to the various political movements changed relatively little in the inter-war years, and the same was true of the general orientations of the parties themselves. The nationalists, centered in the Hlinka and Rázus parties, strove unceasingly and intemperately to increase Slovak self-rule; the Czechoslovaks fought to preserve central control. The position of the Communists, as we shall see in the following chapter, was rather more complicated.

Czechoslovakism Triumphant

The evidence bearing upon Czech-Slovak relations between 1918 and 1938 is mixed. On the one hand, there was no overt discrimination against Slovaks. Constitutionally they had equal rights, and in the cultural sphere they enjoyed absolute freedom to continue their traditions, receive an education in their own language, worship when and as they pleased, and vote in secret elections for the candidates of their own choosing, who in turn had every reasonable chance to win. Slovaks advanced to the highest ranks of government, including the cabinet, and in 1935 Milan Hodža became prime minister. Even two Ľudáks, Josef Tiso and Marko Gažík, served a brief period in the cabinet as heads of the public health and unification ministries, respectively.[85]

On the other hand, the Czech national element was dominant over the Slovak in many respects, whether intentionally or not. Some examples: the use of the Czech language in official matters whenever it was inconvenient to use both Czech and Slovak; the "colonization" of Slovakia throughout the interwar period by many Czech teachers, civil servants, and businessmen; and the naming of Bratislava University after the seventeenth-century Bohemian educator and patriot Jan Amos Komenský (Comenius), rather than after Štúr or some other appropriate Slovak.[86]

Initially, at least, it was quite natural that Czechs should have been so dominant. It was they who had the trained personnel available to fill the many juridical, educational, administrative, and entrepreneurial positions left vacant with the exit of the Hungarians or created newly by the Czechoslovak authorities. In the first twelve years following independence, more than 1400 teachers and other educational personnel went from the Czech lands to Slovakia. Similar migrations occurred in other professions as Czechs found the Slovak job market to be in need of their talents.[87] The Czechophile Slovaks welcomed this influx and readily admitted the need for Czech expertise.[88] The nationalists, on the other hand, considered the matter a question of colonization and resented the fact that so many Czechs held positions of power and responsibility in their land. Not only did the Czechs attain enviable positions in Slovak society, but they also were able thereby to exert assimilationist influences on the Slovaks.[89]

There was undoubtedly a need for Czech officials and teachers in the early years, at least until Slovaks could be sufficiently trained to perform the essential tasks. Some progress was made in this respect, but it was not enough to satisfy the most nationalistic Slovaks.[90] By the second decade of the First Republic the situation had become rather complicated. Professional positions in the Czech lands were adequately filled; the Czechs who had migrated to Slovakia would therefore have had a difficult time finding employment had they returned. Moreover, most of them had settled comfortably into Slovakia, established homes, raised their children, in some cases married Slovaks. Thus the "colonization" of Slovakia by Czech professionals had taken on an air of permanency.

Along with Czech personnel came, of course, Czech capital. The dream of Kálal to help Slovakia along economically became a fruitful business proposition for Czech industrialists and bankers. For the latter (bankers) this was especially true. The larger Czech banks had already made significant inroads into Slovak finance before independence; by 1912 the second-largest Slovak-owned bank, the Úverová Banka (Bank of Credit) in Ružomberok, according to a recent analysis, "was in fact an affiliate of the Živnostenská Banka (in Prague)."[91] With the political consolidation of Czech and Slovak lands, the previous restrictions placed on Czech capital by the Hungarian state were removed. Czech financial institutions now occupied the favorable position previously occupied by bankers in Budapest and Vienna. The smallness and provinciality of Slovak banks, together with the flight of much Hungarian and Viennese capital, left the field open for the Prague banking concerns. These, led by the dynamic Živnostenská Banka, now moved in to dominate Slovak financial affairs.[92]

Increased Czech capital did not automatically represent a boon to the Slovak economy. The development of the Slovak economy between 1918 and 1938 was difficult.[93] On the positive side, a rapidly rising educational standard propelled many Slovaks upward, particularly into the service sectors, finance, social services, and the medical profession. Improvements in farming methods, including the growth of cooperative movements, increased agricultural production. In general, the standard of living rose measurably. On the negative side, nearly all economic indicators rose comparatively less than in the Czech lands, and in the industrial sector the interwar years were characterized by a stagnation.[94] While in fairness it must be remembered that few Europeans at this time really understood the problems of less developed regions, there is ample reason to believe that Slovak criticisms of the First Republic's economic policies were justified.[95]

In the political sphere, Slovaks rose to the highest levels of authority. Here, however, the distinction between Czechoslovaks and Slovak nationalists came directly into play. Politicians of the Czechoslovak orientation prospered in the First Republic, while Slovak nationalists were for the greater part excluded from the Prague government. The nationalists consistently captured an impressive number of seats in the parliament, but it was the Czechoslovaks who were regularly represented within the innermost counsels of the state. The list of those appointed to cabinet positions includes (among others) Štefánik, Hodža, Šrobár, Dérer, Ivan Markovič, Juraj Slávik, Anton Štefánek, and Martin Mičura. The predominance of Agrarians is apparent from this listing; Hodža, Šrobár, Slávik, and Štefánek were Agrarians. Of the others mentioned, Dérer and Markovič were Social Democrats, Mičura was a populist allied with the Czech People's party, and Štefánik a nonpartisan.[96]

At lower levels of political organization, Slovaks were found in abundance. By 1934, 62 of 77 Slovak districts had chief administrative officers who were Slovaks; of 1,234 local auditors, 1,002 were Slovaks. In local governmental positions there were 3,191 Slovaks, 1,581 Czechs, 267 Magyars, and 82 Germans. In the public services, again Slovaks found many positions. The number of Slovaks working with the railroad in Slovakia was twice that of Czechs, and in the postal service more than three times.[97]

Within the Czechoslovak camp, both Czechs and Slovaks went to great lengths to justify their position. The task of creating a unified Czechoslovak nation ultimately did not succeed, but its failure was certainly not for want of exhortatory verbiage. Both at home and abroad, the spokesmen for the single-nation idea spent a great deal of effort on the attempt to prove the national unity of the two peoples.

It has conventionally been assumed that those who adhered to the single-nation concept were more or less homogeneous in their approach to the problem. Eugen Steiner and Samo Falťan, two recent expositors of the "Slovak dilemma," have stressed the singleminded purposes of the interwar Czechoslovaks.[98] Falťan put it this way:

> The root of the evil begins with the fact that Masaryk and the Czech bourgeoisie did not accept the Slovaks as an equal, younger brother, nor as an "immature child," as some claim. They accepted and perceived the Slovak union as a restoration and, indeed, even an "incorporation."[99]

The problem, however, was not so simple. There were many diverging interpretations of the Czech-Slovak relationship even within the camp of those who accepted the single-nation concept. A better approach to an understanding of the problem is that of Lipták, who has differentiated between Czechoslovaks and those whom he calls proponents of the "Great-Bohemia concept" (koncepcia veľkočeská).[100] The latter, centered in large part around a group of academics at Komenský University in Bratislava, believed that the Slovaks were no more than a branch of the Czech nation, that the differences between the two would be overcome as Slovaks were guided into the modern world, and that it was even somewhat superfluous to speak of the two as separate groups with separate traditions. Basing their argument largely on linguistic similarity, the Great-Bohemians phrased their argument along these lines:

> Racially and linguistically the Czechs and Slovaks are one people, the differences, if any, being psychological and not racial, and caused by long political separation into two states. Their languages are so similar that one can be said to be a dialect of the other; in reality they are but two branches of the same language which have been exposed to divergent influences. . . . How small the difference between them is appears from the fact that up until recently the Slovaks used the Czech for their literary language. . . .[101]

There are obvious shortcomings in any attempt to determine one's nationality by language alone, but some of the Great-Bohemians went so far in their assimilationist ideas that they proposed to reunify the Czech and Slovak literary languages into one. As late as 1933 Professor F. Travníček made such a proposal in the interests of furthering the cause of Czechoslovak unity.[102]

In defense of their argument, the Great-Bohemians reminded their critics that many of the Slovak awakeners of a century earlier had had similar visions of Slovak-Czech unity; Kollár had used the word "Slaveczechs" to refer to both, and Štúr's contemporary Michal Miloslav Hodža had made reference to the "Bohemian-Slovak language." The Great-Bohemian proponent Albert Pražák pointed out, moreover, that the very word "Czechoslovakia" (*Československo*) was coined by J. M. Hurban, an important Slovak linguist of Kollár's generation, in an 1839 article.[103]

For the Great-Bohemians, the leap from linguistic similarity to cultural sameness did not seem illogical. Pražák argued, for example, that despite the long political separation, Slovak literature had grown out of "Pan-Bohemian soil" (*všečeská země*); it was the fruit of "the mysterious flux of the whole nation's juices from the greater Bohemian tree."[104]

This view was supported by Václav Chaloupecký, a historian whose specialty was ancient Slovak history. Chaloupecký argued that, because the Slovaks had not experienced the painful national tragedy of the White Mountain, it was more difficult for them to evolve toward a modern democratic society.[105] They were of the same national fabric, however, because their roots were traceable back to a common seed. Professor J. Baudiš, a linguist at Prague University, agreed, and to make his argument even more forceful he added this bit of macaronic logic linking Czechs, Slovaks and Moravians: ". . . the Moravians are historically identical with the Slovaks; and as the Moravians were always regarded as Czechs, there is no reason why the Slovaks should be regarded as a different people."[106]

There was a rather fine line differentiating the Great-Bohemians from the Czechoslovaks. The latter included people with slightly differing opinions about the degree of distinction between Czechs and Slovaks, as well as the desirability of recognizing the differences and accounting for them politically. All, however, agreed that Czechs and Slovaks were best perceived as one nation sharing a common destiny, whatever their differences.[107]

Masaryk was a Czechoslovak, although it might be said that he was very near that fine line dividing Czechoslovaks from Great-Bohemians.

However, he displayed none of the condescension toward the Slovaks that characterized most Great-Bohemians. He genuinely believed in the equality of the two peoples, recognizing that some differences did exist. His religious and humanitarian outlook led him, like Kálal, to view the Slovaks as brothers. No doubt, this derived from his own mixed parentage, and although his personal identification was with the Czech traditions he always felt a closeness to Slovakia: "Both Slovaks and Czechs knew that I had always stood for Slovakia; that, as a Slovak by origin and tradition, my feelings are Slovak, and that I have always worked, not merely talked, for Slovakia. . . ."[108]

Beneš, caught up to a greater extent than Masaryk in the problem of the Slovak autonomists, had a similar view, although his was more complicated. His position shifted over time, now approaching that of the Great-Bohemians and now appearing more amenable to a larger degree of Slovak self-administration. At the Paris Peace Talks of 1919, Beneš put forth the image of a second "Switzerland" in which the various national groupings would cooperate on an equal basis.[109] To his British biographer, Compton Mackenzie, Beneš said, "We would have, like Austria-Hungary, a state of several nationalities" — only better, for national discrimination would not exist.[110] However, another argument of Beneš's seemed to lead him toward the Great-Bohemia concept. He likened Czechs and Slovaks to other European peoples who had gone through an assimilation process much earlier; the French and British had done this, and in time the Czechs and Slovaks would follow suit.[111]

Beneš vacillated considerably on the Slovak question. On the one hand he could say, as he did in 1934, that the policy of the Slovak nationalists was "a shortsighted policy, dictated by local provincial, particularist, or partisan interests" who did not understand the "historical evolution toward unity of our nation and others in Central Europe."[112] On the other hand, he could assume a more tolerant attitude:

> I say to the Slovaks — well, if you are a Slovak, and you have the conscience to be Slovak, I cannot say that you are not, because the question of nationality is not only a question of a separate language. . . . The fundamental thing to be or not to be a Slovak is if you feel you are a Slovak. If you feel you are a Slovak, I have nothing against it, but, gentlemen, *I* feel Czechoslovak; what can you say against that?[113]

The changing political circumstances of Beneš's turbulent career in large part determined his own tergiversation. In the years leading up to 1919 he carefully built up a quasi-legal argument, quite in step with the evolving Allied policy, aimed at winning international approval for Czechoslovak unity and independence. Later, confronted with the obstreperousness of the Slovak nationalists, he resorted to the chiding tone apparent in his 1934 speech cited above. Only one year later he took a more conciliatory line. Faced with the threatening international situation and restlessness among the extremists within the HSĽS, he mixed a strong plea for unity with an implicit acknowledgment of Slovak separateness.[114] Not long thereafter he allegedly promised some sort of autonomy to Slovakia in return for the support of the HSĽS for his election to the presidency.[115] With Hodža as his prime minister, Beneš gravitated toward a position still more favorable to the Slovaks, and in his Christmas Message of 1936 he referred to the need for a "balance between the West and the East of the Republic."[116]

The events of the first few years in exile, including the solidification of the clerical-fascist Slovak state, embittered Beneš toward the Slovaks. During his negotiations with the Communists in Moscow in 1943 concerning the nature of the postwar order, he reportedly refused to recognize the Slovaks as a separate nation and even reverted to his Great-Bohemian stance.[117] By the time of the Košice meeting, however, he had come to agree on the general principle of autonomy for Slovakia.[118]

Slovak nationalists have sometimes claimed that Czechoslovakism was an evil plot fabricated to conceal the underlying fact of coercive Czech chauvinism. According to Falťan, "the Czechoslovak ideology as a state ideology after 1918 had to secure and disguise this 'incorporation' into the Czech nation with force."[119] Mikus said of Masaryk and Beneš, *apropos* their Slovak policies: "Although they had succeeded in destroying Austria-Hungary in the name of the principle of nationalities, they practiced in Czecho-Slovakia a policy of denationalization toward the Slovaks identical with the one of which the Magyars had been guilty. . . ."[120]

Unless we accept either the argument that the Czechophile Slovaks were dupes or traitors, as Mikus would have us believe, or that they were simply denationalized cosmopolitans, as Falťan seems to suggest, neither of these two explanations can shed any light on the appeal of Czechoslovakism to the Slovak masses. We have already seen that significant numbers of Slovaks, many of them well educated and quite a few of the Protestant faith, believed in Czechoslovakism and worked in influential positions to further the cause of the unitary state. Here again we find no homogeneity among the personalities involved; they, like the Czechs, differed among themselves as to specific perceptions of the national task. They shared a common belief that Slovaks alone could never maintain a viable political community, that even an autonomous status within the Czechoslovak Republic would be dangerous, that a separate or autonomous Slovakia would be a threat to the republic's sovereignty as well as a factor encouraging the perpetuation of extreme parochiality and sociocultural stagnation in Slovakia.[121] Beyond these commonalities lay a number of differing outlooks on the nature of the problem as well as the correct solution of the existing conflicts and inequalities.

Perhaps closest to the Czechs was Vavro Šrobár. Šrobár's association with the original Hlasists, together with his early political experience in Slovakia, led him to believe that the solution of Slovakia's national problem lay nowhere but with the Czechs. Implicated in the political and legal events of the Csernova affair of 1907, Šrobár began at this point to envision a modern-day Greater Moravian state. The vision was drawn from the distant past of his own country. It was a romantic vision, conjuring up symbols and legends of a Czech-Slovak unity in times of antiquity.[122] As leader of the pre-independence National party, Šrobár worked during the war to secure Czech-Slovak cooperation. It was he, more than anyone else, who guided the deliberations in Turčiansky sv. Martin and gained the approval of his peers to join with the Czechs at the moment of independence.[123] Upon independence Šrobár was appointed minister for Slovakia, a post that gave him almost dictatorial power during the critical months of the provisional government, the negotiations in Paris, and the abortive attempt to establish a Slovak Soviet Reublic. Šrobár wielded his power astutely but unstintingly, thereby securing order in Slovakia but simultaneously antagonizing many of his opponents.[124] Throughout his career Šrobár fought for Czechoslovak centralism and opposed Slovak autonomy.

One of the most arrogant Czechophiles, condescending to his own conationals, was the Social Democratic leader Ivan Dérer. Impatient with those of lesser mentalities and uncomprehending with regard to the desires of the nationalists, Dérer identified thoroughly with the Czechs. He considered Slovak autonomy unthinkable, for he had no confidence in the Slovaks' ability to rule themselves. He was an admirer of the Great-Bohemian professors at Komenský University, and his disdain for the ignorance of the everyday Slovak was frequently expressed openly:

> . . . The Czech as spoken by the professors at the University is much
> closer to literary Slovak and much more dignified than the imperfect
> Slovak in which the Word of God is preached by many autonomous
> [sic] priests who to this day have not succeeded in acquiring correct
> Slovak speech and grammar. . . .[125]

A more moderate attitude was expressed by Milan Hodža. This
monumental Slovak statesman was not entirely consistent in his
politics and sometimes found himself blowing with the political
winds;[126] nevertheless, his consistent efforts at working for Slovakia
through the Czechoslovak establishment made him one of the outstanding personalities of the First Republic. Like Šrobár, he believed
that Slovakia's national traditions were rooted with those of the
Czechs, and that the two peoples' destinies were inseparably en-
twined.[127] He believed in the national unity of Czechs and Slovaks but
saw great differences between them. He believed that some of the
differences required the determined efforts of the Prague government
to guide not only educational-cultural development, but economic
investment policies as well, in order to equalize the Czech and Slovak
regions. His policies drew him into frequent controversies within the
Prague establishment, but his voice was an influential one.[128] Needless
to say, however, his dreams for the equalization of Czech and Slovak
lands were not realized, or even shared by the Czech bourgeoisie.

Hodža was in many respects an exemplary statesman whose influence, both on the Prague establishment and on his fellow Slovaks,
could not but have been positive. Many Czechs in the Czechoslovak
camp, though, did much to ruin their cause. Štepán Osuský, a longtime
Slovak diplomat associated with Czechoslovakism since the First
World War, vented his frustration with his colleagues after the fall of
the Republic:

> . . . The Slovaks did have an honorable Czechoslovak feeling and
> opinion. They were conscious that with the Czechs they formed a
> state, which was not a sheer extension of Slovakia, but represented the
> foundation of a new family. . . . these Slovaks were better patriots of
> the Czechoslovak Republic than those individual Czechs who thought
> that the Czechoslovak Republic was but an enlarged Czech kingdom,
> and carried on accordingly. . . .[129]

Osuský's complaint is harsh, but it reflects well the hard feelings that
emerged even within the Czechoslovak camp over the arrogance of

Great-Bohemia tendencies. Masaryk and Beneš themselves were not innocent of such tendencies, and although Beneš was not really a "disguised Czech racist," as Osuský charged,[130] he did not fully understand the nature and depth of Slovak nationalism. That there were substantial forces working for the Czechoslovak ideal, as Osuský claimed, cannot be denied; indeed, a younger generation of Agrarians was beginning in the 1930s to strike an interesting balance between Czechoslovakism and Slovak particularism, with significant popular support.[131] On the other hand, the ruling generation in the First Republic must be blamed for the eventual crisis in Czech-Slovak relations which contributed to the demise of the interwar order. The generation of Beneš, with some notable exceptions whose warnings were not heeded, simply overestimated the appeal of Czechoslovak unity and tragically underestimated the significance of Slovak nationalism.

The Demise of Czechoslovakism

For all practical purposes, the Czechoslovak idea died with the passing of the First Republic. The Second Republic, pointedly given the hyphenated name Czecho-Slovakia, embodied the longstanding desire of the nationalists for an autonomous Slovakia. The six years of the Slovak state (1939–45) gave further impetus to the fact of national separateness. Despite the chasm that was to develop into the Slovak National Uprising, none of the major political forces in Slovakia by 1944–45 favored a return to the single-nation principle. Even President Beneš realized that the clock could not be turned back, that after six years of separate existence Slovakia could not be reunited with the Czech lands on the basis of the interwar relationship.[132]

The Košice Program recognized the Slovaks as a distinct nation, with rights as a nation to self-determination in some aspects of government. The Czech and Slovak nations were declared to be equal, the Slovak National Council formed during the war was given wide powers of administration, Slovak military units were to be formed within the armed forces, and a pledge was made to institutionalize the status of Slovakia as an autonomous part of the Republic.[133]

The promise of the Košice Program was abandoned during the first two decades after the war. The government of the Third Republic was unable to implement the changes necessary to solidify Slovak autonomy, for the government was in a perpetual state of crisis after the first few months of its establishment. The Communists, staunchest proponents of Slovak autonomy at war's end, divided on the question of implementation, frightened by the electoral success in Slovakia of the increasingly right-of-center Democratic party. With the coup of February 1948, the Communists set about centralizing control throughout Czechoslovakia. By this time the dominant faction within the party was moving further and further away from any form of autonomy or federalization. Those within the party who resisted the recentralizing tendency — Clementis, Husák, Novomeský, and many more — were now condemned as "bourgeois nationalists" and fell victims to the purge. For Slovakia, the period to which Lipták has bitterly referred as the "years without a name" had begun.[134]

From 1948 until the mid-1960s the Communists were to follow a course more extreme in their political suppression of Slovakia than had ever been the case under the First Republic. If the First Republic's leaders followed a policy of denationalization that was subtle in word and practice, that of the Communists from Gottwald to Novotný was subtle in word only. Gottwald and his contemporaries continued for a while to pay lip service to the Slovaks' wishes, but their statements were belied by their policies. The 1948 constitution represented a significant step toward the recentralization of the state's political institutions; shortly after the adoption of the constitution, Gottwald hailed it as one that "guarantees Slovakia and Slovaks their national rights (and) provides them with the possibility and means to utilize those rights. . . ."[135] In fact, the so-called Ninth-of-May Constitution had reversed the previous assumption regarding the authority of the Slovak National Council (SNR) and made the latter subordinate to central organs in Prague.[136]

The Communist party of Slovakia (KSS) had operated independently of the Czechs since 1939. As an underground organization, the KSS had contributed greatly to the resistance movement and played a role in the national uprising unparalleled by the Communist organizations of neighboring Poland and Hungary.[137] Indeed, Slovaks had aided the Soviet Army in its liberation of the Czech lands. Therefore, justifiably, the Slovak Communists felt they deserved not only recognition and the continuation of their independent status but gratitude as well.[138] Instead, they were suddenly deprived of their independent status in 1948. The KSS remained as a formal organization, but it was now subordinated to the central Czechoslovak (KSČ) organs in what came to be known as the "asymmetrical model" of party organization.[139]

Nor did the few "refinements" in the Czech-Slovak institutional relationship in 1953, 1956, and 1960 alleviate the Slovaks' problem. In

1956 the SNR was given back some of its pre-1948 functions, such as the power to make certain administrative appointments, but it never regained any importance in the legislative area. The 1960 constitution, moreover, abolished the Slovak Board of Commissioners, a rudimentary executive set up in the postwar years but allowed to stagnate from disuse thereafter.[140]

The return to centralism by no means signaled the revival of Czechoslovakism. Communists continued to pay verbal homage, as did Gottwald in 1949, to "the individuality and equal coexistence of both of our fraternal nations."[141] In practice, the denationalization policies applied to Slovakia were applied with equal vigor in the Czech lands. Neither Slovak nor Czech nationalism was tolerated by the regime of the fifties.[142]

The reality of recentralization obscured the underlying political orientations among Slovaks, just as the superstructure of the party monolith simultaneously covered over the repluralizing social tendencies. Party members and the masses in Slovakia were no more easily assimilated into "internationalism" than they had been into Great-Bohemianism a generation earlier. The Slovak partisans of the 1940s who survived the purges of the fifties remained a relatively cohesive political group quite unassimilated into the KSČ mainstream. In the fifties, of course, they risked imprisonment or death for pursuing their nationalistic aims, and when many of them were purged, their bitterness, now repressed, intensified. In the 1960s they gradually regained the ability to articulate their grievances. The rehabilitations were too late to help those who, like Clementis, had lost their lives, but some, like Husák, who lived through their disgrace and imprisonment, emerged within the nationalist movement of the 1960s.

The Slovak movement of the sixties has been discussed in detail elsewhere,[143] but it is worthwhile recalling here that the Slovak dissent was a critical component of the upheaval that took place in the winter of 1967-68, and again in the political infighting of 1968-69. In a curious, even ironic, way the Slovak dissidents within the Communist party became the bearers of the nationalist tradition. They were, like their Ľudák predecessors in this role, united in their opposition to the centralistic regime but divided as to the ways and means of realizing Slovak political interests. All of them by 1968 favored a federal solution, but they divided according to the relative importance they attached to federalism as an issue separate from democratization. With the implementation of a new federal order in 1968-69, it seems that the long conflict between the Slovak nationalists and the advocates of the single-nation concept has been settled once and for all. That there have been shortcomings in the post-1968 situation goes without saying; in any event, the new order reflects the undying reality of Slovakia's separate nationhood, and it would seem impossible that the issue of Czechoslovakism will ever again become a matter of serious discussion.

Lipták has argued that "All shades of Czechoslovakism were profoundly undemocratic, against the interests of the people."[144] The foregoing discussion disputes this. As practiced in the First Republic, Czechoslovakism can hardly be called undemocratic. A consistent majority of voters across the republic supported parties subscribing to Czechoslovak principles, and a substantial minority of Slovaks did so as well. That Czechoslovakism was "against the interests of the people" (*protiľudový*) depends on whom one identifies as "the people." It was certainly not against the interests of *all* the inhabitants of the First Republic; it was decidedly against the interests of those who sought to express and develop an independent sense of Slovak cultural identity without the political constraints of the self-righteous, and sometimes chauvinistic, Czechs. To some extent, Czechoslovakism worked in the interests of the Slovak bourgeoisie — namely that part which profited from the influx of Czech capital. However, the same argument can be made regarding the benefits reaped by those who obtained employment in the service sectors, transportation, and other improved areas of the economy. The educational benefits were monumental and not restricted to any particular class. The experience with a truly open political system, including the scrupulous observance of the freedom of self-expression, helped to bring the Slovaks into a new stage of self-awareness. If they did not "feel Czechoslovak" as Beneš wished they would, they did not have to do so and could shout about it in public squares.

Czechoslovakism derived from an indigenous mixture of Western bourgeois-democratic political thought and Czech messianic idealism. The First Republic's leaders accepted the Anglo-French equation of nation and state, mentioned at the beginning of this chapter. Their ideal was a state dominated by a single, Czechoslovak nation embodying the best elements of Czech traditions. The basis of democracy would be the political rights of the individual, who would have no greater but no less stature in society than his neighbor, Czech or Slovak. To recognize ethnic groups as corporate entities with special collective rights was beyond the range of political values accepted by the Czechoslovaks. They assumed that their adherence to a constitutional order based on individualism would be sufficient guarantee of each person's most deeply felt interests.

In this respect, even the existence of large minorities outside the Czech-Slovak community posed no problem in theory. Germans and Magyars may not like the idea of living in a Czechoslovak state, but they would have the same rights as Czechoslovaks — again, on an individual, rather than corporate, basis. Interestingly, law-enforcement cases involving the seditious activities of national minorities were prosecuted as cases of individual felony under a statute aimed generally at countering treason, conspiracy, and violent attacks against the republic.[145]

The assumption of the First Republic's leaders, then, was that the numerically dominant "nation" of Czechoslovaks would guide the development of a truly democratic state in which even the politically disgruntled minorities would eventually come to live freely and peaceably. It was assumed that this would be a long and difficult process, but in the interim the numerical preponderance of the Czechoslovaks would enable them to handle the minorities through legal processes or with force if necessary.

The Czechoslovak idea, however, proved insufficiently persuasive to unite all Slovaks behind a common identity with the Prague government. The latter's failure to resolve the problems of Czech-Slovak relations stemming from this disunity rendered the government incapable of dealing with the minorities when faced with the crisis of 1938–39. The lesson of that critical period after Munich was one that should have been learned earlier. Because it was not, the ultimate ideal of Czechoslovakism was lost. Looking back upon the lesson of that era, no serious statesman of either nation would be willing to try it again.

VII

Slovak Nationalism

The rise of Slovak nationalism in the nineteenth century and its survival throughout the twentieth testify to the profound strength of nationalism in the modern age. A millennium of foreign rule did not erase the distinctiveness of the Slovaks, a generation of partnership with the benign but assimilation-minded Czechs failed to dilute the spirit of national separateness, and fifteen years of coercive "internationalism" left that spirit similarly intact. Through feudalism, monarchy, bourgeois democracy, and coercive socialism the nation has persevered.

This example of national perseverence is especially remarkable in light of the smallness of the population — fewer than 1.5 million in 1880, approximately 2.5 million in 1930, and 4.4 million in 1974. (See table below.)

Table 7.1

Slovak Population

	1880	1930	1974 (est.)
Slovakia, total	2,435,286	3,322,034	4,715,000
Slovaks in Slovakia	1,489,707	2,337,816	4,045,000
Slovaks in Czech lands			377,000
Slovaks in Czechoslovakia			4,422,000

Sources: Emil Mazúr, "Národnostné zloženie," in *Slovensko,* vol. 3 (*Ľud*), part 1 (Bratislava: Obzor, 1974), pp. 441, 447, 451; *Statistická ročenka* ČSSR 1975 (Praha, 1975), p. 110.

Mere survival is no small feat for a minor nation located in the very center of Europe, and the Slovak phenomenon would seem to suggest a character of extreme resiliency and pluckiness. It is significant that the favorite hero of Slovak folklore is Juraj Janošík, a Robin Hood-like character from the eighteenth century. Janošík, in most respects a common highwayman whose two-year career of brigandage led him to the gallows in 1713, is remembered in legend for his more admirable traits. It is said that his acts of robbery were aimed only at the very wealthy, the noble and the princely, and that he frequently showed mercy or even generosity to the serfs. It is said, further, that his motives were not those of the usual highwayman, but that his banditry represented his way of righting the social injustices associated with rank and wealth. According to the legend, he never killed his victims, preferring instead to let them live with the lesson of their unrighteous ways. That he was captured and executed after such a brief career by no means diminishes his legendary qualities, for during his two years of lawless activity he and his gang operated with tremendous bravura, announcing themselves upon arrival at the estates of those whom they intended to rob and evading capture through cleverness and chicanery.[1]

It is not my intention to portray Juraj Janošík as the epitome of the Slovak national character. Nor is Janošík the Slovak equivalent of Švejk (see next chapter) as a fictional paradigm illustrative of a certain social type. The legend of Janošík, however, does say something about the Slovaks, for they seem to admire Janošík's bravery, passion, and commitment to the underdog. His concern for the common people is inspiring, and the survival of his legend long beyond his death might be seen as a metaphor for the survival of the Slovak nation long after the conquest of Svätopluk's ancient realm.

When one looks for more systematic evidence concerning Slovak national character, one finds frustration. There are the inevitable clichés drawn from laymen's comparisons of Slovaks with Czechs. The Slovaks prefer wine to beer, suggesting a greater tendency to sociability. (A Slovak once asked this author, rhetorically, "Who has ever made a proper toast with beer?") They also have a greater proclivity for hard liquor, suggesting a tendency to alcoholism. They are more emotional than Czechs, but their emotionalism is expressed on a personal level rather than turned outward onto society. In contrast to Czechs, they are religious, modest, backward, distrustful of others, and lacking in messianic impulses; by way of drawing similarities with Czechs, it has been said that they are generally dovish, industrious, amply intelligent, and have a tendency toward discord.[2] Obvious exceptions can be made to these generalizations, and the fact that they have not been confirmed by either hard evidence or scholarly repetition leaves them rather unsatisfactory as descriptions of the national character.

One study of the Slovak character was made by a psychologist, Anton Jurovský. Jurovský's conclusions support several of the characteristics drawn in the preceding paragraph and add a few more observations: Slovaks have an impulse to gallantry, but this is mediated by a strong sense of inferiority; they are individualistic; they are optimistic, especially regarding the ultimate likelihood of justice. Unfortunately, Jurovský's study was published under the rigid censorship of the wartime Tiso regime, and Jurovský's mostly adulatory tone suggests a lack of objectivism.[3]

In a more recent study, Zdeněk Salzmann has compared Czech and Slovak value orientations. Drawing upon his own data gathered by means of a questionnaire administered in Czechoslovakia in 1969, Salzmann found that in no categories of value orientation did Slovaks and Czechs exhibit statistically contrary responses, but there were varying degrees of "resemblances," "similarities," "likenesses," and "identities" in the rank ordering of value indicators.[4] It is useful to consider Salzmann's conclusions regarding the relative similarity of Czech and Slovak value orientations, for so much of today's literature assumes *dissimilarity* between the two peoples. However, Salzmann's data show only hard statistical evidence based on a limited sample of respondents (approximately 400). The results must be taken as dubious, not only because they do not reflect general socio-cultural conditions but also because the questionnaire was administered at a time of extreme flux in the political and cultural circumstances of Czechoslovakia.

The relatively late emergence of the Slovak nation renders it difficult to trace the development of a distinct national character. The Czech self-analysts cited in chapter six could look back across centuries of history and refer to documented features of the Bohemian mentality. Slovaks cannot do this. What there is of an earlier history is undocumented, impossible to place in a modern context, and too distant to be a real focus of national identity. One and one-half centuries of national development might be sufficient to produce observable patterns, but when more than half that time has been spent in bondage the continuity of the tradition is difficult to establish. Moreover, the long controversy between nationalists and Czechoslovaks, as well as the denationalization atmosphere of the Stalinist years, kept the matter of national identity an open question until only recently. The Slovaks of the 1970s, therefore, found themselves scarcely a decade into the process of reestablishing connections with an extremely disjunct past.

As a final factor in the difficulty of defining the national character, one cannot but stress the pace of social and economic development in Slovakia over the course of the past few decades. In 1937, Slovakia's share in the gross industrial output of Czechoslovakia was only 7.8 percent; in 1969, it was 23.1 percent.[5] This dramatic change in the position of Slovakia within the whole republic is underscored by the changes wrought in the Slovak economy. These began during the Second World War, when German capital infused the Slovak economy with a rapid growth of heavy industry.[6] Industrial development continued apace after the war, and the growth rate of Slovak industry has consistently surpassed that of the Czech lands ever since. Between 1948 and 1971, Slovakia's proportion of the total social product of Czechoslovakia grew from 19 percent to 26.2 percent. As a proportion of the national income, the Slovak increase was from 19.2 percent to 25.9 percent.[7]

The past few decades have seen corollary changes in the demographic patterns of Slovakia. As in most modernizing societies there has been a measurable shift of population to the towns and cities. In 1950, 55.9 percent of Slovakia's population lived in localities of fewer than 2,000 inhabitants; in 1970, only 42.7 percent still lived in such rural and small-village settlements.[8] The cities have mushroomed; Bratislava grew from 192,896 in 1950 to 285,448 in 1970, Košice from 79,352 to 144,445, Prešov from 22,843 to 54,942, Žilina from 26,034 to 49,867, and so on.[9] Of all cities with more than 5,000 inhabitants, only six lost population.[10]

The numbers of Slovaks trained for skilled labor and for the professions have greatly increased. In 1953 there were only 67,900 skilled laborers in Slovakia; by 1970 the number had surpassed 350,000. In 1953 there were 14,700 people who had received higher education degrees; in 1970 the number was 80,900; the statistics for middle-school education are, respectively, 53,200 and 266,500.[11] Illiteracy, which characterized fifteen percent of the population in 1921 and eight percent in 1930, was totally removed by 1948.[12]

These are only random statistics, but they speak for the intensity of modernization in Slovakia. The process has been uneven; one does not need statistics to see the persisting gap between the motorized cities and the oxcart society still prevalent in many rural areas. Nor has the overall gap between Slovak and Czech economies been closed, despite the proportionately greater rate of growth in Slovakia.

The economic and demographic changes in Slovakia have uprooted

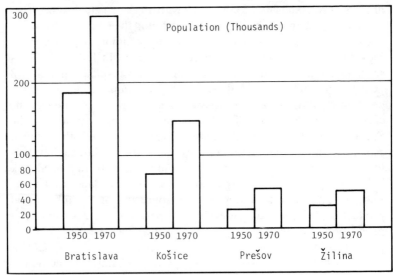

Figure 7.1

Population Growth of Four Slovak Cities, 1950–70

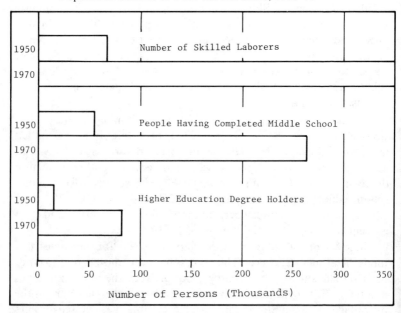

Figure 7.2

Three Social Indicators: Slovakia 1950 and 1970

the traditional order, reversing the balance between rural and urban populations and drawing ever more people into the current of modernization. The gap between the more modern and the more traditional localities remains a salient factor, but the patterns of village life no longer dominate Slovak society. It is a society of differential modernization, but the center of Slovak culture has now shifted to the cities and larger towns. The process continues with no apparent slackening of the general trend in sight.

The foregoing discussion illustrates the fluidity of Slovak society and suggests that the national character cannot be easily defined. Yet within the context of that fluidity there is a pattern of nationalist politics which has been, in some ways, constant over the past half-century. The continuities in Slovak nationalist politics tell us something about the Slovak political culture, a culture that has been more in flux over the past fifty years than that of the Czechs, but is still partially rooted in patterns developed over many years of political experience.

The Nationalist Position, Bourgeois and Communist

In 1968 the government of the Czechoslovak Socialist Republic adopted a plan to convert the unitary state into a federal republic of two constituent parts, the Czech Socialist Republic and the Slovak Socialist Republic. The latter two were given a rather broad range of autonomous responsibilities, including the administrative and legislative institutions necessary to carry out those responsibilities. Overarching the two constituent republics is the federal (Czechoslovak) republic, with all its continuing institutions and a range of powers and responsibilities stipulated by law. The plan was passed by the (federal) National Assembly on October 27, 1968 and became operative in January of 1969. Thus was the dream of many a Slovak nationalist achieved — a formally designated, institutionally realized, legally guaranteed, separate political status for Slovakia.[13] Of all the reforms enacted or proposed in 1968, the federal reform is the only one of major significance to have survived the months following the Warsaw Pact invasion. The autonomous status of socialist Slovakia does not incorporate all the desires of the most fervid Slovak nationalists, but it does represent the fruits of a fifty-year struggle for national recognition within the Czechoslovak state.

The Slovak problem had been a thorny one ever since the beginnings of Slovak politics in the Austro-Hungarian Empire. It was not resolved by union with the Czechs and persisted as a major political issue throughout the interwar years. The reemergence of the Slovak problem in the 1960s was, therefore, rooted in the failure to solve the nationality question earlier in this century. The intervening years of war, the Slovak Republic and the National Uprising, liberation, revolution, promises made and forsaken — all had important conditioning effects upon the nature of the Slovak problem. The wounds of 1939–45 were slow to heal among a population so deeply divided as were the Slovaks. Socialism did not heal the wounds and indeed, as socialism came to be practiced after 1948, the wounds were reopened and left to fester until the sixties. The new nationalists of the sixties inherited this long and bitter legacy, now all the more bitter because of the Communists' broken promises. Nevertheless, the new nationalists resolved to work for a solution of the Slovak problem within the context of the Marxist-Leninist reality of their era. The fact that they themselves were Marxist-Leninists gave their cause an ideological legitimacy *vis à vis* Prague that their precursors had lacked. This ideological legitimacy enabled them to succeed where the earlier generation of Slovak nationalists had failed.

The matter of a "Czech problem," as we saw in the preceding chapter, came up during the sixties, but because the longstanding fact of Czech dominance over Slovaks was so obvious, the Czech question never assumed the salience of the Slovak problem.[14] The road to federalism was built by Slovaks and engineered to help *them* — not the Czechs — reconcile their long need to clarify the meaning of their national purpose and its political implications.

In this light, it is instructive to compare the ideals and purposes of *Ľudáctvo* (populism) and the Communist nationalism of the sixties. To do so requires skipping across the years separating the two movements, as well as some degree of simplification, but it is nonetheless useful to make the comparison in order to examine the continuities in Slovak nationalism over the half-century following 1918.

The dissimilarities in the two movements are easy to find. Most obviously, the Ľudáks and the Communists occupied the opposite ends of the political-ideological spectrum in Czechoslovakia. The position of the HSĽS was that of a reactionary force in society, tied to the primitive authority patterns of the Slovak village, resistant to modernism, defensive of individualism within the limitations of traditional authority, theocratic, and hostile to socialism. The revolutionary ethos of communism was inimical to *Ľudáctvo*, and even such reformist measures as the redistribution of rural lands were viewed by the Ľudáks with some suspicion. The Communists always looked

forward to the arrival of modern, industrial society with its burgeoning
proletariat and its progressive class struggle; the Ľudáks resented the
advance of industrial society, regretted the materialistic influence it
had on the masses, saw in factory life the seeds of godlessness and the
despoliation of peasant innocence. The Communists espoused the
overthrow of the traditional elite and the eventual democratization of
authority; the Ľudáks dreamed of a society in which divinely ordained
leaders would look after the masses, unworthy as the latter were for
positions of responsibility. With the attainment of something approximating the Ľudák ideal state in 1939, the supporters of that state could
refer to it as the embodiment of the thousand-year Slovak quest for
national fulfillment; [15] in the eyes of the Communist Gustáv Husák, on
the contrary, the wartime Slovak Republic was characterized by
"tyranny" and ruled by men who were "traitors and cowards." [16]

The Ľudáks considered Roman Catholicism an inseparable feature
of the Slovak national character, and to the extent that the political
merger with the Czechs called this equation into question, the Ľudáks
resented the First Republic. They disliked being ruled by Protestants,
looking upon the Czech ruling group as heretics and the Slovak
Protestants as something akin to traitors. The diligent efforts of
Masaryk to secure the separation of church and state throughout
Czechoslovakia was met by the opposition of the Ľudáks, whose
political roots were in a prewar party formed in protest against the
secularization of marital laws in old Hungary. [17] A wave of strong anticlericalism swept through Czech society in 1918–19, as anti-Catholic
zealots vented their rage against the religion so closely associated with
the bygone days of Habsburg rule. Many Czechs left the Catholic
Church during this time, some of them finding a home in the new,
liberal-Protestant Czechoslovak Church and others becoming atheists
or agnostics. In some places religious statues were toppled and other
damage was done to churches and church properties. [18] Understandably, the Ľudáks viewed this with horror, and when Jan Hus Day
was proclaimed as a national holiday throughout the Republic, the
Ľudáks were duly incensed. [19]

The Tiso regime embodied the most extreme extensions of Ľudák
philosophy, beginning with fanatical theocratism. In the mind of Tiso,
all mundane affairs were subordinate to the will of God as interpreted
by His priests and other churchly representatives. Tiso looked to the
authority structure of the Roman Catholic Church as a model for
adaptation to secular society. Within the Church, the individual stood
at the base of the structure; over him was the parish, and overarching

the parish was the church universal. As a secular parallel to this neat arrangement Tiso saw the individual at the base of society, the family over the individual, and the nation over the family.[20] To Tiso, his little Slovak state was the perfect place to develop a national community along these corporate lines. Although the reality of force and subservience to the German Reich belied Tiso's ideal, the leaders of the Slovak Republic imagined themselves to be building what one observer has called a solidary state, based on a mystical union of people and community under the ultimate authority of the Roman Catholic Church. If the ideal were to be realized, the organic bond between the individual and the nation would overcome all class conflicts and all divisions of society according to other socio-political criteria, thus creating a society in which the will of the people would be achieved through corporate consensus, bypassing the problematical question of majoritarianism.[21]

Communists, too, believe in a social order that transcends "bourgeois" majoritarianism and embodies corporatist unity, but of course that unity derives from entirely secular sources. There is a mysticism involved in the communist ideal of proletarian unity, but all images of a divinely ordained system are rejected. The cement that holds the working class together in its corporate solidarity is the identity of self-interests, forged during the lengthy pre-revolutionary struggle and solidified in the process of creating a radically new society. Unlike the Ľudáks, who hoped to carry over traditional authority patterns into their new society, the Communists would discard the ways of the old.

Within this context, the Communist nationalists argued, nationalism reaches its fullest potential as a *revolutionary* force — not as a force of maintaining tradition. Husák argued that the origins of nationalism within the Austro-Hungarian Empire had cast the national groups into roles of a revolutionary nature, and this revolutionary character has persisted ever since as the driving force of nationalism. The basic issue in the late twentieth century is similar to that of a century earlier: the creation of an order in which nations are equal. Only when the nation is equal to other nations, Husák argued, can individuals within that nation be truly free. In the Czechoslovak Republic, as in Austria-Hungary, the Slovaks were not equal and, therefore, not free.[22]

That these notions seem to contradict Marxist principles was a sensitive matter. Marx had had ambivalent views on nationalism. Generally, he saw it as a distraction from the international unity of the working class. At the same time, he realized the revolutionary potential in certain "progressive" nationalist movements such as the German, Polish, and Irish movements. Slovak nationalism did not fit his paradigm of progressive national movements, however, largely because it seemed to interfere with the Hungarian national revolt in 1848, with which Marx sympathized.

The Slovak Communists argued, in essence, that what Marx had said was correct in his day and for his geographical location, but Marx had not spoken to the problems of smaller nations within socialist states — obviously a hypothetical situation in Marx's day. The reality of Czechoslovakia in the 1960s was that two nations, theoretically equal, existed within one state, and the smaller of the two was not accorded the rights and privileges of the larger. In this context, as Husák put it, a "realistic application of Marxist principles" had to take nationality into account. This could be done only by establishing complete, institutionalized equality for both the *Staatsvölker*.[23]

Whereas the Communist nationalists believed that their system — because it was socialist — could be changed to account for the national problem, the Ľudáks were profoundly distrustful of the First Republic and its value system, derived as it was from Western-liberal ideas.[24] They saw Czech libertarianism as an evil, anarchistic tendency quite contradictory to their own conservative view of authority, and their attitude toward democracy was skeptical. As Sidor put it, "Democracy? That is only a method of ruling. A method will not rule; rather, people rule. People rule over other people."[25] The Ľudáks' skepticism about democracy reached the outright rejection of majoritarianism in the Tiso regime. Tiso did not reject the idea of democracy, but he did have a different interpretation of it compared to that of the First Republic's leaders. To Tiso, democracy meant the rule of the whole people, the corpus, irrespective of what the majority might appear to want:

> There is a difference between liberalism and real democracy. Real democracy is the equality of the people, measured according to merit and capability and not according to sheer majority. The majority can be stupid and need not be right.[26]

In the earlier years the Ľudáks believed that the way to Slovak self-rule lay in autonomous status within the Czechoslovak Republic. Hlinka had envisioned a degree of autonomy for Slovakia sufficient to allow the Slovaks to escape the secularizing trends emanating from Prague.[27] The policies of the HSĽS throughout the twenties reflected

Hlinka's belief that autonomy within a loose Czechoslovak state was preferable to the alternatives of Slovak independence (an unrealistic proposition) and reunification with Hungary (not very promising, judging from past experience).[28] In any event Hlinka realized that, whatever the flaws of the First Republic, the freedom of the Slovaks to organize and articulate their desires was cause to believe in the possible improvement of the national situation. The system's failure to satisfy the Ľudáks caused Hlinka to shift in the 1930s toward a position more hostile to the First Republic.[29] It was only after his death, however, that the HSĽS, assiduously wooed by Hitler, definitively entered the path of separatism.

The Communists' position on this question went through several permutations. By the 1960s, Slovak Communists were united in their support of Czechoslovakia, but at earlier moments they had shown evidence of doubts about the viability of the Czech-Slovak state. In 1918–19, Slovak contingents within the Bolshevik party and the Hungarian Communist party had advocated the secession of Slovakia from the First Republic and its incorporation into the Soviet Union. Twenty years later, in 1939, the Communist underground in Slovakia adopted the slogan "For a free, independent Slovakia." In the following year the Central Committee of the KSS shifted to another position behind the slogan of a "Soviet Slovakia," thereby reviving the earlier idea. Husák himself was reported to have supported the incorporation of Slovakia into the USSR at one point during the Second World War. All of these positions were repudiated by the exiled leadership of the KSČ. One might in any event wonder how serious the idea of secession was, for the international situation in 1939 was so confusing (with Stalin and Hitler in alliance) that the Slovak Communists' own confusion is entirely understandable.[30]

Whatever secessionist tendency these wartime policies might have represented, there was no parallel to them in the Slovak movement of the 1960s, for despite the deformities of the preceding decade, the Communist nationalists were loyal to the Republic. The nearest approximation to a secessionist idea at this time came from the pen of a non-Marxist historian, Daniel Rapant, who broached the subject most cautiously and hypothetically. In the past as well as at present, he wrote, the union of Czechs and Slovaks was "politically the most acceptable solution out of all feasible and unfeasible combinations." Rapant suggested that this arrangement might not be the best for all times. If in a future European order all nationality problems — including that of a divided Germany — might be settled, then perhaps all nations, great and small, might be fully self-determining.[31]

The manner and tone in which the nationalist objection could be publicly expressed highlights the different political contexts of the Ľudák and Communist national movements. The Ľudáks were blunt and shrill, frequently engaging in hyperbole, arguing their case from the soap-box or on the floor of the Prague parliament. They criticized their antagonists unmercifully and cast aspersion on the Czechophile Slovaks. Once during a parliamentary debate, when Hodža alluded to Czechoslovak tendencies among Slovaks, Hlinka challenged his and (especially) his Czech colleagues' presumption to speak for the Slovaks:

> Just as an individual, when he has reached maturity, has the right to say who he is, what he is, and what his name is, so the Slovak nation has the right to say whether it is Slovak or Czecho-Slovak. Esteemed colleagues, neither the National Assembly nor any individual Czechs have the right to determine this; no one except the sovereign Slovak nation can decide this.[32]

The debate of the sixties never became quite so bitter as that of the twenties and thirties. The dissent of the Communist nationalists was expressed with some fear, at first, then gradually more and more openly, but at no time did the Communists plunge into the fiery rhetoric of the Ľudáks. The unspoken rules of the system dictated that the Slovaks couch their argument in terms of socialist brotherhood, democratic equality, and dialectical progress. By 1968 the discussion had become open and frank — but always within the framework of accepted rhetoric.

Beyond the differences of ideology, historical context, and rhetoric, it is possible to find some important similarities between the politics of the Ľudáks and that of the Communist nationalists. The first is their mutual insistence on a well-rounded, institutionalized solution to the Slovak problem. Hlinka would not have been satisfied with mere economic progress, for aside from the evils of industrialization he was aware that Slovak national identity could not be found in creature comforts. Nor did he trust in promises of future equality, for the future offered by the Czechoslovaks promised equality only as a reward for denationalization. Likewise, the Communist nationalists insisted on a multifaceted program of equality, cultural as well as political. They argued that the economic progress since the war had not led to a standard of living equal to that of the Czech lands, Slovak educational standards lagged far behind Czech, and the cultural policies of the post-1948 regime had led to a stagnation of Slovak literature, radio and television.[33]

Indeed, broken promises were a *leitmotif* of Slovak grievances both after 1919 and after 1948. The Ľudáks pointedly and repeatedly reminded Masaryk of the clause in the 1918 Pittsburgh Agreement promising autonomy for Slovakia, and they also referred upon occasion to the alleged secret clause in the agreement of Turčiansky sv. Martin, qualifying the Czecho-Slovak union as one contingent upon autonomous status for Slovakia.[34] When Ľudák delegates attempted to present a plan for autonomy to the National Assembly in 1922, Sidor reports, they were shouted down by the Czechs and Czechoslovaks.[35] An administrative reform adopted by the Assembly in 1927 had been drawn up by a government that included two Ľudák ministers, but this measure, based as it was on a compromise that fell far short of actual autonomy, failed to satisfy the Ľudáks. The latter left the government coalition in 1929, never to return.[36]

Similar promises were made at Košice in 1945 and broken in Prague thereafter. Given the need for tact and metaphor, it was not as easy for the Communist nationalists to refer to these promises as it had been for the Ľudáks, but with the return of the Slovak question in the sixties the issue was raised. In May 1968, an article in *Ľud* recalled the broken promise of the Pittsburgh Agreement, as if to suggest that the lesson of the First Republic bore direct relevance to the ongoing discussion of federalization during the Prague Spring.[37] Earlier, the party's Action Program had included a vague clause sanctioning some as yet unspecified way of resolving the asymmetric model of rule, and a party commission chaired by Husák began work soon thereafter to draft a plan of federalization.[38] The matter was obviously one of considerable controversy, but the eventual adoption of the federal solution meant a repudiation of the previous practices and an attempt to undo the effects of the broken promises.

Both the Ľudáks and the Communist nationalists ran certain risks by articulating their grievances. To be sure, the fate that befell the "bourgeois nationalists" of the 1950s had not befallen the Ľudáks; that is, Ľudáks were not arbitrarily imprisoned just because they were nationalists. However, the Ľudáks were by no means complete strangers to Czechoslovak prisons. Father Hlinka himself was confined in Mírov for six months following his attempt to intervene in the delicate negotiations of the Peace of Paris. Father Tiso was imprisoned briefly for his Magyarone activities in the early years of the Republic, Tuka was interned for treason in 1929, and Karol Sidor was jailed in

1935 for seditious journalism. On the eve of the German occupation, three prominent HSĽS partisans — Vojtech Tuka, Šaňo Mach, and Matúš Černák — were arrested by the security forces of the Second Republic and imprisoned for conspiring in Berlin with Hitler about the possibility of German support for Slovak secession.[39]

In all these instances, it seems, the prosecution had a strong case. Hlinka's arrest was brought about by his officially unsanctioned efforts to influence the Paris peacemakers to guarantee Slovak autonomy in the new Czechoslovak state. Accompanied by the well-known Magyarone, Father František Jehlička, Hlinka had set out for Paris by way of Poland, where he may have consulted with representatives of the new government there in order to enlist their support. In any event, Jehlička's connections in Budapest and Hlinka's sojourn in Poland raised suspicions in Prague about their motives at a time when the new Czechoslovak state was faced with great hostility from both Poland and Hungary.[40] As for the other incidents of Ľudák imprisonment, they too had been brought about by provocative acts on the part of those involved. Although the Ľudáks generally chose to refer to these as incidents of arbitrary recrimination against Slovak nationalists, there were serious matters of state involved in each case. As such they hardly bear comparison to the purge of bourgeois nationalists in the fifties.[41]

A better comparison can be found in the constraints of peer pressure on nationalist politicians in the interwar period and the 1960s. Here the Ľudáks did have a legitimate complaint. Their colleagues in the Prague Assembly looked down on them as provincials and bumpkins, mocked their dialect and preached to them. The Czechoslovaks accused the Ľudáks of being backward and out of step with the modern European mentality. The Ľudáks were understandably offended by this treatment, and they ultimately realized that their protestations were in vain because their viewpoint was simply not taken seriously. Attempts to justify the nationalist position, even arguments pointing to the European tradition of nationalist philosophy from Herder on, fell upon deaf ears. Likewise, confronting the Czechoslovaks with statements of Masaryk and Beneš concerning the right of national self-determination had no impact in Prague, for the Czechoslovaks were unshakably persuaded that the Slovaks were not a separate nation.[42]

The nationalists of the sixties faced a similar problem. Their Czech peers, persuaded by the internationalist idealism so characteristic of much of the world's intellectual elite in the late 1950s and early 1960s, saw nationalism as obsolete. In a world of interdependent peoples linked together by the marvels of electronic communication, jet travel, and daily economic exchange, the Slovak nationalist position seemed anachronistic and parochial.[43] Later in the 1960s the world's intellectuals would be startled back into reality by witnessing the conflicts in Vietnam, Northern Ireland, and the Indian subcontinent, as well as the rebirth of nationalistic fervor in Quebec, Yugoslavia, and Belgium. News of these events was conveyed throughout the world instantly by means of man-made satellites relaying electronic waves from beyond the earth's atmosphere. The marvels of the technetronic age had failed to supplant the nationalist impulse.

Nationalism, then, is a phenomenon not easily intellectualized or removed from the realm of pure human emotionalism. The recurrence of symbolic issues in the Slovak question is illustrative. One such issue common to the Ľudáks and the Communist nationalists concerned the position of Ľudovít Štúr in the national pantheon. Štúr, the creator of the modern Slovak written language, was not a favorite historical figure to the Czechoslovaks, because the repercussions of his linguistic work had contributed to the separation of Slovak and Czech national movements.[44] Štúr, therefore, was not one of the symbolic figures idealized in the history texts of the First Republic. Hus, Chelčický, Žižka, and Komenský were the heroes of the past. Jan Hus Day became an official holiday, but no such pains were taken to commemorate the life and times of Štúr. One of Štúr's most important books, *Slavdom and the World of the Future,* was never published in Slovak during the interwar years. The Ľudáks claimed that the book was the victim of Czech censorship, because it contained some passages of a stridently nationalistic nature.[45] It did not matter that the book was published in German, its original language, for the Ľudáks argued that publication in German was tantamount to censorship, since few Slovaks could read German. Nor were the Ľudáks pleased with the fact that the German edition, published in 1931, contained a preface in the Czech language by the eminent Moravian scholar Josef Jirásek.[46] It is difficult to say whether the issue was indeed a matter of censorship or whether it was simply a matter of the unavailability of scholars willing and able to translate Štúr's book into Slovak. The fact that it was not published in Slovak might have been a trivial matter, but it provided the Ľudáks with yet another issue in their fight.

If the attitude of the First Republic's leaders toward Štúr was unfavorable, that of the Communists after 1948 was condemnatory. The latter reminded the Slovaks that Marx had considered Štúr a reactionary because of Štúr's opposition to the Hungarian revolt of

1848. Mere mention of Štúr's name during the 1950s was seen as symptomatic of bourgeois nationalism. It was only in the 1960s that the struggle to resurrect the memory of Štúr met with success. One of the protagonists in this struggle was the rehabilitated Husák. Ultimately the Slovaks had their way, and the 150th anniversary of Štúr's birthday was celebrated in Bratislava on October 19, 1965.[47]

Another symbolic issue centered around the Matica Slovenská. Established in 1863 in the interest of promoting the development of the national literary and artistic culture, the Matica had been closed by the Hungarian government in 1875 as a supposed center of panslavist subversion. Its reopening in 1919 was announced by the then minister for the administration of Slovakia, Vavro Šrobár, as a visible symbol of Slovakia's cultural independence. Throughout the years of the First Republic the Matica contributed greatly to the national culture. Miraculously, the institution remained for the most part immune to the deep political cleavage developing among the Slovaks. Its primarily Protestant leadership accepted manuscripts on a wide range of subjects without discrimination as to the authors' religious or political identity. Even through the Second World War the Matica remained intact, its activities restricted somewhat by the stringencies of Tiso's censorship laws but its reputation untarnished. Proof of the institution's political integrity could be seen in the fact that 53 of the Matica's 102 leading members joined the uprising against the "parish republic."[48]

The Matica Slovenská, therefore, was not a significant issue in the Ľudáks' struggle for autonomy. Catholics undoubtedly felt some resentment toward this Protestant-led institution with such an unimpeachable reputation, but its very unimpeachability removed it from the political arena. The Communists, however, would not leave the Matica untouched. Soon after the 1948 coup they proceeded to relieve the Matica of its independence, first by merging it with the insignificant Slovak League, then by nationalizing it, and in 1953-54 by dismantling it and giving several of its functions to other cultural agencies. The longtime, quality journal *Slovenské pohľady* was taken away and put under the auspices of the Slovak Writers' Union, and the Matica became little more than a national library.[49] In a formal sense the institution lived on, and despite the irony of its latter-day misfortunes, its hundredth anniversary was commemorated by a series of publications.[50]

In 1968 a Slovak writer noted the irony in the circumstances of the Matica Slovenská:

> In the schools we teach the young people that in the dark times of
> our bondage and national oppression Hungary destroyed the Matica
> Slovenská and the three secondary schools. Who, then, should
> imagine today that we, the Slovak Communists, have destroyed the
> Matica Slovenská a second time?[51]

By the time the above passage appeared in *Kultúrny život,* a gradual
momentum had been building toward the revival of the Matica. Here
again, as with the rehabilitation of Štúr, the process of re-creating a
national symbol was an uphill battle. The Novotný regime was notori-
ously hostile toward anything that smacked of Slovak nationalism.
When in 1967 President Novotný was invited to speak at a Matica celebration, he did so for political reasons, but his tactless behavior in the
historic town of Martin (formerly Turčiansky sv. Martin) only served
to humiliate the Slovaks further.[52]

Conditions under the reform government of 1968 were more
favorable for the Matica. As early as February there appeared the first
of numerous "Matica Slovenská Clubs," grassroots organizations
begun by intellectuals and supported by large numbers of citizens.
Within four months the membership in these clubs had grown to
100,000. The members worked through petitions and other forms of
mass pressure to persuade the government to repeal the laws of the
1950s which had enfeebled the venerable institution. These pressures
brought positive results. On June 17, 1968, the Slovak National
Council returned many former responsibilities to the Matica, including its right to publish scholarly materials. Although further plans to
broaden the popular base of the Matica's membership were curtailed
after the Soviet invasion, the restoration of the institution to a greater
portion of its earlier glory has survived the years of "normalization"
and "consolidation."[53]

A new symbolic issue arose after 1948 over official interpretations of
the Slovak National Uprising of 1944. This dramatic and highly
controversial event was the culminating point in the Slovak wartime
resistance. The resistance groups were made up of Communists,
Protestants, and dissident members of the armed forces. Although
some Catholics had come to oppose the Tiso regime, relatively few
actually joined the resistance.[54] The movement was by no means united
on the finer points of policy, much less ideology, but the groups'
convergence in the Uprising produced a moment of singular heroism.
The Uprising failed, but the partisans' valorous fight bore witness to

the decline of Tiso's support in the hinterlands, simultaneously paving the way for the Soviet-led liberation of Slovakia.[55]

The Slovak National Uprising was an event that the Prague Communists wished to forget after 1948. There was a similarity between the Communists involved in the Uprising and those of Tito's partisans in Yugoslavia. They had been active in the underground and participated in a major rebellion with minimal assistance from the Soviet Union. Moreover, the Slovak Communists had been separated from their Czech colleagues throughout the war, and those who survived the defeat of 1944 emerged from the war as seasoned national leaders who felt that the Slovaks' exemplary resistance entitled them to respect and honor. From their ranks came those who would be purged as "bourgeois nationalists," however, for the Stalinists had no tolerance for Slovaks whose independent reputations might have cast them in the role of equals or competitors. By purging such men as Husák, Novomeský, Šmidke, Okáli, and Horváth, the party rid itself of this troublesome faction. To celebrate the Uprising in which the purged comrades had participated would have been tantamount to admitting the righteousness of their struggle.

The nationalists' campaign to assert the symbolic importance of the Uprising, therefore, had to be preceded by the rehabilitation of the disgraced leaders of the Uprising. Again the process was difficult, but again the Slovaks were successful. The bourgeois nationalists were rehabilitated (partially, at least) in 1963, and the Slovak National Uprising was honored in official ceremonies celebrating its twentieth anniversary in August 1964.[56] Thereafter the anniversary has been regularly commemorated throughout Czechoslovakia.

Both concrete and symbolic issues have thus permeated the politics of Slovak nationalism since the establishment of the First Czechoslovak Republic. They changed only slightly in the half-century following independence. With the exit of the HSĽS and the advent of the Communists, a few new issues emerged and a few old ones subsided. The fundamental complaint of the nationalists, however, remained relatively constant. Whether their resentment focused on their inferior economic status, the disproportionately small numbers of Slovaks in positions of political power, or the condescending attitude of the Czechs, Ľudáks and Communist nationals alike felt excluded from the ruling circles in Prague and unable to find their own political identity. All these concrete problems were intensified by the difficulty of relating to Slovak national symbols, for Czech history and Czech culture were fed to the Slovaks to compensate for what was officially assumed to be a lack of their own symbols. A Slovak intellectual, Pavol Vongraj, summed up the feeling in an interview published in the Czech journal *Reportér* (March 1969): "We in Slovakia know Czech culture, Czech life, and the Czech problem better than Czechs know the Slovak problem" — and therein, he argued, lies the basis for a "feeling of national inferiority, ahistoricality *[nehistoričnost]* and baseness."[57] It remains to be seen whether or not federalism will provide a solution to the concrete issues of Slovak politics, but at least the acknowledgment of Slovakia's nationhood, now supported by institutionalized realities, has served to alleviate the longstanding feeling of unworthiness.

Who Are the Nationalists?

It is obvious that when we speak of Slovak nationalists in the twentieth century we are speaking of at least two very different groups, or, more accurately, several different groups within each of two major time periods (roughly 1913–45 and 1945–present). In the first of these time periods, the Slovak nationalists — as distinct from the Czecho-slovaks — were concentrated primarily in the Slovak People's party (HSĽS). These were nearly all Roman Catholics of authoritarian temperament and conservative-to-fascist ideological persuasion, dis-trustful of what they considered tendencies toward anticlericalism and unbridled libertarianism among the Czechs. Smaller nationalist groups centered around the Rázus National party (Protestant) and ephemeral Juriga Catholic party. The latter two groups added an element of variety to the politics of Slovak nationalism, but in reality they were of little significance.

In the second of the two time periods under discussion, we are concerned primarily with Slovak Communists who departed from the mainstream postwar trend of centralism within Czechoslovak com-munism. Although the Communist nationalists stemmed from their own roots within the interwar Communist party of Czechoslovakia (KSČ), they were virtually impotent as a political force before the Second World War. Their separation from the KSČ in 1939 led them into six years of dangerous, underground activity inside Tiso's Slovak state, and their central role in the Uprising of 1944 lent them an air of authority that they had never previously had. Thus they emerged from the war as a force with which the Prague politicians, both Communist and noncommunist, had to reckon. As we have seen, the purges of the early fifties sent them into eclipse, and the destruction of opposition parties ensured that no noncommunist survivors of either the interwar nationalist movement or the Uprising would threaten the basis of centralist rule. Communist nationalism re-emerged, however, in the 1960s, as some rehabilitated victims of the purges were joined by others to press for the cause of Slovak rights. In the course of this latter-day movement, diverging wings of the nationalist group again developed, giving rise to a complicated interplay of Slovak-vs.-centralist politics which reached a culmination in 1968–69.

Thus in neither time period is it entirely accurate to speak of "the nationalists" as a cohesive group. The configuration of Slovak politics has been quite pluralistic and interwoven with patterns of subtle differentiation ever since 1913, the year the HSĽS was formed. Nonetheless, it is useful to focus once again on the main centers of Slovak nationalist politics in the two major time periods, namely the HSĽS and what we shall for the moment call simply the "Communist nationalists" in order to draw some conclusions about their respective constituencies.

1. Catholics and Nationalism

The Ľudáks drew their public support from a numerically large section of Slovak society. More than seventy percent of Slovakia's inhabitants were members of the Roman Catholic Church. (See table below.)[58]

Table 7.2

Religions in Slovakia, 1921–1940

	1921	1930	1940
Roman Catholic	2,128,205	2,384,355	1,956,233
Greek Catholic*	193,778	213,725	183,736
Greek Orthodox	2,879	9,075	5,778
All Protestant	529,349	553,506	403,073
(of which Lutheran	(382,248)	(400,360)	(387,677)
(" " Calvinist	(144,549)	(145,829)	(15,396) **
" Czech Brethren)	(2,372)	(6,050)	**
Jewish	135,918	136,737	85,045
Of no confession	6,818	16,890	9,994

* i.e., Uniate

** Protestants other than Lutherans included in statistic for Calvinists in 1940.

Source: Slovenská Vlastiveda (Bratislava: SAV, 1944), pp. 179–80.

Despite the large proportion of Roman Catholics, however, the Ľudáks were never able to capture a majority of the votes in Slovakia. Indeed, the HSĽS never gained the support of a convincing majority of even the Catholic population. The party consistently won a plurality of the vote, but, in keeping with the fragmented multiparty system of the First Republic as a whole, the HSĽS was always a minority party within its own land (Slovakia). The following table shows this in terms of the vote for each National Assembly election beginning with 1925.

Table 7.3

Slovak Elections in First Republic*

Party**	1925	1929	1935
HSĽS	489,111	403,683	489,641 ***
Agrarian	248,034	278,979	286,739
Communist	198,111	152,242	210,785
Social Democratic	60,635	135,506	184,739
National Socialist	36,909	43,968	51,930
Rázus National	35,435	---	***
National Demo-			
cratic	13,608	53,745	25,490
National Workers'	24,954	---	---
Fascist	---	---	32,609
Czech People's	18,036	36,548	37,489
Small Traders'	11,576	30,134	41,996
Juriga Catholic	---	5,395	---
National Union	---	1,810	---
Debtors'	---	---	546
Independent			
Communist	356	---	---

* excluding 1920. Statistics are for elections to National Assembly, lower house.

** Czech and Slovak parties only. (Minority parties excluded.)

***Autonomist Bloc, including both HSĽS and Rázus National.

Sources: Státní úřad statistický, various statistical yearbooks.

It should be added that, when electoral tallies for all parties in Slovakia are taken into account, the result is a consistent and overwhelming show of support for those parties hostile to Czechoslovak centralism. In the 1935 elections, for example, we can see a representative statistic by combining the votes registered by the HSLS, the Communists (a non-Czechoslovak party by its position on the national question), the Magyar parties, the *Sudetendeutschpartei,* and the Fascists. When we do, we find that 61 percent of the voters in Slovakia supported parties that opposed Czechoslovak centralism.[59] Subtracting the parties of the ethnic minorities, the anti-Czechoslovak parties still represented a majority of Slovaks, although the percentage now falls under 55 percent. The HSLS itself, however, remains a distinct minority. Far from being the exclusive spokesmen of the Slovaks, as the leaders of the Tiso regime were later to claim, the Ľudáks came to power in Slovakia only with the help of external forces, namely the support of Hitler, at the time of the Czechoslovak Republic's collapse.[60]

The social basis of Ľudák strength was in the rural Catholic areas of Slovakia. In the ethnically mixed industrial centers the Ľudáks ran into stiff competition from the socialist parties, while in districts with large Protestant populations the Agrarians tended to dominate. (For example, the district around the traditional center of the national movement, Turčiansky svätý Martin, was largely Protestant and a stronghold of the Agrarians.) In general, large and medium-scale farmers tended to support the Agrarian party — in contrast to the Czech lands, where small and medium farmers formed the backbone of the Agrarians' constituency — whereas the Ľudáks appealed more to the masses of Slovak peasants and smallholders. Eastern Slovakia, with its sizable Magyar population and large numbers of Greek Catholics, was not a stronghold of the HSLS but rather of the Magyar parties, and Ruthenia was favorable turf for the Communists.[61]

The nationalist elites reflected patterns that bear some discussion. The two strains of the Slovak national movement mentioned in the preceding chapter — that deriving from the Protestant-cosmopolitan stratum exemplified by Kollár and Šafárik, on the one hand, and that deriving from the provincial Catholic clergy, on the other — continued to play a role in the delineation of Slovak elites after 1918. As early as 1919 the Catholic nationalists registered vehement complaints about the constituency of the delegations to the Paris Peace Talks and the (provisional) Revolutionary National Assembly. With regard to the latter, the body that drew up the constitutional framework for the First Republic, the nationalists complained that only 54 of 270 delegates occupied "Slovak" seats; of these, moreover, thirteen were of dubious Slovak ethnicity — Czechs, in fact, appointed to represent Slovaks. Of the remaining 41 Slovak delegates, 30 were Protestants.[62]

Protestants continued to dominate high positions after 1919. Of seven Slovak cabinet ministers who served in Prague governments between 1920 and 1925, only two (Martin Mičura and Vavro Šrobár) were of Catholic backgrounds.[63] Of the 23 most prominent Slovak politicians in the First Republic, at least 14 were from Protestant families.[64] The disproportionately large numbers of Protestants in positions of district and local authority after 1919 similarly brought bitter complaints from the Ľudáks.[65] Welcomed in Prague as cohorts but resented at home by the Ľudáks, the Slovak Protestants quickly developed firm ties to their peers in the Czech establishment. They formed a cohesive group (with the exception of the Rázus Nationals), and their relations with the Catholic Nationalists became more and more hostile.[66]

The Catholic-Protestant division, therefore, underlay and intensified the nationalist-Czechoslovak polarization. The correlation between religion and position on the national question was by no means pure; there were some Catholics among the Czechoslovaks and some Protestants among the nationalists.[67] In the 1930s the Rázus Nationals broke their earlier alliance with the Czech National Democrats and joined with the HSĽS for the 1935 elections. This apparent show of cross-denominational ideological unity was rather illusive, however. The Rázus Nationals were a minor political force who never made any serious inroads into the Agrarians' appeal to the larger Protestant community.

Moreover, the Protestant nationalists were not generously rewarded after 1939 for their support. In the 1939 Slovak Diet, only five of 63 delegates were Protestants, and only one Protestant served at any time in President Tiso's cabinet.[68] Once in power, the Ľudáks proved their vengeance by systematically excluding Protestants from high positions.

Religion thus played a critical role in the make-up of the nationalists' leadership and constituency from 1918 to 1945. Catholicism was identified very strongly with Slovak nationalism, and many Slovak voters accepted the Ľudáks' argument that the two were inseparable. This identity has come to be obscured in the Communist period, as religion is officially disapproved. The Communist nationalists have sprung from backgrounds that are not so simply defined, but in an attempt to identify the Communist nationalists it is to this subject that we must now turn.

2. *Communists and Nationalism*

Prior to the Second World War the Communists had never been very strong among the Slovaks.[69] The reasons for this are rather clear. In the first place, the Slovak working class was relatively small, and therefore the class basis for a strong Communist movement was dubious. Moreover, the Communists found themselves unable to appeal to a broader segment of Slovak society. The growing numbers of small tradesmen feared that Communism meant the expropriation of their hard-earned businesses; peasants generally heeded the advice of their religious leaders to shun godless Bolshevism; and the poor in general doubted the promises of equality and class justice held out by the Communists.[70] The churches were strong social forces in First Republican Slovakia, exerting a powerful influence on the faithful to honor traditional sources of authority and not question their social status.

During the first decade after independence there were few capable leaders within the Slovak wing of the KSČ, scarcely any with prior political experience, and no theorists. Leadership was the exclusive province of Czechs in the party's formative years. With their backgrounds in the internationalist traditions of the Austrian Social Democratic party, the Czech Communists knew and cared little about the national problems of Slovakia. The party's slogans in the early years made references to the "Czechoslovak nation," reflecting the leaders' unconsciousness of the national issue. Only pressure from the Comintern in 1924 caused the KSČ leadership to reconsider this position, and in fact only after the intra-party revolution of 1929 did a clear stand in favor of national self-determination emerge.[71]

Because of this slowness to recognize the national problem, and because the official line continued to fluctuate even after 1929, the Communists failed to project themselves as a nationalist force. They were obviously no source of serious competition for the position of the Ľudáks in the politics of Slovak nationalism. Therefore, the KSČ found itself relegated in Slovakia to the role of a peripheral party, third strongest, to be sure, but not representative of the Slovak nation. It was, rather, the gathering-place for those who considered themselves the outcasts of society — Magyars, Ruthenes, Jews, youthful anarchists, and others who could not find a niche in the ranks of the Ľudáks, Agrarians, or Social Democrats.

The first significant source of genuine Slovak nationalism within the

KSČ was the journal *Dav* (The Masses), founded in 1924. The people associated with the journal, known as the Davists, came to form a cohesive, nationalist element within the party. They worked to promote a greater consciousness among the Communists of Slovakia's special problems. Although the Davists were only a very small group, their voice was moderately influential, for the Davists included some of the brightest personalities of the left intelligentsia in Slovakia. Among them were the journalist Vlado Clementis, poets Laco Novomeský and Ján Poničan, and later Gustáv Husák.[72] Many of the Davists were to play prominent roles in the Uprising, and all were the subject of Stalinist attacks when the party made a blanket indictment of *Dav* in 1951.[73]

Very few Davists lived to see the reemergence of a Slovak Communist nationalism in the sixties, but two who did, Novomeský and Husák, were among the most outspoken members of the new faction. They were joined by survivors of the Uprising, including Samo Falťan, Ondrej Klokoč, and Mieroslav Hysko. Not coincidentally, these two groups — veterans of *Dav* and of the Uprising — had comprised the majority of those convicted in the early fities of "bourgeois nationalism." They were not the only nationalists in the 1960s, however. Among those who rallied behind the Slovak cause must be included Alexander Dubček, Miloš Hruškovič, Peter Colotka, Štefan Sádovský, and Evžen Löbl, all identified with the reformist strain in the KSS; of these, only Dubček was active in the Uprising, and none had served any time in prison.

When we examine the backgrounds of the Communist nationalists and compare them with the Slovak antinationalists of the 1960s, some interesting facts appear.[74] If we add Viktor Pavlenda and Miloš Gosiorovský to the ten names mentioned in the preceding paragraph, we have a list that we might consider the twelve most prominent Slovak nationalists of the sixties. Among these twelve people there are some common demographic and career patterns which distinguish them from the antinationalists. Most were born in the 1920s, but Husák (1913), Löbl (1907), and Novomeský (1904) are significant exceptions. At least six played significant roles in the wartime resistance movement, but at least four (Löbl, Pavlenda, Colotka, and Sádovský) were not involved. They were, on the whole, a well-educated group. At least eight were products of post-secondary schools, and four earned advanced degrees (Husák, Löbl, Colotka, and Sádovský). Moreover, all except Dubček can be considered members of the intelligentsia; this includes two (Hysko and Novomeský) about whom details concerning their educational backgrounds are obscure, and one (Gosiorovský) whose profession entitles him to be considered in this category. (Hysko and Novomeský were both writers; Gosiorovský was a university professor.) The nationalists were thus dominated by members of the intelligentsia, for the most part well educated and engaged in intellectual activities.

The seven most prominent Slovak antinationalists show quite different patterns. Only one of them (Ďuriš) pursued his education beyond the level of the gymnasium, and he did not complete his university training. By occupation, three were unskilled laborers; the rest included a skilled industrial worker, a railroad worker, a journalist, and a party apparatchik. All but one were born before 1920, and all but two before the First World War. All but two were imprisoned by pre-1945 governments for political activities, and none were jailed after 1945. The one characteristic they had in common with the nationalists was their participation in the wartime resistance; most, if not all, were involved.[75] All of them, in addition, held positions of at least the rank of candidate member in either the KSČ or the KSS during the critical period 1954–62, that is, after the purges but before the rehabilitations of bourgeois nationalists. In contrast, only three of those who became nationalists (Dubček, Pavlenda, and Hruškovič) held high positions during the same time period.

From these facts one can draw three conclusions. The first, and most obvious, is that those who were most favored by the centralist regimes of the Gottwald-Novotný years were the antinationalists. They were the ones who held high positions and ran no risk of imprisonment, even though their earlier involvement in Slovak partisan activities might have made them candidates for purging along with the "bourgeois nationalists."

Secondly, the strong correlation between education and position on the Slovak question suggests that the antinationalists' weak educational backgrounds may have made them prone to accepting the official position of the pre-1968 governments. They were not inclined to question the judgment of those who rewarded them with political favors, and as a result they failed to take heed of the growing national problem in their own homeland. The nationalists, who were better educated, saw the problem and understood its implications. They were not inclined to accept the regime's judgment that socialism had solved the national question, and they were not satisfied with partial solutions and euphemistic discussions.

Finally, the differences in occupational strata, combined with prison records, suggest a third conclusion. The antinationalists, mostly solid members of the working class, believed that the only dynamic force within modern society was that of the class conflict. They had been veterans of the struggle against the interwar bourgeoisie — indeed, victims of the First Republic's anticonspiracy law — and carried the lesson of that experience with them into the socialist phase of development. They were persuaded by the "internationalist" ideology of orthodox communism, and they looked upon nationalism as a regressive force that had no place in a socialist society. In contrast, the nationalist intelligentsia was less persuaded as to the exclusive role of class conflict. Some of the nationalists had been involved in the struggles against the bourgeois government — although none had been imprisoned then — and they believed in the cause of the working class. They did not believe that the victory of socialism had eliminated all other major social conflicts, though. On the contrary, they believed that the resolution of the class conflict could never be quite final until the nationality conflict was resolved. To the nationalists, true social equality was impossible without true national equality.

Beyond this point of agreement, the Slovak nationalists divided. The division surfaced in the politics of 1968 and intensified during the troubled months following the invasion, with enormous consequences for the entire Czechoslovak Socialist Republic.

The Slovaks in 1968 and Beyond

In retrospect, the configuration of political factions in 1968–69 seems perplexing, both among the Slovaks themselves and throughout the leadership of the ČSSR. The key personalities sometimes shifted their sides in the various discussions, now taking difficult and courageous stands for high principles and now blowing with the winds of political opportunity. Vasil Biľak, a Ruthene from Slovakia who had openly opposed federalism before 1968, found himself in the federalist camp but ambivalent or hesitant in his support of reforms in other areas. Some, like Oldřich Černík, a Czech, were leading forces of progressivism and reform before the twenty-first of August but edged gradually into a more conservative position thereafter. Husák, always a strong federalist, vacillated in his attitudes toward other political reforms but was generally supportive of them. Jozef Lenárt, a Slovak who achieved prominence in the Novotný entourage despite his early support of fundamental economic reform, became a conservative in the atmosphere of 1968, was converted to a position of favoring — or at least tolerating — federalization, and maneuvered through the crisis years with most of his reputation and authority intact. Others such as Alois Indra, Jan Pillér, and Drahomír Kolder entered the reform era hostile to the new politics and never changed their positions on the basic questions.[76] Likewise, a number of progressives including Dubček, Josef Smrkovský, Ota Šik, František Kriegel, and others maintained their reformist stance throughout the crisis.[77]

Among the Slovaks, four groupings became apparent. The old anti-nationalists represented one. These men were closely tied to Novotný and did not survive him in positions of power. Several of their cohorts (Bacílek, David, Ďuriš, and Široký) had lost their power in 1962–63, at the beginning of the Slovak nationalists' rise. Sabolčík was demoted a few years later; Chudík and Cvik held onto key posts longer and exited with Novotný in the spring of 1968.

The remaining three groups tended to favor a federal solution to the Slovak problem, although some had arrived at this position only in 1968. The first of these groups was comprised of people who favored federalization but considered the national issue inseparable from the general questions of political reform and democratization. This was a comparatively small group in Slovakia — an "island" in a sea of nationalists less concerned with issues of democracy, as one close observer has described it. Dubček was, of course, preeminent in this group but by no means the most progressive member. Others included Colotka, Lipták, the philosopher Miroslav Kusý, and the economist Löbl. On the edge of the group were people like Pavlenda, Falťan, Sádovský, and Hysko. The progressives moved to the forefront as a result of their natural alliance with the Czech progressives, thus maintaining their high positions during the reform era despite their numerical minority within the Slovak elite.

On the other side of questions concerning democratization was a group of people whose positions on the various reform issues fluctuated but tended to be rather conservative. Most of these men were late-comers to the cause of federalism; Biľak, Emil Rigo, Michal Pecho, and Bohuš Chňoupek, for example. Some, such as Biľak, were known to support the party's program of reform in general, although with strong reservations and little apparent enthusiasm. Following the invasion this group quickly moved away from the reform program and became the internal nemesis of the progressives.

The "moderate" group that was destined to prevail centered around Husák. Husák had played a very careful game throughout the spring of 1968, and he was widely identified by the public as a reformer. His support of the political reforms was never as enthusiastic as that of the progressives, however, and his greatest efforts prior to the invasion were aimed at promoting federalism. Indeed, the central theme of the group around Husák was the struggle for a federal system as the primary aim of Slovak politics in 1968. On Husák's side were several prominent Slovak literati: Novomeský, Miroslav Válek, and Vojtech Mihálik.[78]

The division between Slovak moderates and progressives over the relative importance of federalism vs. democratization was reflected in the two major intellectual periodicals, *Kultúrny život* and *Nové slovo*. The latter, a revived journal that had been defunct — and discredited — since 1950, began again in March 1968, when several members of the editorial board of *Kultúrny život* resigned because of *Kultúrny život*'s increasing preoccupation with democratization. The most important men associated with *Nové slovo* included Husák and Novomeský, who used the journal to carry on a public debate about the importance of federalism for Slovakia.[79]

In the months after the invasion, and especially leading up to the changes of spring 1969, Husák gathered forces around him from both the conservative group and the progressives (for example, Sádovský). This newly ascendant grouping around Husák generated a further alliance with Czech conservatives. The result, of course, was the ouster of the last of the reformers. The Husák coalition, moving ever more and more in a conservative and dogmatic direction, led the country away from reformism to "normalization." In this they had the full support of the Soviet Union, whose leaders might have looked askance at Slovak nationalism but were willing to trade the issue for political control and censorship.[80] In subsequent years, the Husák group came to lose even that point for which it had traded away the other reforms, as Slovak nationalism fell again into disfavor in the mid-1970s.

The temporary triumph of the "moderate" Husák position came about only after the Soviet intervention. It is quite impossible to say definitively which nationalist faction would have prevailed in the absence of outside force. Certainly there was a consistent momentum within the country as a whole toward an increasingly progressive policy, and given more time to consolidate their position the progressives might have won out.[81] Support for the progressives was evident among the Slovak public, but the extent to which public opinion could be transformed into party reality was not clear.[82]

Certainly, one fact is clear: the Slovak elites were seriously divided, just as Slovak political elites had always been divided since before

1918. References to past political divisions in Slovakia crept into casual conversation and even party dialogue. According to a reasonably well-founded rumor, the members of the progressive-nationalist group were at one point condemned by a member of the Slovak opposition as "Protestants." (It is, perhaps, significant — and well known in Slovakia — that Dubček came from an old Protestant family and Husák from Catholic backgrounds.)

That the issue of federalism figured so centrally in the "Slovak Spring" of 1968 served to distinguish Slovak politics from Czech. In the Czech lands, both official and public discussion concerned itself primarily with the complex cluster of issues gathered around the slogan "democratization." The problem of Czech-Slovak relations was not ignored, but at no time did the Czechs accord it the high degree of importance it had for Slovaks.[83] Many Czechs gave the idea of federalization only their halfhearted approval at best, seeing in federalism the spectre of three bureaucracies instead of just one.[84] This was obviously not so in Slovakia, where public discussion centered at least as much around the federal issue as any other. A participant put it thus:

> In the contemporary Czech language the word most frequently used is "democratization." In Slovakia this word is rivaled by the word "federalism." It is necessary to understand why both words are spoken in the same breath in one part of the state. And in this case, that is not possible without an awareness of certain historical facts. Today, as a matter of fact, the issue is that of a new stage of the conflict which four million Slovaks have been waging for more than a century.[85]

It is significant that the above lines were written by the eminent historian Lipták. A progressive in the 1968 configuration of Slovak politics, Lipták was consciously drawing the attention of his (Czech) audience to the real political differences between Czechs and Slovaks. Central to the distinction was the longstanding subordinate position of the Slovak nation. That subordinate status had bred into many Slovaks a deep-seated resentment toward outside wielders of power, including Czechs. Few Czechs appreciated the strength of Slovak resentment, preferring instead to persist in their view of the Slovaks as younger brothers.

Underlying the Slovak resentment has been the disparity in historical experiences between them and the Czechs. Their different historical experience produced a culture only marginally comparable to that of the Czechs — more recently and less profoundly influenced by modernist strains of thought, less volatile and more tradition-oriented, more conservative. The emergence of Husák's moderate-nationalist wing in 1968–69 must be understood in the context of the historical backgrounds. Among the Czechs there was a much greater polarization of party factions in the critical months after the invasion, reflecting the historical tendency of Czechs to move to the extremes of a question. Among the Slovaks the opposite was true; there was a greater tendency to coalesce around the center, to accept the federal program and eschew other reform issues. The Czech center was far weaker in comparison.[86] Under Soviet pressure, the most realistic tactic for Husák and the Slovak moderates was to create an alliance with the Czech conservatives. This they did at the cost of a return to dogmatism and repression.

In the end, the federal program itself was compromised. Not long after the implementation of the federal reform some Slovaks saw shortcomings in the new system.[87] The Constitutional Law of October 27, 1968 left many specific questions unresolved and allowed the federal government to assume jurisdiction over matters that are not clearly accounted for.[88] More importantly, the creation of a federal state structure did not carry over to the organization of the Communist party, where the asymmetric model of rule still prevails. The Communist party of Slovakia, subservient to the Communist party of Czechoslovakia, does not have a counterpart in the Czech lands. Efforts begun in 1968 to rectify this asymmetrical arrangement were abandoned in 1969 as Husák himself yielded to strong pressures from the Soviets and from Czech conservatives to return to the principles of "democratic centralism." In the following year, further pressures on Husák drove him to change his ideological position toward a more orthodox Marxist-Leninist interpretation of the national issue. He began to argue the need to reorient the public mentality toward Czech-Slovak unity and away from what now came, once again, to be ominously called bourgeois nationalism.[89]

Even the reforms so boldly promulgated in the governmental structure have been eroded to a significant degree, both by constitutional measures and in the practical application of federalism. Recentralizing policies began with the designation of the Czech and Slovak premiers as federal vice-premiers in the autumn of 1969. Early in 1970, the decision to abolish state secretaries in federal ministries — positions earlier set up to balance Czech-Slovak authority in the top ranks of the ministries — added a further impetus to recentralization.[90] Additional measures followed, gradually cutting down the competence and authority of the national governments and thereby frustrating the aims of the Slovak nationalists. Ultimately the momentum carried policies of antinationalism beyond the government and into other aspects of life; by 1977, for example, much of the effort that had gone into the writing of Slovak history between 1965 and 1975 was being officially disparaged, and many historians had lost their jobs because of their "incorrect" interpretations during those years.

For a few years, it had appeared to many Slovak Communists that their national aspirations might ultimately be realized. In the early 1970s a richer selection of new literary and scholarly works emanated from Bratislava than from Prague. The Slovak economy was livelier, and workers' morale was higher. The creation of many new governmental positions in Slovakia opened up some avenues for social mobility, ramifying throughout other occupational sectors. Industry, particularly construction, experienced a boom that could be readily seen in the urban centers.

With the exception of intellectual life, which has since come once again to feel the pressure of the new dogmatism, most of these trends continue. Yet all is not well. Especially in the light of the official ideological abandonment of Slovak nationalism, there is still a large gap between workers and government. The bureaucracy remains as impervious to influence as ever, and the Communist party is obeyed rather than loved. National symbols have come to be deemphasized or recast into a forced conformity with the party's notions of internationalism.

In Summary

This chapter and the preceding one have been aimed at demonstrating the obstacles that have arisen in the quest for national identity in Czechoslovakia. The focus has been on the Slovaks more than on the Czechs, not because the "Czech question" has been resolved but rather because the Slovak question has been the more difficult and conflict-ridden.

The national question for both Czechs and Slovaks is likely to persist as long as the Communists are unwilling to acknowledge the depth to which the problem reaches in their society. By deemphasizing or fighting nationalist tendencies the Party has succeeded only in driving the wedge that tends to divide itself from the public ever deeper.

It is Moscow-oriented, orthodox Marxist-Leninist ideology that motivates the Czechoslovak Communists' policies. Their purpose has been to make the workers more class-conscious and less concerned with their *national* identity as such. In the orthodox Marxist-Leninist view of the world, nationalism is a tool of the bourgeoisie used to distract the working class from its true interests. The bourgeoisie invokes the symbols and values of the nation in order to benumb the class-consciousness of the proletariat and woo its acquiescence in the preservation of capitalist authority patterns. Glorification of the nation does not focus the workers' attention on those objective interests that put them in conflict with the bourgeoisie, but rather it causes them to be misled by "subjective" impulses toward national unity reaching across class lines. The true interests of the workers, according to this theory, is based on their destiny as a social class; these interests transcend national identities, uniting proletarian against bourgeois the world over.[91]

The thought that Marx's and Lenin's ideas on nationalism might be less than entirely appropriate within a socialist context has occurred to numerous Communists, ranging from Husák to Tito, but no generally acceptable theory has arisen to account for this problem area. Lacking such a theory, those who are inclined to orthodoxy are driven back to the ideas that were developed in an earlier day. Like pluralism, nationalism can arise only in bourgeois social orders; in socialist societies it can only be considered symptomatic of deviance. The tolerance of Slovak nationalism for ten years was a sign that the orthodox ideological position on this question was being seriously challenged. The challengers, however, did not succeed either in buttressing their arguments with sufficiently persuasive theoretical points or in holding onto effective political power. The return in recent years to an antinationalist policy, ironically supported by the former Slovak nationalist Husák, shows both the dominance of the political dogmatists and the paramountcy of Soviet influence in Prague.

To turn the foregoing analysis around, it is interesting to note the relationship between impulses to nationalism and the effectiveness of Communist rule. Here again, the discontinuity of policy since 1948 points out yet another obstacle the Communists have encountered in their attempt to revolutionize society. Nationalism is indeed deeply rooted, and there are no signs that its appeal has been significantly diminished by the efforts of the revolutionary elite. The ideology of proletarian internationalism has not provided its own images and symbols to compete with those of the nation. Other communist elites, notably those in Romania and Hungary, have had some modest success in linking their rule with certain popular national symbols, but in Czechoslovakia this issue has been persistently plagued by political inconsistency and official insensitivity.

VIII

From Švejk to Dubček: The Humor and Pathos of Political Nonviolence

Once again, let us consider for a moment the course of Czech and Slovak history since the turn of the century. From separate national movements emerging out of the divided Habsburg Empire, Czechs and Slovaks were politically united into an independent republic which met an unhappy end twenty years after its founding. There followed less than one-half year of uneasy confederation under the watchful eye of Hitler, and then six years of humiliating Nazi domination. After the war another uneasy, transitional period of home rule lasted less than three years before the country came once more to be thoroughly dominated by the norms of a foreign power. For twenty years Soviet-style communism ruled, exiting temporarily for the short-lived Dubček era. Seven and one-half months of quasi-independence in 1968 was ended by the invasion of "fraternal" allies, and after several further months of uncertain transition the pattern of Soviet domination was reestablished. Of the entire period since the beginning of the Czechoslovak Republic, fewer than twenty-four years have been independent in any meaningful sense of the word.

It has been argued throughout this book, at least implicitly, that the development of a political culture takes place best under conditions of national independence. However, independence has been the exception rather than the rule in Czechoslovak history. The periods of freedom have represented very intensive movements of creative political development, tending in the direction of pluralistic democracy in any of several forms. These efforts have been repeatedly interrupted and frustrated by forces that have brought on outside control. Thus the development of a Czechoslovak political culture has been discontinuous; indeed, it has been periodically postponed while society learned to accommodate the wishes of a more powerful foreigner.

If times of adversity bring out the true character of the human species, Czechs and Slovaks have certainly had ample opportunity to display their innermost strengths and foibles. They have had to learn

patience, to forebear the most ignominious defeats, to hold onto something of their own values while being either subtly coaxed or massively
bombarded by the foreigner's demands on their behavior. They have
not always succeeded in repelling the assaults on their value systems.
They have sometimes changed or modified their ideas, but to a
remarkable extent it can be said that distinct Czech and Slovak values
have persisted — despite the temptation simply to give in and accept
the ways of the foreigner.

The patterns of Czech and Slovak behavior under alien control have
included several types of action: armed resistance to the oppressor,
direct and indirect collaboration with the enemy, attempts to negotiate
compromise political arrangements, passive resistance, and dis-
heartened resignation to a seemingly hopeless fate. Of these patterns,
the least characteristic of both nations has been the resort to violent
resistance.

Indeed, a marked strain of nonviolence runs through the course of
Czech and Slovak history. Nonviolence as a normative pattern of
behavior is perhaps more pronounced among the Czechs, but it is by
no means lacking among Slovaks and might even be said to be
dominant in both national cultures.

To say this is not to overlook the times when Czechs and Slovaks
have taken up arms for the national cause; the Czechoslovak Legions
fought valiantly in the First World War, and bold resistance movements during the Second World War also provided moments of great
heroism. Without in any way discrediting or underestimating these
efforts, however, it must be said that they were exceptional in the
recent history of Czechoslovakia. The Czechoslovak Legions were a
relatively small force compared to the numbers of their countrymen
who fought (willingly or not) in the Austro-Hungarian Army. The
Czech resistance in the Second World War lasted only until 1942 and
then was stifled by the brute force of the Nazis. Even the Slovak
resistance — the usual term "National Uprising" is not entirely
accurate because a part of the nation still sympathized with the Tiso
regime — took on a significant dimension only in the final year of the
war, and within a still-divided populace.

Because of the prevalence of foreign domination, it is necessary to
discuss the patterns of response among Czechs and Slovaks to the
stimuli associated with alien political norms. Here we are on rather
slippery empirical ground, for it is quite impossible to measure the
relative frequency of acts of resistance vs. collaboration or passive vs.
active resistance. Here also we run into differences between Czech and

Slovak behavior, for some patterns are more characteristic of one nation than of the other. This is especially true of the pattern known as "Švejkism," to be discussed below as primarily a Czech phenomenon. With these preliminary caveats in mind, let us take a look at Czech and Slovak behavior in times of political crisis brought on by great-power interference in Czechoslovak affairs.

Resistance and Collaboration

When Czech workers staged strikes leading to military suppression in June 1953, Czechoslovakia became the first Soviet-bloc country in which discontent with the Communist system was openly expressed. The outbreaks in industrial centers bespoke a violent side of the Czech temperament that seemed out of character. In fact, however, violent resistance has occurred at earlier moments on the part of both Czechs and Slovaks.

The Second World War was the time of the most concentrated active resistance in recent history. In Bohemia and Moravia, organized resistance groups formed almost immediately following the German occupation in the spring of 1939. The movement attracted people from a broad spectrum of political persuasions. Several groups sprang up, coordinated by an organization called the Central Leadership of Domestic Resistance, or ÚVOD (*Ústřední vedení odboje domácího*).[1] Demonstrations and other relatively minor acts of resistance characterized the activities of the movement in the first two years of the occupation. Thereafter, Gestapo tactics gradually succeeded in stifling the Czech resistance. The terror that descended upon the Protectorate in 1941 virtually snuffed out resistance activities on a large scale, and subsequent events took on the character of individual acts of violence and sabotage.[2] The most striking of these was the killing of *Reichsprotektor* Reinhard Heydrich in May 1942, accomplished by exiled Czechs trained in Britain and parachuted surreptitiously into Bohemia. This was a daring and spectacular deed, but it provoked a wave of retaliatory terror that included the wholesale destruction of Lidice and the extermination of the remaining resistance groups.[3] The resistance as an effective movement did not again emerge significantly until the hastily contrived, almost spontaneous uprising of May 1945 coinciding with the entry of the liberating Russian and American troops.[4]

The same was not true of the Slovak resistance, as we saw in the preceding chapter. In Slovakia the resistance took shape much later than in the Protectorate but gathered force continuously up to the moment of the Uprising. The latter was an event of impressive magnitude which, despite the fact that it failed in its immediate objectives, weakened the position of the Germans and the Tiso regime at a critical point in the course of the war.

Although the wartime resistance movements and the brief 1953 unrest were unique in the post-1918 history of the Czechs and Slovaks, there were some precedents in the earlier affairs of both nations. The distant heritage of the Hussites, the violence accompanying the events of 1848, the scuffling that attended the earliest political-party activities of the Slovaks under Hungarian rule, and the exploits of the Czecho-slovak Legions can all be claimed as parts of a historical legacy that is not exclusively nonviolent.[5]

Yet nonviolence under attack would still seem the stronger part of the national heritage. When compared with many other nations in analogous situations, Czechs and Slovaks certainly appear less prone to armed resistance. The rapid disintegration of Bohemian resistance after the defeat on the White Mountain seemed to foretell a future of relative nonviolence. The revolution of 1848 in Bohemia and Slovakia was very minor in comparison with that in France, Italy, and Hungary proper; the workers' unrest in 1953 was nothing in comparison with that which broke out in Poznań and Budapest three years later; and, of course, the public reaction to the occupation of August 1968 and thereafter never approximated the fierce combat that had raged for several days in Hungary twelve years earlier.

Indeed, during both world wars resistance activities were counter-balanced by collaborationism. During World War I numerous Czech politicians, supported by pro-Vienna newspapers, opposed the aims of the Czech "Mafia" and attempted to rally the public behind the Emperor. They were joined by not a few Czechs, many of whom had positions of privilege in the socio-economic order of the Crownlands—but some of whom did not.[6]

During the Second World War collaboration was widespread among both Czechs and Slovaks, but for different reasons. The supporters of Tiso were eager collaborators, enthused at their separation from the Czechs and quick to join the Nazis in their systematic expropriation of the Jews. Czechs who collaborated, on the other hand, tended to do so more for reasons of survival or out of sheer opportunism than from political conviction. The safest thing to do was to swim with the Nazi tide, and for some who did so there were material rewards in addition. Still, for many Czech and Slovak collaborators there seems to have been a gnawing sense of guilt associated with their support of regimes they knew to be in violation of their higher moral instincts.[7]

There was collaboration during the Stalin years, when despite some misgivings many citizens flocked to the party bandwagon. The terror of the 1950s, moreover, produced many informers anxious to protect themselves and their families by betraying their neighbors. Again, there were collaborators in 1968. These were rather few in number at the time of the Soviet-led occupation, but their ranks grew in the course of the fall and winter of 1968–69. By the spring of 1969 the collaborators in the top ranks of the party had emerged as a force strong enough to unseat Dubček and "normalize" political life.[8] This meant, of course, the return of Czechoslovakia to colonial status — and the re-emergence throughout society of individuals who found it personally advantageous to acquiesce in the re-establishment of a system seen by others as repugnant.

If resistance and collaboration were the only forms of mass response to be found consistently among Czechs and Slovaks in times of national crisis, they might not be so different from, say, Hungarians, Poles, Dutchmen, or Norwegians — nationals of other minor European powers who have been similarly invaded or oppressed by larger powers. However, there is another pattern of behavior that is widespread at least among the Czechs at such times. Sometimes called "Švejkism," the pattern is characterized by elements of both collaboration and resistance, blended together in such a way as to suggest an unusual, if not unique, feature of the Czech national character.

It is easy to take one of two simplistic attitudes toward the notion of Švejkism: that it is, on the one hand, a quick and comprehensive explanation of Czech submissiveness or, on the other, a hackneyed stereotype undeserving of scholarly attention.[9] Yet Švejkism, a notion derived from fiction but used to describe real-life behavior, is taken seriously by numerous literary scholars, not just as a fictional syndrome but as a description of something very real and enduring. Let us now turn to the subject of Švejkism and see whether or not it sheds any light on the Czech situation.

Resistance Disguised as Collaboration:
The Good Soldier Švejk in Fiction and Real Life

Švejkism refers to the outlook and behavior of the Good Soldier Švejk, that bumbling, imperturbable, contemptible-yet-lovable hero of the well-known World War I novel by Jaroslav Hašek.[10] More specifically, Švejkism is used to describe real-life manifestations of behavior and outlook reminiscent of the fictional syndrome. As discussed by literary scholars, the word itself has taken on an international familiarity; there is, of course, a Czech word for it (*švejkiada*) and even a Russian word (*shveikovshchina*). Švejkism suggests a basic passivity, an outwardly serene and compliant demeanor coupled with a proclivity for joking about tragic circumstances, but also an inner revulsion toward one's social and political environment. Švejk, in the novel, is a secret rebel who fundamentally rejects the world around him. The world is oppressive and absurd, and he is aware of that. Instead of fighting it, however, Švejk chooses to ridicule it together with all its established values. There are indeed sufficient grounds for ridicule, and Švejk's special talent is uncovering the many absurdities that surround him.

The story of the Good Soldier Švejk is a familiar yarn, but in order to establish the relevant pattern of behavior, let us begin by reviewing some of the episodes from the Hašek novel. It goes without saying that Švejk should be seen as a caricature, a grotesque exaggeration of reality, but like all good fictional characters he embodies certain profound truths of human nature.

Josef Švejk, stricken with a severe attack of rheumatism, refused to let his infirmity interfere with his patriotic duty. The Austrian Archduke had just been shot in Sarajevo, and the war had broken out. The Emperor called his male subjects to arms; Švejk responded by appearing at the recruiting office in a bathchair wheeled by his trusty charwoman, Mrs. Müller. From Švejk's previous military record it is ascertained that he is mentally unfit for service. When asked what else ailed him, Švejk mentioned his rheumatism but insisted that he would gladly serve his Emperor despite this malady. He was forthwith locked up as a malingerer.

Thus begins the career of the Good Soldier Švejk in the First World War. From this beginning the misadventures follow one upon another in a hilarious and complicated sequence of events. Released from the malingerers' ward, he passes through the garrison prison, where he meets the company chaplain, Otto Katz. Katz, a converted Jew but unconverted drunkard, takes a liking to Švejk and makes him his attendant, a job which largely consists of undoing the chaplain's mistakes and rescuing him from self-destruction. Then the chaplain, having lost everything in a card game with Lieutenant Lukáš, gives Švejk to the lieutenant in a final defeat. Švejk becomes attendant to Lt.

Lukáš, and the misadventures accelerate. Švejk gets Lukáš into trouble by procuring for him a dog that turns out to have been stolen from a colonel. Later, he loses one of the lieutenant's suitcases by leaving it unattended while reporting to Lukáš that the luggage is all right. Then he becomes separated from his company enroute to the battlefront and wanders around in circles for a long time before he is finally arrested and shipped back to where he belongs.

Always eager to please his master, Švejk takes pains to follow his orders literally — so literally that his obedience often results in silliness. Typical of this is a telephone conversation just behind the front lines. Lukáš tells Švejk to be brief to avoid wasting precious military time, but it is Lukáš who makes the conversation long and pointless while Švejk responds punctually and crisply. Then, as Lukáš prattles on, Švejk carries his punctuality to an extreme:

> [Lukáš] ". . . Now, listen very carefully to what I say. . . . As soon as you hang up the receiver. . ."
>
> There was a pause and then renewed ringing. Švejk picked up the receiver and was drowned in a heap of abuse: "You animal, you guttersnipe, you blackguard, you. What the hell are you doing? Why do you break the connection?"
>
> [Švejk] "Please, sir, you said I was to hang up the receiver."[11]

Švejk's special talent is his ability to respond to the general absurdity of his situation in a way that makes everything seem utterly ridiculous. He is by no means alone. All around him are people who respond similarly, seeking the most ludicrous ways possible of subverting the system. For example, when Švejk is thrown into the malingerers' ward, he discovers some very sick men along with the genuine malingerers. All of them were subjected to various torments, ranging from starvation diets to the punitive application of enemas, in order to purge them of their supposed hypochondria. A man pretending to be nearsighted broke down after having his stomach pumped, and a second gave up his pretense at deafness following an enema. When Švejk then announces that he has rheumatism, he is greeted by derision, as his new roommates assure him that this excuse will not get him out of combat duty. Even a dying consumptive wrapped in cold sheets to "cure" his hypochondria laughed at the idea that rheumatism would be accepted as a legitimate excuse.[12]

Throughout the novel we are frequently shown two sides of the Good Soldier Švejk. One side is for public display, and to the extent it is possible, this side attempts to appear innocent, patriotic, and stupid. The other side is shown only to close friends and other people who can be trusted with Švejk's true opinions. Švejk would never slander the Emperor before his authorities, for example, but in the company of another Czech flunky he does not mince words. He declares that the Emperor is "completely off his rocker" and so senile that he needs two wet nurses. Švejk then pronounces the harshest of judgments on the Austrian state itself: "A monarchy as idiotic as this ought not to exist at all."[13]

It is not just the Emperor who serves as the butt of Švejk's jokes. He aims his barbs at religious institutions as well: ". . . in the orphanage at Benešov, after they'd brought them water from Lourdes, the orphans got diarrhea the like of which the world has never seen."[14] Austrian politicians come in for their share of ridicule, also; Švejk is heard to marvel at the fact that the inmates of a lunatic asylum are allowed to babble and carry on virtually unrestrained, just as if they were in parliament.[15] And of course one should not forget the military official-dom, for example Colonel Friedrich Kraus, who "was so colossally stupid that the officers avoided him from afar. . . ."[16]

In addition to iconoclasm and ridicule, there is a streak of gallows humor in Švejk. He is quite capable of joking lightly about the most dreadful circumstances, even when they affect him personally. When informed by Lukáš that they would soon be sent to the Serbian front, where all the previous regimental officers had been killed, Švejk says "It'll be really marvelous when we both fall dead together for His Imperial Majesty and the Royal Family. . ."[17] Nor is his gallows humor derived only from his own situation. On one occasion he spends a night in criminal detention, where throughout the night he listens to the moans and cries of prisoners being tortured in nearby cells. This he recalls as one of his "most affectionate memories."[18]

Švejk and his peers are consistently seen by their superiors as either scoundrels or idiots — but Hašek prefers to leave judgment to his readers. In fact, on balance they seem very clever indeed. In most cases they act as they are supposed to act; they play the military, political, or religious game by the rules. Inwardly, however, they reject everything about the established order. They show this rejection not by outright resistance but by playing upon the ridiculous aspects of their world, mocking the authorities by taking them literally. In the words of a Czech literary critic,

. . . they do not resist the authorities and their commands, they do not revolt, they do not show opposition, on the contrary they demonstrate ardent obedience, obstinate determination to carry out the orders required of them. And it is through this exaggerated willingness, this consistent seizing upon the official letter of the law that they carry the matter *ad absurdum,* they turn the world of authority upside down, they ridicule it and demonstrate its nonsensical nature, its cruelty, its falsity.[19]

So far, we are admittedly dealing with fiction. How seriously should we take the Good Soldier Švejk? Is he to be seen merely as an entertaining character figuring in a story now more than a half century old, or is there indeed something more real and enduring about his personality? Does Švejk, as a literary character, have anything to tell social scientists about the empirical world? It is the thesis of the present argument that both Švejk and Hašek, his creator, are to be taken seriously and that the fictional character does have something to tell us about real life. *The Good Soldier Švejk,* as an interwar Czech encyclopedist put it, is "important not only in its esthetic value . . . but above all significant as a sociological document."[20]

This is, of course, a very controversial argument. Even the literary value of *Švejk* has been a matter of some controversy ever since its publication. Hašek himself was something of an outsider to the predominantly bourgeois literary circles of Prague both before and after the First World War. He was a "bohemian" with a severe drinking problem who had come from a working-class family, been inducted into the Austro-Hungarian Army, and defected to the Russian side during the war. In Russia he joined the Czechoslovak Legions, but then he apparently became disillusioned with the rightist political tendencies among the legionaries and drifted away from them, at one point joining the Bolshevik party. Perhaps something about the Bolsheviks disillusioned him, too, for upon his return to Prague he withdrew from political activism and devoted himself to writing. He never joined the Communist party of Czechoslovakia.[21]

Hašek's literary work, in addition to *Švejk* and one other novel, amounted to some 1500 short stories, all of them based on the idiom of the streets and pubs of his home town. Because he wrote in the dialect of the common man, with a great deal of blasphemous and scatological language, Hašek was considered by the literary elite of his day as unartistic. At the time of his premature death in 1923, Hašek had alienated almost the entirety of the Czech literary establishment. Nonetheless, his stories — especially *Švejk,* who quickly became the subject of many oral anecdotes among the working class — had their own following among the common folk. It was this fact that led first the left-wing intellectuals of Bohemia, and later others, to recognize the true genius of Hašek.[22]

Immediately upon the publication of the first volume of *Švejk,* the Communist publicist Ivan Olbracht saw the novel as a new type of literary work, directed to the common man and filled with a progressive social message. Five years — and Hašek's death — transpired before bourgeois critics could bring themselves to take the novel seriously, but in 1926 an article by J. O. Novotný appeared which opened what was to be a long-running literary controversy among the Czech literati of all social classes.[23] It is interesting that some of the interpretations that have been drawn divide the critics into groups that do not coincide in every respect with their social or political identities; it is true that there is a general distinction between Marxist and non-Marxist interpretations, but in some instances Marxist and bourgeois critics find themselves arguing much the same point.

For example, the most limited social interpretation of *Švejk* can be seen in the criticism of the aforementioned Communist, Olbracht, as well as in that of the bourgeois philologist Albert Pražák. Olbracht saw Švejk as a wartime character responding to the exigencies of life during the world war; so did Pražák. Švejk thus emerges as a little man caught up in a war of which he really wants no part; thrust into it against his will, he seeks to live with the reality as best he can. His behavior, then, is a self-defense mechanism employed to get himself through an impossible situation while at the same time illustrating the senselessness of the war.[24]

A somewhat broader view of Švejk as a social actor comes out of a certain strain of bourgeois criticism in the mid-1920s. J. O. Novotný saw in Švejk not just an embodiment of anti-war sympathies but a statement of national rebellion against the old Austria. According to Novotný, Švejk is

> . . . actually the consummate expression and prototype of Czech passive resistance against the war, and of the tenacious life-and-death struggle between the Czech people and the Austrian regime even before the outbreak of the war. . . . Josef Švejk embodies . . . his nation's organized evasion of duty. . . .[25]

Novotný's view of Švejk as a more enduring social type was echoed by the Catholic writer Jaroslav Durych. Durych was understandably unsympathetic to the anti-religious outlook of Hašek, but nonetheless he saw in *Švejk* "a document which, among all the books in the world, gives the greatest view of reality. It is an embodiment of the nation. Here we are shown how the nation was and how it will be. . . ."[26] Novotný and Durych considered Švejk something of a national symbol, expressing the repugnance of the nation toward Austrian rule as well as the timelessness of the national spirit.

On a still broader level of analysis we have the orthodox Marxist-Leninist interpretation of Švejk. To some extent Olbracht's argument reflected this view, centering on Švejk as a common man revulsed at the idiocy of imperialistic warfare. However, the Marxist-Leninist interpretation really reached its standard form in the late twenties and early thirties, in the analysis of the Communist writer Julius Fučík. Fučík argued that Švejk, a "half-proletarian petit-bourgeois," stood for the intrinsic sympathies of the working class, in revolt against imperialism and bourgeois values generally. This revolt was brought to a head by the world war, but Švejk and others like him realized they did not have sufficient power to bring about a successful revolution and furthermore were unable to extricate themselves entirely from their ingrained habits of behavior. Pawns of the imperial order, their inner revulsion nevertheless drove them to express their opposition through the means available to them — the sometimes conscious, sometimes unconscious little subversive measures that befuddled an already confused military bureaucracy.[27]

Fučík's interpretation of Švejk as an international type born of the contradictions within imperialist orders was echoed by other Communists and indeed became the standard Soviet interpretation of Hašek and *Švejk*.[28] In the introduction to a 1967 Russian translation, for example, we read that Švejk personifies "the unwillingness of the masses to be reconciled with the 'madness of imperialism'."[29]

The broadest interpretations of all are to be found in the analyses of post-World War II Marxist critics, beginning with Bertolt Brecht and continued by what appears to have been the majority of Czech-Marxist literary critics in the 1960s. Brecht considered *Švejk* one of the three most important literary works of the twentieth century and modeled his play, *Schweyk im zweiten Weltkrieg* (Švejk in the Second World War), after it. He saw Švejk as a symbol of resistance to oppression that could take more than one form; Švejkism thus arises in response to fascism as well as to the more traditional forms of imperialism.[30]

Brecht's analysis was by no means a major reinterpretation of

Fučík's but rather amounted to an updating of Fučík's interpretation. A more radical revision appeared in Czechoslovakia with the 1960 publication of Milan Jankovič's treatise, *Umělecká pravdivost Haškova Švejka* (The Artistic Truthfulness of Hašek's Švejk). Jankovič argued that Švejk was meant to portray Czech society generally rather than just the working classes, and to typify the revolutionary sentiments of his people while oppressed by powerful ruling groups:

> Švejk is not the representative of a distinct social class. . . . The author leaves it unclear to the reader as to what Švejk's concrete social position is. . . . Švejk appears as one among other national types; in the development of the action, he becomes a spokesman for the national collectivity, a typical representative of the national collectivity.[31]

> . . . In the style of the popular humorist, Hašek made of Švejk a natural blend of the typical features of a people seeking to free themselves from dependency on the ruling class. . . .[32]

Jankovič's thesis was by no means unanimously accepted among Czech literary critics, but it set off a renewed discussion of the Hašek novel and influenced many Czechs to see the meaning of the work as one that transcends simple class analysis.[33]

The debate has not been completely resolved. The Good Soldier Švejk remains a controversial character, and the meaning of the novel a matter of sometimes heated polemic. There are those who would deny Švejk's resemblance to actual personalities, or write him off as a distortion or an insult. Many Czechs see in Josef Švejk a slanderous attack on the common man.[34] Others see him as a product only of the wartime circumstances, and an exceptional one at that.[35] Still others have decried the influence of the novel upon Czech readers, claiming that it puts forth a negative, immoral, or at least inappropriate pattern of behavior as one that should be emulated.[36]

To be sure, Švejk is hardly an exemplary hero type. Many of his characteristics — his insincerity, his sacrilegiousness, his apparent self-centeredness, and his disdain for moral issues — are not the features one looks for as a model for one's life. Švejk is not meant to serve as such a model, however; he is a portrayal of empirical reality as seen through the prismatic vision of a brilliant satirist. All the details of his personality are aimed at making one single, broadly expressed point: the world of authorities, bureaucracies, armies, social rituals, and political oppression is nothing more than an absurdity writ large, and the only way the "little man" can deal with such a world is to ridicule it.

Švejk is a soldier, and the primary stage of his exploits is within the context of the Austro-Hungarian Army. However, it seems persuasive that Hašek meant to use the military context as a convenient and timely convention. The army is absurd, but so also is life in the civilian world — a fact that seems amply confirmed by Švejk's occasional peregrinations into cities and villages.

Nor is Švejk merely a story about the effects of war upon society. It is, first and foremost, a comment on authority and an expression of deep skepticism toward the value system underlying the reality imposed upon society by those in power. Švejk is not, as one critic has argued, just a cynic and an opportunist who is out to get for himself as much from the system as possible.[37] True, he will never pass up an easy chance to get a free meal or a few days' holiday at others' expense, but this trait does not describe the whole Švejk. The benefits of the system come to Švejk irregularly and quite unpredictably; there is nothing he can do to ensure himself an easy time of it. His behavior rarely changes, but the rewards are constantly oscillating from pleasure to pain. If he chose, he could do otherwise, and maybe he would be better off — like Lieutenant Dub, the arch-loyalist — but he does not. Instead, he deals with the distasteful system in his own way, seeming to conform but actually ridiculing it.

This is exactly where the fictional character begins to bear some resemblance to real-life Czechs. In Josef Švejk we can see a parody of actual behavior in a real-world setting. He is a caricature, and to refer to Švejkism as a social phenomenon is to resort to the language of hyperbole, but it is worth considering the proposition that there is a significant element of truth in the caricature. Let us treat this proposition as a hypothesis and try to discern its empirical veracity.

First, it should be pointed out that Hašek's creation of Švejk was not an entirely original invention but, rather, came in the midst of a long tradition of Czech fiction. In its form, *The Good Soldier Švejk* evolved out of a series of pub stories which Hašek first tried out on his drinking buddies in the working-class beer halls of Prague. The pub story itself is a peculiar Czech custom dating back some centuries.[38] Secondly, the character of Švejk himself, as a recent Czech scholar has pointed out, really represents the modern reincarnation of the "wise fool" — a hero-type associated with medieval folk tales generally, and epitomized in Bohemia in the legends of the iconoclastic satirist Jan Paleček, a fifteenth-century court fool.[39] Thirdly, numerous Czech artists have since inherited Hašek's general approach to satirical writing. Allowing for some obvious differences in style and medium, one can perhaps see

Hašek's influence in the stories of Kundera, Hrabal, and Škvorecký, the autobiography of Jaroslav Brodský (*Solution Gamma*), the plays of Havel, and the films of Forman, Menzl, and Passer. All of these latter-day artists share with Hašek a peculiar capacity to ridicule the world in which they live, and an equal capacity to laugh at human foibles.

It is this capacity to laugh even when reality is cruel that one finds disarmingly often among Czechs. The national history has not been a happy one, and perhaps one would not expect to find humor widespread among a populace whose fortunes have been mostly tragic, but humor there is and always has been. Amid the most brutal historical circumstances, the "wise fool" has appeared again and again to satirize, confound, and befuddle the authorities.

Indeed, the wise fool can be a very disruptive force. During the Second World War, Nazi soldiers discovered that Czechs had suddenly forgotten the German they had learned in school and were of no help to them when they were lost.[40] A generation later, those Czechs who had forgotten how to speak Russian had a similarly difficult time directing the Soviet troops who occupied their country in 1968. On the other hand, those who had learned their Russian lessons better were able to make life uncomfortable for the visitors by haranguing them with arguments about the reality of the situation in Czechoslovakia. To add to the confusion, many citizens tore down street signs and directional markers, in some instances replacing them with signs pointing toward the homelands of the invaders.

Like Švejk, real-life Czechs have shown that they know when to keep their mouths shut and when they can speak freely. An American diplomat in Prague during the Nazi occupation noted that publicly, Czechs were compliant toward their German masters, but privately they expressed scorn and ridicule toward the Germans, mixing irony and bitterness in their intimate conversations.[41]

Collaborationist officials have often been the butt of popular jokes. Like Hašek, whose scorn for Czech military officers was gleefully expressed in *Švejk,* some Czechs of later generations have at times openly showed their contempt for traitors and collaborators. After the Munich agreement and the advent of the quisling Beran government, newsreel sequences of Beran shown in movie theaters were hissed and jeered, especially when the prime minister was shown with *Reichsprotektor* von Neurath.[42] A similar incident reportedly took place in a Prague theater sometime in 1969 or 1970. A newsreel showed party chief Husák greeting Leonid Brezhnev with the customary kiss on each cheek, whereupon a loud voice from the darkened theater shouted, "Why not his arse, too?" The newsreel was stopped, the lights went on, and the theater's manager stepped before the audience to demand that the perpetrator of this distasteful insult identify himself and apologize. Nobody did so, and the manager finally gave up. The theater was again darkened, and the newsreel rerun. When the dramatic moment came around again, the entire audience shouted in unison, "Why not his arse, too?"

The 1968 occupation was the setting for a prolific display of ironic humor, often at the expense of the invaders but sometimes in the form of self-ridicule. A program on Prague television several days after the arrival of the foreign troops satirized the tragedy. To a background of pop music, viewers were treated to a travelogue around Prague, complete with film shots of Soviet tanks, howitzers, antiaircraft guns, pockmarked buildings, and other scenic attractions.[43] A bus damaged by tanks and charred by fire bore the sign "House of Soviet Culture." Graffiti abounded throughout the country, and anti-Russian jokes were told countless times.[44] Later the jokes were turned inwardly upon the Czechs themselves: "Czechoslovakia is the most peace-loving country in the world; she doesn't even intervene in her own affairs."

Hašek had understood well the capacity of his countrymen to recognize the potential for humor amid tragedy. Švejk could make light-hearted comments about macabre situations, and his real-life descendants were just as capable of seeing irony in their misery. The graffiti writers and sign painters of 1968 thus joined the beer-hall wits of earlier generations in the spirit of Soldier Švejk.

Humor and ridicule of this sort have traditionally appeared in the Czech press. Before the First World War, Czech journalists frequently expressed their negative feelings toward the Austrian rulers through subtle satire, double entendre, and ironic associations.[45] These weapons re-emerged during World War II and the 1968 occupation, evidencing a touch of sly subversiveness on the part of those who informed the public. In 1939, for example, a Czech paper once reprinted a story taken verbatim from a recent Berlin newspaper, listing "fourteen lies of the democratic press." One of the lies denied in the story was that German troops would soon occupy Memel. The story was slightly outdated by the time the Czechs printed it, however, for a headline on the same page — again taken verbatim from a German paper — announced that Memel had just been occupied.[46]

Similar incidents occurred following the reimposition of censorship in 1969. One newspaper reported that Czechoslovakia's exports of footwear to the Soviet Union would be doubled by 1972, in the spirit of socialist cooperation. On another page of the same issue appeared an article complaining about the shortage of shoes in Czech stores. The proud announcement of the increased exports thus was rendered ironic by the implication that the Russian consumer's gain was the Czech's loss.[47]

One of the most interesting happenings during the weeks immediately after August 21, 1968 was the resistance carried on by members of the press. Their courageous efforts to continue reporting facts under the pressure of the occupying troops have been discussed at length elsewhere and need not concern us in detail.[48] Newspapers, radio crews, and television stations went quickly underground on August 21, reporting daily events from secret, movable locations that were not brought under control by the foreign troops until after several weeks' time. Journalists and broadcasters thus kept the public informed about the events of the occupation, and they were aided by technical crews who kept the presses rolling and the radio stations on the air. Here again, the wise fool appeared, sabotaging the facilities prior to the arrival of the troops and feigning inability to repair them until after the troops had left.

Sabotage was not limited to the activities of journalists. Railwaymen got into the act as well, thereby reviving yet another tradition. Inexplicable work stoppages and track diversions on more than one occasion caused the delay of supplies being shipped to the occupying forces from the USSR.[49] The railwaymen of 1968 thus relived for a short time some episodes out of the Second World War, when railwaymen were sometimes called the "blue army" because of their activities. Breakdowns and delays occurred commonly, and numerous political exiles owed their escape early in the war to cooperative railwaymen.[50]

But we have now gotten slightly off the track, so to speak. Let us once again return to the proposition that Švejk represents real life. To some extent, it seems that the proposition is borne out by the behavior patterns just documented. Many Czechs themselves will admit to the aptness of the Švejk caricature (though some will deny it vehemently). Some rediscovered their kinship with Švejk in 1968, as illustrated in a back-page newspaper story that appeared on August 27. Švejk was cast into the current situation, talking in his typically offhand way to Mrs. Müller about the Soviet occupation and expressing his gratitude to the fraternal troops for helping him understand the complexities of political reality.[51]

Švejkism does not tell the whole story of the Czech situation. Tragic circumstances do not give themselves to constant public mirth, and it would be a mistake to imagine the Czechs incessantly chuckling during the unfortunate events of the occupation periods. Anger and pathos have been equally evident. Impromptu memorials to victims of the Gestapo and those of the Soviet Army sprang up at the sites of fatalities; the sounds of the national anthem or Smetana's "My Country" brought tears to the eyes of strong men; pilgrimages to the graves of national patriots were made in the deepest solemnity; and even the art of graffitists sometimes took on somber tones ("We do not need Russian grain for our dead").

There is a seriousness in the situation that cannot be dismissed. The crises of the Czech nation have meant not merely absurdity; they have brought on the loss of life, the death of loved ones, the loss of personal and national dignity, the bitter adoption of the colonial mentality. The Švejk model cannot adequately account for these elements of genuine human tragedy. Švejk is real, and he exists among Czechs of every generation, but his saga gives us only a partial insight into the nature of the Czechs as a small nation dominated by more powerful neighbors. To understand this condition fully we must take account of the pathos that accompanies the small-nation syndrome, a pathos that is not unique to Czechs but that finds its particular Czech expression in the national tradition of nonviolence.

The pathos of Czech nonviolence is what ultimately connects Slovaks with the tradition. It is inaccurate to identify Slovaks with the Good Soldier Švejk; Hašek's novel is about Czechs. The story applies to Slovaks only to the extent that it portrays human character traits that are universal rather than specific — for example, the little man's inability to fight against a great power directly, or his tendency to seize onto the benefits of the system when offered to him. However, there is nothing characteristically Slovak about the gallows humor in *Švejk,* nor is it easy to find examples of any more general Slovak inclination to laugh at one's own misfortunes. (From among the members of the student generation in 1968 there did ensue the same outpouring of graffiti that appeared in Prague, but then the events of 1968 are historically isolated.)

Far more apparent in Slovak history is a general tendency to polarize into loyalist and oppositional groupings — the Magyarones vs. the nationalists, the Czechophiles vs. the Hlinka Populists, the Tiso supporters vs. the resistance, the federalists vs. the nationalist-progressives. Some of these groups enumerated above have obviously been anything but nonviolent; those of the Second World War were blood enemies. Yet throughout the course of Slovakia's troubled history there have been relatively few extended periods of violent rebellion or open resistance against the oppressor.

Czechoslovakia's leaders have long reflected the nonviolence that is central to their society's political traditions. Among these leaders is where one finds the most evident marks of the pathos running through the two nations' histories. Political leaders do not have the range of alternatives open to them that anonymous citizens have; they cannot readily disguise their true feelings toward the foreign invader while bowing to his command — at least they cannot effectively subvert his authority by mocking it. They are faced with the arduous choice between compliance and noncompliance. Those who have sought a middle course, like the post-Munich leaders, have failed. The plight of national leaders under such circumstances is pathetic indeed, for it brings the plight of the nation into focus as one that ultimately has its effect on the personal level.

The Pathos of Leadership: Nonviolent Traditions

Nonviolence in philosophy and action has been particularly characteristic of Czech political leaders. It is extraordinary in a nation with a cultural history more than a thousand years old that during the last five hundred of these years not a single person has emerged who can be considered a major revolutionary hero. Not since the days of Hus and Žižka have the Czechs produced such a figure. There has been no one comparable, in these terms, to Lenin, Mao, Robespierre, Kossuth, Kościuszko, or even Gandhi. When passive resistance has prevailed there have been those who appealed in vain for a more active strategy — Rieger in the 1860s, Gottwald in 1939, and small groups of dissidents in 1968–69. None were able to persuade many of their countrymen, the vast majority of whom followed their more characteristic inclinations to nonviolence.

It is even difficult to consider the great President-Liberator Masaryk a revolutionary in the usual sense of the word. In a broader sense he was, certainly, the leader of a revolution that overthrew Austro-Hungarian rule and instituted a new social order. Masaryk was a fighter, and he held steadfastly to his own lofty principles even under fierce pressures, yet his revolution developed almost in spite of himself. He led no uprisings, he moved no men to erect barricades in the streets. His revolution occurred as the result of careful planning, diplomacy, tireless organizational work, and propitious timing. He chose to pursue independence only after many years' experience had persuaded him that meaningful reform within the Austrian system was implausible, and he liberated his people at a time when the odds were most favorable and the prospect of losses minimal. Significantly, independence was not won "independently" but rather came about partly as a result of exogenous events — the world war and the disintegration of Austria-Hungary — and Western support for the Czechoslovak cause.

Masaryk often seemed perplexed by the problem of reconciling his own religious humanism with his belief that violence in the cause of moral principles, or in self-defense, was necessary; he once had a lengthy argument with Tolstoy about the latter's pacifism.[52] At the same time, Masaryk placed little faith in revolution, which on at least one occasion he equated with dictatorship: "Revolution or dictatorship can sometimes abolish bad things, but they can never create good or lasting ones."[53]

Of Czechoslovakia's Communist leaders, none have been important revolutionary figures. Gottwald, the present leadership's candidate for such a distinction, can be called many things — a dedicated party worker, a ruthless power politician with a brilliant sense of timing, and the founder of Socialist Czechoslovakia — but not a revolutionary hero. The "Gottwald Revolution" (to coin a phrase of dubious accuracy) was in many respects a civil war against his own people, a protracted struggle against a population just emerging from the Second World War with neither the energy nor the desire to resist.

Dubček, a Slovak revolutionary of a sort, suddenly found himself thrust into the forefront of a radical political program with implications of a moral and theoretical revolution. He was, however, a reluctant revolutionary — a "hero against his will," as Pavel Tigrid has described him.[54] Moreover, the revolution that was in the offing in 1968 was not the product of his singular efforts. Rather, it emerged from genuinely collective leadership and blossomed into a movement that foretold the massive participation of the Czechoslovak public in the making of the revolution. Again, this was to be a revolution characterized not by the violent overthrow of an *ancien régime* but by careful planning and reasoned tactics.[55]

The "revolutions" of 1918, 1948, and 1968 thus fall into the broad pattern of nonviolence in Czech and Slovak history. The most dramatic changes of the two nations' recent political development took place in contexts of careful maneuvering rather than spontaneous uprisings, accompanied by a minimum of bloodshed and a maximum of efforts to avoid violence. This is a pattern that had been discovered by Czech politicians in the nineteenth century in their dealings with the government in Vienna, and it has ever since seemed the most compelling strategy.[56]

Beneš and Dubček

Of all the political leaders in the modern history of Czechoslovakia, Edvard Beneš and Alexander Dubček stand out as the most tragic symbols of the eternal national pathos. Both enjoyed the passionate support of their people before being betrayed by their own colleagues, foreign and domestic. Both experienced the exultation of progress toward a vague national destiny only to have their world come crashing down on top of them. Both men were very human, possessing more than ordinary capabilities but no less than ordinary weaknesses.

Beneš was a fitting representative of the Czech nation. His religious outlook was skeptical and humanistic, combining a belief in the divine with a coolness toward organized religion. His politics were those of a moderate, non-Marxist socialist with some sympathy for the moral goals of communism. He was not the majestic statesman-philosopher that Masaryk was. Masaryk's other-worldly idealism and intellectual brilliance placed him far above the everyday individual. This is not to say that Masaryk was not loved by his countrymen; in fact, Masaryk's people saw in him the uncompromising goodness that characterized the best in Czech self-images, and they were drawn to him because of it. Beneš was less brilliant, more earthly, less strong — all qualities that made him more typical of his people than Masaryk. Insofar as there could have been a worthy heir to Masaryk, Beneš qualified; but the two were by no means equal.

There were occasions when Beneš, under pressure, embodied the national tendency to give in outwardly while maintaining an inner stubbornness and firmness at the same time. Toward Hitler, he initially made a determined attempt to resist the dictator's demands for the Sudetenland, and he likewise resisted the pressures of his alleged allies, the French and British, for his country's capitulation. Then, faced with the crushing betrayal at Munich, he gave in, realizing that his friends would not come to his aid if he chose to resist further. This was not a heroic moment in Czechoslovakia's history, but it did reflect a sense of realism and an overwhelming instinct for survival.[57] Beneš appealed for calm and nonviolence, aware that any attempt to stage a national resistance in the absence of great-power support was doomed to a quick catastrophe. Five days later he resigned from the presidency, amid the criticisms of Communists and some others who publicly protested their country's capitulation. Rightly or wrongly, Beneš simply felt that in the long run his nation's chances for survival were better served by the path he chose. He quickly disassociated himself with the newly imposed order and went into exile in order to prepare for the long road to a restoration.[58]

It is an entirely moot question whether or not Beneš's stance was in the best interests of his country. Beneš was hopeful that Nazi Germany would collapse before long, and he believed this strongly at the outbreak of war. Ironically, Beneš's decision not to defend Czechoslovakia might very well have prolonged Hitler's endurance, for the occupation of the Czech lands in 1939 placed the German army in control of a highly strategic location and represented a prize addition to Germany's military-industrial plant. Had Beneš's wishful thinking about an early German collapse been correct, his decision in 1938 might have proven to be a wise and patient one, for his homeland would then have been spared the destructiveness of a resistance effort. In the long run the decision not to resist ensured the physical survival of Czechoslovakia, but the moral damage of the long war was immeasurable. Relatively little physical destruction occurred, but the Czechoslovakia that Beneš had known before 1938 was not saved. After 1945 Beneš found his country broken, demoralized, bitter, and sharply divided. It was this Czechoslovakia that turned to communism in 1948 and thereafter veered dramatically away from the ideals and purpose underlying the previous political culture.

Beneš himself bore a large part of the responsibility for this. He emerged from exile in 1945 as the leader of his people, a man whom most of his countrymen were ready to forgive and to reestablish as Masaryk's heir.[59] Of all the surviving noncommunist politicians, he alone might have wielded the authority to preside over the restoration and reformation of the democratic order, and he alone might have been able to withstand the pressures from Moscow and curtail the Communists' abuse of their positions. However, as early as 1943 Beneš took steps that ultimately made it possible for the Communists to make their ascent. In his eagerness to ensure the Communists' support for a broadly based postwar order, Beneš had signed a treaty of friendship with the Soviet Union in 1943 and taken great pains to incorporate the Czechoslovak Communists' desiderata into his plans for the future. It was established that the left would predominate, that

National Assembly elections would be held as soon after the war's end as possible, that National Committees — important to the Communists' power drive — would be organized as a political infrastructure, that radical land reform and a partial nationalization of industry would be carried out, and that collaborators would be dealt with severely.[60] All of this Beneš accepted as consistent with his deeply held desire to build a newer, better Czechoslovakia, a Czechoslovakia that would live up to the ideals of the First Republic while strengthening its international position. The latter would be done by means of a diplomatic neutralism, with Prague poised as an intermediary between the powers of East and West.[61]

The treaty of friendship with the USSR was the first step in this new neutralism, but it was not an entirely novel departure for Beneš. A certain pro-Russian orientation had long underlaid Czech attitudes, and although this was neither unanimously felt nor unambivalent, it was a factor that distinguished Czech nationalism from, say, Polish nationalism. Earlier, it had been expressed in the Prague-Moscow alliance of 1935. The 1935 alliance had been illusory, but the Soviets nonetheless could excuse their failure to defend Czechoslovakia in 1938–39 on the grounds that their obligation presupposed French action. The capitulation of the French and their British allies in 1938 exonerated Stalin — to his great relief, no doubt — and turned the Czechs toward a pro-Soviet orientation that was destined to be just as illusory and tragic as the 1935 alliance.

For Beneš, the tragedy of 1948 was doubly disheartening. The activities of the Communists between 1945 and 1948 must certainly have signaled their ultimate intentions, thereby destroying the naive confidence Beneš had had in them earlier. Their final victory came as a personal humiliation to Beneš, impelled as he was toward yet another capitulation. Since 1945 his noncommunist colleagues had been timid and ineffectual when they were not fighting among themselves, and Beneš himself had consistently shied away from a direct showdown with the Communists. In the National Assembly the noncommunist delegates were frequently backed into ideological corners, unable to propose alternatives to the Communists' plan and unable to unify themselves in opposition to the latter's mounting power. A political vacuum developed as a result, and the Communists were able to move easily into it.[62]

Thus the Communists were the only viable, nonpassive political force prepared to offer the firm leadership needed in the crucial postwar years. Beneš, never an aggressive actor during moments of crisis, did not lead the offensive that would have been necessary in 1947–48 to head off the Communist victory. Perhaps he could not; by 1948 he was known to be unwell, and indeed he died shortly after his resignation from the presidency that summer. The road was open for an aggressive political force; the prize was total power. The Communists moved, and Beneš's last tragic act was to preside over his country's entry into the Stalinist era.

Twenty years later, under very different circumstances, a brave Communist whom the knowledgeable observer Pavel Tigrid has called "every inch a Slovak" was to meet similar frustration. Alexander Dubček was, of course, not a singularly powerful man; he never achieved the personal authority Novotný had exercised, and there were other men in 1968 who were equally strong — Smrkovský, Černík, Husák, and Biľak in particular. Nevertheless, Dubček was the most visible personality of the reform era, and certainly the greatest popular symbol. It was he who popularized the slogan "socialism with a human face," thereby signaling to the public a dramatic change in the party's policies and intentions.[63]

Dubček was a man of great decency, compassion, modesty, and accessibility. He preferred to trust other people — this was to be a part of his downfall — and, in turn, he himself was candid and straightforward. Many Czechs and Slovaks alike came to love and idolize him, as they had loved Masaryk and Beneš.[64] Crowds responded to him very warmly, despite his tendency to shyness and lack of oratory brilliance. As a leader, he was at times strong and determined, but at other times he could be indecisive and (as Jiří Hendrych once referred to him) a "hesitater."[65] He was so upset by the occupation of his country and the apparently rough treatment he received during his abduction into the Soviet Union that he suffered a complete physical collapse.[66]

Dubček's faith in communism was unshakeable and remained so even after his removal from office. For him, communism held the answer to all political problems. He had not been among the first in the party to work for major reforms, but he did speak out boldly at the critical moment of truth for Antonín Novotný; Dubček was the first to challenge Novotný at the Central Committee plenum of October 30–31, 1967, at which time the then first secretary's political fortunes began to fall.[67] As soon as Dubček found himself in Novotný's former position he began to play a leading role in rectifying the party's past mistakes according to what he considered true Communist policies. He was passionate in his support of the Slovak national cause, but as first secretary of the Czechoslovak Communist party he came to see himself as a leader in the cause of all citizens' interests. "Socialism with a human face" was not just a catchy slogan; Dubček took it seriously. "Everything that we are undertaking," he said of the party's Action Program, "is for the human being." The party's primary interest, he emphasized, was to work for the people, that they may "live better, more freely, and more happily."[68]

There were limits to the freedom that Dubček foresaw for his people. Democracy, he argued, entails discipline; the majority will rule, and the minority must then submit to that rule. Time and again Dubček's public utterances showed his concern for moderation and order, for proceeding along the path of democratization "prudently, deliberately, without hysteria and, I repeat once again, true to the ethic of our party."[69] There was no question in his mind but that the leading role of the party must not be challenged. He favored the reintroduction of elections that gave voters a choice of candidates, but for those who wanted the return of opposition parties he had no sympathy.[70] When the writers of the "2000 Words" shocked the party with their implicit challenge, Dubček wasted no time disassociating himself from what he viewed as forces threatening "a return to anarchy and destruction, to the disintegration of social unity," and who "seriously endanger the democratization process."[71]

Modest though he was in most respects, Dubček fatally overestimated his ability to persuade Czechoslovakia's allies that all was in proper Marxist-Leninist form back home. On several widely publicized occasions he journeyed to other bloc capitals to explain the Czechoslovak program, each time returning home with the optimistic report that the allies understood and supported his policies. Some Czech commentators did not share his sanguine appraisals of the international situation; their misgivings were later confirmed, but in the meantime Dubček continued to trust in his ability to deal with Brezhnev, Ulbricht, Kádár, et al.[72] Thus his shock at the news of the occupation is quite understandable.[73]

When the invasion came, Dubček went on radio and television immediately to plead for nonresistance and calm. Upon his return from Moscow following his humiliating abduction, Dubček called upon the public to trust him and to end their resistance activities.[74] Even at this point, and during the ensuing several months, Dubček believed that the Soviets could be persuaded to tolerate the continuation of the Czechoslovak reforms. By the time of his downfall, Dubček obviously came to learn otherwise; the truth, once again, was crushing.

Six years later, in an open letter addressed to the Federal Assembly and the Slovak National Council, Dubček once more expressed his abiding faith in communism. The letter, much publicized in the West, showed the disgraced Dubček to be embittered by his own personal situation but still convinced that the program that he helped shape in 1968 contained the solutions to Czechoslovakia's problems. With the same naive self-assurance that had distinguished his arguments during the Prague Spring and Summer, Dubček chided the Warsaw-Pact allies for imposing a dogmatic solution in ignorance of Czechoslovakia's specific national conditions. Over and over again he defended the policies of 1968 and strongly condemned the reimposition of "old practices" which, he wrote, had led to an even greater crisis than the party had faced in 1967.[75]

We are left with a rather pathetic image of Dubček, the fallen hero, shorn of all political influence and employed in rather menial work. It has been argued that Dubček, out of power, has become the de facto leader of an increasingly vocal opposition in Czechoslovakia.[76] This may be true, but as of this writing the opposition has yet to show any practical viability and is in constant danger of being eradicated. Dubček himself remains politically unpersoned and constantly under surveillance.

The image is especially pathetic because it reminds us of that most recent episode in a longer pattern of Czechoslovak humiliations. Once again, rightly or wrongly, the leadership chose a nonviolent response to the foreign invasion. Memories of Munich were quickly revived in 1968–69, and again citizens were forced to acknowledge that their country was miserably helpless against the might of a great power. Their colonial status, of which they have since been repeatedly reminded, is all the more psychically brutal because they feel they can do nothing about it.

Pathos and Absurdity

In the behavior patterns of the masses, compliance has predominated over resistance both from 1948 to 1968 and since 1969. Open resistance has seemed futile; the chances of success are too slim, and the costs of failure too high, to justify public opposition.

Many outsiders have asked how it could be that such people, raised on principles of democracy and pluralism, could submit to autocratic rule without putting up a resistance. Both Czechs and Slovaks, morally and psychologically exhausted from the war years and the rapid pace of postwar reconstruction and social revolution, accepted the imposition of Stalinism without the overt resistance one might expect from peoples with their political backgrounds. Why they did so is not easily answered; perhaps it cannot be answered at all.[77]

In this respect, it is worth considering Skilling's suggestion that the chain of historical events culminating in the war, reconstruction, and revolution undermined citizens' faith in the national traditions and fatally weakened the public will to resist the horrors of the fifties.[78] There is a good deal of truth in this hypothesis, but two objections must nonetheless be raised. In the first place, there unquestionably *was* resistance, a deepseated inner resistance on the part of everyday citizens unwilling to become the "new men" of the Stalinist social model. On the surface, they could conform as if they accepted their role as prescribed for them; they performed the ritual activities of obeying orders, attending rallies, "volunteering" for overtime work, and so on, just as Švejk fulfilled his formal obligations. Underneath, there was widespread rejection of the system and its values, a mass compulsion to turn inwardly into one's personal life, and a great deal of contraband joking about the common misery.[79] It is true that there was no active resistance to Stalinism, but neither did the Stalinists succeed in converting the entire working class to their own professed convictions.

Secondly, it must be remembered that at no time in the modern history of Czechs and Slovaks have they effectively resisted the determined wishes of a thriving great power. The few experiences of national resistance (in 1848, 1939–42 for the Czechs and 1944–45 for the Slovaks) had proved to be costly and, except for the Slovak National Uprising, unproductive. Thus Czechs and Slovaks did not have relevant experiences in their past from which they could draw the lesson that active resistance pays. This is very important if we are to take the concept of apperception seriously in our behavior model, for according to apperception theory, individuals will tend to refer to past experience as a guide to present behavior.[80] It is difficult, therefore, to *expect* resistance on the part of people who are not historically conditioned to resist, even when they are compelled to accept a reality that grossly violates their most cherished traditions.

While conforming outwardly, Czechs and Slovaks managed to keep alive their sense of values. These might have undergone some modification under the influence of daily ideological training; certainly, the absence of significant antisocialist tendencies among the many public patterns of 1968 suggests that in at least this respect public values were transformed. However, independent thinking — something the Stalinists had tried to stifle — had not stopped. During the Prague Spring it was apparent that people had done a lot of thinking about their situation. It required only one further step to translate thinking into acting. For twenty years it had been impossible to act according to one's thoughts, but in 1968 the possibility suddenly came alive. The spiritual and intellectual resistance which Czechs and Slovaks had practiced during the preceding two decades had equipped them to survive those years with many of their basic orientations to political action intact.

It is here that the concept of Švejkism might shed some light. *The Good Soldier Švejk* does not explain how an individual or a community can hold onto cherished values in the face of protracted experiences with resocialization. Indeed, it is hard to argue that Švejk himself has any strongly held values at all. He knew what he did not believe, however, and he also knew how to feign belief when it was necessary. In Stalinist Czechoslovakia, the ability to do this was the precondition to physical survival. One way of making it through that troublesome time was to behave as Josef Švejk might have — to obey orders and display unquestioning loyalty — even while feeling revulsed by the entire political system.

Psychological survival requires something further, and here again the model of Švejk suggests a meaningful lesson. A sense of humor, even though it may be perverse and (by someone else's standards) cruel, can be an enormous help when one must live under the thumb of others. Earlier chapters of this book have explored the incongruence between the Communists' system of beliefs and institutions and the underlying political orientations among Czech and Slovak citizens. To those individuals who are inclined to see the incongruities as reflections of a general absurdity in life, the situation can be best dealt with in terms of the absurd.

As in Švejk's world, there have been sufficient examples of absurdity in the world of Socialist Czechoslovakia — the Stalinist conversion of an already modern economy (at least in the Czech lands) into a system geared for premodern economic mobilization;[81] the elimination of political opposition in a highly pluralistic society, done in the name of the workers' interests; the attempt to generate mass enthusiasm for a government that ruled by coercion; the consciously antinationalistic policies disguised under the watchword of "internationalism"; and the practice of terrorizing, in the name of socialism, a society long predisposed to at least certain aspects of socialism. The incongruities eased somewhat in the course of the sixties and nearly disappeared in the Prague Spring, but after 1969 they returned as prevalent as they had ever been. The situation after 1968 may be even more incongruous than that of the early 1950s. Then, there were many believers in the revolutionary cause; today there are few. A generation ago Czechoslovakia was undergoing radical social change; today the regime struggles to hold the line, fearful of change. Originally, Communist believers hoped that the masses would eventually be persuaded to share their vision; today many believers themselves have fallen away, the apathy of the masses is taken for granted, and their compliance with the norms of the political charade is bought with a relatively high material standard of living, according to the terms of the "new social contract."[82]

Survival entails an ongoing effort at living one's life according to the demands of the system, even when that involves a conflict with one's values. The psychological result is a cónstant source of dissonance between what the individual believes and how he acts. According to cognitive dissonance theory, the tendency at this point should be toward restoring consonance, or reducing the level of dissonance, between beliefs and behavior.[83] Not everybody is capable of doing this, and one finds many citizens either sinking into frequent states of depression or lapsing into nihilism.

For others, the obvious response to an absurd situation is absurdity itself. Instead of fighting the system, many choose to deal with it in its own terms. They behave as the system demands, perhaps sometimes to an extreme and ludicrous degree. They learn the proper slogans of the day, whether they be "Long live the Emperor" or "With the Soviet Union forever," and recite them with gusto. In the *appearance* of carrying out their duties they can exceed the zeal of their superiors, but then, there are many times when the superiors do not care to inspect the results closely. Like the nature of political life in general, this is all a part of the contemporary charade.

The psychic dissonance inherent in the situation is reduced in two ways. On the one hand, people know that to behave in the approved manner can bring material rewards, for the state does encourage the advancement of those who are loyal. At the same time, people know that not to behave correctly is to invite punishment; tens of thousands of political prisoners in the fifties, and smaller numbers of people who lost their specialized jobs after 1969 attest to the reality of the threat. The carrot can be very succulent indeed, and the stick very heavy. The incongruity of living out of harmony with one's beliefs is rationalized by the knowledge that no other alternative makes much sense.

Secondly, the dissonance can be further reduced by perceiving the behavioral demands imposed by the system as symptomatic of a generally senseless world. To view the whole environment as an absurdity is to discount incongruities; if all is absurd, the notion of incongruity is irrelevant, for within that absurd world nothing makes sense. One can therefore live in whatever way is necessary for survival, holding onto one's own beliefs (or holding none, as one chooses) and laughing at the overall situation in the meantime. In the mid-1970s it was fashionable for some people to respond to their friends' query, "How are things?" by replying, "I can't say" — implying, of course, not that they do not know how they feel but that they are not supposed to admit how bad things are.

All the nations of Eastern Europe have had to make adjustments to the persistent rule of outsiders, German, Russian, or Turk. All have developed collective patterns of behavior that, during most of the time spent under foreign domination, reflect an adjustment to the wishes of the conqueror. None, obviously, have engaged in constant struggle against the outsider. However, other nations have on occasion unleashed their collective fury against the oppressor and attempted — sometimes successfully, sometimes not — to throw him off by means of violent national revolution. Czechoslovakia's nearest neighbors, the Poles and the Hungarians, have revolted in the post-1945 era, but in calmer moments they too have had to adjust.

It is within neither the scope of this study nor the expertise of this author to describe and explain the patterns through which other nations in Eastern Europe cope with their situation. To some extent they have all behaved in ways that might be likened to Švejkism, conforming on the surface but harboring their own skepticism within. The use of the Švejk paradigm to describe reality must in any case be made with all due qualifications. In the present case, for example, it is probably true that only in the vaguest sense does Švejkism describe the behavior of Slovaks. Slovaks are not so quick to laugh at their misfortunes and tend to take the matter of personal convictions more seriously. Like the Czechs, however, they too have been consistently nonviolent under conditions that might have provoked other nations to rebellion.

The methods of survival practiced by Czechs and Slovaks within the threatening reality of their geopolitical location have at times cost them what Westerners might self-righteously call the pursuit of "higher ideals." At the risk of appearing cynical, we might suggest that the pursuit of higher ideals is a luxury available to peoples who do not have to contend with survival in the face of irresistible pressures to demean themselves.[84] For Czechs and Slovaks, the pursuit of higher ideals has been possible only exceptionally in their history. This is not to say that they are incapable of high-minded idealism; quite the contrary. When given the opportunity, they have thought great thoughts and displayed the noblest motivations. The opportunity to develop strong, consistent philosophic traditions in the contemporary era, however, has been denied them by the brutal facts of geopolitics.

Herein lies the greatest element of pathos in their situation. Without the chance to develop national spokesmen who can once again articulate the best in their traditions, Czechs and Slovaks are cut adrift from their past. The cultural revival of the 1960s paralleled that of the nineteenth century (although on a smaller scale) and reminded both nations of their worth, but the leaders of that more recent intellectual awakening are now *personae non grata* in their homeland.[85] As of this writing, no one has emerged to take their places, and those who have dared to speak out in their defense have mostly been silenced or sent into exile. As a result, culture languishes amid the mediocrity of those literary and scholarly works which the government finds unobjectionable.

As for political opposition, it can be said to exist but not to flourish. Small-scale acts of protest and the occasional circulation of "open letters" take place, but the regime is still fully capable of using the powers of the police and the propaganda machine to atomize potential opposition groups. The fate that has befallen the Charter 77 group within only a few months after its circulation of the human-rights petition is testimony to the difficulty of organizing for political alternatives.[86] Thus the prospects of significant change in the foreseeable future do not seem promising.[87]

In the meantime, a fellow who looks strikingly like Josef Švejk can be seen in the streets of Prague and elsewhere frequenting his favorite pubs, extemporizing on the quality of socialist education or nonchalantly describing President Husák as an ox. There is no longer a senile Emperor to serve as the butt of his iconoclastic jokes, but the dignitaries of the Czechoslovak Socialist Republic will always provide a laugh or two.

Conclusions

Political Culture, Revolution, and Small Nations

The meaning of Slovak history is to be found in the mission of small nations in history generally.
— Daniel Rapant (1967)

. . . there has never been anything self-evident about the existence of the Czech nation. . . .
— Milan Kundera (1967)

The foregoing chapters present evidence bearing upon three important aspects of the theory of political culture: the relationship between underlying patterns of political orientations within a society and the parameters of likely political change; the special tasks of, and the obstacles encountered by, revolutionary leaders who seek to change mass political orientations in a radical way; and the precarious status of cultural persistence for politically dependent nations.

The first two of these questions have been explored by numerous scholars in earlier articles and monographs, although one looks in vain for systematic attempts at proposition-building. Works cited in the introductory chapter, above, have dealt in detail with questions of political culture and political change (Almond, Verba, Pye, Tucker, *et al.*), and additional studies by Fagen, Solomon, Barghoorn, Jowitt and others have treated aspects of political culture and socialist revolutions.[1] Little attention has been given to the special theoretical problems arising from the study of small nations whose political culture is crucially influenced by great powers.

The first part of this chapter is aimed at formulating a number of general propositions suggested by the case of Czechoslovakia. These are offered in the interest of encouraging further study of political cultures, an enterprise that is in need of some systematic methodological groundwork at the present time. The propositions offered are not intended to exhaust the empirical ground covered either by the theory of political culture or the data of the present study. The inquisitive reader will undoubtedly find many more hypotheses implicit in the growing literature on the subject (including this monograph).

The second part of the chapter will summarize some of the lessons of the Czechoslovak experience more specifically.

Some Propositions

The first three propositions are of a very general nature, dealing with ideas that are implicit in much of the previous literature on the subject of political culture.

Proposition 1 Within every society exist certain culture-related or culturally derived impulses that condition political reality in important ways.

These impulses act as intangible forces operating through the psychological processes of individuals, conditioning them to view political reality according to lessons they have learned from previous experiences. On a mass level, general patterns of such individual predispositions will be observable. Depending on the complexity of society and the uniformity or diversity of previous political experiences, there will be one, two, or more major patterns of interrelated beliefs, values, and orientations to political action. In addition, there may be any number of subcultural patterns that differ from the major patterns and may or may not be significant factors in the overall political configuration. All such patterns (including subcultural patterns) that *are* politically salient will tend to impose constraints on society's political alternatives. Hence, a corollary to Proposition 1:

Proposition 1-a Political institutions and policies will reflect the values and orientations of one or more of the significant cultural patterns within a society.

If the political leadership of a society holds a set of values and operates according to political orientations that are in conflict with those of other significant groups, the latter will tend to resist the programs and policies of the leaders. To the extent that the resistant groups are strong enough to obstruct the successful application of the government's policies, the leaders will be constrained to modify their political expectations. Therefore,

Proposition 1-b Successful political programs are dependent on a substantial degree of social support by groups beyond the governmental leadership. Such support is in turn dependent upon some compatibility of values held by the political leadership and a reasonably broad portion of society.

In the case of Socialist Czechoslovakia, we have found a rather heterogeneous political culture in which there are two major patterns, the Czech and the Slovak, and a ruling subculture, that of the Communists. The impulses derived from these distinct traditions have conditioned citizens to view political reality from at least three diverging angles. Because the political institutions and policies exclusively reflect the values and orientations of the current ruling elite, there exists a serious gap between rulers and ruled. Very little social support for the regime's objectives can be found beyond the circles of the ruling elite. As a result, major social objectives — from satisfactory levels of labor productivity to the internalization of socialist norms — seem unattainable. In one brief period of political reform and renewal (1968–69), the leadership attempted to rectify the fundamental incongruence of official and mass orientations. A remarkable degree of success seemed within reach just as the reforms were stopped and then reversed. In the years since, the gap between rulers and ruled has returned, and the social objectives of the government continue to be elusive.

One of the methods through which a government frequently attracts and maintains its needed base of social support is its identification with, and manipulation of, popular symbols.[2] This leads to a second major proposition:

> *Proposition 2*   The degree of public support for a government
>   will correlate directly with the ability of the government to
>   identify itself with popular political symbols.

In the task of creating or maintaining political cohesion within a society, emotional affect can be as important as effective policies. A government that embodies widely accepted national traditions, carries forth the legacy of past patriots, and makes use of compelling slogans will be much more popular than one that is deficient in any of these affective criteria.

Socialist Czechoslovakia has been characterized by governments who are incapable of identifying with positive public symbols. The Communists' denial of the Masaryk legacy, along with all the other nostalgic memories of the First Republic, has alienated the wider portion of the Czech populace. The status of the Slovak legacy is more ambiguous, but the Communists' denial of the nationalist argument during the 1950s and '60s drove a wedge between Prague and

Bratislava even further than in the First Republic. Moreover, the retreat of the Husák government from its pro-Slovak position since 1969 has once again damaged the regime's support base in Slovakia. Here, too, the reform leadership of 1968–69 had made substantial headway in identifying the government with both Czech and Slovak popular symbols — democracy, pluralism, federalism, humanism — only to find frustration in the return of "normalized" politics.

Significant aspects of a political culture can undergo change or transformation over time. The conditions underlying such cultural change are complex and difficult to separate in terms of causal inference, but some of them can be at least hypothetically identified. At the same time, an attempt can be made to identify those conditions that tend to promote continuity within the political culture. Consider, therefore,

> *Proposition 3* The general conditions underlying the dynamics of continuity and change in a political culture include (i) goals and efficacy of political leadership, (ii) rate of economic and social development, (iii) strength of traditional value systems, and (iv) presence or absence of external constraints;

and two corollaries:

> *Proposition 3-a* The following conditions will tend to promote continuity within a political culture: (i) a leadership which either derives its goals and policies from traditional values or is unable to induce mass acceptance of new ideas; (ii) a relatively slow pace of modernization and a tendency toward stability in patterns of social stratification; (iii) strong traditional value systems; (iv) a relatively strong foreign influence in support of traditional patterns.

> *Proposition 3-b* The following conditions will tend to give rise to changes: (i) a leadership that favors change and is able to persuade the public to support policies of change actively; (ii) a relatively brisk pace of modernization, including rising standards of material welfare and a rearrangement of stratification patterns; (iii) weak traditional value systems; (iv) a relatively strong foreign influence in support of change.

The interplay of these factors in Socialist Czechoslovakia has been complicated, leading to very mixed results. The leadership has consistently held fast to the goal of revolutionary social change, but both the type of changes seen as necessary to achieve this goal and the level of the regime's actual commitment to necessary changes have fluctuated. The Stalinist years (to approximately 1956) and the "Prague Spring" were times of manifest commitment on the part of the leadership to sweeping changes, but the direction of change in 1968 was vastly different from that of 1948–56. The period 1956–67, on the other hand, can be seen as a time when the leadership attempted to hold the line against changes percolating up from mass society. The post-1969 years have involved a general retreat from the changes begun in 1968 and the "consolidation" of an unsteady status quo in which the regime's social support once again was lost, as it had been before 1968. Although there was some degree of social support for the revolutionary goals of 1948, it seems safe to say that much of it dissipated in the subsequent years of totalitarian rule. Only in 1968 did it appear that the regime had in fact attracted the overwhelming support of the constituency the Communists claimed to be representing. Given the sincerity of the reform leadership's commitment to genuine social change and the widespread support the Communists enjoyed in 1968, one can speculate that the long-hoped-for progress toward a basic, society-wide unity of revolutionary purpose might have been in the offing. However, the events since the Soviet-led invasion have restored the yawning gap between rulers and ruled. The post-1969 leadership has chosen to coexist with a passively disaffected public rather than to risk any new initiatives involving fundamental change. The pursuit of the revolutionary objectives, therefore, has been put aside in preference for the maintenance of the political status quo.

Economic and social factors have shown similarly mixed results. Economic development has proceeded more rapidly in Slovakia than in the Czech lands, but in both halves of the republic there have been significant shifts in the stratificational patterns. Curiously, the result was the continuity of a long tradition of pluralism in people's political orientations — but within that, a radical realignment of social and political forces around newly aggregated interest groupings. To the social scientists of the 1960s, the new pattern had just begun to come into focus. Political initiatives aimed at dealing with this reality were, like the other reforms of 1968, discontinued in 1969.

The strength of traditional value systems among Czechs and Slovaks has been discussed at great length in the preceding chapters, as have the nature and strength of the Soviet influence. It should suffice to say that both of these factors have shown some ambiguity, but that the two have generally been in contradiction with each other.

From the propositions offered above, it is only a short step to an additional hypothesis concerning revolutionary societies and political culture:

Proposition 4 Under any circumstances, revolutions incur difficulties generated by strong inertial forces arising from the political culture. Revolutions will succeed only to the degree that (i) they have widespread popular support, and (ii) the goals of the revolution can be perceived as being consistent with some important elements of the traditional political culture.[3]

Proposition 5 contains two interrelated conditions requisite to the success of a revolution. Before discussing them, it should be explained that "success" here refers to the attainment of fundamental goals as defined by the most important prophets and leaders of the revolution. In the case oı Communist revolutions, these would include Marx and Lenin as well as the leading national revolutionary figures.

Widespread popular support for the socialist revolution was presupposed by Marx, for the inertial forces in society would, he theorized, be swept away in the wake of the proletariat's victory. Marx argued that culture was a part of the societal superstructure, created and conditioned by the nature of authority relations in the economic base — and therefore subject to change as a reflection of changes in the basic relations.[4] Lenin discovered that the process of changing human attitudes would not be so straightforward or automatic upon the workers' victory. For Stalin and his successors, the task became very trying indeed. The inertial forces did not succumb upon the defeat of the bourgeoisie, and the latter's spirit has returned again and again in the form of revisionism, apathy, and subjectivism.

This might suffice as an explanation of Czechoslovakia's political difficulties had not the events of 1968 occurred. As soon as the Dubček regime made it known that real changes were in progress, and especially when the party made a serious effort to identify with some of the previously discredited national traditions, the party's stock among the public rose spectacularly. The institutional and moral revolution promised by the leaders of '68 thus attracted popular support by virtue of both the objective nature of the program and the appeal to popular symbols (democracy, national equality, "socialism with a human face"). The experience of 1968 should have put to rest all the old excuses for the failure of the socialist revolution, but instead, the post-1969 leadership has chosen to draw just the opposite conclusion, claiming that the policies of 1968 were disruptive — and precisely because they were dreamed up by "counterrevolutionaries" disguised as party reformers.

The heavy hand of the foreigner is obvious in the Czechoslovak experience, suggesting three further propositions about the nature of political culture in dependent countries. The first of these is:

> *Proposition 5* A political culture will develop a coherent shape only under conditions of prolonged political independence or autonomy. It is not necessary that the autonomy be complete; a dependent nation may be able to function and develop politically while under the rule of foreigners, but only so long as the rule is sufficiently lenient to permit the organic growth and systematic articulation of the dependent political culture.

The presence of foreign influence is a constant threat to the development of positive political values and stable communities of shared political orientations. The foreigner will often disrupt the organic process of political development, causing strains and frictions among the populace and sometimes dividing a nation against itself. This is not to deny the proposition that, under certain propitious circumstances, foreign influence can be a spur to national unity. National liberation movements are formed out of some common opposition to the imperialist, and the threat or actuality of foreign invasion during wartime can also be a force acting to bring a people together. Long-term political development, however, requires the absence of international crises and the evolution of positive (as opposed to anti-imperialist) unifying symbols.

Proposition 5 is sharply reflected in the case of Czechoslovakia. Because of the relatively lenient attitude of the Austrians, Czech society evolved its own coherent political patterns from the 1860s to the outbreak of the First World War. These patterns continued to evolve after 1918, creating a political culture among Czechs and Czechophile Slovaks which, despite certain tendencies toward ideological fissiparousness, had its own coherency and stability. The fatal shortcoming of the First Republic was its inability to integrate Czechoslovakia's minorities, as well as most Slovaks, into that dominant political culture. Because of this lingering internal problem, the international catastrophe took a much greater toll of the Republic's moral self-assurance.

The German occupation ended the continuity of political development for all times. Postwar political development took place in an atmosphere of continuing crisis which has in most respects persisted to the present day. The central feature of the crisis is a deep-seated, seemingly ineradicable estrangement of the broad body politic from those who, by the grace of the Soviet Politburo, occupy the seat of power.

This leads to the following:

    Proposition 6   Under conditions of protracted or intermittent
    political dependency, in which a colonial or quasi-colonial
    elite rules by the norms of an outside power, there will be a
    tendency toward a bifurcated political culture in which elites
    and masses do not share a common set of positive values and
    orientations.

Proposition 6 would seem to follow from all that has been said in the
preceding several hundred pages, but two further comments should be
made. One might ask at this point about "national communism" in the
Soviet bloc, particularly in Poland and Romania. Here the proposition perhaps runs into difficulties because of the emergence of
nationalistic leaders such as Gomułka, Gierek, and Ceauşescu, each of
whom has at one time or another managed to attract a substantial
public following on the basis of his ability to manipulate nationalistic
symbols. However, it could be argued that the strength of the symbols
used in each case inheres not so much in their contribution to a *positive*
national unity as in their representation of a fundamentally *negative*
unifying force — an expression, that is, of national unity as opposed to
the Soviet controllers. Indeed, when one looks beyond this negative
unifying cause, it is hard to find persuasive evidence that elites and
masses share many positive political values. The breakdown of
Gomułka's illusory national consensus in the years after 1956, the
reliance of the Polish regime on placatory economic measures to quiet
unruly workers in the 1970s, and the neo-Stalinist social control
measures standard in Ceauşescu's Romania all testify to the uncertainty of congruence between elite and mass political orientations.

    The situation referred to in Proposition 6 has obvious application to
dependency contexts other than that of the USSR's empire. The overthrow of native colonial elites was an important step in the liberation
of Egypt and other third-world countries, and one would expect some
further implications for the nature of elite-mass patterns in South
Vietnam prior to the American disengagement. American misunder-
standing of political realities in Vietnam — especially the Saigon
government's lack of any sturdy social base — can be readily compre-
hended in terms of a bifurcated political culture which American
officials simply failed to recognize for so many years.[5]

    One further proposition on the subject of dependency suggests itself:

    Proposition 7   Nations with a strong sense of past traditions
    will tend to refer to these as a source of sustenance while
    under alien domination, although a relatively weak national

tradition will not necessarily preclude either a sense of national injury or rebellion in the name of the nation.

The Czechs' sense of national traditions has, as we have seen, been stronger than the Slovaks'. The former is tied up with very mixed feelings of pride, humility, and frustration, and although one could make an argument for the irrelevance of past glories in the face of present-day weakness, there is something in the Czech past to sustain the nation through its perpetual crisis. "Before Austria was we were, and after Austria ceases to be we shall continue," Palacký's immortal rallying cry, might have a modern counterpart if we substitute the Warsaw Treaty Organization for Austria. Not surprisingly, one does not hear many Czechs voicing such optimism today, but neither has the nation forgotten the better moments in its past. In times of the greatest national tragedies — the German and Soviet occupations — Czechs have shown their national pride in one way or another.

Slovaks do not have as long and rich a historical tradition, but their collective sense of national pride is no less strong. The constitutional proclamation of Czech-Slovak equality in 1968 was a matter of great gratification to Slovaks, and the subsequent retreat from nationalism in official policy has not been mirrored in public attitudes. The present situation is less degrading to Slovaks than to Czechs, who take no solace in being the acknowledged equals of the Slovaks. Therefore, it is to be expected that the gloom which has descended over Bohemia and Moravia becomes less dark as one travels eastward into Slovakia. It does not disappear, though, for the reality of political life in Slovakia is nonetheless tied up with that of the not-so-distant ethnic cousins — and fellow colonists — populating the Czech lands.

Prisoners of Geopolitics

It might be said, as Pavel Tigrid has argued with regard to Czech history, that both Czechs and Slovaks have lived in a state of almost perpetual crisis in the modern period.[6] The crisis has not always been identical for the two nations, but there are certain features of it that both have shared. They have shared the constant threat of submergence under the pressure of greater nations located too close not to have a cultural impact. They have shared the exhilaration of national revivals, especially gratifying in the context of their threatened position. They have shared jubilant moments of victory, liberation, and the highest expectations, as well as agonizing defeat, humiliation, conquest and reconquest.

Pavol Vongraj, cited in an earlier chapter, has bemoaned the Slovaks' tendency to feel themselves bereft of a true national history — a feeling that is especially strong when Slovaks are reminded of the long tradition of Bohemia.[7] Christian Willars, a Czech-émigré journalist, has suggested that the Czechs themselves are not as "historical" as they think they are. Willars has, in fact, called his countrymen an "ahistorical" nation, because their discontinuous national development has prohibited the evolution of a genuinely historical view of life. In the place of a historical view of life, he argues, Czechs have substituted what they euphemistically call "realism." This "realism" is not the realism of Masaryk's noble and uplifting philosophy, but rather it is a "type of 'realism' which produces adaptation to every act of villainy, overlooks *real* reality and . . . negates those very values that must be preserved in order to prevent really tragic peripeteia and catastrophes."[8]

Both of the above views are exaggerated, spoken as they were in moments of rhetorical exuberance. Vongraj was expressing the pent-up frustrations of Slovaks at their longstanding condition of cultural derivativeness, and Willars was engaging in the traditional Czech custom of national self-deprecation. Both nations do have a history of which they can be proud. If the moments of ignominy seem to outnumber those of glory, it is not really the fault of Czechs and Slovaks, who have the misfortune of a geographical placement between the historically overwhelming German and Russian cultures. True, Czechs and Slovaks have usually shrunk away from fighting the national cause when it has been threatened, and they might be called either realistic (for understanding the impossible odds) or cowardly (for not fighting anyway, as a matter of principle). They cannot be justly blamed for this predicament, for there is no strong evidence that another course of action at any critical moment in their history would have guaranteed a greater continuity in their national development. If the lessons of Finland (in 1939-40) and Yugoslavia (in 1948) suggest that fighting or resisting might be the better course, the lessons of Hungary and Poland throughout the modern era suggest a less clearcut answer.[9]

Nineteen sixty-eight, the most recent opportunity for fighting the national cause, might have been a turning point in Czechoslovakia's history of a scale even greater than it has seemed. In the first place, the intervention of the WTO allies definitively ended the national preoccupation with the German threat. For hundreds of years Czechs had lived in constant and usually hostile confrontation with Germans,

while Slovaks (although buffered by the Magyars) also found themselves within the sphere of the greater German culture. Even after
Germany's cataclysmic defeat in 1945, the spectre of a German revival
haunted Czechoslovakia; German "revanchism," the myth of which
was assiduously promoted and hyperbolized by the Soviet protectors,
was the justification for the Soviet protectorate and the excuse for an
official anti-Western psychosis under the guise of "vigilance."

Incredibly, many otherwise perspicacious Czechs and Slovaks
blamed the political misdeeds of 1948 and after entirely onto their own
Communist leaders, failing to recognize the ubiquity of Soviet influence. To some extent, this rather naive supposition underlay the
optimism of the "Prague Spring"; the mistakes of the recent past were
the result of policies made in Prague, and therefore they could be
corrected by reforms made in Prague. The intervention dispelled these
notions and awakened the Czechs and Slovaks to the reality that they
were politically accountable to an outside force. Confronting this
revelation, Czechs and Slovaks realized that the real national enemy
lay not to the west but to the east.[10]

In the second place, 1968 was a turning point for Czech-Slovak
relations. That this is true is obvious in the enactment of the federalization law, but the change in Czech-Slovak relations goes beyond institutional matters. To this day many Czechs are convinced that the
Slovaks' only interest in 1968 was federalization, that democratization
meant to them only a means to pursue autonomy, and that in the
critical months after August 21 the Slovaks' lack of concern for pre-
serving the reform momentum was the deathblow to democracy. There
is, of course, some truth in this; the position of the Slovak "moderates"
did indeed become the vehicle for the restoration of autocracy. However, the Slovak "moderates" could not have gained the upper hand
without the collaboration of the Czech extremists, and without the
latter it is doubtful that any coalition of indigenous political forces
would have abandoned the programs of 1968 so thoroughly. The
lingering suspicions are there, nonetheless, coloring the attitude of
Czechs toward Slovaks and intensifying a bitterness that had temporarily dissipated in the Czech-Slovak unity during the first weeks of
the occupation.

Thirdly, the abortion of the political rebirth in 1968 carried with it
the end of the cultural flourish of the preceding years. The impact upon
literature, drama, the cinema, and all the arts is altogether too obvious.
Less obvious is the impact upon the process of national self-rediscovery
that began in the sixties. History and the social sciences have been set

back decades in the years since 1969, and serious philosophy has ceased to exist. Moreover, in the vulgar atmosphere of the "new social contract," other values have taken precedence over self-knowledge, namely self-preservation and material self-indulgence. Otto Ulč has said that the *dacha,* the family automobile, and the pet dachshund have become the replacements for ideological zeal.[11] It might be said that the quest for these possessions has also triumphed over the quest for national self-realization. The advent of a consumer society, so long in coming to Eastern Europe, brings with it not only the benefits of what we in the west have been conditioned to call "better living"; it brings also a source of distraction from those spiritual aspects of life which Czechs and Slovaks have found frustrating and painful.

The regime is not happy with the present condition of public apathy, but the leaders are willing to settle for apathy in the absence of enthusiasm. Indeed, there seems to be a widespread tendency to forget the past — encouraged by the regime's constant attempts to confuse the issues with ideological slogans — and there is even less interest in building the socialist future. The situation might be described as one of political incoherence and ideological malaise. The gap between rulers and ruled has never been so wide, and if President Husák or any new political forces decide to attempt the building of bridges, they will surely discover the difficulty in doing so.

The reasons for the present incoherence should be implicit in the preceding chapters, but it is appropriate to summarize them here. In the first place, Czechoslovakia is ruled by subcultural forces who have the decisive support of the Soviet Communist party. Without that foreign support, those in power today would not be in power; the current leadership knows this and appreciates the fact that it is mortally dependent on Soviet force to guarantee its tenure. The citizens know this, too, and feel the humiliation of rule by men whose mandate derives from an alien source. The fact that these men are Czechs and Slovaks makes the situation doubly humiliating, for it serves as a reminder of the long national tendency to accommodate the unprincipled foreigner and his whims.

Secondly, the subcultural force ruling Czechoslovakia embodies an ideology that goes against the grain of most of the national impulses, Czech and Slovak. The Communists in practice have been antihumanistic and therefore contradict a long strain in Czech intellectual history, and they are anti-religious, which puts them in fundamental conflict with the central religiosity of Slovak culture. The Communists purport to be the bearers of a revolutionary tradition, moreover, which among both Czechs and Slovaks is weak and distant at best. The party's attempts to revolutionize the masses have never been a resounding success, with the possible exception of a few months in 1968–69, and the fact that today's leadership has disowned the "Prague Spring" as "counterrevolutionary" has made its credibility as a revolutionary force dubious.

The ideology of monolithic class unity is another source of political incongruity. Between 1860 and 1938 the course of political development for Czechs and Slovaks led to a pluralism of a type too subtle to be explained by conventional class-conflict theories. In the 1950s and '60s there developed a new social basis for an incipient pluralism within a single-class society, giving an exciting dynamic to the politics of 1968 and destroying the myth of working-class unity. This, too, has been denied by subsequent rulers, who have preferred to ignore the empirical evidence disproving their own dogmatic analyses. In place of the spontaneous mass involvement in politics that characterized 1968, contemporary Czechoslovak politics offers the masses only the routine of controlled activity under the hackneyed slogan of class unity.

Thirdly, the national traditions are once again being denigrated. This is not as true in present-day Slovakia as in the Czech lands, for the preeminence of the Slovak nationalist Husák has served to preserve some of the nationalist revival of the 1960s. Czech national traditions, however, are nowhere in vogue and go officially neglected, and even the celebration of Slovak traditions takes place in a subdued and party-oriented fashion. One notes, for example, much ado over the annual commemoration of the Slovak National Uprising but no publicity around the date commemorating the arrival of Sts. Cyril and Methodius in what is now Slovakia.

Fourthly, the regime has consistently violated the spirit of what Czechs and Slovaks have traditionally understood to be *socialism*. With important exceptions among the Slovaks, socialism has a long and respected place among the positive political symbols of Czechoslovakia.[12] The social and economic justice implicit in the socialist promise has always been attractive to modern Czechs and Slovaks, and despite official practices since 1948 they do not generally confuse socialism with autocracy. With the exception of the Dubček regime, the successive Communist governments have discredited themselves by insisting that socialism is exclusively identified with their rule. Thus when Ludvík Vaculík, in his famous speech to the Fourth Writers' Congress, dared to separate the idea of socialism from the current ruling personalities, he was expressing what his countrymen felt but had not said openly: ". . . I am not persuaded that things need have turned out here the way they did and hence I cannot identify this power-system with the concept of socialism as the system itself tries to."[13]

It follows from the above that the Communists have contributed a sense of bitter division to the political culture, a deep vertical division cutting across all regions of the country. There are few outside the ruling elite who feel an identification with those in power. This condition is more true of the current system than it has been at any previous time in the past century. The Austro-Hungarian monarchy had its admirers among both Czechs and Slovaks, and the Slovak state of World War II did also. Even the pre-1968 Communist regime had some basis of support within society — among the radical intelligentsia, left-wing trade unionists, youthful idealists, and so on. The government of the 1970s has very little social support; it seems more isolated from mass currents than even the Novotný regime was in its last months.

In the mid-sixties public confidence in the government, and in the appointed authorities elsewhere in society, was very low. As Vaculík put it, "I don't know whether you have noticed it, but all of us, Czechs and Slovaks, wherever we work, are inclined to believe that the men who tell us what to do are less competent than we are."[14] Vaculík did not have to add that this applied not only to the workplace but also in public life. Similar sentiments are heard in the pubs today, and bitter jokes about Russians frequently accompany them. Indeed, references to the rulers now carry implicit connections with the Russians — a link that was not automatically made before 1968.

The impact of a nearby giant is, of course, not unique to Czechoslovakia. Small nations generally live, to one degree or another, in the shadow of larger powers, and the threat of becoming subservient or derivative is ever-present. Consider for a moment the examples of the Dutch, Canadians, and Vietnamese. The Dutch, once a great imperial power but doomed by smallness to be a minor force in the modern era, have lived in dangerous proximity to Britain, France, Austria, and Germany, yet they have maintained a continuity of national development for centuries. Their independence has been interrupted only for short periods of time during all-European wars, and their national spirit has not been seriously shaken by these temporary crises. In part, the Dutch have the British to thank for this, because the traditional balance-of-power role played by Great Britain effectively incorporated Holland into an informal protectorate without causing the sacrifice of any part of Dutch sovereignty. In the post-1945 era the Netherlands have maintained their independence without the British role in a sub-continent that has been stabilized by the absence of imperial or ideological expansionism and strengthened by the organizations of the European Community.

Canada presents a rather different case. Nestled against a giant whose national aggressiveness has at times threatened Canadian inde-pendence, the Canadians have assimilated many features of life in the United States. American capital is an enormous force in Canada, American popular culture is Canadian popular culture, American tastes are often Canadian tastes, and American standards are, by and large, Canadian standards. This is not to say that there remains nothing distinctive about Canada. Canada has retained much more of British and French culture than has the USA, Canadian politics is significantly different from American politics, and Canadian citizens resent being confused with Americans. On occasion the Canadian government has defied American wishes, for example in extending early recognition to the People's Republic of China and in accepting American military refugees during the Vietnam War. However, the Canadian government must always remain sensitive to the mood in Washington when embarking upon foreign policy initiatives. More-over, it must always assess the impact of its actions upon American corporate interests; the Canadian economy is so closely linked to that of the USA that every tremor on Wall Street is felt in Montreal and Vancouver — but no similar, reciprocal Canadian impact is felt upon the economy or the politics of the United States.

Vietnam probably presents the most tragic case of small-nation struggle in the twentieth century. Throughout the many centuries of imperial history in East Asia the Vietnamese have felt the ebb and flow of first Chinese, then French, Japanese, and American expansionism. The anti-colonial struggles of the past few generations are only the modern sequel to the ancient conflict with China, and the struggle involving the United States is the last chapter. The end of the anti-colonial struggle occurred in the era of devastating modern warfare. The physical and psychological wounds of the last forty years are so deep as to seem irreparable. The clash of hostile ideologies added fuel to the already fiery struggle, sometimes dividing families and severing close friendships. Because many remained on the peripheries of the ideological conflict, however, there is a chance that the political wounds that have arisen since 1945 may be healed in the course of time. Whether or not the physical and psychological wounds heal is a more difficult question. At least the prospect of self-rule is a welcome relief from the century-long national struggle, and in time the common task of governing themselves may bring the Vietnamese together, thereby mitigating the recent tragedy. In the meantime, the example of this small nation's fate will long serve to emphasize the dreadful catastrophe that looms as an ever-present possibility for small nations generally.

The nations of Eastern Europe have always faced this kind of threat. Historically they have been engulfed in the perennial clash of great European empires, now merely extensions of this or that empire, now independent. The history of the region illustrates the phenomenon; one reads of the rise and fall of Greater Moravia, Bohemia, Poland, Serbia, Croatia, Hungary, and so on. Prisoners of geopolitics, the East European nations have rarely been entirely independent. The nearest approximation of a nation-state system, that of 1918–39, proved to be so unstable that it did not last beyond the maturing of one human generation.

Today most of the nations in the region are outposts of the modern bureaucratic empire centered in Moscow. It is to the credit of the contemporary arrangement that Eastern Europe has settled into a condition of relative stability since 1956. The biggest threat to that stability — the Czechoslovak crisis of 1968 — was stifled with a minimum of force and bloodshed, and the restoration of "normalcy" has proceeded more peacefully than one might have expected. In the larger international context, East-West détente has at least partially relaxed the deep-seated Soviet fears concerning the sanctity of Moscow's empire. Europe, the source of so much world tension in recent centuries, is now one of the least conflict-prone regions on the globe.

Of course, for the East Europeans the price of such regional stability has been a general impingement upon national independence. The limitations on national sovereignty have varied from time to time and country to country. Yugoslavia, of course, made a successful exit from the Soviet bloc in 1948, when global tensions and an American nuclear weapons monopoly made the time propitious. Albania, geographically remote from Moscow, proved to be of little significance to Soviet interests in the region, and the Albanians were allowed to drift giddily along the trail of a Chinese-style radical communism. Romania's leaders have displayed remarkable agility in dancing on an ideological tightrope suspended between conservative domestic policies that are quite to the Soviets' liking and bold foreign policy adventures that have sometimes vexed the Russians.

For both historical and geographic reasons, the countries bearing the greatest comparability to Czechoslovakia are Hungary and Poland. In the years of the Soviet empire, both Hungary and Poland have tested the limits of their national prerogatives. For the Poles, conservative reforms have quieted the occasional rebelliousness of impatient citizens, and political caution on the part of the PZRP leadership has assuaged Soviet doubts about the undulating course of events there since 1949. For the Hungarians, the explosion of 1956 brought on a Soviet response that left no doubt about the nation's lack of independence. Several years of recriminations yielded to the careful reconstruction policies of the Kádár regime. Ever mindful of the lesson of 1956, Kádár has led his nation through a course of moderate reforms without relaxing the authority of the Communist party. Hungarian society is by no means free of repression, nor is it (in any western sense) "liberal" or politically pluralistic, but neither is it intolerable or even more than mildly uncomfortable for the Hungarian worker. In fact, it can probably be said that Hungarian life today is as nearly democratic as it has been at any time in the past, and Hungarian politics is as much in keeping with the national traditions as present circumstances will allow.

This cannot be said of Czechoslovakia. Indeed, one of the dangers of any future relaxation there would run the risk of reawakening the democratic and pluralistic undercurrents so deeply embedded in the political culture. Czechs and Slovaks are trapped by the danger inherent in any honest recollection of their national histories. Attempts may be made to strike a balance between the current repressiveness and the spontaneity that would surely erupt again once the political constraints were relaxed.[15] Nineteen sixty-eight remains a bittersweet memory, in the meantime; the happiness of the Czechoslovak Spring is veiled behind the persisting vision of all the events that followed the occupation. It is difficult for Czechs and Slovaks to accept the lesson of 1968, and whether or not they will be able to fashion a political compromise à la hongroise is still a matter of conjecture.

Notes

INTRODUCTION

1. This is best expressed in *The State and Revolution* (1917).

2. A good example is Edward A. Taborsky's *Communism in Czecho-slovakia 1948-1960* (Princeton: Princeton University Press, 1961).

3. Among social scientists of the postwar era, the first statement of the political culture idea appeared in Gabriel A. Almond's article, "Comparative Political Systems," *The Journal of Politics*, XVIII: 3 (August 1956), pp. 391-409. The first use of the concept in a textbook on comparative politics appeared in Samuel H. Beer and Adam B. Ulam, ed., *Patterns of Government* (New York: Random House, 1958). For important developments of the concept, see Almond and Sidney Verba, ed., *The Civic Culture* (Princeton, 1963); Lucian W. Pye and Verba, ed., *Political Culture and Political Develop-ment* (Princeton, 1965); Carole Pateman, "Political Culture, Political Struc-ture, and Political Change," *British Journal of Political Science*, I: 3 (July 1971), pp. 291-305; and Pye, "Culture and Political Science: Problems in the Evaluation of the Concept of Political Culture," *Social Science Quarterly*, LIII: 2 (September 1972), pp. 285-96. A balanced but not very successful critique is that of Dennis Kavanagh, *Political Culture* (London: Macmillan, for *Government and Opposition, 1972*). For a discussion on the level of "basic concepts" which, unfortunately, avoids some of the more recent innovations in the concept, see Walter A. Rosenbaum, *Political Culture* (New York: Praeger, 1975).

In the field of Communist studies, see Frederick C. Barghoorn, *Politics in the USSR* (Boston: Little, Brown and Co., 1966, 1972), as well as his contri-bution to Pye and Verba, *op. cit.* (1965); Richard R. Fagen, *The Transforma-tion of Political Culture in Cuba* (Stanford: Stanford University Press, 1969); Richard H. Solomon, *Mao's Revolution and the Chinese Political Culture* (Berkeley: Univ. of Calif. Press, 1971). See also the symposium volume edited by Archie Brown and Jack Gray, *Political Culture and Political Change in Communist States* (New York: Holmes and Meier, 1977). Pertinent articles elsewhere include Robert C. Tucker, "Communism and Political Culture," *Newsletter on Comparative Studies of Communism*, IV: 3 (May 1971), pp. 3-12; *id.*, "Culture, Political Culture, and Communist Society," *Political Science Quarterly*, LXXXVIII: 2 (June 1973), pp. 173-90; Francis Castles, "On Communism and Political Culture," *Newsletter. . .*, V: 1 (November 1971), 55-56; Dorothy W. Knapp, David W. Paul, and Gerson S. Sher, "Digest of the Proceedings of the Arden House Conference on Communism and Political Culture," *Newsletter*, V: 3 (May 1972), pp. 2-17; Stephen White, "An Empirical Note on Communist Political Culture," *Newsletter*, VI: 2

(February 1973), pp. 41–44; Paul, "A Further Empirical Note on Communist Political Culture," *Newsletter,* VI:4 (August 1973), pp. 6–11; and Kenneth Jowitt, "An Organizational Approach to the Study of Political Culture," *American Political Science Review,* LXVIII:3 (September 1974), pp. 1171–91.

4. See Alfred G. Meyer's discussion of this role in "Communist Revolutions and Cultural Change," *Studies in Comparative Communism,* V:4 (Winter 1972), 345–70.

5. Sidney and Beatrice Webb, *Soviet Communism: A New Civilization?* (New York: Charles Scribner's Sons, 1936), II, pp. 911–15. I am indebted to A. H. Brown for having alerted me to this early use of the term. See his *Soviet Politics and Political Science* (London: Macmillan, 1974), p. 89ff.

6. Harry Eckstein first suggested this approach in a preparatory memorandum for the 1971 Arden House conference. Cf. Jowitt, *op. cit.,* p. 1174.

7. Almond, "Comparative Political Systems," p. 396; cf. Edward C. Tolman, "A Psychological Model," Part 3 of Talcott Parsons and Edward Shils, ed., *Toward a General Theory of Action* (Harvard Univ. Press, 1951). In systems terminology, we are referring here to the conventional S → R model of social behavior (Stimulus → Response). Between the time of the stimulus and the individual's response to it there occurs a mediatory process (M) conditioning the response, an unseen and perhaps inscrutable process which is contained in the paradigmatic "black box" of what now becomes an S → M → R social behavior model. According to Almond, *loc. cit.,* the mediatory process involves cognition (in which the individual perceives the stimulus in a particular way), cathexis (in which he attaches some degree of significance to it), and evaluation (in which he applies his value judgments concerning alternative courses of action). Diagrammatically:

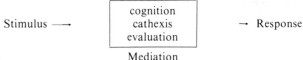

Stimulus ⟶   cognition / cathexis / evaluation   → Response

Mediation

8. See, e.g., Clyde Kluckhohn, *Culture and Behavior* (New York: The Free Press of Glencoe, 1962), p. 263.

9. A further diagram may help to illustrate:

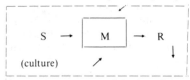

The mediatory forces at work inside the "black box" of M function under the influence of the cultural environment. The latter envelops the entire situation, thus not only influencing the cognitive processes (M) but also, in many cases, conditioning the nature of the stimulus (S). In turn, the response (R) may make some contribution to the further development of the culture itself, for behavior patterns are a component of culture. (See discussion below.)

10. Here I am purposely taking a stand on the controversial question of whether to view political culture as a system of beliefs or to adopt an anthropologically oriented definition, thereby including objective phenomena such as patterns of behavior. I have opted for the latter, and in so doing I have joined Fagen, Meyer, Tucker, Jowitt, and Geertz as against Almond, Verba, Pye, and

Beer. See my essay, "Political Culture and the Socialist Purpose," in Jane P. Shapiro and Peter Potichnyj, *Change and Adaptation in Soviet and East European Politics* (New York, Washington, and London: Praeger, 1976), pp. 3–17. See also Fagen, *op. cit.,* p. 5; Meyer, *op. cit.,* pp. 347–50; Jowitt, *op. cit.,* p. 1173 and *passim;* Tucker, "Culture, Political Culture, and Communist Society," pp. 176–79; and Clifford Geertz, "A Study of National Character," *Economic Development and Cultural Change,* XII (January 1964), pp. 207–08. Cf. Almond, "Comparative Political Systems," p. 396; Pye, in his introductory essay to Pye and Verba, *op. cit.,* p. 7; Verba, in his concluding chapter to *ibid.,* pp. 523–26; and Beer, in Beer and Ulam, *Patterns of Government,* pp. 12ff.

11. *Culture and Behavior,* p. 46.

12. There are obvious differences among these particular examples, and they are not meant to be taken as equivalent. Personality, for example, may influence the speed and intensity with which an individual will respond to a stimulus, as will his health. Weather and time of day will probably be less salient over a long run, but they may have a significant impact upon specific actions undertaken at specific moments: the citizen who stays home on a rainy election day, the California voter who casts his ballot after hearing some early returns from the Eastern time zone.

13. Meyer, *op. cit.,* p. 349. (Emphasis in the original.)

14. Fagen refers to "patterned ways of life and action as well as the states of mind that sustain and condition these patterns." *Op. cit.,* p. 5.

15. In Kluckhohn's words, culture is "an abstraction from behavior." *Culture and Behavior,* p. 25.

16. Verba, p. 521; Tucker, "Culture, Political Culture, and Communist Society," pp. 179–81; also Edward W. Lehman, "On the Concept of Political Culture: A Theoretical Reassessment," *Social Forces,* Vol. 50 (March 1974), p. 364.

17. I construe politics quite conventionally, that is, as a set of activities relating to the authoritative allocation of values among the members of a society.

18. For a more abstract discussion of political salience in this general context, see Moshe M. Czudnowski, "A Salience Dimension of Politics for the Study of Political Culture," *American Political Science Review,* LXII:3 (September 1968), pp. 878–88.

19. The literature on political socialization is a growing list, from which any attempt to assemble a representative sampling would be superfluous. Among students of Communist societies, Fagen has most successfully investigated the process, which he succinctly defines as "the inculcation of political information, values, and practices, whether formally or informally, in planned or unplanned fashion." (*Op. cit.,* p. 2 and passim.) For a discussion of how the process takes on a special character in Communist societies more generally, see Ivan Volgyes's introductory chapter in Volgyes, ed., *Political Socialization in Eastern Europe* (New York, Washington, London: Praeger, 1975). Cf. the present author's review of Volgyes *et al.* for a skeptical discussion of the empirical problems involved (*Problems of Communism,* XXV: 5 (Sept.–Oct. 1976), pp. 79–82).

20. My formulation of this proposition has been influenced by Cyril E.

Black's paper, "Theories of Political Development and American Foreign Policy," presented to Dartmouth Bicentennial Conference on International Affairs (unpubl., 1970), p. 13.

21. Cf. Meyer, *op. cit.,* p. 360ff.

22. "The Immediate Tasks of the Soviet Government," in V. I. Lenin, *Collected Works,* vol. 27 (Moscow: Progress Publishers, 1965), cited from p. 254.

23. For an analysis of the "new man" see Raymond A. Bauer, *The New Man in Soviet Psychology* (Cambridge, Mass.: Harvard University Press, 1952).

24. Fagen, *op. cit.;* Solomon, *op. cit.*

25. This is most clearly expressed in *The German Ideology* and the preface to *A Contribution to the Critique of Political Economy.* For a discussion, see Terry Eagleton, *Marxism and Literary Criticism* (Berkeley and Los Angeles: University of California Press, 1976), pp. 3–6.

26. Pye tells us that in studying political culture we must "treat both the historical development of the system as a whole and the life experiences of the individuals who currently embody the culture." — *Political Culture and Political Development,* p. 9.

27. Tucker, "Culture, Political Culture, and Communist Society;" Meyer, *op. cit.*

28. Pye, "Culture and Political Science," *passim.*

29. *Supra,* especially footnotes 7 and 8.

30. This strategy of inquiry would seem compatible with that suggested by Pye: ". . . political culture must be studied on the basis of an understanding of how the particular political system performs. The initial hypotheses about a political culture must thus take the form of statements which hold that the system behaves 'as if' certain values, sentiments, and orientations were the most critical in giving the collectivity its most distinctive character." (Pye, "Culture and Political Science," p. 293.)

31. Rosenau, *The Scientific Study of Foreign Policy* (New York: The Free Press, and London: Collier-Macmillan, 1971), pp. 116ff.

32. On this subject, see Rosenau, ed., *Linkage Politics: Essays on the Convergence of National and International Systems* (New York: The Free Press, 1969).

33. For some critical thoughts on the extent to which attitudinal data should be used in studies of any political culture, see my "Further Empirical Note on Communist Political Culture," *op. cit.* Cf. Archie Brown and Gordon Wightman, "Czechoslovakia: Revival and Retreat," in Brown and Gray, *op. cit.,* pp. 159–96. Although I do not disagree with their general argument, Brown and Wightman rely to an unjustifiably large extent (in my opinion) on a relatively small number of attitude surveys.

CHAPTER ONE

1. See Stephen F. Cohen, *Bukharin and the Bolshevik Revolution: A Political Biography, 1888–*1938 (New York: Knopf, 1973), pp. 123–59, especially 132ff.

2. Nowhere is this more poignantly documented than in Roy A. Med-

vedev's *Let History Judge,* edited by D. Joravsky and G. Haupt (New York: Knopf, 1971).

3. Ralph T. Fisher, Jr., *Pattern for Soviet Youth* (New York: Columbia University Press, 1959), p. 2.

4. For an interesting study of the "new man" stereotype as it appeared in Socialist Realist literature in the USSR and Hungary, see Paul Hollander, *The New Man and His Enemies,* unpublished Ph.D. dissertation (Princeton, 1965).

5. Bauer, *The New Man in Soviet Psychology,* pp. 147–150.

6. Robert C. Tucker, "Stalin and the Uses of Psychology," in *The Soviet Political Mind,* revised (New York: W. W. Norton and Co., 1971), pp. 143–172.

7. *Ibid.,* p. 166. See also I. V. Stalin, *Economic Problems of Socialism in the USSR* (New York: International Publishers, 1952); *id., Marxism and Linguistics* (New York: International Publishers, 1951).

8. On this subject see, e.g., Barghoorn, *Politics in the USSR,* Second Ed. (Boston: Little, Brown and Co., 1972), pp. 87–115.

9. See Fagen, *The Transformation of Political Culture in Cuba,* and Volgyes *et al., Political Socialization in Eastern Europe.*

10. For a lengthy discussion of the party's efforts between 1948 and 1960 to create the "new man," see Taborsky, *Communism in Czechoslovakia,* pp. 471–594.

11. Ivo Duchacek, "Education," in V. Busek and N. Spulber, ed., *Czechoslovakia* (New York: Praeger, 1957), pp. 162–63.

12. See, e.g., Dean Jaros, *Socialization to Politics* (New York: Praeger, 1973), especially pp. 97–123.

13. See Jindřa Kulich, "The Communist Party and Adult Education in Czechoslovakia," *Comparative Education Review* (June, 1967), pp. 231–243.

14. Galia Golan, *The Czechoslovak Reform Movement* (Cambridge: Cambridge University Press, 1971), pp. 109–19.

15. See, e.g., "Letter of the Minister of Education to All Employees in the University," and "Minister of National Education, Prague, to All the Rectors of the Universities and All the Deans of the Faculties," reprinted in *The New York Review of Books,* XIII (December 4, 1969), pp. 21–23; also the accompanying article by Hans J. Morgenthau, "Inquisition in Czechoslovakia."

16. For a more detailed treatment of these developments, see Otto Ulč, *Politics in Czechoslovakia* (San Francisco: W. H. Freeman and Co., 1974), pp. 114–18; and *id.,* "Czechoslovakia: From the Winter of Discontent to the Despair of Husák's Autumn," in Volgyes, ed., *Political Socialization in Eastern Europe,* pp. 45–50.

17. For example, a directive issued by the Ministry of Education in 1967 stipulated that of the three people constituting the loan commission in every school, two must be appointed by the school's ČSM committee. Source: U.S. Department of Commerce, Joint Publications Research Service, Sociological Translations on Eastern Europe, No. 41,825 (June 1967). Hereafter this source will be referred to as JPRS/ST.

18. JPRS/ST No. 18,073 (1962).

19. Ulč, *Politics in Czechoslovakia,* p. 117.

20. Radio Free Europe, Research Files on Czechoslovak Youth (New York), Feb. 7, 1967; Richard Cornell, *Youth and Communism* (New York:

Walker and Co., 1965), p. 161 ff.; Anita Dasbach, "Czechoslovakia's Youth," *Problems of Communism*, XVIII (March–April 1969), pp. 24–31.

21. Brochure published by Krajské středisko státní památkové péče a ochrany přírody v Plzni (Plzeň, 1965).

22. The term "Prague Spring" is, of course, a synechdoche. Not only Prague, but the entire country — Czech and Slovak, urban and rural — was caught up in the changes of 1968, and the local differences within the ČSSR were reflected in the complex pattern of reform politics. Moreover, the "spring" of reform actually began in January and lasted until sometime after the August intervention, passing through several distinct phases. On this, see esp. H. Gordon Skilling, *Czechoslovakia's Interrupted Revolution* (Princeton, 1976).

23. On political participation during and after 1968, see Otto Ulč, *Politics in Czechoslovakia* (San Francisco: W. H. Freeman and Co., 1974).

24. Radio Free Europe Research, Situation Report: Czechoslovakia No. 44 (Munich: December 5, 1973). Hereafter, RFE/SR.

25. *Rudé právo*, August 18, 1973, p. 1.

26. RFE/SR, *loc. cit.*

27. See, for example, Husák's speech to the party conference of Bratislava's first district, April 14, 1973, in which Husák boasted of the high degree of moral and political unity on the public's part in support of the party's policy. Reported in RFE/SR, No. 15 (April 18, 1973).

28. See footnote 24.

29. RFE/SR, No. 4 (February 4, 1976).

30. "Lidé a čas," *Rudé právo*, October 12, 1974, p. 1.

31. RFE/SR, No. 11 (March 11, 1975).

32. "Lidé a čas."

33. Radio Prague, August 7, 1972, as reported in RFE/SR, No. 36 (Oct. 18, 1972).

34. Radio Hvězda, November 10, 1871, in RFE/SR, No. 16 (June 8, 1972).

35. *Smena* (Bratislava), January 8, 1975.

36. "Lidé a čas"; also Radio Prague, in RFE/SR, No. 11 (March 19, 1975).

37. Radio Prague, March 10, 1975, reported in *ibid.*

38. *The Memorandum* (*Vyrozumění*), a play that was first performed in one of Prague's avant-garde little theaters in the mid-sixties, depicts everyday life in an office where no work gets done, slavish obedience to regulations causes nothing but confusion, and the staff spends most of its time eating lunch, celebrating birthdays, and going out to do the shopping.

39. Abstracted from *Odbory a společnost*, April 1973, in *ABSEES*, Soviet and East European Abstracts Series, V:1 (Glasgow: January 1974), p. 174.

40. *Ibid.*

41. RFE/SR, No. 25 (July 15, 1973). In early 1978 reports of a renewed official interest in economic reform seemed to indicate that the government was ready to welcome some of the former managers once again.

42. George Moldau [pseud.], "Vysoká náročnost — nejlepší zbraň" (Lofty Pride Is the Best Weapon), *Listy*, IV:1 (Rome: February 1974), p. 1.

43. "Léto uprostřed zimy" (Summer in the Middle of Winter), *Svědectví*, XI:41 (Paris, 1971), p. 3.

44. In Bratislava, for example, crime increased fourfold between 1950 and

1971, and two and one-half times between 1960 and 1971. *ABSEES*, III:4 (April 1973), p. 168.

45. RFE Situation Report: Czechoslovakia No. 11 (March 22, 1972); *Statistická ročenka ČSSR*, 1975, pp. 490–92.

46. RFE/SR No. 30 (August 29, 1973), again from official sources. More statistics from Slovakia alone show a continued increase in alcohol consumption. In 1974, Slovaks drank 18,000 hectolitres more hard liquor than they had in 1973, and they spent Kčs 6.6 billion on all alcoholic beverages. So serious was the problem that the Slovak National Council was driven to produce new legislation increasing the penalties for alcohol abuse and strengthening other forms of control. Reported by J. Mesko in *Právda* (Bratislava), September 19, 1975, p. 4.

47. RFE/SR, *ibid.*

48. For example, Federal Minister of Health Jan Prokopec once argued that Czechs and Slovaks drank no more hard liquor than the average Europeans. Prokopec admitted that beer consumption was high, however. *Rudé právo*, December 7, 1973, p. 3.

49. These appear in *Rudé právo*, *Právda* (Bratislava), *Mladá fronta*, *Zemědělské noviny*, *Práce*, and other newspapers.

50. *Večerní Praha*, January 3, 1972 (in *ABSEES* II:4, April 1972, p. 153); *Právník*, June 1973 (*ABSEES* IV:2, October 1973, p. 162; *Zdravotnické noviny* (*ABSEES* V:1, January 1974, p. 148).

51. None of these social problems are unique to Czechoslovakia. One can find evidence of them, as well as official lamentations about them, in nearly all East European countries. They exist in the West, too, in many cases to much greater degrees (cf. the crime rates in the U.S.). The point, however, is that the problems do exist in Czechoslovakia, they are taken seriously by the regime, and they do reflect upon the success of the revolutionary process.

52. I was told of a lumber firm that purposely cut down twice as many trees as it needed for lumber production, because when the logs were floated down a river to move them to the mill, it almost invariably happened that one-half of them would disappear!

53. From an article in *Tvorba*, June 26, 1974, as reported in *ABSEES*, V:4 (October 1974), p. 169.

54. *Ibid.* Also RFE/SR No. 27 (August 16, 1972). Cf. Malcolm W. Browne's report on the redevelopment of Sudeten German properties in Western Bohemia (*The New York Times*, August 18, 1975, p. 13). Most of the houses are in bad condition, but wealthy Czechs are willing to pay the going price, estimated by Browne to be approximately $20,000, in order to acquire vacation property.

55. "Léto uprostřed zimy," *loc. cit.*

56. *New York Times*, January 27, 1977.

57. As of this writing, the regime had gathered its forces together and virtually silenced the movement through a combination of arrests (although relatively few), forced exile, and isolation of the charter's main proponents. Whether or not the matter has been disposed of remains to be seen. The events were well covered in the Western press; see esp. the *New York Times* and the *Christian Science Monitor* during the first half of 1977.

58. In *Novinář*, December 1972, as summarized in *ABSEES*, IV:1 (July 1973), p. 160.

59. *Ibid.*

60. Data are from *Statistická ročenka ČSSR*, various years. The trend lines B, B′, and B″ were calculated by the standard regression formula (least-squares method) in which the slope is computed thus:

$$b = \frac{N\Sigma XY - (\Sigma X)(\Sigma Y)}{N\Sigma X^2 - (\Sigma X)^2}$$

and the intercept thus:

$$a = \frac{\Sigma Y - b\Sigma X}{N}$$

61. *Právda* (Bratislava), October 25, 1972, summarized in *ABSEES*, IV:3 (April 1973), p. 169.

62. RFE/SR No. 26 (August 1, 1973).

63. *Tribuna*, February 26, 1975, as reported in RFE/SR (April 2, 1975).

64. Nor did the uncovering of corruption in 1974–75 among officials in the foreign-trade administration contribute to the regime's ideological cause. See *ibid.*

65. *Nová mysl*, No. 4 (April 1972), reported in RFE/SR No. 17 (May 17, 1972).

66. *Tribuna*, January 10, 1973, reported in *ABSEES*, IV:3 (April 1973).

67. *Sociológia* (Bratislava, No. 1/1970), reported in RFE/SR No. 44 (Dec. 13, 1972).

68. *Osvětová práce*, No. 22 (1972), in *ABSEES*, IV:3 (April 1973).

69. *Právda*, January 5, 1973, reported in *ABSEES*, III:4 (April 1973).

70. *Tribuna*, October 25, 1972, in *ABSEES*, III:3 (January 1973).

71. *ABSEES* III:2 (October 1972).

72. Nada Slavetínská, in *Tribuna*, No. 121 (May 22, 1974), as reported in RFE Research, Czechoslovak Press Survey, No. 2521 (June 6, 1974).

73. *Rudé právo*, September 5, 1972, p. 3.

74. RFE/SR No. 26 (July 24, 1974).

75. *Rudé právo*, July 6, 1973.

76. Interview with F. Hájek, deputy head of the Institute of Marxism-Leninism, Charles University, in *Svět práce*, July 25, 1973, reported in *ABSEES*, IV:2 (October 1973).

77. *Tribuna*, July 13, 1973; *ABSEES, loc. cit.*

78. *Učitelské noviny*, December 17, 1970; *ABSEES*, I:4 (April 1971), p. 160.

79. RFE/SR No. 26 (December 21, 1972).

80. *Rudé právo*, July 6, 1973, p. 1.

81. Bohemicus [pseud.], "Proti vládě lži" (Against the Rule of the Lie), *Listy* IV:2 (May 1974), p. 1ff.

82. In an interview granted to a reporter for the American Communist paper *Daily World*, Vasil Biľak expressed the official view that "socialism with a human face" was no more than a "demagogical slogan" used to mislead the people in 1968. Cited in *Rudé právo*, September 13, 1975, p. 2. See also *Rudé právo*, January 5, 1978, on the tenth anniversary of Dubček's advancement to party leadership.

83. See Piekalkiewicz, *Public Opinion Polling in Czechoslovakia*, pp. 28–32.

84. *Ibid.,* pp. 14–28.

85. Speech given on the thirtieth anniversary of the Slovak National Uprising, published in *Právda* (Bratislava), May 21, 1974; excerpted in RFE, Czechoslovak Press Survey No. 2521 (June 6, 1974).

86. *Ibid.*

87. "Oprávněná hrdost," *Rudé právo,* August 18, 1973, p. 1.

88. See, for example, the front-page coverage of the anniversary of the October Revolution in *Rudé právo* each year on November 7; see also the accompanying editorial commentaries, e.g. Karel Doudera, "Trvalý zdroj naší svobody" (Enduring Source of Our Freedom), *ibid.,* November 7, 1974, p. 3. Cf. also L. Štrougal's speech on the thirtieth anniversary of the Soviet Army's Carpatho-Dukla operation, *ibid.,* October 7, 1974, p. 1.

89. "Proti vládě lži," p. 1. "Bohemicus," a Czech correspondent who occasionally smuggles out columns for *Listy* from his base in Prague, has satirically debunked two common lies. The first, that the occupying troops would be removed upon "normalization," he suggests, was no lie; the original soldiers who came in 1968 have long gone and been replaced several times by new troops. Thus have the (original) occupying troops indeed been removed.

Secondly, "Bohemicus" notes citizens' indignation over the Soviet promise in 1968 that the occupying troops would not interfere (*vměšovat se*) in Czechoslovakia's internal affairs. The columnist ironically suggests that what has taken place was not interference or intervention but rather the (re-)establishment of Soviet rule over Czechs and Slovaks. In this case the word "interfere" is irrelevant; a boss cannot be accused of "interfering" in the operations of his own business enterprise, nor can a ruler be said to "interfere" in the affairs of his subjects — he simply *rules* them.

90. From an article by Zdeňka Fučíková in *Učitelské noviny,* March 14, 1974, as reported in RFE/ČS No. 14 (April 3, 1974).

91. Interview with Biľak, conducted by a reporter for the American Communist newspaper *Daily World,* reprinted under the headline "Socialismus v ČSSR je neotřesitelný," *Rudé právo,* September 13, 1975, p. 2. According to Biľak, some 70 percent of those removed from party lists kept their jobs. Cf. dispatch by Eric Bourne in *The Christian Science Monitor,* April 13, 1976.

92. The 1971 arrests became the focus of yet another lie. Three months passed before the regime admitted the arrests. Then, in a somewhat elliptical statement, First Secretary Husák explained that those arrested had engaged in criminal activities against the state. He added that "not a hair on the head ... of any law-abiding citizen" would be harmed, and despite widespread rumors concerning recriminations for political activism in 1968, nobody would be prosecuted for political opinions held either currenty or in 1968–69. (*Rudé právo,* February 24, 1972, p. 1). It was not long thereafter that official lists of criminals were made public, including many of the 1968 activists.

93. Of those respondents with post-secondary educations, only 5 percent felt they had any political influence. *Svědectví,* XIII:50 (1975), pp. 253–58.

This is an interesting poll, and although its accuracy cannot be taken for granted, an effort was made to guarantee the most accurate information possible. It was conducted in late 1974 by an anonymous person, allegedly qualified by professional training to do such polling, whose current occupation brought him into contact with people of different social groups from all regions of the ČSSR. Respondents' replies were kept confidential, and the questions were intelligently formulated. The researcher contacted some 120 individuals for this particular survey, but he apparently did not put all questions to every respondent. Further reference to this survey will be made, below.

94. For a very interesting discussion of underground oppositional activities, see Jan F. Triska, "Messages from Czechoslovakia," *Problems of Communism*, XXIV: 6 (November–December, 1975), pp. 26–42. See also *Tribuna*, No. 4 (January 21, 1976), as reported in RFE/SR No. 30 (February 2, 1976), pp. 3–5.

95. The number of historians alone who were thus deprived of their professional positions as of 1975 was 144. Much worldwide sympathy for their cause (but no concrete change) was generated by the circulation of several documents at the International Congress of the Historical Sciences in San Francisco (1975). These included a moving letter from the eminent Czech historian Vilém Prečan (since exiled) and a directory of purged historians. For reportage, see *The New York Times*, August 22, 1975, and the *Washington Post*, August 24, 1975.

96. Georg Moldau, *op. cit.*, p. 2.

97. *New York Times*, October 1, 1976.

98. Among the open letters published in the West in 1975 were those written by Havel, Kohout, Ludvík Vaculík, and Karel Kosík. Addressed either to President Husák or to West European cultural figures, the letters expressed frustration at the authors' inability to publish or have their works performed in their own country. In autumn 1976, two new plays by Havel were premiered in Vienna; not surprisingly, the playwright was refused permission to accept an invitation to the premiere performance. Likewise, when a new play of Kohout's opened on Broadway, he also was unable to view the staging.

On the open letters of 1975, see Triska, *op. cit.*; cf. *Svědectví*, XIII: 50 (1975), pp. 377–94; *Der Spiegel* (Hamburg), June 9, 1975; and *The New York Times*, August 29, 1975.

99. The regime is clearly concerned by the fact that some do read Solzhenitsyn's works, and official attempts are made to discourage the practice by warning of the slanders allegedly made by Solzhenitsyn. See, e.g., Zdeněk Kropáč in *Rudé právo*, January 22, 1974, p. 6.

100. To counter rumors that the government is discouraging the international flow of information, a *Tribuna* writer has pointed out that the ČSSR maintains forty-two agreements on cultural cooperation with other countries, is a party to four multilateral cultural agreements, and subscribes to 1349 international organizations. *Tribuna*, January 16, 1974, as abstracted in *ABSEES*, V: 2 (April 1974), p. 159.

101. See Malcolm W. Browne in the *New York Times*, August 18, 1975, p. 13.

102. *Ibid.* Also *ABSEES*, VII: 1 (January 1976), p. 166, from an article in *Svět práce*, August 20, 1975.

103. *ABSEES, ibid.*, pp. 165–66, from *Život strany*.

104. Antonín J. Liehm, *Closely Watched Films* (White Plains, N.Y.: International Arts and Sciences Press, 1974), p. 4.

105. Browne, *op. cit.*

106. *Svědectví,* XIII:50 (1975), pp. 253 58.

107. *Ibid.* The difference between white-collar and blue-collar responses to this and the preceding question is interesting. Still more interesting is the difference in responses to the question, "How do you see the future for your family and children?" A majority of blue-collar workers felt that their children will be better off than they are now (52 percent), whereas a plurality of white-collar workers (36 percent) thought their offspring would be less well off. This probably reflects the discrimination in the current admissions practices of post-secondary schools, favoring the children of blue-collar workers.

108. Jiří Nežárka, "Režim, který má strach," *Listy,* VI:4 (August 1976), p. 4.

109. In other Communist-ruled countries one can find much greater success in reconciling national traditions with revolutionary purposes; perhaps the best examples are Poland, Hungary, and Romania.

CHAPTER TWO

1. H. Gordon Skilling, "The Dialectic of Czechoslovak History," *The Canadian Forum,* XLIX (October 1969), pp. 155 157.

2. The only major efforts at English-language histories of Czechoslovakia are R. W. Seton-Watson, *A History of the Czechs and Slovaks* (Hamden, Conn.: Archon Books, 1965), and S. Harrison Thomson, *Czechoslovakia in European History* (Princeton University Press, 1943, 1953). A standard Communist history is the multi-volume *Přehled československých dějin* (Prague: Nakladatelství Československé akademie věd, 1958 1968, 4 v. in 5). A recent textbook for pedagogical institute students worth consulting is F. Kavka, J. Butvin, J. Havránek *et al., Dějiny Československa* (Prague: Státní pedagogické nakladatelství, 1964 1968, 3 v.). A one-volume, pre-Communist history which I have found useful is Kamil Krofta, *Dějiny československé* (Prague: Sfinx, 1946). Shorter, but useful, surveys can be found in the Czechoslovak "Book of Knowledge" (*Československá vlastivěda*), editions of which were published in Prague during the 1930s and again during the 1960s.

3. For a well-balanced Marxist view of the First Republic in its international environment, see Věra Olivová, *The Doomed Democracy: Czechoslovakia in a Disrupted Europe, 1914 38* (Montreal: McGill Queen's University Press, 1972).

4. See, e.g., *Dr. Jozef Tiso o sebe* (Passaic, N.J.: Slovak Catholic Sokol, 1952), for a defense of the wartime Tiso regime as an embodiment of the Slovak national cause.

5. This unhappy experience will be examined in light of the Slovak nationalist objection in chapters six and seven.

6. The Second Republic was the system in effect during the five-month interlude between Munich and the German occupation of Bohemia and Moravia, i.e. 1938-39.

7. In this tally I have considered the events of 1918, 1938 39, and 1948 as the three structural changes. The eight Presidents have been T. G. Masaryk, Edvard Beneš, Emil Hácha, Beneš again, Antonín Zápotocký, Klement Gottwald, Antonín Novotný, Ludvík Svoboda, and Gustáv Husák. Among the foreign powers I have counted Austria and Hungary separately, due to their differing internal authority structures, and added Germany and the USSR.

8. For analyses of the Austrian and Austro-Hungarian systems, see Oscar Jászi, *The Dissolution of the Habsburg Monarchy* (Chicago: University of Chicago Press, 1929) and Robert A. Kann, *The Habsburg Empire: A Study in Integration and Disintegration* (New York: Praeger, 1957).

9. On the wartime occupation and its impact, see O. Janeček, "Československo," in Československá akademie věd, *Střední a jihovýchodní Evropa ve válce a v revoluci 1939–1945* (Praha, 1969), pp. 31–122.

10. See e.g., Jiri Horak, *The Czechoslovak Social Democratic Party 1938–1945* (New York: unpublished Ph.D. Dissertation, Columbia University, 1960), pp. 132–42, 161–3, and 228ff. The Social Democrats in particular were severely hit by Nazi purges. Their leaders on the national level were nearly all exiled or incarcerated, and their intricate network of local party organizations was virtually annihilated. The SDs, one of the two strongest parties prior to 1938, emerged from the war broken and impotent.

11. Vojtech Mastny, *The Czechs under Nazi Rule: The Failure of National Resistance, 1939–1942* (New York: Columbia University Press, 1971). The most important exception was the assassination of Heydrich in 1942, a spectacular event committed by two Czech exiles flown into Bohemia from their conspiratorial base in London. This daring and provocative act triggered a series of retaliatory atrocities, including the infamous annihilation of Lidice. This wave of terror seemed to break whatever remnants of the Czech resistance were left.

12. Janeček, "Československo," pp. 70–1.

13. A great deal of obscurity still enshrouds the Slovak Uprising, an object of official celebration in Czechoslovakia today. (See Janeček, *ibid.,* p. 99ff.) The subject will be discussed again in chapter seven.

14. See, e.g., Joseph A. Mikus, *Slovakia, A Political History: 1918–1950* (Milwaukee: Marquette University Press, 1963), *passim.*

15. Paul E. Zinner, *Communist Strategy and Tactics in Czechoslovakia 1918–1948* (New York: Praeger, 1936), pp. 400–402.

16. See, e.g., the radio speeches of Beneš following the 1943 treaty with the USSR and during the last year of the war in Beneš, *Šest let exilu a druhé světové války* (Praha, 1946), pp. 223–230, 250–258.

17. See, e.g., Zinner, *op. cit.,* p. 117ff., and Josef Korbel, *The Communist Subversion of Czechoslovakia 1938–1948* (Princeton, 1959). For a discussion of the coup in the context of the international environment, see Morton Kaplan, *Macropolitics* (Chicago: Aldine, 1969), pp. 81–121. For a Communist party version, cf. Pavel Reiman *et al., Istoriya Kommunisticheskoi partii Chekhoslovakii,* Russ. ed. (Moscow, 1962), pp. 541–618. A more recent, and very knowledgeable treatment, is that of Pavel Tigrid in Thomas Hammond, ed., *The Anatomy of Communist Revolutions* (New Haven: Yale, 1975), pp. 299–332.

18. I am indebted to Stephen Fischer-Galati for this particular formulation of the Soviet-East European relationship. See also chapter four, below.

19. Taborsky, *Communism in Czechoslovakia, passim;* Vlastislav Chalupa, *Rise and Development of a Totalitarian State* (Leiden: H. E. Stenfert Kroese N. V., 1959), pp. 113–217. For some extraordinarily documented information concerning the purges, see Jiří Pelikán, ed., *The Czechoslovak Political Trials 1950–1954, The Suppressed Report of the Dubček Government's Commission of Inquiry 1968* (Stanford, 1971).

20. The Košice meeting took place among Communist and non-Communist leaders in April 1945, approximately a month prior to the defeat of the Germans.

21. By the time of the 1950 census, fewer than 5 percent of the pre-1938 German minority remained. (Source: Peter A. Toma, "The Czecho-Slovak Question under Communism," *East European Quarterly*, III (March, 1969), p. 27.)

22. Ústav dějin KSČ, *Dějiny KSČ* (Prague, 1967), p. 199; Juraj Zvara, *Maďarská menšina na Slovensku po roku 1945* (Bratislava, 1969), pp. 62–65. The Hungarian government's position was that if Czechoslovakia was to retain the territories (retaken from Hungary after the war) in which large numbers of Magyars lived, it must also keep those Magyars. It is likely that the 1948 decision was made in Moscow, because it satisfied no one. Czechs and Slovaks were not enthused about keeping this potentially troublesome minority, and Hungary's leaders would undoubtedly have preferred to take custody of the Magyars across the border — and the territories as well. At any rate, approximately 68,000 Magyars had been expelled, and an additional 6,000 left voluntarily. Only 354,332 Magyars were counted in the 1950 census, compared to at least 739,000 in 1930; Zvara, however, admits that the 1950 figure "is not real," since pressure was put on many Magyars to register as Slovaks. (Zvara, *Maďarská menšina*, p. 89.)

23. In the years just prior to the Communist coup, a lively effort was made by the literati to define a new progressive culture. See Jaroslav Kladiva, *Kultura a politika 1945–48* (Praha, 1968).

24. This theme appeared in a Soviet novel by Vasili Ardamatsky, *The Pay-off*, pointedly reviewed by M. Shiryanov in *Sovyetskaya Rossiya* (April 14, 1968).

25. The three major socialist parties of 1946 (Communists, Social Democrats, and National Socialists) drew a combined total of more than 4.8 million votes, or 68.7 percent of all votes.

26. Reassessments of Masaryk began to appear in the early 1960s, still critical but serious and reasoned. See, e.g., Lubomír Nový, "Filosofie T. G. Masaryka," Masarykova universita, Filosofická fakulta, *Spisy*, No. 78 (Brno, 1962). The renewed attention to Masaryk culminated in 1968 and 1969 with the reissuance of several of the former Presidents' essays, including *The Czech Question*, as well as the publication of an important book by Milan Machovec, *Tomáš G. Masaryk* (Praha: Svobodné slovo, 1968). Machovec's work presented an analysis of Masaryk's life and a critique of his work from a Marxist perspective. Hardly an apologetic for the President-Liberator, the book is nevertheless an example of the trend toward admitting the importance of Masaryk in the development not only of the Czechoslovak Republic as an independent state, but of the value system that underlay the interwar political order.

During the Prague Spring, the discussion of Masaryk reached the public in both learned journals and the daily press. See, e.g., O. Janeček, "T. G. Masaryk; Několik poznámek a úvah k historickému hodnocení jeho osobnosti," *Nová mysl*, June 1968; Věra Olivová, "T. G. Masaryk a náš polednový dnešek," *Rudé právo*, August 21, 1968; and J. Špičak, "TGM a dnešek," *Svobodné slovo*, March 7, 1969.

27. Ján Uher, "Zdokonaľovať vedecko-ateistickú propagandu," *Predvoj,* IV: 26 (Bratislava: June 23, 1960).

28. See, e.g., Erika Kadlecová, "Výzkum religiozity Severomoravského Kraje," *Sociologický časopis,* I: 1 (Praha, 1965), pp. 13–23+, and "Z výsledků výzkumu religiozity dospělých u Severomoravském Kraji," *ibid.,* I: 2, pp. 135–47; also Rudolf Pravdík, "Some of the Research Results: Youth in the Mirror of the World Outlook," transl. U.S. Joint Publications Research Service, Doc. No. 43,162 (1967). While the research generally showed a relative waning in the strength of churches over the years, respondents to surveys very frequently upheld the desirability of religious ethics. Similar findings emerged in an independent survey conducted in 1969 by a Czech-American anthropologist, Zdeněk Salzmann, "A Contribution to the Study of Value Orientations among the Czechs and Slovaks," *Research Reports* No. 4, Department of Anthropology, University of Massachusetts (Amherst: April, 1970).

29. Of the many books and articles dealing with the 1968 events, see especially H. Gordon Skilling, *Czechoslovakia's Interrupted Revolution* (Princeton Univ. Press, 1976); Galia Golan, *Reform Rule in Czechoslovakia* (Cambridge U. Press, 1973); and Ivan Sviták, *The Czechoslovak Experiment* (N.Y.: Columbia Univ. Press, 1971).

30. These polls are reported by V. V. Kusin, *The Intellectual Origins of the Prague Spring,* p. 16.

31. Reported by Milan Jan Reban, *Czechoslovakia 1968: Some Aspects of Pluralism and Change,* Ph.D. dissertation, Michigan State University (East Lansing, 1972), p. 80.

32. The first poll, conducted by the Institute for the Research of Public Opinion (Prague), found that 85 percent of the respondents were for socialism, the remaining 10 percent neutral or noncommittal. The second poll, done by the Institute of Sociology, Charles University, showed 89 percent for "continued socialist development," while 6 percent were uncertain. The first survey is discussed in *"Svoboda" — die Presse in der Tschechoslowakei 1968* (Zürich: Internationales Presseinstitut, 1969), p. 73. The second appeared in the journal *Polls,* III: 4 (Amsterdam, 1968), p. 17.

Two surveys conducted by Radio Free Europe among Czech and Slovak visitors to the West show evidence that tends to contradict the Czech polls. These surveys, taken in late 1967 and early 1968, indicate predominantly negative reactions to the concepts "socialism" and "communism," as measured by the Osgood-Suci-Tannenbaum Semantic Differential scale. It should be noted, however, that the RFE survey did not directly ask the respondents whether they would prefer capitalism (or some other system) to socialism. See RFE, Audience and Public Opinion Research Department, "Attitudes toward Key Political Concepts in East Europe" (Munich: December, 1969), pp. 56–59.

33. There is a wealth of literature on the First Republic from a number of different perspectives. For "bourgeois" views, see Robert J. Kerner, ed., *Czechoslovakia: Twenty Years of Independence* (Berkeley and Los Angeles: University of California Press, 1940), a collection of essays on assorted topics, and Edward Táborský, *Czechoslovak Democracy at Work* (London: Allen and Unwin, 1945), a concise description of the political system. A more recent collection of articles also covering the 1938–1948 period is Victor S. Mamatey and Radomír Luža, ed., *A History of the Czechoslovak Republic* (Princeton,

1973). For official Communist party histories, cf. Československá akademie věd, Historický ústav, *Přehled československých dějin* (Prague, 1960), d. III, and also P. Reimann *et al., Istoriya Kommunisticheskoi Partii Chekhoslovakii* (Moscow, 1962), also in original Czech edition (Prague, 1961). A somewhat modified, later party view is presented in Ústav dějin KSČ, *Dějiny KSČ* (Prague, 1967), and an unusually sympathetic Marxist interpretation appears in Olivová, *The Doomed Democracy.* A similarly balanced Marxist survey can be found in *Československá vlastivěda,* d. II, Dějiny svazek 2 (Prague, 1969).

A standard analysis of the German problem is that of Elizabeth Wiskemann, *Czechs and Germans* (New York: St. Martin's Press, Second Edition, 1967). On Czech-Slovak relations, two pamphlets representing the government's position are *Nationality Policy in Czechoslovakia,* Czechoslovak Sources and Documents No. 22 (Prague, 1938), and I. Dérer, *The Unity of the Czechs and Slovaks,* Documents No. 23, 1938. Varying degrees of hostility toward the government's position are exemplified by S. Osuský, *Beneš and Slovakia* (Middletown, Pa., 1943), and Joseph A. Mikus, *Slovakia, A Political History 1918–1950* (Milwaukee, 1963), both works by disaffected Slovak émigrés. A somewhat more balanced work is Jozef Lettrich, *History of Modern Slovakia* (New York: Praeger, 1955). For an insider's account of the Slovak autonomy movement, see Karol Sidor, *Slovenská politika na pôde pražského snemu 1918–1938,* 2v. (Bratislava, 1943).

34. Of the numerous biographies and studies of Masaryk, perhaps the best in a single volume is Jan Herben, *T. G. Masaryk: život a dílo Presidenta osvoboditele,* 5. vydání (Prague, 1946).

35. *Ibid.,* p. 419.

36. Táborský, *Czechoslovak Democracy at Work,* p. 112.

37. Olivová, *The Doomed Democracy,* pp. 131–134, 177–178.

38. The four leaders (Klement Gottwald, Josef Krosnář, Josef Štětka, and Václav Kopecký) managed to escape to the Soviet Union to avoid arrest and prosecution. See *ibid.,* pp. 188–190.

39. It has recently been argued that Masaryk controlled the major political parties through his own personal followers, who entered the various parties after 1918 in order to propagate Masaryk's political ideas and gain the acceptance of his policies. *Československá vlastivěda,* d. II, Dějiny svazek 2 (Prague, 1969), pp. 408–409.

40. Cf. Jozef Kirschbaum, *Náš boj o samostatnosť Slovenska* (Cleveland: Slovenský ústav v Clevelande, 1958), *passim.* Kirschbaum invokes most often Masaryk's wartime book, *Das neue Europa.*

41. This distinction will be examined in more detail in later chapters.

42. Z. Nejedlý, *T. G. Masaryk* (Prague: Melantrich, 1930–1937, 4v. in 5).

43. *Československá vlastivěda,* op. cit., d. II (1969), p. 408.

44. Taborsky, *Communism in Czechoslovakia,* pp. 136–137.

45. ČSAV, Historický ústav, *Přehled československých dejin,* III (Prague, 1960), pp. 47–51 and *passim.*

46. *Ibid.,* p. 44 and *passim.*

47. *Ibid.,* pp. 265–304, 429–469. Cited from p. 466. For a brief account of the Czech cinema during this time, see Josef Škvorecký, *All the Bright Young Men and Women: A Personal History of the Czech Cinema* (Toronto: Peter Martin Associates Ltd., 1971), pp. 1–27.

48. In 1968, when it became possible to challenge the post-1948 view of the past, a spate of articles was written in an effort to redress the recent historiographical distortions. These articles prompted a hysterical barrage of criticism in the Soviet press. It was charged, for example, that in reassessing the post-1950 interpretation of Masaryk, the reformers of 1968 were really seeking to lead society back down the primrose path of "Masarykism," i.e., bourgeois and anti-socialist humanism. (See, e.g., M. Shiryanov, in *Sovyetskaya Rossiya,* April 4, 1968.) In a brilliant reply to Shiryanov, Vlastimil Vávra forcefully argued that Masaryk's historiographical rehabilitation by no means signified a return to bourgeois political norms, but rather it represented an attempt to reach a fuller and more accurate understanding of Czechoslovakia's past. (V. Vávra, "Masaryk a Savinkov," *Mladá fronta,* May 16, 1968).

49. Milan Kundera, *The Joke,* translated by David Hamblyn and Oliver Stallybrass (New York: Coward-McCann, 1969). Originally published in Prague, 1967.

50. For a fascinating insight into the minds and work of the writers and filmmakers of the 1960s, see A. J. Liehm, *The Politics of Culture* (New York: Grove Press, 1972), and by the same author, *Closely Watched Films: The Czechoslovak Experience* (White Plains, N.Y.: International Arts and Sciences Press, 1974).

51. Thus we witnessed films such as Klos and Kadár's *Shop on Main Street* (*Obchod na Korze*) and Brynych's *The Fifth Horseman is Fear* (*A patý je strach*), dealing with the ambiguity of guilt for the persecution of Jews during the war; novels such as Mňačko's *The Taste of Power* (*Jak chutná moc*) and Havel's play *The Memorandum,* bluntly criticizing a system that perverted its own values and those of the nation in general; and the brilliant film by Menzel, *Closely Watched Trains* (*Ostře sledované vlaky*), dealing with a young man's coming of age in a time of moral ambiguity.

52. Traditionally, it had been assumed that the Greater Moravian Empire had been centered primarily on territories which today make up modern Slovakia. According to Slovak historians, the empire probably extended from a northwesterly point somewhere near present-day Magdeburg to a southeasterly point south of Lake Balaton, with important centers located at and around Nitra, Velehrad, and as far west as Praha and Líbušín. See, e.g., František Kavka, *et al.,* ed., *Dějiny Československa do roku 1437,* Prozatímní učebnice pro posluchače dálkového studia na Pedagogických fakultách, I. díl (Prague, 1964), pp. 65ff. An American scholar, Imre Boba, has disputed the traditional placement of the Greater Moravian Empire, arguing that it was instead located a considerable distance to the south. (cf. Boba, *Moravia's History Reconsidered: A Reinterpretation of Medieval Sources* (The Hague: Martinus Nijhoff, 1971).) Slovak historians have reacted with nationalistic hostility to Boba's revisionistic study, and they have generally rejected its conclusions. Regardless of where the ancient empire actually was located, there is evidence of a relatively advanced culture on Slovak lands during the time in question (seventh through ninth centuries A.D.). Whether or not this was a part of the Moravian Empire, or any empire, is clearly questionable, but this does not obliterate the fact that Slovaks can claim a history dating back to that early time.

53. For a review of some of these historiographical strains, see Otakar

Odložilík, "Modern Czechoslovak Historiography," *Slavonic and East European Review*, XXX:75 (June 1952), pp. 376–392.

54. See Josef Macek, *The Hussite Movement in Bohemia* (Prague: Orbis, Second Edition, 1958); also Kavka, op. cit., 236–339; ČSAV, *Přehled československých dějin*, d. I (Prague, 1958), pp. 73–180ff.; S. Harrison Thomson, *Czechoslovakia in European History* (Princeton, 1943, 1953), pp. 69–110, 249ff.; and Kamil Krofta, *Nesmrtelný národ* (Prague, 1940), pp. 245–254.

55. "The Táborites had not yet reached the stage of development in which they could lay the foundations for a classless society; they had no idea of the social process and they anticipated history by hundreds of years in trying to establish the utopia of apostolic poverty and equality of a thousand years before. It is therefore natural that this fantastic attempt to establish a classless society was doomed to disaster in the economic conditions and the existing situation." (Macek, *op. cit.*, p. 52.)

56. Kavka, *op. cit.*, I, p. 338.

57. *Ibid.*, II, p. 34.

58. A passage from one of Chelčický's writings will serve to illustrate:
It is manifest that there is a superabundance of various classes of priests and nobles, and that all want to be lords, knights and mercenaries. For it is easy to ride about on robust horses and talk big, abuse the common people calling them varlets and donkeys, skin them like limetrees, crack their heads, eat and drink of the very best, be idle and lounge about from place to place, indulge in empty talk and commit all sorts of sins without shame . . . all this let us leave to the pagans, for it has nothing to do with the faith of Christ and with it his spiritual body.

— from Chelčický, *On the Three Classes*, cited by J. L. Hromádka in Karel Čapek, et al., *At the Crossroads of Europe: A Historical Outline of the Democratic Idea in Czechoslovakia* (Prague, 1938), p. 127.

59. Cf. T. G. Masaryk, *The Making of a State; Memories and Observations 1914–1918*, translated and abridged by Henry Wickham Steed (New York: Frederick A. Stokes Co., 1927), p. 406.

60. *Ibid.*, pp. 58–59, 174, 322, and *passim*.

61. Kamil Krofta, *Dějiny československé*, p. 313.

62. Macek, *op. cit.*, pp. 104–105.

63. Numerous works on the Thirty Years' War could be cited, but those on which I have relied include C. V. Wedgwood, *The Thirty Years War* (London: Jonathan Cape Ltd., 1938), Josef Pekař, *Bílá hora: Její příčiny a následky* (Prague, 1921), and Kavka *et al.*, d. II, pp. 170–195. Robert J. Kerner also deals with the results of the war in the first portion of his authoritative *Bohemia in the Eighteenth Century* (New York: Macmillan, 1932).

64. I am aware that there is some ambiguity in my use of the term "nation" at this point. In the medieval and early modern sense, the nation consisted of the ruler and privileged estates of a land, united under the symbol of the Crown. Generally, it was much later — dating, conventionally, from approximately the time of the French Revolution — that the meaning of nation took on its modern-day sense, i.e., a group of ethnically homogeneous people, whatever their class status, united by a common sense of historical and

political destiny. Nonetheless, there are elements of an incipient national consciousness, in the modern sense, in the revolt of the Hussites. Hus staked out a new theological position, and it so happened that those who became his followers were also those who spoke his mother tongue. By recognizing their religious uniqueness, Czechs were implicitly creating for themselves an ethnic uniqueness; their rituals of worship, hymns, and even their Bible were Czech. They were thus consciously severing themselves from the idea of Christian universality as it was embodied in the medieval Church. In doing this, they were in fact creating a national religion, specific to ethnic Czechs (and a number of Slovaks who also came to adopt Hussitism). The reconsolidated Bohemian Kingdom that evolved following the turbulence of the mid-fifteenth century took on a peculiar character that we might call "national," almost in the modern sense, however inchoate the feeling of national unity might have been. It does not seem far-fetched, then, to agree with Krofta's argument (above) that Czech nationalism, or perhaps something *akin* to Czech national-ism, actually had its beginnings in the Hussite reformation. This inchoate nationalism was destroyed in the seventeenth century, before it could evolve into a truly and clearly modern form, and the national revivalists of the nine-teenth century had to create a new nationalism among a people cut off from their spiritual predecessors. Significantly, however, the nineteenth-century revivalists appealed to a sense of identity with their fifteenth-century forebears in establishing the basis of modern Czech nationalism.

65. Edvard Beneš, *Bohemia's Case for Independence* (New York: The Arno Press, 1971, orig. published 1917), pp. 1–2ff. See also Lettrich, *History of Modern Slovakia,* p. 26.

66. See, e.g., Kavka's illustrated chapter on Czech culture between 1437 and 1526, in *Dějiny československa,* II, pp. 64–77.

67. Krofta, *Nesmrtelný národ,* p. 2.

68. The poet Jan Kollár (1793–1852) and the archeologist Pavel Josef Šafařík (1795–1861), for example, chose to write their major works in Czech. It is interesting that Šafařík used the Czech spelling for his name; the letter ř does not occur in modern Slovak orthography.

69. A Roman Catholic priest, Anton Bernolák (1762–1813), was the most important of the earliest Slovak linguists.

70. The Czech and Slovak cultural awakenings are discussed separately in Kavka *et al., d.* III, pp. 14–179. See also Thomson, *Czechoslovakia in European History,* pp. 152–215 and *passim.*

71. The largest English-language treatment of this period in the Austrian and Austro-Hungarian Empire is Robert A. Kann, *The Multinational Empire: Nationalism and National Reform in the Habsburg Monarchy 1848–1918,* 2 v. (New York: Columbia University Press, 1950). Other useful works are Josef Redlich, *Das Österreichische Staats- und Reichsproblem,* 2v. (Leipzig, 1920, 1926), and Jászi, *op. cit.*

72. Robert A. Kann, *The Habsburg Empire: A Study in Integration and Disintegration* (New York: Praeger, 1957), pp. 69–70.

73. R. W. Seton-Watson, writing under the pseudonym of Scotus Viator, reported that according to Hungarian statistics, more than 500 Slovaks were arrested between 1896 and 1908 for political crimes ranging from criticizing the government to brawling in the streets during elections. See Viator, *Racial Problems in Hungary* (London, 1908), pp. 454–462.

74. R. W. Seton-Watson, *A History of the Czechs and Slovaks,* pp. 267-8.

75. Palacký wrote the first few volumes in German during the 1840s. Sometime in the 1850s he began writing in Czech, translating the earlier volumes into Czech as well. The entire *History (Dějiny národa českého)* was completed in the 1860s.

76. Hans Kohn, "The Historical Roots of Czech Democracy," in Kerner, ed., *Czechoslovakia: Twenty Years of Independence,* p. 94.

77. Krofta wrote: "Palacký became the great spiritual leader of his people. For them he interpreted the meaning of their history splendidly. . . . Today Palacký's work about Czech history has for the most part been superseded by more recent historical research and is therefore obsolete. Even his best writings must be supplemented and corrected according to the results of the newest scholarly work. But his own original core remains undisturbed, and we shall never forget his educative significance." — *Nesmrtelný národ,* pp. 660-661.

The fact that Palacký wrote his *History* in Czech was in itself very significant. Prior to Palacký's work, very little scholarly writing had been done in the Czech language. The generation of scholars who preceded Palacký felt that Czech was a suitable medium for vernacular literature but not for scholarly or scientific communication. By using the Czech language, therefore, Palacký contributed to its linguistic development. In many instances he was obliged to formulate passages for which there was no adequate syntax in the language as previously codified. Thus Palacký's historical writing had a significance even beyond its monumental, overt purpose. Source: *Československá vlastivěda,* II, Dějiny sv. 2 (1969), pp. 80-82.

78. Many books and articles have been written about the reform rule of 1968, and to list them all here would be unnecessarily voluminous. Especially noteworthy are Skilling, Golan, and Sviták, *op. cit.;* also Vladimir V. Kusin, *Political Grouping in the Czechoslovak Reform Movement* (New York: Columbia, 1972); and Alex Pravda, "Reform and Change in the Czechoslovak Political System: January-August 1968," *Sage Research Papers in the Social Sciences* (Beverly Hills and London, 1975). A helpful resource in locating and identifying the many relevant materials is Zdeněk Hejzlar and V. V. Kusin, *Czechoslovakia 1968-1969; Chronology, Bibliography, Annotation* (New York and London: Garland, 1975).

79. See Václav Vrabec, "Paměť společnosti," *Rudé právo,* March 24, 1968, who calls for the "rehabilitation of history" in Czechoslovakia. An important step in the subsequent "rehabilitation of history" was the revocation of a 1965 restriction on the independent functioning of the historical journal *Dějiny a současnost.* Numerous articles began to appear in this newly revivified journal in 1968 which reopened some vexing historical questions; see Hejzlar and Kusin, *op. cit.,* for references. For a discussion of the abiding popular respect for Masaryk which again became apparent in 1968, see Brown and Wightman, "Czechoslovakia: Revival and Retreat," in Brown and Gray (ed.), *Political Culture and Political Change in Communist Systems,* pp. 176-80.

CHAPTER THREE

1. Frederick C. Barghoorn, *Politics in the USSR,* second ed. (Boston: Little Brown and Co., 1972), p. 20ff.

2. See Ulč's discussions of the political authority structure in his *Politics in Czechoslovakia* (1974), passim.

3. Barghoorn, pp. 25–26.

4. The obvious exceptions to this generalization are Yugoslavia and the Asian Communist states, but then one might argue that their systems are so different as to exclude them from the Marxist-Leninist category.

5. Barghoorn, p. 20.

6. On this fascinating subject, see Robert N. Bellah, "Civil Religion in America," *Daedalus,* vol. 96 no. 1 (Winter 1967), pp. 1–21; W. Lance Bennett, "Political Sanctification: The Civil Religion and American Politics," *Social Science Information,* vol. 14 no. 6 (1975), pp. 79–102; also *id.,* "Imitation, Ambiguity, and Drama in the Political Order: An Essay on the Civil Religion," as yet unpublished.

7. Variations on this in some Communist systems are noteworthy, e.g. the occasional multiple-candidacy districts in Yugoslav, Hungarian, and Polish elections.

8. The ramifications of this pluralistic tendency will be explored in detail in chapter five.

9. Authoritarianism in the context of Marxism-Leninism refers to theories or policies emphasizing the authority of the central political agency (Communist party, government) while disregarding or deemphasizing freedom of the individual.

10. The relevance of libertarianism in the Marxist-Leninist context will be explained in the subsequent discussion.

11. Otto Ulč, drawing from the definition offered by the Czech social theorist Jiří Cvekl, defines Stalinism as a political system characterized by "a subordination of the interests of the society to those of the state, a fusion of state and Party, strict centralism, bureaucratic rule, and a rigid hierarchy of authority." Ulč, *Politics in Czechoslovakia,* p. 6. To this it might be added that Stalinism is further characterized by ideologically determined standards of education and esthetics, state-owned industry, collectivized agriculture, and enforced social conformity.

12. This ambivalence within the Communist movement is by no means unique to Czechoslovakia, but it does seem to be particularly pronounced there. Cf. Skilling, *Czechoslovakia's Interrupted Revolution,* pp. 21–42.

13. David Rodnick's extensive interviews in 1947–48 disclosed that few Czechs and Slovaks then considered communism a potential threat to the political system as they knew it. Rodnick, *The Strangled Democracy: Czechoslovakia 1948–1969* (Lubbock, Texas: The Caprock Press, 1970), passim.

14. Much of Western literature on the Communist ascent to power in Czechoslovakia and the nature of post-1948 rule proceeds from the retrodictive fallacy that because Communist rule was totalitarian, the pre-1948 KSČ was therefore a totalitarian party. See, e.g., Josef Korbel, *The Communist Subversion of Czechoslovakia 1938–1948* (Princeton: Princeton University Press, 1959), and Vlastislav Chalupa, *Communism in a Free Society: Czechoslovakia 1945–48* (Chicago: Czechoslovak Foreign Institute in Exile, 1958). Skilling's treatment of this (*loc. cit.*) is a welcome antidote. Cf. my discussion below.

15. See Paul E. Zinner's subtle study of interwar communism, *Communist*

Strategy and Tactics in Czechoslovakia 1918–1948 (New York: Praeger, 1963).

16. Although passing reference will be made in this chapter to the Slovak exception, the subject of a Slovak political culture will be postponed and taken up in detail in chapter seven.

17. T. G. Masaryk, *Česká otázka; snahy a tužby národního obrození* (Praha: Melantrich, 1969, orig. publ. 1895), pp. 22–24, 27–28, 220–37 and *passim; id., The Meaning of Czech History* (Chapel Hill: University of North Carolina Press, 1974), pp. 13–14, 15–33. Edvard Beneš, *Bohemia's Case for Independence* (New York: Arno Press and the New York Times, 1971, orig. London, 1917), pp. 1–4 and *passim.*

18. Masaryk, *The Making of a State: Memories and Observations 1914–1918* (London: Geo. Allen and Unwin Ltd., 1927), pp. 403–38. For a discussion of church and state in the First Republic, see V. Busek, "Church and State," in Busek and N. Spulber, ed., *Czechoslovakia* (New York: Praeger, 1957), pp. 130–53.

19. Beneš, *Bohemia's Case for Independence,* p. 2.

20. *Id., Světová válka a naše revoluce,* vol. 2 (Praha: Orbis, 1928), p. 531. Beneš, like Palacký before him, also preferred to emphasize the dichotomy between peaceloving Czechs and bellicose Germans.

21. R. W. Seton-Watson, *Masaryk in England* (London and New York: Macmillan, 1943), p. 30.

22. Masaryk, *The Making of a State,* p. 391.

23. Seton-Watson, *Masaryk in England,* p. 27.

24. *The Making of a State,* pp. 416–17.

25. Beneš, *Democracy Today and Tomorrow* (New York: Macmillan, 1939), pp. 137–38.

26. See, e.g., Ivan Dérer, *The Unity of the Czechs and Slovaks* (Prague: Czechoslovak Sources and Documents, No. 23, 1938, by Orbis); Ľubomír Lipták, *Slovensko v 20. storočí* (Bratislava: Vydavateľstvo politickej literatúry, 1968), pp. 128–29; also Horst Glassl, "Die Slowaken und die 'Burg'," in *Die "Burg"; Einflussreiche politische Kräfte um Masaryk und Beneš,* hrsg. von Karl Bosl (München, Wien: R. Oldenbourg Verlag, 1973), pp. 131 ff.

27. Edward Táborský, *Czechoslovak Democracy at Work* (London: Geo. Allen and Unwin Ltd., 1945), pp. 94–97.

28. Věra Olivová, *The Doomed Democracy* (Montreal: McGill Queen's University Press, 1972), pp. 156, 182–90; Václav L. Beneš, "Czechoslovak Democracy and Its Problems," in Victor S. Mamatey and Radomír Luža, *A History of the Czechoslovak Republic 1918–1948* (Princeton: Princeton University Press, 1973), pp. 121–22; Mamatey, "The Development of Czechoslovak Democracy 1920–1938," *ibid.,* pp. 152–53. For a discussion of authoritarianism in the ancestral Young Czech party, see H. Gordon Skilling, "The Politics of the Czech Eighties," in Skilling and Peter Brock, ed., *The Czech Renascence of the Nineteenth Century* (Toronto: University of Toronto Press, 1971), pp. 276–78.

29. V. Beneš, *ibid.,* pp. 67–68; Olivová, p. 191; also Gotthold Rhode, "The Protectorate of Bohemia and Moravia, 1939–1945," in Mamatey and Luža, *op. cit.,* pp. 302–03. It should be mentioned that by far not all Agrarians collaborated during the war; some, in fact, were active in the resistance movement. See Luža, "The Czech Resistance Movement," *ibid.,* p. 345.

30. Edvard Beneš, *Masarykovo pojetí ideje národní a problém jednoty československé*, lecture to the Šafařík Learned Society in Bratislava (Bratislava: Učená společnost Šafaříkova, sv. 1, 1935).

31. For a lengthy inside history of Slovak nationalist politics in the First Republic, see Karol Sidor, *Slovenská politika na pôde pražského snemu*, 2 v. (Bratislava: Andrej, 1943).

32. On the wartime Slovak state, see Yeshayahu Jelínek, *The Parish Republic* (Boulder, East European Quarterly, 1976). It is interesting that many of the Slovak populists had been distrustful of the Germans before 1939, but the far-right contingent that gained control in 1939 realized the necessity of German support if Slovakia were to avoid annexation by Hungary or Germany itself. See Jörg K. Hoensch, "The Slovak Republic, 1939–1945," in Mamatey and Luža, pp. 271–73ff. See also O. Janeček, "Československo," in *Střední a jihovýchodní Evropa ve válce a v revoluci 1939–45*, publ. Československá akademie věd (Praha, 1969), pp. 31–122.

33. For a lengthy and well-chosen excerpt from the Economic and Philosophic Manuscripts, see Robert C. Tucker, ed., *The Marx-Engels Reader* (New York: W. W. Norton and Co., 1972), pp. 52–103.

34. Good examples of these thinkers' works are Gajo Petrović, *Marx in the Mid-Twentieth Century* (Garden City, N.Y.: Doubleday-Anchor, 1966); Svetozar Stojanović, *Between Ideals and Reality: A Critique of Socialism and Its Future*, tr. Gerson S. Sher (London, Toronto, and New York: Oxford University Press, 1973); and Mihailo Marković, *From Affluence to Praxis: Philosophy and Social Criticism* (Ann Arbor: University of Michigan Press, 1974).

35. Leszek Kołakowski, *Toward a Marxist Humanism*, tr. Jane Z. Peel (New York: Grove Press, 1968).

36. Karel Kosík, *Dialektika Konkrétního* (Praha: Nakl. ČSAV, 1963). Nikolaus Lobkowicz offers a brief but enlightening review of this difficult work in *Studies in Soviet Thought*, IV:3 (September 1964), pp. 248–51.

37. See Robert C. Tucker, *Philosophy and Myth in Karl Marx* (Cambridge and New York: Cambridge University Press, 1961), for a lucid essay showing the development of Marx's thought from the early period to the later works.

38. Milovan Djilas, *Anatomy of a Moral*, edited by Abraham Rothberg (New York: Praeger, 1959), a collection of articles originally published in *Borba* and *Nova misao* (Belgrade) during the winter of 1953–54; cited from pp. 53–54 of the Rothberg edition.

39. This was explicitly stated, for example, by Imre Nagy, *On Communism* (New York: Praeger, 1957), pp. 194–203.

40. George Lichtheim, *Marxism, An Historical and Critical Study*, Second Ed. (New York: Praeger, 1965, 1967), p. 103.

41. Karl Marx and Frederick Engels, *Selected Works*, I (Moscow: Foreign Languages Publishing House, 1962), pp. 377–85; also Tucker, *Marx-Engels Reader*, pp. 374–81. Tucker points out that Marx's moderate tones in this address may well have been only a conscious, temporary tactic. The fact remains, however, that the words were spoken and recorded for future practitioners to interpret.

42. Robert C. Tucker, "The Deradicalization of Marxist Movements," in *The Marxian Revolutionary Idea* (New York: W. W. Norton, Inc., 1969), pp. 172–214.

43. For a clear and succinct discussion of the politics of this period, see Mamatey, "The Development of Czechoslovak Democracy 1920–1938," esp. pp. 99–113.

44. The strike was most serious in Kladno, Rosice-Oslavany, Brno, Hodonín, Vrútky, Spišská Nová Ves, Zvolen, Gelnice, and Vráble. Olivová reports fatalities in Prague, Most, and Oslavany. Olivová, *The Doomed Democracy*, pp. 130–134; also P. Reimann, *et al., Istoriia Kommunisticheskoi Partii Chekhoslovakii* (Moscow, 1962, orig. Praha: Ústa dějin KSČ, 1961), pp. 177–81. Cf. Mamatey, *op. cit.*, pp. 102–06, and Zinner, pp. 28–35.

45. For an account of the beginning of the KSČ, see H. Gordon Skilling, "The Formation of a Communist Party in Czechoslovakia," *The American Slavic and East European Review*, XIV (October 1955), pp. 346–58.

46. Julius Braunthal, *History of the International*, Vol. 2, 1914–43, transl. John Clark (London: Thomas Nelson and Sons, Ltd., 1967), pp. 309–10. Braunthal says of the KSČ in the 1920s that "it was actually not a revolutionary party. . . . It was scarcely distinguishable, in fact, from a right-wing reformist Social Democratic party in opposition." The party's official history notes that the "primary danger" within the KSČ at this time was rightist tendencies, a holdover from Social Democratic traditions. See Reimann, *Istoriya KPCh*, pp. 252–53.

47. Reimann, *ibid.*, p. 252; *Statistická příručka Republiky Československé*, vol. 3 (Praha, 1928), pp. 254–56. By 1928, the KSČ had approximately 150,000 members, according to Braunthal (p. 319).

48. *Statistická příručka*, 3, p. 260.

49. The 1919 insurrection, despite its origins outside Czechoslovakia, served to inspire the Communists of a later era. See, e.g., Martin Vietor, "Hrdinný pokus o nastolení vlády lidu," *Život strany*, No. 12 (1964), pp. 725–29. Cf. Peter A. Toma, "The Slovak Soviet Republic," *The American Slavic and East European Review*, XVII (April 1958), pp. 203–15.

50. Skilling, "Gottwald and the Bolshevization of the Communist Party of Czechoslovakia," *Slavic Review*, XX (December 1961), pp. 642–55. See also *id.*, "The Comintern and Czechoslovak Communism: 1921–1929," *American Slavic and East European Review*, XIX (April 1960), pp. 234–47.

51. "V duchu Bolševismu kupředu!," speech at Sixth Party Congress, March 9, 1931, in K. Gottwald, *Spisy*, sv. 2 (Praha: Svoboda, 1951), p. 279.

52. Figures on party membership are from Skilling, "The Comintern and Czechoslovak Communism," p. 245. Electoral statistics from Czechoslovak Republic, *Manuel Statistique*, IV (Prague, 1932), pp. 401–02, and *Annuaire Statistique* (Prague, 1936), p. 269.

53. See Skilling, "Communism and Czechoslovak National Traditions," *Journal of International Affairs*, XX: 1 (1966), pp. 118–36. The link with the Comintern extended even to the point of the KSČ's adoption of the Comintern's nationality policy endorsing separatism.

54. "Dělníci, pracujíci, rolníci a živnostníci — spojte se!," speech to public meeting in Prague, March 2, 1936, in Gottwald, *Spisy*, sv. 7, pp. 56–69. See also Zinner, p. 55f.; Olivová, p. 210.

55. See, e.g., Gottwald's article in *Rudé právo*, October 8, 1938: "Svět k tomu nesmí mlčet!" Also "Po Mnichovském Diktatu," speech before Permanent Committee of the National Assembly, October 11, 1938. (Both are

reprinted in K. Gottwald, *Deset let; sborník statí a projevů 1936-1946* (Praha: Svoboda, 1949), pp. 162-71. Other speeches and articles concerning the fascist threat appear throughout the volume.)

56. This is implicitly admitted by Jaroslav Nedvěd, *Cesta ke sloučení sociální demokracie s komunistickou stranou v roce 1948,* Rozpravy ČSAV, Řada společenských věd, LXXVIII:8 (Praha, 1968), pp. 4-7.

57. The two more moderate socialist parties received more than twice as many votes in 1935 as the Communists. The Social Democrats received 1,034,774, the National Democrats 755,880 (total for the two: 1,790,654), and the Communists 849,009. Czechoslovak Republic, Státní úřad statistický, *Annuaire Statistique de la République Tchècoslovaque,* 1936, p. 269.

58. Skilling, "The Comintern and Czechoslovak Communism," pp. 242-44.

59. Even the fact that several important past and future KSČ leaders were in Moscow did not necessarily foretell the later events, for those who spent the war years in the USSR did not comprise a majority in the post-1945 Communist leadership group. (See discussion in next chapter.)

60. Jiří Pelikán, ed., *The Czechoslovak Purge Trials 1950-1954* (Stanford University Press, 1971); cf. Zbigniew K. Brzezinski, *The Soviet Bloc,* revised ed. (Harvard University Press, 1967), pp. 3-150.

61. *Ibid.,* p. 49.

62. *Ibid.,* p. 80. Prior to the Pelikán Commission's report a number of articles and commentaries appeared in the media, probing the Soviet role in the purge trials. See, e.g., *Rudé právo,* April 14, 1968; also U.S. Foreign Broadcast Information Service, *Daily Report,* April 29 and May 8, 1968, from ČTK and Radio Prague dispatches.

63. H. Gordon Skilling has described in detail the clash between Stalinist norms and the prevailing orientations of the body politic in his chapter, "Stalinism and Czechoslovak Political Culture," in Robert C. Tucker, ed., *Stalinism and Communist Political Culture* (New York: W. W. Norton and Co., forthcoming).

64. Brzezinski, pp. 93-97. Brzezinski estimates that approximately 550,000 KSČ/KSS members were eliminated between 1950 and 1954, compared to 370,000 in Poland and substantially lower numbers in other East European countries.

CHAPTER FOUR

1. The best English-language account of the 1948 coup is Tigrid's "The Prague Coup of 1948: The Elegant Takeover," in Hammond, ed., *The Anatomy of Communist Takeovers* (1975), pp. 399-432. The particular virtue of Tigrid's discussion is that the author has made use of rare documentary evidence that became momentarily available in 1968.

2. Talcott Parsons, *The Social System* (Glencoe, Ill.: The Free Press, 1951), pp. 520-25.

3. Č. Adamec, B. Pospíšil, and M. Tesář, *What's Your Opinion? — A Year's Survey of Public Opinion in Czechoslovakia* (Prague: Orbis, 1947), pp. 12-13.

4. Nedvěd, *Cesta ke sloučení demokracie s komunistickou stranou,* p. 8; also Jiri Horak, *The Czechoslovak Social Democratic Party 1938-1945,*

unpublished Ph.D. Dissertation, Columbia University (New York, 1960).

5. The Slovak SDP had merged with the KSS during the 1944 Slovak National Uprising. A few Slovak Social Democrats later split away and started the Labor party, but this proved to be devoid of mass support. See Radomír Luža, "Between Democracy and Communism 1945–1948," in Mamatey and Luža, *A History of the Czechoslovak Republic,* pp. 402–03.

6. Of course, one should not overlook the fact that Nazis imprisoned a good many Communists, too. Such notable future leaders as Novotný, Zápotocký, and Šik were incarcerated. The toll of Communists imprisoned and/or executed, however, was not as heavy as that of Social Democrats. The latter were special targets because they had aided in the evacuation of Austrian SDs following the *Anschluss* of March 1938. Nearly all the Czech SD leaders were imprisoned or exiled, and some were shot by firing squads; numerous others died from the conditions in the prisons. Those who returned from exile in 1945 found that the old network of local party organizations had been destroyed. The party by 1945 was hardly a shadow of its former self, a powerless group of political has-beens (or ne'er-would-be's) who were easily swallowed up by the Communists three years later.

In the prison camps, meanwhile, the Communists were perhaps the most resourceful and the most cohesive group of inmates. No doubt their relatively high survival rate was due in large part to this. See Eugen Kogon, *The Theory and Practice of Hell; The German Concentration Camps and the System Behind Them,* transl. Heinz Norden (New York: Farrar, Straus and Co., 1949), pp. 231–35.

7. Vratislav Bušek, "Action Committees," in Miloslav Rechcígl, Jr. (ed.), *Czechoslovakia Past and Present,* vol. 1 (The Hague and Paris: Mouton, 1968), pp. 296–333.

8. Luža, p. 401; also Vlastislav Chalupa, *Communism in a Free Society: Czechoslovakia 1945–1948* (Chicago: Czechoslovak Foreign Institute in Exile, 1958), pp. 37–38. The Communists' role in the redistribution of rural lands undoubtedly helps to explain the party's unprecedentedly strong showing in rural districts in 1946.

9. V. V. Kusin, *The Intellectual Origins of the Prague Spring* (Cambridge, 1971), p. 1.

10. Nedvěd, p. 9ff.

11. Rodnick, *The Strangled Democracy,* p. 68ff. Rodnick reports that of his interviewees who voted Communist in 1946, 10–15 percent did so for religious or moral reasons.

12. The speech is reprinted in K. Gottwald, *Deset let,* pp. 370–88. Paul Zinner has cited articles published in the Moscow-based Czech journal *Československé listy* in August 1943 as the earliest indication of Communist intentions. See Zinner, *Communist Strategy and Tactics,* pp. 85–86.

13. Cf. Korbel's statement that "On July 10, 1947 Czechoslovakia lost her independence." Josef Korbel, *The Communist Subversion of Czechoslovakia 1938–1948* (Princeton, 1959), p. 182.

14. The old cold-war debate about whether or not Czechoslovakia "had to go Communist" (i.e., whether or not Stalin would have pursued this end at any cost) need not concern us here, but for a typical exchange on this question, see William E. Griffith, "Myth and Reality in Czechoslovak History," *East*

Europe, XI (March 1962), pp. 3–11+, comments by Adolf Procházka and Petr Zenkl in the following (April) issue, and Griffith's reply in the May issue.

15. Public opinion surveys conducted in the winter of 1947–48 indicated that the Communists' popular base had slipped notably since 1946. See Tigrid, p. 410; also Zdenek Suda, *The Czechoslovak Socialist Republic* (Baltimore: The Johns Hopkins University Press, 1969), p. 34.

16. Tigrid, pp. 431–32.

17. E. Beneš, *Úvahy o slovanství*, second ed. (Praha: Čin, 1947), pp. 279–90; cited from p. 284.

18. This is first apparent in a radio speech by Beneš broadcast from Moscow upon the completion of the Czechoslovak-Soviet Friendship Agreement of December 1943. The speech is reprinted in Beneš, *Šest let exilu a druhé světové války* (Praha: Družstevní práce, 1946), pp. 223–30.

19. For an interesting discussion of the 1948 coup set in the context of world politics, see Morton Kaplan, *Macropolitics* (Chicago: Aldine, 1969), pp. 81–121.

20. See Brzezinski, *The Soviet Bloc*, revised ed., pp. 58–64 and 67ff. Brzezinski argues that the founding of the Cominform, more than the subsequent difficulties with Yugoslavia, signaled the tightening of the bloc.

21. R. V. Burks, *The Dynamics of Communism in Eastern Europe* (Princeton, 1961). See especially Burks's table on Social Composition of Interwar Parties, p. 35.

22. The data referred to here and in the subsequent discussion have been drawn from the Archive on Political Elites in Eastern Europe, compiled by the University of Pittsburgh Center for International Studies under the direction of William Jarzabek. A number of errors in the Pittsburgh data have been corrected through cross-references with other sources. The author wishes to thank Martin J. E. Král for having pointed out most of these errors.

23. On status inconsistency, see Gerhard E. Lenski, "Status Crystallization: A Non-Vertical Dimension of Social Status," *American Sociological Review*, vol. 19 no. 4 (August 1954), pp. 405–13. For a review of the literature, see James A. Geschwender, "Continuities in Theories of Status Consistency and Cognitive Dissonance," *Social Forces*, vol. 46 no. 2 (December 1967), pp. 165–67.

24. Although there are few missing values for the ethnicity variable in the Pittsburgh data, the author's own familiarity with the ethnic situation suggests that there are many inaccuracies. In particular, Jews seem to be undercounted, as some (e.g. František Kriegel) have been coded as Czechs; quite likely, others have been coded as Slovaks. In any event, ethnicity is a difficult identity to establish in many individual cases, given a certain degree of exogamy as well as historical intermixing of language patterns and cultural assimilation.

25. Burks has argued (*op. cit.*, pp. 157, 214–15 and *passim*) that the Magyar minority represented fertile ground for the Communists' electoral appeal. The Pittsburgh data on elites suggest that the heavy Communist vote in Magyar districts was not a vote for co-national political candidates.

26. "Toward a Theory of Dependency in Eastern Europe," conference panel chaired by Jan F. Triska, Eighth National Convention of the American Association for the Advancement of Slavic Studies, St. Louis, October 7, 1976.

27. William Zimmerman, "Dependency Theory and the Soviet-East Euro-

pean Hierarchical Regional System: An Initial Testing," unpubl. conference paper (see preceding note); Karl W. Deutsch, "Imperialism and Neocolonialism," *Papers* of the Peace Society (International), vol. 23 (1974), pp. 1–26. Cf. Johan Galtung, "A Structural Theory of Imperialism," *Journal of Peace Research,* vol. 2 (1971), pp. 81–117.

28. For a useful survey of the major theories of imperialism, see Deutsch (*ibid.*).

29. The author by no means wishes to reintroduce the vocabulary of the cold war and, indeed, feels himself to be a member of a generation chronologically removed from the anticommunist literature of the 1950s. In order to justify this smugness, however, the author has attempted to define his terms in a sufficiently thorough and objective way as to make them meaningful in their own right.

30. George Lichtheim, *Imperialism* (New York: Praeger, 1971), pp. 135–36.

31. S. N. Eisenstadt, *The Political Systems of Empires* (New York: The Free Press of Glencoe, 1963), pp. 10–12 and *passim.*

32. *Ibid.,* pp. 13–18.

33. *Ibid.,* pp. 18–24.

34. The post-invasion issuance of the Brezhnev Doctrine (1968) was perhaps the clearest statement of the defense perimeters and the mutuality of interests among the bloc partners in maintaining domestic, as well as international, stability.

35. See Brzezinski, pp. 5–9, for a brief discussion of the Soviet interest in Eastern Europe.

36. See Ghita Ionescu, *The Politics of the European Communist States* (New York: Praeger, 1967), pp. 87–167.

37. See Ulč's discussion of political participation in Czechoslovakia, *op. cit.,* pp. 24–44; see also chapter one of the present study.

38. Lichtheim, *Imperialism,* p. 5.

39. *Ibid.,* p. 4.

40. *Ibid.,* p. 9.

41. For a critical review of Lichtheim's study, see Irving Louis Horowitz in the *American Journal of Sociology,* vol. 78 (July 1972), pp. 245–49.

42. See, for example, the contributions by Vernon V. Aspaturian, A. Ross Johnson, and Paul Marer to Charles Gati, ed., *The International Politics of Eastern Europe* (Praeger, 1976). See also Nish Jamgotch, Jr., "Alliance Management in Eastern Europe (The New Type of International Relations)," *World Politics,* vol. 27 (April 1975), pp. 405–29.

43. Marer, "Has Eastern Europe Become a Liability to the Soviet Union? (III) The Economic Aspect," in Gati, *op. cit.,* pp. 59–81.

44. Finley, "Economic Linkage and Political Dependency in Eastern Europe," unpublished conference paper (see note 26).

45. Nor can it be said, according to Aspaturian and Johnson, that Eastern Europe has become a political-ideological or military liability to the USSR. See Aspaturian, "Has Eastern Europe Become a Liability to the Soviet Union? (I) The Political-Ideological Aspects," pp. 17–36, and Johnson, ". . . (II) The Military Aspect," pp. 37–58, both in Gati, *op. cit.*

46. It is noteworthy that the so-called Brezhnev Doctrine stressed the multilateral context of bloc intervention, and the decision to intervene in August

1968 was made jointly by the five hostile allies. However, it was Brezhnev himself whose pronouncement served as the basis of justification, just as it was imperative that the bulk of the military operation be carried out by Soviet forces.

47. Kent N. Brown, "Coalition Politics and Soviet Influence in Eastern Europe," unpublished conference paper (see note 26).

48. Otto Ulč has described this specialized language, which he calls "Stalinese," in his excellent chapter on political communication; see Ulč, *op. cit.*, pp. 131-34.

CHAPTER FIVE

1. For a succinct discussion of the institutionalization process of political parties, see Samuel P. Huntington, *Political Order in Changing Societies* (New Haven and London: Yale University Press, 1968), pp. 419-20.

2. It was, of course, the German problem that brought about the end of the First Republic. This is not meant to minimize the importance of other problems — the depression, Slovak and Magyar national grievances, etc.; these, too, contributed significantly to the weakening of the republic. As I have argued elsewhere, however, the internal weaknesses of the system — serious though they were — did not themselves cause its downfall. Even the German population was on the verge of becoming reconciled to its status as a national minority, and the cooperation of the German "activist" parties between 1926 and 1933 testified to this. It was the *international* situation that destroyed the First Republic: the spread of extremist German nationalism outward from the Third Reich, the interaction between this phenomenon and the effects of the depression which gave rise to the *Sudetendeutsch* movement, and finally the abandonment of Czechoslovakia by the French and the British at Munich in 1938. See David W. Paul, *Nationalism, Pluralism and "Schweikism" in Czechoslovakia's Political Culture,* unpublished Ph.D. dissertation (Princeton, 1973), pp. 46-49.

3. Jaroslav Krejčí, *Social Change and Stratification in Postwar Czechoslovakia* (London: Macmillan, and New York: Columbia University Press, 1972).

4. Ladislav Lipscher, "Zur allgemeinen Analyse des politischen Mechanismus in der Ersten Tschechoslowakischen Republik," in Karl Bosl, ed., *Die "Burg": Einflussreiche politische Kräfte um Masaryk und Beneš* (München, Wien: R. Oldenbourg Verlag für Collegium Carolinum, 1973), p. 151. This statistic will, perhaps, find a close competitor in Israel, where as many as 24 parties have offered candidates for election to the Knesset at the same time. See Gregory S. Mahler and Richard J. Trilling, "Coalition Behavior and Cabinet Formation; The Case of Israel," *Comparative Political Studies,* VII:2 (July 1975), pp. 200-33.

5. Czechoslovak Republic, Státní úřad statistický, *Manuel Statistique de la Republique Tchécoslovaque,* I (Prague, 1920), p. 102.

6. Václav L. Beneš, "Background of Czechoslovak Democracy," in Miloslav Rechcígl, Jr., ed., *The Czechoslovak Contribution to World Culture* (The Hague: Mouton, 1964), pp. 267-76.

7. Milan E. Hapala, "Political Parties in Czechoslovakia, 1918-1938," in

Rechcígl, ed., *Czechoslovakia Past and Present* (The Hague and Paris: Mouton, 1968), Vol. I, p. 139.

8. This will be discussed at length in chapters six and seven.

9. See, e.g., Myron Weiner and Joseph LaPalombara, "The Origins and Development of Political Parties," in Weiner and LaPalombara, ed., *Political Parties and Political Development* (Princeton, 1966), pp. 3–42 *passim*.

10. In 1871 the Czechs nearly obtained a solution of this type, in the form of the Hohenwart Program (named after the Austrian prime minister of that time). The Hohenwart Program would, in effect, have introduced a trialist system in the Empire, replacing the dualism of the 1867 Compromise; the Bohemian Crownlands would have been on a par with Hungary. After considerable hesitancy and despite what some Czechs thought was a promise to the contrary, the Emperor rejected the Hohenwart Program because of pressure from German liberals and the Magyar nobility — both of whom felt threatened politically by the rise of the Czechs. See A. E. F. Schäffle, *Aus meinem Leben* (Berlin, 1905), Vol. II. (Schäffle was chief advisor to Hohenwart, who incidentally fell along with his trialist program.)

11. Zdeněk Šolle, "Kontinuität und Wandel in der sozialen Entwicklung der böhmischen Länder 1872–1930," in Karl Bosl, ed., *Aktuelle Forschungsprobleme um die Erste Tschechoslowakische Republik* (München, Wien: R. Oldenbourg Verlag, 1969), pp. 30–34.

12. Ferdinand Seibt, "Zur Sozialstruktur der Ersten ČSR," in *Beiträge zum deutsch-tschechischen Verhältnis im 19. und 20. Jahrhundert* (München: Verlag Robert Lerche, für Collegium Carolinum, 1967), pp. 121–23.

13. Šolle, *op. cit.*, pp. 43–45.

14. Seibt, *op. cit.*, pp. 111–12; Antonín Boháč, *The Population of the Czechoslovak Republic*, translated for Human Relations Area Files, Inc. (New Haven, Conn.) from *Československá vlastivěda*, Ser. 2, Národopis (Praha: Sfinx, 1936), p. 69. Percentages exclusive of Subcarpathian Ruthenia are according to my own calculations.

15. Boháč, *ibid*.

16. Seibt, *loc. cit.* Seibt shows, interestingly, that industrialization does not necessarily mean a high degree of urbanization. In the Czech lands many small industrial towns and agglomerates of adjacent towns grew up around small and medium-sized industrial enterprises. Indeed, the overall pattern of Czech industrialization was toward a much smaller degree of concentration than was the case in most Western societies. This is true with regard to size of industrial enterprises as well as to size of population centers; hence the growth of family enterprises, factories with ten to fifteen employees, and industrial towns such as České Budějovice, Kladno, Ústí nad Labem, Zlín, Třebíč, and Karlovy Vary. (Seibt, pp. 117–18.)

17. Modern sectors include industry, trades, commerce, banking, and transportation; rural sectors include agriculture, forestry, and fishing. Source: Boháč, pp. 67, 69. For a more detailed breakdown of the 1930 data see V. L. Beneš, "Czechoslovak Democracy and Its Problems," in Mamatey and Luža, *op. cit.*, pp. 42–43.

18. Seibt, p. 119; also Heinz O. Ziegler, *Die berufliche und soziale Gliederung der Bevölkerung in der Tschechoslowakei* (Brünn, Prag, Leipzig, Wien: Verlag Rudolf M. Rohrer, 1936), p. 231 and *passim*.

19. Seibt, *ibid.*

20. Source: Ziegler, p. 231.

21. Ziegler, p. 232. Ziegler prefers to draw his distinction between large- and middle-scale enterprises on the basis of mechanization, relations of authority between employer and employee, etc., rather than in terms of precise numbers of employees. Small enterprises, however, are distinguished in terms of numbers (ten or fewer).

22. *Ibid.*, p. 23ff.

23. ". . . The sum total of [the] relations of production constitutes the economic structure of society, the real foundation, on which rises a legal and political superstructure and to which correspond definite forms of social consciousness. The mode of production of material life conditions the social, political and intellectual life process in general. . . ." Preface to *The Critique of Political Economy,* in Karl Marx and Frederick Engels, *Selected Works,* 2v. (Moscow: Foreign Languages Publishing House, 1962), I, p. 363.

24. References hardly need be cited here, but see, e.g., "Manifesto of the Communist Party," in *ibid.,* pp. 34–45.

25. See Stanley Z. Pech, *The Czech Revolution of 1848* (Chapel Hill: University of North Carolina Press, 1969).

26. Among the many books on politics in the Habsburg empire after 1848, see esp. Kann, Jászi, and Redlich. For shorter treatments, see C. A. Macartney, *The Habsburg Empire 1790–1918* (London: Weidenfeld and Nicolson, 1968), and Alan W. Palmer, *The Lands Between* (London and New York: Macmillan, 1969, 1970).

27. H. Gordon Skilling, "The Politics of the Czech Eighties," in Peter Brock and H. G. Skilling, ed., *The Czech Renascence of the Nineteenth Century* (Toronto: University of Toronto Press, 1970), p. 265f.

28. Šolle, "Kontinuität und Wandel," pp. 23–27.

29. *Ibid.*

30. *Ibid.*, p. 36.

31. On the origins of Czech political parties, see *ibid.,* pp. 35–38, *inter alia.* For discussions of the interwar party system, see V. L. Beneš, "Czechoslovak Democracy and Its Problems," pp. 66–75; Malbone W. Graham, "Parties and Politics," in Robert J. Kerner, ed., *Czechoslovakia: Twenty Years of Independence* (Berkeley and Los Angeles: University of California Press, 1940), pp. 137–70; Hapala, *op. cit.,* pp. 124–40; Charles Hoch, *The Political Parties in Czechoslovakia* (Prague: Czechoslovak Sources and Documents, No. 9, 1936, by Orbis); and Joseph Rothschild, *East Central Europe Between the Two World Wars* (Seattle: University of Washington Press, 1974), pp. 95–100.

32. Jiri Horak, *The Czechoslovak Social Democratic Party 1938–1945,* unpublished Ph.D. Dissertation, Columbia University (New York, 1960).

33. V. Beneš, *ibid.,* pp. 67–68; see also Anthony Paleček, "Antonín Švehla, Czech Peasant Statesman," *Slavic Review* XXI (December 1962), pp. 699–708.

34. Beneš, *ibid.;* also V. Olivová, *The Doomed Democracy,* pp. 195–96. The party's right wing sought an alliance that would exclude the socialists from the government and swing Czechoslovakia's foreign policy toward Germany.

35. Czechoslovak National Socialist Party, Executive Committee in Exile, *Half Century of Struggle against Marxism; Who Are the Czechoslovak National Socialists?* (n.d.)

36. R. V. Burks, *The Dynamics of Communism in Eastern Europe* (Princeton, 1961), p. 66.

37. Czechoslovak Republic, Státní úřad statistický, *Annuaire Statistique,* 1936; see also Beneš, "Czechoslovak Democracy," p. 72. The National Democrats had formed in 1919 from the members of five prewar parties, including the Young Czechs and the remnants of the Old Czechs. The party took on a staunchly Czech-nationalist and rightwing character in subsequent years, and following the 1935 elections it merged with the Czech fascist movement, now known as the National League.

38. Beneš, *ibid.,* pp. 70–71.

39. Šolle, p. 36; J. W. Bruegel, "The Germans in Pre-War Czechoslovakia," in Mamatey and Luža, ed., *op. cit.,* pp. 178–83. It should be mentioned that German party development, like Czech, was basically continuous between 1861 and 1930; however, the rise of Henlein and the *Sudetendeutschpartei* ended that continuity.

40. Lipscher, "Zur allgemeinen Analyse des politischen Mechanismus," p. 150.

41. See Ľubomír Lipták, *Slovensko v 20. storočí* (Bratislava: Vydavateľstvo politickej literatúry, 1968), pp. 21–42; also Scotus Viator (pseudonym for R. W. Seton-Watson), *Racial Problems in Hungary* (London, 1908), *passim.*

42. Lipscher, *loc. cit.;* also Kann, *The Habsburg Empire: A Study in Integration and Disintegration,* pp. 375–79.

43. Masaryk noted diverging strains of Slovak political thought by about 1900: the Hlasists, the first articulate "Czechoslovak" group; a similar group around Milan Hodža; Svetozar Hurban-Vajanský and the panslavists; Andrej Hlinka and the Catholic nationalists; and a smaller collection of Protestant nationalists. See Karel Čapek, *President Masaryk Tells His Story* (New York: G. P. Putnam's Sons, 1935), p. 193.

44. The Slovak populists joined the Czech People's party in a short-lived merger and ran together with them in the 1920 elections. Friction was evident almost from the beginning, and they split in 1922.

45. V. Beneš, "Czechoslovak Democracy," pp. 73–75.

46. The foregoing analysis is not meant to exaggerate the similarities between Czech and Slovak societies. The differences were crucial and will be explored in chapter six.

47. For a dissenting opinion on this question, see Olivová, *op. cit.,* pp. 128–34, and for an argument linking class and national conflict in Slovakia, see Samo Falťan, *Slovenská otázka v Československu* (Bratislava: Vydavateľstvo politickej literatúry, 1968), pp. 61–69.

48. Falťan, *ibid.;* also V. Beneš, "Czechoslovak Democracy," p. 44.

49. Edvard Beneš once asserted that the overlapping party constituencies made coalition politics easier than in other European democracies. See *Edward Beneš in His Own Words,* compiled by Karel Hudec (New York: Czech-American National Alliance, 1944), p. 27.

50. Coalition politics, like pluralism itself, had had a previous history among the Czechs in the Austrian system, when the nationality issue drew Czech parties together; this was particularly true in the Bohemian and Moravian *Landtage.* See Lipscher, p. 151.

51. Jan Hajda, "The Role of the Intelligentsia in the Development of

Czechoslovak Society," in Rechcígl (ed.), *The Czechoslovak Contribution to World Culture*, pp. 307–12.

52. Of course, not all the Czech politicians of the First Republic were drawn from the intelligentsia. Notable exceptions were the Agrarian leader Švehla, the Social Democrat Antonín Hampl, and Klement Gottwald.

53. See the discussion of this in chapter three, above.

54. The annexation of these territories fulfilled the Polish and Hungarian irredenta that had resulted from the borders drawn at Trianon in 1919.

55. Emil Hácha became President upon the forced resignation of Beneš in October 1938.

56. See Hubert Ripka, *Munich, Before and After* (New York: Howard Fertig, 1969).

57. Two more Slovak parties entered the scene prior to the 1946 elections. They were the Labor party, formed by Social Democrats who objected to the Slovak SDs' 1944 merger with the Communists, and the Freedom party, formed around Šrobár from the ranks of dissident members of the Democratic party. See Luža, "Czechoslovakia between Democracy and Communism," in Mamatey and Luža, *op. cit.*, pp. 402–03.

58. Zinner, *Communist Strategy and Tactics*, pp. 99–116. In a survey conducted in the Czech lands during March of 1946, 57.5 percent thought the number of parties "sufficient," while only 5.6 percent thought them "too few"; 34.2 percent even considered the number "too many." It is noteworthy that of those who thought there were "too many," Communists and their supporters predominated. See Č. Adamec, B. Pospíšil, and M. Tesář, *What's Your Opinion? — A Year's Survey of Public Opinion in Czechoslovakia* (Prague: Orbis, 1947), pp. 12–13. The survey was conducted by the Czech Institute of Public Opinion.

59. Vladimir Kusin estimates that in 1948 there were between 60,000 and 70,000 social organizations in Czechoslovakia. Kusin, *Political Grouping in the Czechoslovak Reform Movement* (New York: Columbia University Press, 1972), p. 194. Kusin adds that by 1967 the number declined to 700–800.

60. Taborsky, *Communism in Czechoslovakia;* Rechcígl, *Czechoslovakia Past and Present*, 2 vol.; Zdeněk Suda, *The Czechoslovak Socialist Republic* (Baltimore: Johns Hopkins Press, 1969); Vlastislav Chalupa, *Rise and Development of a Totalitarian State* (Leiden: H. V. Stenfert Kroese N.V., 1959); and David Rodnick, *The Strangled Democracy: Czechoslovakia 1948–69* (Lubbock, Tex.: The Caprock Press, 1970).

61. Kusin, *The Intellectual Origins of the Prague Spring* (1971), p. 13.

62. Krejčí, *Social Change and Stratification;* cf. Reban, *Czechoslovakia 1968: Some Aspects of Pluralism and Change* (1972), p. 29 ff.

63. Jean-Paul Sartre has characterized this system as "the Thing," whose human perpetrators themselves became akin to the inhuman Thing, ultimately devoting themselves to the preservation of the Thing itself, a creature that, in Sartre's words, "has no other end than to persevere in its being. . . ." Sartre, "The Socialism that Came in from the Cold," introduction to A. J. Liehm, *The Politics of Culture*, transl., Peter Kussi (New York: Grove Press, 1973), pp. 3–37; cited from p. 11.

64. On this, see especially Kusin, *Political Grouping*. See also Skilling, *Czechoslovakia's Interrupted Revolution;* Golan, *Reform Rule in Czecho-*

slovakia; and Reban, *op. cit.* Documentary material appears in Robin A. Remington, *Winter in Prague; Documents on Czechoslovak Communism in Crisis* (Cambridge, Mass.: M.I.T. Press, 1969). A useful collection of public opinion data from 1968 has been assembled by Jaroslaw A. Piekalkiewicz, *Public Opinion Polling in Czechoslovakia, 1968-69* (New York: Praeger, 1972).

65. Karel Bartošek reflected upon an incipient opposition that formed in the late fifties and played a role in two important events of the early sixties: the rehabilitation of former political prisoners in 1962-63, and the formulation of a new economic program soon thereafter. Bartošek, "Revoluce proti byrokratismu?", *Rudé právo,* July 26, 1968.

66. Paul, "The Repluralization of Czechoslovak Politics in the 1960s," *Slavic Review, loc. cit.* See also Kusin, *Political Grouping.*

67. Ivan Sviták, *The Czechoslovak Experiment 1968-69* (New York and London: Columbia University Press, 1971), p. 4.

68. The Club of Committed Nonpartisans (*Klub angažovaných nestraníků*) was a loose network of local clubs formed to discuss politics and influence legislation. Many of the KAN's more outspoken members were thought to have personal political ambitions, but KAN itself was never advanced as an opposition party. The most important function assumed by KAN was to act as a lobby for democratic and humanitarian causes, although there were instances where a local organization did become more directly involved in politics or administration; the local KAN group of a small village near Karlovy Vary, for example, participated in the planning of a municipal water works project.

69. *"Svoboda"* — *die Presse in der Tschechoslowakei 1968* (Zürich: Internationales Presseinstitut, 1969), pp. 35-36.

70. "Co chceme"(What We Want), *Literární noviny,* V: 16 (April 21, 1956).

71. Examples could be found in the social satire of Bohumil Hrabal (*Closely Watched Trains, Dance Lessons for the Older and More Advanced*), the political novels of Ladislav Mňačko (*The Taste of Power, Death is Called Engelchen*), and the absurdist drama of Václav Havel (*The Garden Party, The Memorandum*).

72. For a revealing collection of interviews with a number of these personalities, see Liehm, *The Politics of Culture.*

73. Liehm, *Closely Watched Films; The Czechoslovak Experience* (White Plains, N.Y.: International Arts and Sciences Press, 1974); Josef Škvorecký, *All the Bright Young Men and Women; A Personal History of the Czech Cinema* (Toronto: Peter Martin Associates Ltd., 1971).

74. Svaz československých spisovatelů, *IV. sjezd Svazu československých spisovatelů, Protokol* (Praha, 1968). See especially the dramatic speech by Ludvík Vaculík, pp. 141-51. This speech, among a few others, is also reproduced (in English translation) in Dušan Hamšík, *Writers against Rulers* (New York: Vintage, 1971).

75. Even this move did not entirely succeed. The regime failed to bring the Slovak Writers' Union under control, perhaps because the Slovak organization had eschewed any outright challenges to the regime. When the government moved against the Czechoslovak union, however, the Slovak organization began to show more sympathy toward the revolt and offered space in its publications to several Czech dissidents, who gladly accepted.

76. Jan Křen, "Kult a historie," *Kulturní tvorba,* I (May 23 and 30, 1963); Bartošek, *op. cit.* Křen reexamined the legacy of Masaryk in a critical but reasoned way, at the same time deploring the "simplistic falsifications, deformations, and omissions" that characterized history in the fifties. He even disputed the former doctrines that led historians to interpret "every event in history . . . as goal-oriented and deliberate." (Křen, *op. cit.,* May 23, p. 4.)

77. On October 31 some Prague students were arrested for publicly protesting a power shut-off in their hostel. Further demonstrations ensued in protest against the arrests, and the police responded with beatings and more arrests. The students' demands now escalated to include academic and political freedom. The government at first criticized the students, then criticized the police, and finally, after more than a month had passed, released the incarcerated demonstrators. A general wave of indignation swept through Prague in response to this incident, and many influential party members shared in the censure of the regime. It is very likely that the Strahov hostel incident thus contributed to the timing of Novotný's downfall, for the latter occurred within a month of the students' release.

78. Zbyněk Vokrouhlický, "Jednota v pluralitě," *Mladá fronta,* Sept. 17, 1968.

79. A moving account of Club 231 activities is given in the autobiography of one of the club's founders, Jaroslav Brodský, *Solution Gamma* (Toronto, 1971).

80. Krejčí, *Social Change and Stratification,* pp. 27–62; also Otto Ulč, "Czechoslovakia: The Great Leap Backward," in Charles Gati, ed., *The Politics of Modernization in Eastern Europe: Testing the Soviet Model* (New York, Washington, and London: Praeger, 1974), pp. 89–116. It should be noted that Bohemia and Moravia were already highly egalitarian, even during the interwar period. In terms of income distribution, the Czech lands in 1937 were far more egalitarian than any West European country in recent times. And by 1947, before the Communist takeover but after the implementation of the National Front program, even the mild inequalities of the First Republic had been further reduced.

The Gini index of income equality, a widely used statistical indicator, shows some interesting comparisons in this light. (The basic principle behind the meaning of the Gini index is quite simple: the higher the coefficient, the more unequal the income distribution; 0.00 is absolute equality, with everyone receiving exactly the same income, 1.00 is absolute inequality in which one person would receive all income and everybody else nothing.) The Gini coefficient for Bohemia and Moravia in 1937 was .22871; in 1947 it was .17984. (Krejčí, p. 16.) No doubt, if Slovakia had been included the coefficient in each case would have been higher, but the statistics for the Czech lands speak for themselves.

In comparison, West European coefficients for various postwar years were: United Kingdom .366 (1955); Norway .386 (1950); Sweden .399 (1960); Italy .403 (1948); Denmark .421 (1952); Netherlands .431 (1950); and West Germany .473 (1950). These indices may be somewhat misleading, for they reflect income distribution before taxes. They are considerably lower after taxes because of progressive income taxing policies — but in no case do they yet approach the equalization trends of the Czech lands. West Germany, e.g., falls only to .432 (the highest), Norway to .313 (the lowest). Source: Bruce M. Russett, *et al.*, *World Handbook of Political and Social Indicators* (New Haven: Yale University Press, 1964), pp. 245, 247.

81. Pavel Machonin *et al.*, *Československá společnost; sociologická analýza sociální stratifikace* (Praha, 1969, unpubl.), pp. 613 14. This impressive work was published in Bratislava under the same title (in Slovak, *Československá spoločnosť.* . .) early in 1969, shortly before the reimposition of censorship. The Czech edition did not make it beyond the stage of page proofs. Some of the latter made their way to the West, and it is this unpublished document that I have used.

82. Jiří Večerník, "Problémy příjmu a životní úrovně v sociální diferenciace," *ibid.,* p. 303.

83. *Ibid.,* p. 304.

84. *Op. cit.* Two preliminary efforts, both edited by Machonin, are somewhat more readily obtainable: *Sociální struktura socialistické společnosti* (Praha, 1966) and *Změny v sociální struktuře Československa a dynamika sociálně-politického vývoje* (Praha, 1967). For a review of the 1969 volume see Ernest Gellner, "The Pluralist Anti-Levellers of Prague," *Government and Opposition,* vol. 7 no. 1 (Winter 1972), pp. 20 37. See also Machonin, "Social Stratification in Contemporary Czechoslovakia," *American Journal of Sociology,* vol. 75 no. 5 (1970), pp. 725 41.

85. Machonin, "K obecnému vymezení pojmu 'sociální struktura'" in *Změny v sociální struktuře Československa,* pp. 15 43.

86. Gross occupational statistics are officially given in three primary categories of occupation type: (I) workers in the national(ized) economy, subdivided into those employed in the production of material goods and those in nonproductive sectors (transportation, education, culture, etc.), (II)students and apprentices, and (III) others, including those employed in nonplanned sectors or independently. Statistical references break down by sector, but all are considered workers (*pracující*). In 1967, the percentages of working-age population in the categories were (I) 78.82 percent, (II) 9.47 percent, (III) 11.71 percent. (Working-age population is defined as men between the ages of 15 and 59, women 15 54.) Source: *Statistická ročenka Československé republiky 1968* (Praha: Nakladatelství technické literatury, 1968), p. 129ff.

Of all persons employed, 88 percent worked in the state-owned sectors, 10.1 percent for cooperatively owned enterprises, and only 1.9 percent independently. Source: Věra Rollová, "Sociální diferenciace podle ekonomického postavení a problém společenských tříd," in Machonin, *Československá společnost,* p. 350.

87. Jiří Cvekl, "Osobnost a sociální struktura," in Machonin, *Změny v sociální struktuře Československa,* pp. 255 74.

88. The word *nivelisace* translates roughly to "leveling" or "equalization," but the connotations of neither English word add up to a satisfactory translation. I hope the reader will pardon my use of the neologism "nivelization."

89. Cvekl, *op. cit.,* pp. 269 73, cited from p. 271.

90. Zdeněk Strmiska a Milan Petrušek, "Společenské skupiny," in Machonin, *op. cit.* (1967), pp. 79 105.

91. Machonin, "K obecnému vymezení pojmu 'sociální struktura,'" p. 38.

92. *Ibid.*

93. Machonin, *Československá společnost,* p. 599.

94. *Ibid.,* p. 609.

95. Machonin defines a stratified society as "one in which *strata* are formed which represent groupings of persons with similar characteristics of the positions on different character scales of objective vertical differentiations, i.e. groupings exhibiting a certain extent of *status consistency* — that is, of coordinated interpenetration of positions into the productive and attributive systems." *Ibid.,* p. 599. Machonin is not renowed for prosaic beauty, but I trust that this passage will serve to inform the reader that the matter of defining stratification has not been neglected.

96. To verify their working hypotheses concerning status rankings and prestige, the sociologists conducted a massive interviewing campaign in 1967, thereby adding a body of subjective opinion data to their statistical facts.

97. Other defining characteristics are democracy in form and content, collective ownership of the means of production, and achievement as the basis of social mobility. Machonin, *Československá společnost,* p. 600.

98. Cf. Branko Horvat, *An Essay on Yugoslav Society* (White Plains, N.Y.: International Arts and Sciences Press, 1967), pp. 145–75, and Jan Szczepański, *Polish Society* (New York: Random House, 1970), pp. 105–46. See also *Stratification in Hungary* (Budapest: Hungarian Central Statistical Office, 1967).

99. Jaroslav Kapr, "Obecná struktura prestiže povolání v Československu," in Machonin, *Československá společnost,* p. 393. Kapr's respondents indicated the following as the most important criteria for judging the prestige of a given occupation: good pay, service to humanity, social prestige (unclarified), education and difficulty of task performed. *Ibid.,* pp. 401–02.

100. Machonin, "Sociální stratifikace v Československu 1967," in *ibid.,* p. 134ff.

101. Jiří Večerník, "Problémy příjmu a životní úrovně v sociální diferenciace," *ibid.,* p. 301ff. See also Krejčí, *op. cit.,* pp. 67ff.

102. Machonin, p. 133. The researchers found that party membership correlated to some degree with access to management positions (thus indirectly with prestige), but not as strongly as the research team had expected. (pp. 615–16.)

103. *Ibid.,* p. 604.

104. Machonin, p. 140ff. Even taking the higher statistic in each grouping, there is a residuum of approximately 7.8 percent which is not adequately explained.

105. Rollová, *op. cit.,* p. 350ff.

106. Machonin, p. 608.

107. *Ibid.*

108. Lubomír Brokl, "Moc a sociální rozvrstvení," pp. 239–70.

109. Machonin, p. 608.

110. Machonin, "Sociální stratifikace v Československu 1967," p. 133.

111. One reference that is not so oblique is the following: "The insufficiently democratic character of the political structure (especially the fact that a relatively great part of the population do not participate in power) makes it … impossible to achieve a closer connection between the political-organizational system on the one hand and the occupational system and that of lifestyle on the other." Machonin, p. 603.

112. In the sixties there occurred a steady rise in the political influence of an economic-technocratic elite, typified by such men as Šik, Richta, and Kýn. Along with them, Machonin noted the development of a technocratic organization which threatened to replace the traditional bureaucracy. In a tacit admission that true democratic socialism did not exist, Machonin posited three vague types of system: a bureaucratic system (presumably that existing in 1967, despite Machonin's denial of a bureaucratic stratum), true democratic socialism (unspecified), and technocracy. Machonin, pp. 607–08.

113. See footnote 87.

114. Those of us concerned with contemporary social theory are indebted to Ralf Dahrendorf, among others, for their refutation of the classical Marxian assumption that property ownership alone is the basis of class relations in industrial society. More important, as Dahrendorf points out, is the reality of control and authority within a system, whether these be based on private or public ownership. See Dahrendorf, *Class and Class Conflict in Industrial Society* (Stanford University Press, 1959). Věra Rollová of the Machonin team approached this conception without adopting it. She strongly rejected the "Stalinist" view that ownership of the means of production is the sole determinant of all differentiation, but she did not accept the possible relevance to the subject of classes. *op. cit.*, pp. 353–55.

115. *Literární noviny* (Prague) and *Kultúrny život* (Bratislava) were particularly interesting in this light. For a discussion, see Dušan Hamšík, *Writers against Rulers*, transl. D. Orpington (London: Hutchinson and Co.; New York: Vintage, 1971).

116. Zdeněk Mlynář, *Stát a člověk; Úvahy o politickém řízení za socialismu* (Praha: Svobodné slovo, 1964).

117. Mlynář, "Problems of Political Leadership and the New Economic Mechanism," *World Marxist Review*, vol. 8 (December 1965), p. 81. (Emphasis in the original.) See also several further articles by Mlynář in 1968, esp. *Rudé právo*, February 13; *Práce*, April 13 and June 18; and *Nová mysl*, no. 5, pp. 607–27. The *Nová mysl* article, entitled "Toward a Democratic Political Organization of Society," can be found, in English translation, in Andrew Oxley, Alex Pravda, and Andrew Ritchie, *Czechoslovakia; the Party and the People* (London: Allen Lane, The Penguin Press, 1973), pp. 114–22. For further discussion, see Alex Pravda, "Reform and Change in the Czechoslovak Political System: January–August 1968," *Sage Research Papers in the Social Sciences*, Contemporary European Studies (Beverly Hills and London, 1975), pp. 25–28.

118. Richta and his colleagues at the Academy of Sciences published a massive study, *Civilisace na rozcesti* (Praha: Svoboda, 1966). Excerpts can be found in Remington, *Winter in Prague*, pp. 8–12.

119. Machonin, "Sociální stratifikace v Československu 1967," p. 85.

120. M. Lakatoš, "K niektorým problemom štruktúry našej politickej sústavy," *Právny obzor*, vol. 68 no. 1 (Bratislava, 1965), pp. 26–36, cited from p. 28.

121. *Ibid.*, p. 30.

122. *Ibid.*, pp. 31–33.

123. Lakatoš, "Niektoré problemy socialistickej demokracie z hľadiska postavenia občana v našej spoločnosti," *Právny obzor*, vol. 69 no. 3 (1966), pp. 213–22, cited from p. 220.

124. *Ibid.*

125. Kusin, *Political Grouping,* pp. 211 24 and passim.

126. See Morris Ginsberg, *Sociology* (London: T. Butterworth Ltd., 1934), pp. 40 41, for the earliest use of the term "quasi-groups."

127. Dahrendorf, *op. cit.,* pp. 179ff. Dahrendorf distinguishes conflict groups from others by virtue of their interest in the political relations of domination and subjection.

128. *Mladá fronta,* May 4, 1968. Only "further democratization," a sort of catch-all response, drew a larger percentage of replies (46 percent).

129. Jaroslaw A. Piekalkiewicz, "What the Czechoslovaks Want," *East Europe,* vol. 20 no. 5 (May 1971), p. 7.

130. Drahoš Šmejc, "Jaké volby by veřejnost přivítala," *Reportér,* vol. 4 (May 15, 1969), supplement. Piekalkiewicz has collected a large number of surveys relating to the political party system and published them in his volume, *Public Opinion Polling in Czechoslovakia, 1968 69;* see esp. pp. 153 251.

131. Otto Ulč, "Political Participation in Czechoslovakia," *Journal of Politics,* vol. 333 (May 1971), pp. 430 34. The new leaders of these parties resisted pressures of the rank and file to organize on the factory level, but the pressures were growing steadily stronger. Because these parties did not command very large public followings, however, it would have taken some considerable effort to rejuvenate them as serious political competitors. (See following note.)

132. In a hypothetical election including the KSČ and the two other Czech parties, respondents gave the Communists a plurality of 43 percent, with fully 27 percent uncertain as to how they would vote. Adding a new party to the field drew only 4 percent of the voters away from the Communists, reducing their hypothetical plurality to 39 percent. See Piekalkiewicz, *Public Opinion Polling,* pp. 246 51.

133. *Ibid.,* pp. 252-73.

134. Golan, *Reform Rule,* pp. 155 56.

135. *Ibid.,* 158 61; also Ulč, p. 427.

136. Ulč, pp. 426-38; Golan, 153ff.; Lakatoš, "Možnosti národní fronty," *Kulturní noviny* (Prague), April 5, 1968, p. 8.

137. Golan, *Reform Rule in Czechoslovakia,* pp. 140 44; Skilling, *Czechoslovakia's Unfinished Revolution,* pp. 333 35, 346 63.

138. *Slavic Review, op. cit.;* also *Nationalism, Pluralism, and Schweikism in Czechoslovakia's Political Culture,* pp. 187ff.

139. As Golan, Skilling, and others have shown, the reforms as such were not immediately ended with the occupation. Dubček and his colleagues stayed in office for several months into 1969, and many of the reforms continued to be implemented as well. But the question of interest groups, and certainly of opposition parties, was a dead letter after August 1968.

140. From the Soviets' viewpoint, the impact of the Czechoslovak reforms was particularly irksome in the Ukraine. For a persuasive argument to this effect, see Grey Hodnett and Peter J. Potichnyj, "The Ukraine and the Czechoslovak Crisis," Occasional Paper No. 6, Department of Political Science, Australian National University (Canberra, 1970).

CHAPTER SIX

1. Pye and Verba, *Political Culture and Political Development*, p. 529.
2. The best discussion of the Slovak problem in the twentieth century is to be found in Ľubomír Lipták, *Slovensko v 20. storočí* (Bratislava: Vydavateľstvo politickej literatúry, 1968).
3. It is interesting that the Slovak nationalists were riding a wave that crested approximately five years after the downfall of the Dubček government. No doubt Husák, who had been associated with the nationalists, was largely responsible for their longevity. However, they too fell out of official favor in the mid-seventies, the victims of the same tendency of Communist orthodoxy that had cost the Czech democrats their political careers. By late 1977, the tide had turned so far that nationalistically-oriented Slovak histories were being removed from the shelves of libraries, and there were even rumors that the federal system itself might be reconsidered.
4. It is not only the Allied statesmen of Wilson's day, but modern Western political scientists, too, who have often mistakenly associated the concept of nation automatically with that of state. The hyphenated term "nation-state" is thus used indiscriminately by many theorists of world politics, regardless of whether they are speaking of Japan (a real nation-state), Canada (a binational state), or West Germany (a state based on only part of a nation).
5. The vast majority of political sovereignties in today's world can be described as nation-states only by distorting the meaning of *nation* and disregarding the fact that multiple nations may exist within one state (e.g. the Soviet Union) or that many states have not yet succeeded in developing a single national consciousness from among numerous smaller communities (e.g. the new states of Africa).
6. A world of explanation about Silesia seems appropriate. The old Kingdom of Bohemia at one time included all of Silesia, and this region went over to Habsburg rule along with Bohemia and Moravia in the sixteenth century. Most of the Silesian territory later passed from Viennese control to Frederick II's Prussia (i.e., in 1741). Only a relatively small part of Silesia remained a part of the Habsburg-ruled Bohemian Crownlands thereafter, but this part became Czechoslovak territory in 1918.
7. Masaryk, *The Making of a State* (1927), passim.
8. See, e.g., Elizabeth Wiskemann, *Czechs and Germans,* Second Ed. (London, Toronto and New York, 1967), and J. W. Bruegel, "The Germans in Pre-War Czechoslovakia," in Mamatey and Luža, *A History of the Czechoslovak Republic* (Princeton, 1973), pp. 167–187.
9. The "activist" parties were those who adopted a positive attitude toward the Prague system. These included three parties whose leaders participated in governmental coalitions — the German Agrarian party (in coalition 1926–35), the Christian Socials (1926–29), and the German Social Democrats (1929–35). Prior to the onset of the international crisis of the mid-1930s, these three parties were clearly predominant among the Germans in Czechoslovakia.
10. See the essays by Václav L. Beneš, Victor S. Mamatey, and Piotr S. Wandycz in Mamatey and Luža, *A History of the Czechoslovak Republic 1918–1948,* pp. 39–166, 216–238, passim. Cf. also Robert Paul Magocsi, *The*

Development of National Consciousness in Subcarpathian Rus 1918–1945, Ph.D. Dissertation, Princeton University (Princeton, 1972).

11. Statistics differ with regard to the Magyar population in Czechoslovakia. The Hungarian census of 1910 showed 1,063,000 Magyars in territories that were later transferred to Czechoslovakia. Czechoslovak census takers found only 739,000 Magyars in 1921 and 604,000 in 1930. See Hugh Seton-Watson, *Eastern Europe Between the Wars,* 3rd ed., p. 343 (first two figures), and (third figure) Ludvík Němec, "Solution of the Minorities Problem," in Mamatey and Luža, p. 416n.

12. See Němec, *ibid.,* pp. 416–427.

13. Ústav dějin KSČ, *Dějiny KSČ* (Prague, 1967), p. 199; Juraj Zvara, *Maďarská menšina na Slovensku po roku 1945* (Bratislava: Epocha, 1969), pp. 62–65. The decision to abandon the expulsion of the Magyar minority came about after some considerable tension between Prague and Budapest. The Hungarian government's position was that if Czechoslovakia was to retain the territories where Magyars were living, it must also keep the Magyar inhabitants. The decision to end the policy of expulsion may very well have been made in Moscow, for it satisfied no one. The potentially troublesome Magyar minority remained, and Hungary gave up its claim to the territories.

14. For about ten years beginning in the mid-sixties we saw a flourishing of works on the Slovaks, the history of Czech-Slovak relations, and the role of national dissent in the reform movement. See, e.g., Lipták, *Slovensko v 20. storočí* (1968); Samo Falťan, *Slovenská otázka v Československu* (Bratislava: Vydavateľstvo politickej literatúry, 1968); Jaroslav Barto, *Riešenie vzťahu čechov a slovákov 1944–48* (Bratislava: Epocha, 1968); and Ladislav Lipscher, *K vývinu politickej správy na Slovensku v rokoch 1918–1938* (Bratislava: Vydavateľstvo Slovenskej akadémie vied, 1966). These early books were followed by more historical studies, including a detailed general history comprising the first volume of a new Slovak encyclopedia. See Ján Tibenský et al., *Slovensko,* t. 1: *Dejiny* (Bratislava: Obzor, 1971). See also Butvin's third volume of Kavka, Butvin, Havránek et al., *Dějiny Československa* (Praha, 1964–68). Although many of the studies published at this time were written from a strong nationalistic bias, they represented important new attempts to uncover the realities of Slovakia's past.

For a study in English, see Eugen Steiner, *The Slovak Dilemma* (Cambridge University Press, 1973).

15. See Yeshayahu Jelinek, *The Parish Republic: Hlinka's Slovak People's Party 1939–1945* (Boulder, 1976).

16. G. W. Prothero, *Slovakia,* Handbook No. 3, Historical Section of the Foreign Office (London, n.d.); New Haven, Conn.: Human Relations Area Files, p. 8.

17. Although roads and railroads were built up around Pozsony and other important industrial centers, the farther one moved into the hinterlands the fewer and worse the roads became. *Ibid.,* pp. 23ff.

18. By 1890, 59 percent of Cisleithanian Austria's total industrial production took place in the Czech Crownlands. Source: C. A. Macartney, *The Habsburg Empire 1790–1918* (London: Weidenfeld and Nicolson, 1968), p. 619.

19. One of the cornerstones of the Slovak Republic (1939–45) was its

unabashedly theocratic political culture, so pervasive as to suggest a conscious attempt to distinguish the Slovak state from its secular predecessor. See Jelinek, *op. cit.*

20. Vladimir V. Kusin, "Nationalism and the Reform of Communism in Eastern Europe," unpubl. paper, pp. 7–8.

21. The best-known tract of this sort published in the First Republic was probably that of Ferdinand Peroutka, *Jací jsme* (Praha: Fr. Borový, 1924, 1934). Others included Emanuel Chalupný, *Národní povaha československá* (Praha, 4th ed., 1935); and Jiří Mahen, *Knížka o českém charakteru* (Vyškov: F. Obzina, 1924). For an earlier discussion, see Masaryk, *Česká otázka* (1895, republ. 1969). See also Vladimír Šalda, "Znovu o české otázce," *Svobodné slovo*, August 18, 1968, among other such timely reconsiderations of the Czech national question. Émigré writers have been especially active in more recent self-examination; see, e.g., Pavel Tigrid, "Jací jsme, když je zle," *Svědectví*, vol. 12, no. 46 (1973), pp. 303–19; in the same issue, see Christian Willars, "Znovu: smysl českých dějin," pp. 289–301; and also V. V. Kusin, "The European Context of Czech Political Culture," unpubl.

22. The *humanita* described by Masaryk was, he argued, the driving force of the Czech (and Slovak) national revival, a characteristic personified by all the great men of the nineteenth century. See *Česká otázka, passim.*

23. From Mahen, *Knížka o českém charakteru,* summarized by Zdenek Salzmann, *A Contribution to the Study of Value Orientations among the Czechs and the Slovaks,* Research Report, Department of Anthropology, University of Massachusetts, No. 4 (Amherst: April, 1970), p. 7.

24. Tigrid, "Jací jsme, když je zle," pp. 307–308.

25. Cited by Salzmann, *op. cit.,* p. 5, from Karásek's 1907 essay, "Příspěvek k psychologii českého lidu."

26. Tigrid, *loc. cit.* Also F. Peroutka, *Budování statu,* cited by Tigrid.

27. Peroutka, *Jací jsme* (1934), pp. 17–18. (". . . zaplaneme ale pohasneme . . . lehko pronikneme do hloubky ale nevydržíme tam . . . nás charakterisuje neúplnost, nedomýšlení, a nedopovídání. . . .")

28. Mahen and Chalupný are both cited by Salzmann, pp. 5–7; Chalupný is cited by Tigrid, p. 305n. Chalupný analyzed this trait in terms of a rather questionable link between the Czech language — specifically, pronunciation patterns — and orientations to behavior. Chalupný pointed to the pattern of stress on the initial syllable of all Czech words and argued that this linguistic "anticipation" (*anticipace*) paralleled an anticipatory tendency in Czech behavior, characterizing Czechs as people who venture into projects readily and enthusiastically but then expect positive results to come about in the natural course of events, i.e., they slack off hoping the results will follow by themselves. Thus, Czechs tend "to consider something that has not yet happened as certain, the first step as final and definitive, a probable victory as undisputed." (Tigrid, *loc. cit.*)

29. See my reference to this theme as discussed by Skilling, *supra* (ch. 2).

30. Šalda, "Znovu o české otázce," *Svobodné slovo,* August 18, 1968, p. 1.

31. Tigrid, pp. 312–16; Mahen, cited by Salzmann, p. 7. See my chapter on Švejkism (ch. 8) for a more specific elaboration of Czech non-militancy.

32. Tigrid, pp. 305–07; Tigrid finds these generalizations confirmed by Chalupný.

33. *Ibid.*, p. 309.
34. *Česká otázka,* p. 221.
35. Tigrid, p. 311.
36. *Ibid.*, 308–09. In support, Tigrid cites Chalupný (1936), as well as Karásek's *Gotické duši* (1900).
37. Masaryk, *Česká otázka,* pp. 224–25.
38. Masaryk's word *humanita* has no direct equivalent in English. It contains elements of humanism in its Renaissance sense, that is, a belief in the creative poential of human beings individually and in community; it also connotes humanitarianism in a modern sense, a feeling for the welfare and inviolability of the human person.
39. Edvard Beneš, *Světová válka a naše revoluce,* vol. 2 (Praha: Orbis, 1928), pp. 540–43. Ironically, the same argument was made by Slovak separatists later, often invoking Beneš's line of reasoning. See, e.g., Jozef Kirschbaum, *Náš boj o samostatnosť Slovenska* (Cleveland: Slovenský ústav v Clevelande, 1958), p. 26 and *passim.*
40. K. Kosík, "Iluze a realizmus," *Listy,* vol. 1 (Rome, November 7, 1968), p. 1.
41. Masaryk, *Česká otázka, passim.*
42. Z. Nejedlý, *O smyslu českých dějin* (Praha: Státní nakladatelství politické literatury, 1953), pp. 53–54, from a 1914 essay "Spor o smyslu českých dějin."
43. "Iluze a realizmus," *loc. cit.*
44. *Česká otázka,* pp. 7–8.
45. Tigrid, p. 312.
46. S. Harrison Thomson, *Czechoslovakia in European History,* Second Edition (Princeton: Princeton University Press, 1953), pp. 203–24.
47. See the discussion by J. Butvin in F. Kavka *et al., Dějiny Ceskoslovenska,* vol. 3 (Praha: Státní pedagogická nakladatelství, 1968). See also Peter Brock, *The Slovak National Awakening* (Toronto, 1976).
48. Masaryk's father was a Slovak peasant who married a Moravian woman and lived in Moravia. His mother, it seems, may have had more German blood than Czech, although Masaryk himself considered her to be a Czech. See Thomas D. Marzik, "Masaryk's National Background," in Peter Brock and H. Gordon Skilling, ed., *The Czech Renascence of the Nineteenth Century* (Toronto, 1971), pp. 239–53.
49. *Slovensko,* published by Umělecká beseda (Praha, 1901), cited from the introduction. One of the contributing editors to this volume was the aforementioned Jaroslav Vlček.
50. See, e.g., the articles by P. Križko on history and school system.
51. Karel Kálal, *Spisy slovákofilské* (Praha: Náklad Leopolda Mazáče, 1928), 6 t. Volume 2 of this imposing collection, "Slovenské obrazky," comprises some thirty articles written by Kálal between 1899 and 1922, most of them originally published in *Osvěta.* Kálal's childhood memories of "starý Ondřej" (Old Andrew), the tinker, appear in volume 1. Some Slovak intellectuals of Kálal's day noted his observations on Slovakia with a mixture of amusement and indignation. See, e.g., *Národnie Noviny* No. 61 (May 29, 1902). The present author is indebted to Thomas D. Marzik for having pointed out the role of Kálal.

52. This was not a new idea, either to Masaryk or to Czechs in general. The panslavist argument of Kollár held some lingering appeal among Slovak intellectuals, especially those of the older generation who made up the core of the Martin group. Masaryk, however, rejected panslavism itself as impractical; see *Česká otázka*, pp. 66–69.

53. Cf. Butvin's argument to the contrary in Kavka et al., *Dějiny Československa*, vol. 3, p. 448. Butvin considers Kálal's ideas about Czech-Slovak unity a "reactionary Slavophile orientation" and implies that both Kálal and Masaryk were mainly interested in economic penetration.

54. The radical nationalists of the following generation painted a dark picture of what they called the "Hlasist deviation" of the turn of the century. See, e.g., Joseph Mikus, *Slovakia: A Political History 1918–1950* (Milwaukee: Marquette University Press, 1963), p. xxxii.

55. Falťan, *Slovenská otázka v Československu*, pp. 10–11.

56. Lipták, *Slovensko v 20. storočí*, p. 10ff.

57. For a study of the social origins of these men see Jan Hučko, *Sociálne zloženie a pôvod slovenskej obrodenskej inteligencie* (Bratislava: Vydavateľstvo SAV, 1974).

58. See also table 1, chapter five, for statistics comparing Slovak occupational distribution with that in the Czech lands.

59. Lipták, pp. 10–11.

60. *Ibid.*, pp. 11–12. Also Prothero, *Slovakia*, pp. 44–45.

61. Prothero, *ibid.*, pp. 32–34.

62. Lipták writes: "This illustrative listing (of economic enterprises) cannot negate the backwardness of Slovakia, but . . . Slovakia at the threshold of our century had already crossed many of the barriers associated with this concept today. . . ." *Op. cit.*, p. 12.

63. Prothero, p. 21; also R. W. Seton-Watson, *A History of the Czechs and Slovaks*, reprint ed. (Hamden, Conn.: Archon Books, 1965), pp. 267–68.

64. My sources differ on the exact numbers and dates involved. Prothero reported 1,921 Slovak-language schools in 1869 and 240 in 1912, with a more or less gradual diminution between those two years. (*Ibid.*, p. 20.) Lipták reports 1,115 schools in 1890 and only 241 already by 1905–06. (Lipták, p. 18.)

65. Prothero, *ibid.*

66. According to Lipták, only 14.9 percent of all Slovaks spoke Magyar, and these were mainly inhabitants of ethnically mixed communities. In less integrated areas the percentage was lower: Orava 3.9 percent, Liptov 6.4 percent, Turiec 8.5 percent, Trenčín county 4.2 percent. (Lipták, p. 19.)

67. *Ibid.*, p. 18. At this time Slovaks accounted for approximately ten percent of the population of Hungary. (Lipták admits that these statistics may be inexact, but they are not grossly unrepresentative.)

68. See the interesting discussion of social and family life in Slovakia by Božena Filová in *Ceskoslovenská vlastivěda*, vol. 3 (Praha: Orbis, 1968), pp. 539–54.

69. Rodnick, *The Strangled Democracy*, pp. 132–33.

70. Václav L. Beneš, "Czechoslovak Democracy and Its Problems, 1918–1920," in Mamatey and Luža, *A History of the Czechoslovak Republic*, p. 75. As Beneš has pointed out, the personality syndrome was inherited from a similar tradition in Hungarian politics.

71. Of course, there were some Slovak priests who did not make this distinction and favored a return to Hungarian political jurisdiction after 1919.

72. The relationship between religious and political affiliations will be taken up again in the next chapter.

73. Victor S. Mamatey, "The Establishment of the Republic," in Mamatey and Luža, pp. 8–10; Karel Čapek, *President Masaryk Tells His Story* (New York: G. P. Putnam's Sons, 1935), p. 193.

74. Mamatey (*ibid.*, p. 10) notes that the Slovak Social Democrats were forced to join the Hungarian SDP but, despite the internationalist preferences of the latter, the Slovak SDs maintained their close relations with the Czechs. These continued after 1918.

75. Fifteen Slovaks were killed by Hungarian militiamen and 59 brought to trial for protesting the replacement of their priest, the young Hlinka, with a Magyar. Hlinka himself made a number of speeches in Bohemia and Moravia aimed at stimulating support there and was promptly imprisoned upon his return to Hungary. Lipták, p. 32; Mamatey, p. 9.

76. Lipták, pp. 32–33. Lipták considers the temporary eclipse of the Hlinka group during this time a decisive factor in the subsequent development of national politics, pushing Hlinka to the right and into a position of ideological incompatibility with the others.

77. Mamatey, p. 8.

78. Lipták, pp. 33–37.

79. *Ibid.*, pp. 21–22. Lipták estimates that forty Slovak delegates would have been the rightful proportion if based on population.

80. *Ibid.*, pp. 30, 34.

81. R. W. Seton-Watson. (See discussion in chapter two, p. 74 and fn. 73).

82. Lipták, pp. 45–53. Lipták's estimate of the numbers of Slovak troops seems high but may be accurate.

83. Another factor that stirred the imaginations of the Slovaks was the Russian Revolution. While the Ľudáks looked upon it with some doubts and even horror, the Hlasists and socialists saw in it a cause for hope at a time of increasing antimonarchism and the rise of democracy.

84. A great deal of controversy has ever since surrounded the circumstances of this so-called Declaration of the Slovak Nation (made, like the May decision, in Turčiansky sv. Martin). The controversy concerns a secret clause relating to some form of autonomy for Slovakia, but, as Lipták has put it, there remain to this day "many completely unexplained hypotheses" about that clause. Lipták, p. 78.

85. Mamatey, "The Development of Czechoslovak Democracy, 1920–1938," in Mamatey and Luža, p. 134.

86. For a lengthy list of Slovak nationalists' grievances against the First Republic, see Mikus, *op. cit.*, pp. 16–35.

87. Antonín Štefánek, "Education in Pre-War Hungary and in Slovakia To-Day," in *Slovakia Then and Now*, ed. R. W. Seton-Watson (London: George Allen and Unwin Ltd., and Prague: Orbis, 1931), pp. 137–38.

88. Hodža wrote approvingly of the Czech influx, citing "the great shortage of officials" in Slovakia. See Hodža, "The Political Evolution of Slovakia," in *ibid.*, pp. 85–86. Dérer explained with regard to the juridical profession that, as of 1918, "there were only a few judges in Slovakia who had a decent command

of Slovak, and there was no one who knew Slovak legal terminology, which indeed did not exist, and which had to be created after the revolution on the basis of Czech terminology." Ivan Dérer, *The Unity of the Czechs and Slovaks; Has the Pittsburgh Declaration Been Carried Out?*, Czechoslovak Sources and Documents No. 23 (Prague, 1938), p. 54.

89. Mikus, p. 30.

90. Dérer has pointed to the judicial situation as an example of significant progress. By mid-1937 the judges within the jurisdiction of the Bratislava and Košice High Courts included 227 Slovaks, 211 Czechs, 66 Ruthenes, 75 Magyars, and 50 Germans. *Op. cit.*, p. 55.

91. Milan Strhan, "Živnostenská banka na Slovensku v rokoch 1918–1938," *Historický časopis*, vol. 15, no. 2 (Bratislava, 1967), p. 178.

92. *Ibid.*, pp. 177–218, *passim*.

93. Cf. Kornel Stodola, "Economic Progress," in *Slovakia Then and Now*, pp. 252–67, and Zora P. Pryor, "Czechoslovak Economic Development in the Interwar Period," in Mamatey and Luža, pp. 210–14.

94. Pryor (*ibid.*) notes that employment in most industries was lower in 1930 than in 1921, that employment in large-scale industry in Slovakia by 1937 represented only 8 percent of the country's total, and that by 1932 fewer than 20 percent of Slovak communities had electricity (cf. 60 percent in the Czech lands).

95. Mikus, pp. 30–35. See also Lipták, pp. 109–22, and Falťan, pp. 92–101.

96. The brief political career of Milan R. Štefánik ended tragically in an airplane crash near Bratislava on May 4, 1919. The circumstances surrounding the mishap and Štefánik's evolving political position have been the cause of much controversy. Štefánik, an astronomer living in Paris before 1914, joined the Czechoslovak movement during the war and quickly became the third member of the Masaryk-Beneš-Štefánik triumvirate of politicians-in-exile. Upon liberation Štefánik was named minister of war in the provisional Czechoslovak government. Relatively little was known of his politics, other than his Czechophile sympathies. However, it was rumored that he had developed some major disagreements with Masaryk and Beneš at the Paris Peace Talks concerning the status of Slovakia in the new republic. Some reports of his fatal mishap suggested that the Italian aircraft in which he was riding was shot down as it crossed the border and approached Bratislava. If that was the case, then a further question arises as to whether or not the national colors carried by the aircraft were mistaken for the Hungarian national colors, for the mishap occurred at a time of Hungarian irredentist activities that constituted a genuine danger to Czechoslovakia's southern border. It seems rather farfetched to suggest that either Masaryk or Beneš had conspired to sabotage Štefánik's flight, although it has been circumstantially argued that upon Štefánik's death Beneš found it easier to pursue his plans for winning the Paris peacemakers' consent to a centralized Czechoslovak order. See Horst Glassl, "Die Slowaken und die 'Burg'" in *Die "Burg,"* hrsg. von Karl Bosl, bd. 1 (München und Wien, 1973), pp. 142–43.

97. Lipták, p. 129.

98. Steiner, *The Slovak Dilemma*, pp. 17–26; Falťan, *Slovenská otázka v Československu*, pp. 69–78.

99. Falťan, *ibid.*, p. 77.

100. Lipták, p. 124 ff.

101. Jaroslav Císař and J. Pokorný, *The Czechoslovak Republic* (Prague: Orbis, and London: T. Fisher Unwin Ltd., 1922), p. 18.

102. Lipták, p. 124.

103. Albert Pražák, writing in Císař and Pokorný, *op. cit.*, Appendix D, pp. 204–07.

104. Cited by Lipták, p. 125.

105. Glassl, "Die Slowaken und die 'Burg'," p. 143.

106. In Císař and Pokorný, Appendix C, cited from p. 203.

107. Lipták, 126 ff.

108. Masaryk, *The Making of a State*, p. 209.

109. Štepán Osuský, *Beneš and Slovakia*, transl. Philip J. Anthony (Middletown, Pa.: Jednota Press, 1943), p. 5.

110. Compton Mackenzie, *Dr. Beneš* (London: George G. Harrap and Co. Ltd., 1946), p. 292.

111. O. Janeček, "Československu," in *Střední a jihovýchodní Evropa ve válce a v revoluci*, pp. 98–99.

112. Beneš, *Reč k Slovákom o našej národnej prítomnosti a budúcnosti* (Bratislava: Czechoslovak National Council in Bratislava, 1934), p. 41.

113. Mackenzie, *Dr. Beneš*, p. 286.

114. Beneš, *Masarykovo pojetí ideje národní a problém jednoty československé*, lecture to Šafařík Learned Society (Bratislava: Učená společnost Šafaříkova, 1935, sv. 1), p. 15.

115. Osuský, *Beneš and Slovakia*, p. 5. Karol Sidor reported that the vote by HSĽS representatives in the National Assembly was taken hastily and without time to consider alternatives. Sidor, *Slovenská politika na pôde pražského snemu*, vol. 2, pp. 155–58.

116. Beneš, *Christmas Message 1936*, Czechoslovak Sources and Documents, No. 15 (Prague, 1937), p. 17.

117. Janeček, p. 98.

118. Mackenzie, pp. 285–86.

119. Falťan, p. 76.

120. Mikus, p. 6.

121. Lipták, pp. 126–28.

122. Vavro Šrobár, *Osvobodené Slovensko: pamäti z rokov 1918–1920*, sv. 1 (Praha: Čin, 1928), p. 8.

123. See Šrobár's memoirs, *ibid.*, pp. 97 ff., 187 ff.

124. Václav L. Beneš, "Democracy and Its Problems," p. 76 ff.

125. Dérer, *The Unity of the Czechs and Slovaks*, p. 53.

126. Šrobár noted, for example, that Hodža was among the last supporters of the monarchy before the fall of Austria-Hungary. Šrobár, *Osvobodené Slovensko*, sv. 1, pp. 88 ff.

127. Milan Hodža, "The Political Evolution of Slovakia," in Seton-Watson, ed., *Slovakia Then and Now*, p. 66 ff.

128. Glassl, *op. cit.*, pp. 144–45.

129. Osuský, *Beneš and Slovakia*, p. 19.

130. *Ibid.*

131. Lipták, p. 131.

132. Radio address of February 17, 1945, in Beneš, *Šest let exilu a druhé*

světové války (Praha: Družstevní práce, 1946), p. 255.

133. See Barto, *Riešenie vzťahu čechov a slovákov*, pp. 30–34.

134. Lipták's chapter "Roky bez mena" (*op. cit.*, pp. 284–321), a bold and stinging critique of the Stalin years, cost him his position in the Historical Institute of the Slovak Academy of Sciences.

135. Speech in Bratislava, July 10, 1948, in Gottwald, *Spisy*, vol. 15 (Praha, 1961), p. 46.

136. See Edward Taborsky, *Communism in Czechoslovakia* (1961), pp. 333–39.

137. See Vilém Prečan, ed., *Slovenské národné povstanie: Dokumenty* (Bratislava: VPL, 1965), and also Gustáv Husák, *Svedectvo o slovenskom národnom povstaní*, 2nd ed. (Bratislava: VPL, 1969).

138. "Dva národy v jednej republike," interview with three Slovak historians, *Smena* (Bratislava), Jan. 27, 1968, p. 4; statement of Ján Tibenský.

139. See, e.g., Miroslav Kusý, "Československá politická kríza," *Nová mysl*, no. 11 (Praha: November, 1968), pp. 1315–28.

140. Taborsky, *Communism in Czechoslovakia, loc. cit.*; also Otto Ulč, *Politics in Czechoslovakia* (1974), p. 15.

141. Speech to the Presidium of SNR, Topolčiany, August 27, 1949, in *Spisy*, vol. 15, p. 265.

142. See my discussion, *supra*, ch. 2.

143. Lipták, 322–50; Steiner, *passim;* Dean, *Nationalism and Political Change in Eastern Europe;* Golan, *The Czechoslovak Reform Movement*, pp. 209–30; Kusin, *Political Grouping in the Czechoslovak Reform Movement* (1972), pp. 143–49; Skilling, *Czechoslovakia's Interrupted Revolution*.

144. Lipták, p. 126.

145. Elizabeth Wiskemann, *Czechs and Germans*, 2nd ed. (London and Toronto: Macmillan, and New York: St. Martin's Press, 1967), pp. 121, 267.

CHAPTER SEVEN

1. See the entry of "Janošík" in *Ottův slovník naučný*, vol. 13 (Praha, 1898), pp. 15–16.

2. From a 1921 study by Anton Kompánek, cited in Salzmann, *A Contribution to the Study of Value Orientations*, p. 8.

3. Jurovský's study, in the form of a contribution to the 1943 *Slovenská Vlastiveda*, is cited by Salzmann, *ibid.*, pp. 8–10.

4. Salzmann, *ibid.*, pp. 37–39 and *passim*.

5. *Hospodářské noviny* (Praha), December 24, 1971.

6. Adela Hornová, "Ekonomický vývin Slovenska v podmienkach kapitalismu," in *Slovensko, op. cit.* (1974), pp. 289ff.

7. Vlastislav Bauch, "Ekonomický vývin Slovenska v podmienkach socialistickej výstavby," *ibid.*, p. 334.

8. Jan Verešík, "Geografia sidel: Mestá," *ibid.*, p. 524.

9. *Ibid.*, pp. 532ff.

10. *Ibid.* These six were Banská Štiavnica, Kolárovo, Kremnica, Myjava, Turzovka, and Vrútky.

11. Bauch, p. 334.

12. Ján Verešík, "Vzdelanie obyvateľstva," *ibid.*, pp. 429–30.

13. See Jaroslav Chovanec, Laurinec Káčer, Stanislav Matoušek, and

Rudolf Trella, *ČSSR: Federatívny socialistický štát* (Bratislava: Slovenské pedagogické nakladateľstvo, 1969). See also Golan, *Reform Rule in Czechoslovakia*, 186–99 and *passim;* Ulč, *Politics in Czechoslovakia*, 14–18, 71–72. The federal law of October 27, 1968 is reprinted in Chovanec *et al.,* pp. 95–138.

14. Only in 1968 and thereafter did the "Czech question" receive public attention. Throughout the earlier sixties there was much discussion about the Slovak problem, but it was generally assumed that there was no corollary Czech problem. See, e.g., Dušan Havlíček, "Bratrům čechům," *Kulturní tvorba,* vol. 4, no. 10 (March 10, 1966), p. 3.

15. The ideology of the Slovak Republic is articulated in Štefan Polakovič, *K základom slovenského štátu* (Turčiansky sv. Martin: Matica Slovenská, 1939).

16. In *Nové slovo,* September 24, 1944, reprinted in Husák, *Z bojov o dnešok* (Bratislava: Nakl. Pravda, 1973), pp. 19–22.

17. The Hungarian People's party was formed in protest against a law passed in 1894 requiring civil registration of marriage and permitting divorce for any citizens. It was from this clericalist movement that the Slovak populists emerged, driven first into an alliance with other Slovak nationalists and later into their own party.

18. Kamil Krofta, *Dějiny československé* (Praha, 1946), pp. 736–38.

19. Hlinka, writing in October 1919 from a prison cell in Mírov, Moravia, reflected upon the news he had received from the outside and warned that "in Prague there is a movement to destroy religion, and above all, Catholicism." Andrej Hlinka, *Zápisky z Mírova,* ed. Karol Sidor (Bratislava: Andrej, 1941), cited from p. 44.

20. J. Paučo, ed., *Dr. Jozef Tiso o sebe,* speech in his own defense before the National Court in Bratislava, March 17–18, 1947 (Passaic, N.J.: Slovak Catholic Sokol, 1952), pp. 124–26 and *passim;* also Polakovič, *op. cit.*

21. Jelínek, *The Parish Republic.*

22. Husák's position on this issue is discussed by Golan, *The Czechoslovak Reform Movement,* pp. 196–202.

23. Golan, *ibid.,* pp. 201–02. The use of the German term *Staatsvölker* here is my own. I use it to distinguish Czechs and Slovaks, the protagonists in the "national" conflict, from the Magyar and other "minorities." Among Czechs and Slovaks one sometimes finds references to themselves as the *štátotvorné národy* (loosely, "state-constituting nations"), a concept roughly equivalent to the historical notion of *Staatsvölker.* See, e.g., Anton Hykisch, "Každodennost mladšího bratra," *Plamen,* no. 1 (January 1968), p. 11, where, in the middle of another general argument, Hykisch reminds his readers that the "Czechs and Slovaks are the *štátotvorné národy* of this republic."

24. "The source of our present-day crisis is liberalism, the beginnings of which date back to the eighteenth century, but the consequences of which, both economic and ideological, we are experiencing today and will still be borne by whole [future] generations. Liberalism, in full measure releasing the restraints to egoism and individualism, has essentially poisoned man's righteous love for his nation." Polakovič, *K základom slovenského štátu,* p. 57.

25. Karol Sidor, *Slovenská politika na pôde pražského snemu,* vol. 2, pp. 151–52.

26. Cited from a 1938 article by Polakovič, *Tisova náuka* (Bratislava: Nakladateľstvo HSĽS, 1941), p. 124.

27. Hlinka, *Zápisky z Mírova*, pp. 42–46.

28. This opinion was not always shared by all the members of the HSĽS, some of whom came from Magyarone backgrounds and only gradually left their attachment to Hungary behind them.

29. Mamatey, "The Development of Democracy 1920–1938," in Mamatey and Luža, *A History of the Czechoslovak Republic*, pp. 149–50.

30. Indeed, the situation was so confusing that many Communists in Slovakia joined the Nazis. Documentation on this early phase of the war is elusive, but see Janeček, p. 72, and Steiner, *The Slovak Dilemma*, pp. 45–47.

31. Daniel Rapant, "Slováci v dejínach: Retrospektíva a perspektívy," *Slovenské pohľady*, vol. 83 (April 1967), pp. 28–38. Rapant's hypothetical prognosis was a small part of his general argument concerning the broader meaning of Slovak history.

32. Cited by Sidor, *Slovenská politika*, vol. 1, p. 276.

33. Miroslav Kusý, "Československá politická kríza," *Nová mysl*, no. 11 (November 1968), pp. 1325–26.

34. In June 1918 Masaryk met in Pittsburgh with a group of Slovak-Americans and signed a declaration in support of an independent Czechoslovak state. One of the conditions of the agreement was that Slovakia would receive a fair amount of autonomy, including separate administrative, legislative, and judicial organs. Masaryk was later to back away from the Pittsburgh Agreement, arguing that the document had represented no more than a crude statement of intent and was not legally binding. In the letter of the issue Masaryk was correct: the Pittsburgh Agreement was not a legal document but rather a loose statement of intent. The Ľudáks, however, considered it morally binding and minced no words in saying so. See, e.g., Joseph Mikus, *Slovakia: A Political History*, p. 3 and *passim*.

35. Sidor, *Slovenská politika*, vol. 1, p. 152ff.

36. The Ľudáks' exit from the coalition followed a substantial drop in their electoral tally in the 1929 assembly elections. It also followed the imprisonment of Ľudák (and Magyarone) Vojtech Tuka on charges of sedition, a matter that caused bitter dissension within the Ľudák camp as well as in Prague. See *ibid.*, pp. 337–48.

37. "Pittsburská dohoda," *Ľud*, May 30, 1968, pp. 3–4.

38. Golan, *The Czechoslovak Reform Movement*, pp. 311–23; *id.*, *Reform Rule in Czechoslovakia*, p. 49.

39. Sidor, vol. 1, pp. 81–82, 337ff.; Mikus, pp. 8–13; V. Beneš, "Czechoslovak Democracy and Its Problems 1918–1920," in Mamatey and Luža, pp. 84–85; Theodor Procházka, "The Second Republic, 1938–1939," *ibid.*, pp. 267–68.

40. Particularly disturbing to the Czechoslovaks was the ongoing dispute over the territory of Těšín (Cieszyn, Teschen) along the Polish border. It is possible that Hlinka might have offered to support Poland's claims to the whole territory in return for support on the Slovak issue.

41. See Lipták, *Slovensko v 20. storočí*, pp. 301ff., for a most illuminating and authoritative discussion of the proceedings against the "bourgeois nationalists."

42. For a restatement of these Slovak arguments, see Kirschbaum, *Náš boj o samostatnosť Slovenska* (Cleveland, 1958), pp. 26–30 and *passim*.

348 THE CULTURAL LIMITS OF REVOLUTIONARY POLITICS

43. See Hykisch, "Každodennost mladšího bratra," p. 10.

44. "Not Štúr, but Kollár" was Masaryk's attitude, reflecting his preference for the Czechophile activities of Kollár. See interview with the historian Bohuslav Graca, "Dva národy v jednej republike," *Smena,* January 26, 1968.

45. Mikus, *op. cit.,* from his introduction, p. xxix.

46. L. Štúr, *Das Slawenthum und die Welt der Zukunft* (Bratislava, 1931).

47. Golan, *The Czechoslovak Reform Movement,* pp. 196–98.

48. Wolf Oschlies, "Matica Slovenská," *Orientierungspunkte internationaler Erziehung; Essays und Fallstudien zur vergleichenden Erziehungsforschung,* ed. Hans-Joachim Krause *et al.* (Hamburg: Stiftung Europa-Kolleg, 1973), p. 231.

49. *Ibid.,* pp. 232–33; also Steiner, *The Slovak Dilemma,* p. 152.

50. See, e.g., *Matica slovenská v našich dejínach,* ed. Július Mésároš and Miroslav Kropilák (Bratislava: Vyd. SAV, 1963).

51. Cited by Oschlies, p. 231, from *Kultúrny život.*

52. Novotný reportedly gave an inappropriate speech and later got into an argument with a number of Slovaks about cultural contacts with Slovaks abroad. When he departed, Novotný carelessly left behind his official gift, a collection of rare Slovak books published by the (old) Matica. See Steiner, pp. 151–52.

53. Oschlies, pp. 234–45.

54. Janeček considered the dearth of Catholics in the resistance movement "probably the greatest weakness of the revolution's development in Slovakia. . . ." Janeček, *op. cit.,* p. 112.

55. On the Slovak National Uprising, see Husák, *Svedectvo o slovenskom národnom povstaní* (Bratislava, 1964, 1969); Wolfgang Venohr, *Aufstand für die Tschechoslowakei* (Hamburg: Christian Wegner Verlag, 1969); and Anna Josko, "The Slovak Resistance Movement," in Mamatey and Luža, pp. 372–83. For a massive compendium of documents relating to the Uprising, see Vilém Prečan, ed., *Slovenské národne povstanie: Dokumenty* (Bratislava: Vyd. politickej literatúry, 1965); for a less exhaustive selection of documents, see Venohr, *op. cit.,* pp. 287–369.

56. Golan, *The Czechoslovak Reform Movement,* p. 195.

57. Cited by Oschlies, p. 244.

58. The uniformly lower numbers for 1940 reflect the loss of population accompanying the transfer of territories to Hungary according to the terms of the so-called Vienna Award of November 1938.

59. Czechoslovak Republic, *Statistisches Jahrbuch 1936,* pp. 269–70.

60. On this, see Jelinek, *The Parish Republic.*

61. *Ibid.* Also R. V. Burks, *The Dynamics of Communism in Eastern Europe* (Princeton, 1961), p. 78ff.

62. Mikus, *op. cit.,* pp. 11–12. According to this source, Beneš and Alice Masaryková (Masaryk's daughter) were two of the "dubious" Slovak delegates. It might be added that of the Slovak delegates to the first assembly, only six had had any prior parliamentary experience, because of the exclusive political practices in old Hungary, whereas 55 of the Czech delegates had sat in the Vienna *Reichsrat.* See Ladislav Lipscher, "Klub slovenských poslancov v rokoch 1918–1920," *Historický časopis,* vol. 14, no. 2 (1968), pp. 133–68.

63. *Ibid.,* p. 20. Mikus, like many of the Ľudáks, refused to consider Šrobár

a proper Catholic because of his consistent political association with Protestants of the Czechoslovak persuasion.

64. These and other unreferenced statistics in the ensuing discussion are from my own research drawn from a variety of biographical and general reference sources. In my survey I have included cabinet ministers, heads of parties, and former leaders of the wartime independence movement who continued to play influential, if informal, roles in the counsels of the First Republic.

65. See Hlinka, *Zápisky z Mírova, passim.*

66. V. L. Beneš, "Democracy and Its Problems," in Mamatey and Luža, p. 78.

67. By expanding the data mentioned in fn. 64 (above) to include cabinet-rank officials of the Tiso regime, some interesting correlations of religion and nationalist orientation can be seen. These data show:

18 Catholic nationalists
2 Protestant nationalists
13 Protestant Czechoslovaks
3 Catholic Czechoslovaks.

68. Jörg K. Hoensch, "The Slovak Republic 1939–1945," in Mamatey and Luža, p. 278 n. The lone Protestant in Tiso's cabinet was Ferdinand Čatloš, an army colonel (later general) who served for only six months as minister of national defense. For some time thereafter Čatloš was active in the extreme, pro-German faction of the HSĽS and moved close to the fanatical Hlinka Guards. In 1944, apparently frustrated by his inability to advance within the Tiso regime, he joined the ranks of the government's opposition and went over to the side of the National Uprising. See Anna Josko, "The Slovak Resistance Movement," *ibid.,* p. 374 n.; also the "Čatloš Memorandum" of July 1944, in Prečan, *Slovenské národné povstanie: Dokumenty,* pp. 262–64.

69. Electoral statistics from interwar elections show slightly higher percentage votes in Slovakia than in the Czech lands. This, however, is misleading, as R. V. Burks has shown, for many of the Communist votes came from Magyars and other disgruntled minorities. The percentage of Communist votes in districts primarily inhabited by ethnic Slovaks tended in fact to be considerably lower than the KSČ vote in Bohemia and Moravia. See Burks, *The Dynamics of Communism,* p. 66, 150–51, and 218–19.

70. Lipták, p. 138 ff.

71. *Ibid.,* pp. 140–41 ff. See also Y. Jelinek, "Nationalism in Slovakia and the Communists, 1918–29," *Slavic Review,* vol. 34, no. 1 (March 1975), pp. 65–85.

72. *Ibid.,* p. 140; Mamatey, "The Development of Democracy," p. 120; Steiner, pp. 29, 44; Jelinek, "Nationalism in Slovakia," pp. 80–81.

73. Lipták, pp. 310–11; Golan, *The Czechoslovak Reform Movement,* p. 21.

74. By "Slovak antinationalists" I mean those prominent Slovak Communists who were closely associated with the Novotný regime and opposed to any serious discussion of federalization. In my sample I have included Karol Bacilek, Michal Chudík, Pavol David, Július Ďuriš, Michal Sabolčík, Rudolf Cvik, and Viliam Široký. (Široký is actually of Magyar ethnic stock, but I have included him because his longtime association with the KSS, including partici-

pation in the wartime resistance, put him in a position where he purported to speak for Slovakia.)

75. Only Cvik seems not to have been active in the wartime resistance. (I have not been able to confirm whether or not Cvik was involved.)

76. Regarding individuals' positions on ideological and political issues (aside from those connected to the Slovak national question), I prefer to use the terms "progressive" (favorable to the reforms proposed or discussed in 1968) and "conservative" (hostile to or skeptical of the reforms). This political bifurcation is, of course, a simplification; a moderate position emerged somewhere between the progressives and conservatives, something akin to a radical position appeared on the edge of the progressives, and a tendency toward reaction showed itself on the fringe of the conservative group.

77. See Golan, *Reform Rule*, pp. 218–22 and *passim;* also Pavel Tigrid, *Why Dubček Fell* (London: Macdonald, 1971).

78. Golan, *Reform Rule*, p. 107.

79. On the formation of *Nové slovo*, see Steiner, p. 181; also Robert W. Dean, *Nationalism and Political Change in Eastern Europe; The Slovak Question and the Czechoslovak Reform Movement*, Univ. of Denver Monograph Series in World Affairs, No. 1 (1972–73), pp. 35–37.

80. Steiner, p. 212.

81. Golan, *Reform Rule, passim.*

82. *Ibid.,* p. 296. Public opinion polls taken in Slovakia between August 1968 and the spring of 1969 showed clear and strong preference for Dubček over all other top officials, including Husák.

83. Piekalkiewicz reports that a survey question administered to both Czechs and Slovaks in April showed that 79 percent of Slovak respondents "agreed fully" with the proposition that the relationship between Czechs and Slovaks needed to be put in order, and an additional 15 percent "agreed partially." Among Czechs, 52 percent agreed fully and 31 percent partially. Piekalkiewicz, *Public Opinion Polling in Czechoslovakia*, p. 111.

84. My own conversations with a limited sampling of Czechs on this matter are supported by Piekalkiewicz, *ibid.,* p. 340 n.

85. L. Lipták, "Demokratická federace," *Mladá fronta,* April 13, 1968, p. 2.

86. For a good discussion of this comparison between Czech and Slovak factions in the post-invasion period, see Juraj Charvát, "Demokratisace a Slovensko," *Reportér,* vol. 4, no. 11 (March 20, 1969), p. 9.

87. Rudolf Trella and Jaroslav Chovanec, *Nové štátoprávne usporiadanie ČSSR* (Bratislava: Smena, 1971), pp. 150–60. The authors suggest a need for three separate constitutions: one for the Federal Republic, one for the Czech and one for the Slovak Republic.

88. See the delineation of responsibilities in paragraphs 7–28 of the Constitutional Law No. 143 in Chovanec, Káčer, Matoušek, and Trella, *ČSSR: Federatívny socialistický štát* (Bratislava, 1969), pp. 101–08.

89. Dean, *Nationalism and Political Change,* p. 41 ff.; Ulč, *Politics in Czechoslovakia,* p. 17.

90. Dean, *ibid.* Previously, every ministry headed by a Czech was to be balanced by the appointment of a Slovak state secretary (and vice versa).

91. V. I. Lenin, *On Proletarian Internationalism* (Moscow: Progress Publishers, 1967), pp. 56–57, 74–81, 86–89, and *passim.*

CHAPTER EIGHT

1. The Communist party, outlawed in 1938, did not cooperate with the other resistance groups until the German attack on the Soviet Union in 1941. See Jiri Horak, *The Czechoslovak Social Democratic Party 1938–45,* pp. 164–76; also Vojtech Mastny, *The Czechs under Nazi Rule: The Failure of National Resistance 1939–1942* (New York and London: Columbia University Press, 1971), pp. 145–55.

2. *Meldungen aus dem Reich; Auswahl aus den geheimen Lageberichten des Sicherheitsdienstes der SS 1939–1944,* hrsg. von Heinz Boberach (Neuwied und Berlin: Luchterhand, 1965), p. 341n.

3. Mastny, *op. cit.,* pp. 207–23.

4. O. Janeček, "Československo," in *Střední a jihovýchodní Evropa* (1969), p. 118.

5. On the events of 1848 in Bohemia, see Stanley Z. Pech, *The Czech Revolution of 1848* (Chapel Hill: University of North Carolina Press, 1969); for documentation of the revolt in Slovakia, see Daniel Rapant, *Slovenské povstanie roku 1848–49; Dejíny a dokumenty,* 5v. (Martin: Matica Slovenská, 1937–72). For some rather piecemeal discussions of the activities of the Czechoslovak Legions, see Masaryk, *The Making of a State,* pp. 169–200, and Ferdinand Peroutka, *Budování státu,* vol. 1 (Praha, 1933), pp. 286–316.

6. R. W. Seton-Watson, *Masaryk in England* (London and New York: Macmillan, 1943), p. 80. The reader may feel justified in questioning my use of the term "collaborationism" in this sense, since the people under discussion were in support of their ruler, the Emperor. Their position is analogous to that of the Tories during the American Revolutionary War, who chose to side with the King at a time when the tide of opinion among their fellow colonists had turned against the Empire.

7. This sense of guilt is remarkably portrayed in several literary and cinematic works of the 1960s, especially the films *The Shop on Main Street* and *The Fifth Horseman Is Fear.*

8. Cf. Tigrid, *Why Dubček Fell,* pp. 99–167, and Skilling, *Czechoslovakia's Interrupted Revolution,* pp. 813–23.

9. This author will admit to having been discouraged by several colleagues from using the term "Švejkism" on the grounds that it oversimplifies or demeans the Czechs' attempts to deal with crises. On the other hand, a number of scholars — and the majority of Czech-born scholars with whom the author has consulted — have offered words of encouragement.

10. All the references will be to the two following editions: *Osudy dobrého vojáka Švejka za světové války,* 2 v. (Praha: KLHU, 1960), hereafter abbreviated as *Osudy;* and *The Good Soldier Švejk and His Fortunes in the World War,* transl. Cecil Parrott (New York: Thomas Y. Crowell Co., 1974), hereafter *Švejk.*

11. *Osudy,* vol. 1, pp. 406–07; *Švejk,* p. 418.

12. *Osudy,* vol. 1, pp. 69–70; *Švejk,* pp. 62–63.

13. *Osudy,* vol. 1, p. 208; *Švejk,* pp. 207–08.

14. *Osudy,* vol. 1, p. 142; *Švejk,* p. 139.

15. *Osudy,* vol. 1, p. 37; *Švejk,* p. 31.

16. *Osudy,* vol. 1, p. 204; *Švejk,* p. 201.

17. *Osudy,* vol. 1, p. 214; *Švejk,* p. 213.

18. *Osudy,* vol. 1, pp. 98–99; *Švejk,* p. 95.

19. Emanuel Frynta, *Hašek, the Creator of Švejk* (Prague and Brno: Artia, 1965), p. 110.

20. *Ottův slovník naučný nové doby: Dodatky,* vol. 2, part 2 (Praha, 1933), p. 1042.

21. *Ibid.,* p. 1041; *Bol'shaia sovetskaia entsiklopediia,* vol. 10 (Moskva, 1952), p. 279. Hereafter, *BSE.*

22. For a good chronological survey of Czech literary critics' evolving views on Hašek and *Švejk,* see Pavel Petr, *Hašeks "Schwejk" in Deutschland: Neue Beiträge zur Literaturwissenschaft,* vol. 19 (Berlin, 1963), pp. 35–60. Cf. Frynta, p. 29, who suggests that Hašek was not highly regarded in his own country until after World War II. *BSE* (p. 279) reports that *The Good Soldier Švejk* was banned from classrooms and military libraries in interwar Czechoslovakia.

23. Petr, pp. 36–41 ff.

24. *Ibid.,* pp. 36–37. Also, A. Pražák in Karel Čapek et al., *At the Crossroads of Europe: A Historical Outline of the Democratic Idea in Czechoslovakia* (Prague: Pen Club, 1938), p. 222.

25. Cited by Petr, p. 40.

26. *Ibid.,* p. 42.

27. *Ibid.,* pp. 44–46.

28. *BSE.* Also I. Bernstein, *"Pokhozhdeniia bravogo soldata Shveika" Iaroslava Gasheka* (Moskva, 1971).

29. P. Bogatyreva, from translator's introduction to Ia. Gashek, *Pokhozhdeniia bravogo soldata Shveika* (Moskva, 1967), p. 19.

30. Petr, pp. 143–76.

31. Milan Jankovič, *Umělecká pravdivost Haškova Švejka* (Praha, 1960), p. 46.

32. *Ibid.,* p. 52.

33. Cf. Frynta, pp. 105–06.

34. *Ibid.,* p. 75.

35. Such were the opinions of Pražák, F. X. Šalda, and Karel Poláček, all illustrious bourgeois luminaries of the 1930s. Čapek, *loc. cit.;* Petr, p. 47.

36. See, e.g., the views of the bourgeois poet Viktor Dyk and the Marxist historian Zdeněk Nejedlý, in Petr, pp. 43–44, 56. Nejedlý, writing after 1945, felt that the horrible experience with Hitler had rendered the humorous idyll of Švejk inappropriate to the times.

37. Cf. the following comment on Švejkism:

Only a superficial reader of the famous World War I novel by Jaroslav Hašek can consider the behavior of its hero a form of resistance. In reality, "Švejkism," the ostensibly zealous though skeptical compliance often typical in repressive societies, was little more than the sly opportunism of the "little man" — which, however, extended to the highest ranks. — Mastny, *op. cit.,* p. 160.

Without wishing to join in a polemical exchange, especially in the absence of any further elaboration on Mastny's part in the above-cited passage, I should simply like to add that I believe his argument misses the point.

38. Frynta, pp. 93–103.

39. *Ibid.*, pp. 110–11.

40. And then there were the streetcar conductors in Prague during the German occupation who purposely mispronounced the street names they were required to announce in German, thereby causing great mirth among their passengers. In Jiří Hronek, *Volcano under Hitler* (London, 1941), p. 47.

41. George F. Kennan, *From Prague after Munich* (Princeton, 1968), pp. 117–18.

42. *Ibid.*, p. 118.

43. *The New York Times,* August 26, 1968, p. 16.

44. Many of these witticisms are shown in the documentary film shot by Czech cameramen and circulated in the West under the title *Seven Days to Remember*.

45. Frynta, p. 94.

46. Kennan, p. 115.

47. Josef Josten, "Kampf ohne Waffen; der passive Widerstand in der Tschechoslowakei vom 21. August 1968 bis zum Herbst 1972," *Beiträge zur Konflikt Forschung,* no. 4 (Köln, 1972), p. 142.

48. *"Svoboda" — Die Presse in der Tschechoslowakei 1968* (Zürich: Internationale Presseinstitut, 1969), p. 128ff.; Alan Levy, "The Short, Happy Life of Prague's Free Press," *The New York Times Magazine,* September 8, 1968, pp. 34–35+; Sláva Volný, "The Saga of Czechoslovak Broadcasting," *East Europe,* vol. 17, no. 12 (December 1968), pp. 10–16.

49. *The New York Times,* August 25, 1968, p. 36.

50. Hronek, *op. cit.,* pp. 38–44, 67–74. A fictional portrayal of railway sabotage from the Nazi era is to be seen in Jiří Menzel's film *Closely Watched Trains.*

51. *The Czech Black Book,* prepared by the Institute of History of the Czechoslovak Academy of Sciences, ed. Robert Littell (New York, Washington, and London: Praeger, 1969), pp. 242–43. Westerners seized upon the Švejk image immediately, seeing in it an easy cliché to describe the Czech national character. The cover of *East Europe,* vol. 17, no. 10 (October 1968) featured one of Josef Lada's famous cartoon drawings of the good soldier, and Harry Schwartz's early book about the events of 1968, *Prague's 200 Days* (New York: Praeger, 1969), included a chapter entitled "The Schweikism of Autumn."

52. Masaryk, *The Making of a State,* p. 73.

53. Quoted in R. W. Seton-Watson, *Masaryk in England,* p. 13.

54. *Why Dubček Fell,* Chapter 1.

55. My use of the term revolution to refer to the events of 1968 thus reflects a rather hesitant agreement with the general thesis of Skilling, q.v.

56. See Stanley Z. Pech, "Passive Resistance of the Czechs, 1863–1879," *Slavonic and East European Review,* vol. 36, no. 87 (June 1958), pp. 434–52.

57. See, e.g., the announcement of the government's capitulation made by Prime Minister Syrový, especially his reference to the alternative of "making a desperate and hopeless defense. . . ." In Hubert Ripka, *Munich: Before and After* (New York: Howard Fertig, 1969), p. 232.

58. Beneš, *Memoirs: From Munich to New War and New Victory,* tr. Godfrey Lias (London: Geo. Allen and Unwin Ltd., 1954), pp. 50, 273–75. Cf. Compton Mackenzie, *Dr. Beneš* (London: George G. Harrap and Co. Ltd., 1946), pp. 265, 314.

59. In May 1946, a survey asking Czechs to name those personalities in public life who enjoyed their greatest confidence revealed that 80 percent readily named Beneš. In Č. Adamec, B. Pospíšil, and M. Tesář, *What's Your Opinion? — A Year's Survey of Public Opinion in Czechoslovakia* (Prague: Orbis, 1947), p. 15.

60. Ladislav K. Feierabend, *Beneš mezi Washingtonem a Moskvou,* vol. I of personal memoirs (Washington, 1866, by the author), p. 106ff.; Beneš, *Memoirs,* pp. 268–73.

61. Feierabend, *ibid.,* pp. 92, 98–99; Mackenzie, *Dr. Beneš,* pp. 301–05. Beneš, aware of the potential for conflict between the USSR and the West, believed in a convergence theory. He thought that the USSR would evolve politically so as to resemble Western democracies while retaining its socialist economy, and he saw Czechoslovakia emerging as a "bridge" between East and West.

62. Vlastislav Chalupa, *Communism in a Free Society: Czechoslovakia 1945–1948* (Chicago: Czechoslovak Foreign Institute in Exile, 1958), pp. 404–44; Pavel Tigrid, "The Prague Coup of 1948: The Elegant Takeover," in Thomas T. Hammond, ed., *The Anatomy of Communist Takeovers* (New Haven and London: Yale University Press, 1975), pp. 399–432.

63. For biographical studies of Dubček, see Tigrid, *op. cit.,* pp. 9–20 and, especially, William Shawcross, *Dubček* (London: Weidenfeld and Nicolson, 1970).

64. Numerous surveys taken in 1968 showed Dubček's personal popularity to be consistently high in both halves of the republic. These are reported in Jaroslaw Piekalkiewicz, *Public Opinion Polling in Czechoslovakia.*

65. Reported by Tigrid, p. 13.

66. Rumors to this effect were finally confirmed several years later when Dubček's colleague Josef Smrkovský, in an interview by Davide Lajolo of the Italian leftist newspaper *Giorni — Vie nuovo,* related the events that transpired during the bizarre events of the abduction. The interview was published in the above-mentioned paper and in *Der Spiegel,* vol. 29, no. 9 (February 24, 1975), pp. 82–93.

67. Tigrid, pp. 19–20; Shawcross, pp. 131–35.

68. Interview, *Rudé právo,* April 11, 1968, pp. 1–2.

69. *Ibid.*

70. Speech to West Slovakian party conference, Bratislava, as reported in *Rudé právo,* April 21, 1968, p. 2; cf. *The New York Times,* April 1, 1968, p. 2.

71. *Rudé právo,* June 28, 1968, p. 3.

72. For example, several radio commentators expressed open doubts about the outcome of Dubček's talks with Brezhnev in Moscow early in May. See the coverage in U.S. Foreign Broadcast Information Service, *Daily Reports: Czechoslovakia,* May 8, 1968.

73. Smrkovský interview, as reported in *Der Spiegel.* Smrkovský reported that upon the news of the invasion Dubček, along with Černík, "broke down" and "was in a state of consternation." (Page 82.)

74. Littell, ed., *The Czech Black Book,* pp. 31, 249–56. Dubček reacted to the occupation with shock and resignatiòn. In an interesting contrast Smrkovský, according to his own report, reacted with fury and indignation — angrily telephoning Soviet Ambassador Chervonenko and assigning him full

responsibility for the invasion, speaking sarcastically to Brezhnev and Kosygin upon his arrival in Moscow, refusing to have a drink in the Kremlin with other bloc leaders. When told (incorrectly) that he and his colleagues would have to face an alleged "revolutionary tribunal" headed by Alois Indra, Smrkovský exploded with wrath and had to be calmed by Dubček. (*Spiegel*, pp. 84, 86, 91.)

75. A lengthy summary of the letter was printed in *The New York Times*, April 13, 14, and 15, 1975.

76. Jan F. Triska, "Messages from Czechoslovakia," *Problems of Communism*, vol. 24, no. 6 (November–December 1975), pp. 26–42.

77. See H. Gordon Skilling, "Stalinism and Czechoslovak Political Culture," in Robert C. Tucker, ed., *Stalinism and Communist Political Culture*.

78. *Ibid.* Cf. a similar expression (cited by Skilling as well) offered by the Pelikán Commission, investigating the purge trials.

79. One common joke: In a worker's state a worker has to be strong and stupid, a party worker stupid and loyal, and the First Secretary of the Party a blithering idiot.

80. See the discussion in my introductory chapter, above.

81. A 1968 cartoon in *Dikobraz* showed a bureaucrat explaining to one of his colleagues, "Thanks to the continuous development of socialism, we became a developing country."

82. See discussion in chapter one, above.

83. Leon Festinger, *A Theory of Cognitive Dissonance* (Stanford, 1957); also Jack W. Brehm and Arthur R. Cohen, *Explorations in Cognitive Dissonance* (New York, London, and Sydney: John Wiley and Sons Inc., 1962), p. 4.

84. The author has noted with interest the reactions of American audiences to Lina Wertmüller's film *Seven Beauties*. The film graphically and horrifyingly depicts the moral depravity to which an Italian defector, imprisoned in a Nazi concentration camp, is driven in order to survive.

85. Some, such as the noted author Bohumil Hrabal, have undergone self-criticism and been readmitted to the Writers' Union and other official circles, but they are greatly compromised and as yet have not regained their prominence as spokesmen of society.

86. See, among other Western coverage, Vilém Prečan, "Czechs: Still in the Grip of the Graveyard," *The Times* (London), April 13, 1977.

87. As this manuscript was being prepared for copy editing, the author learned that potential opposition forces within the KSČ were beginning to jockey for position. The regime's nervousness about the opposition, and about the remnants of the Charter 77 group as well, caused it to continue tightening its control over society. The outcome of this tense situation was not predictable, and despite some observers' convictions that changes were in the making, on the surface nothing was apparent.

CONCLUSIONS

1. See footnotes 3–4 to the introductory chapter of this book.

2. Cf. Richard Rose, "England: A Traditionally Modern Political Culture," in Pye and Verba, *Political Culture and Political Development*, pp. 100–05.

3. Cf. Kenneth Jowitt's reference to congruences between the ideological and organization format of a Marxist-Leninist system and the "community" political culture. Jowitt, "An Organizational Approach to the Study of Political Culture in Marxist-Leninist Systems," *American Political Science Review*, vol. 68 no. 3 (September 1974), pp. 1177–78.

4. For a strong and succinct statement of this relationship, see Terry Eagleton, *Marxism and Literary Criticism* (Berkeley and Los Angeles: University of California Press, 1976), pp. 3ff. Cf. Henri Arvon, *Marxist Esthetics*, transl. Helen Lane (Ithaca: Cornell University Press, 1973), pp. 24ff.

5. On this, see Frances Fitzgerald, *Fire in the Lake: the Vietnamese and the Americans in Vietnam* (Boston: Little, Brown and Co., 1972).

6. Tigrid, "Jací jsme, když je zle," *Svědectví, vol. 12 no. 46* (1973), pp. 303–19.

7. See p. 236.

8. Willars, "Znovu: Smysl českých dějin," *Svědectví*, vol. 12 no. 46 (1973), pp. 289–301, cited from p. 295.

9. For some propositions about the likely effectiveness of small-state strategies under the pressure of great powers, see Annette Baker Fox, *The Power of Small States; Diplomacy in World War II* (Chicago: The University of Chicago Press, 1959), pp. 183–85.

10. On this, see Willars, p. 300.

11. Ulč, *Politics in Czechoslovakia*, p. 146.

12. Kusin, *The Intellectual Origins of the Prague Spring*, p. 1.

13. Cited in Hamšík, *Writers Against Rulers*, p. 197.

14. *Ibid.*, p. 187.

15. For a discussion of a compromise plan proposed a few years ago by penitent reformers and authored by Zdeněk Mlynář, see Vladimir V. Kusin, "Czechoslovakia: A New Analysis," in *Soviet Analyst*, vol. 4 no. 15 (July 7, 1975), pp. 4–6.

Index

Alcoholism, 31–32, 305.
Almond, Gabriel A., 3, 10, 299, 300.
Apperception, 4, 134, 277.
Aspaturian, Vernon V., 325.

Barghoorn, Frederick C., 78, 79, 299.
Beneš, Edvard, 57, 58, 62, 77, 85–88,
   95, 103, 106–07, 131, 147, 151,
   179–80, 181, 186, 189–91, 209–10,
   213, 216, 231, 271–74, 309, 348,
   354.
Biľak, Vasil, 45, 244, 245, 274.
Brecht, Bertolt, 262–63.
Brethren (*Jednota bratrská*), 70, 71,
   185, 186.
Brezhnev, Leonid I., 44, 265, 275.
Brezhnev Doctrine, 325, 326.
Brodský, Jaroslav, 265.
Brown, Archie H., 299, 300, 302, 317.
Brown, Kent N., 127.
Brzezinski, Zbigniew K., 322, 324.
Burks, R. V., 108, 324.

Čapek, Karel, 60, 67, 157.
Chalupný, Emanuel, 187, 339.
Charles IV, 62, 190.
Charter 77, 25, 26, 34–35, 39, 45, 305.
Chelčický, Petr, 60, 71, 186, 232, 315.
Clementis, Vlado, 214, 215, 242.
Collaboration, 57, 253, 255–56, 265.
Comenius (Jan Amos Komenský),
   60, 204, 232.
Cominform, 59, 107.
Comintern, 93, 97.
Communist Party of Czechoslovakia
   (KSČ), 51, 78, 79, 88, 89 ff., 107 ff.,
   154, 155, 165, 168, 171, 174, 228,
   236, 241 ff.; 351;
_____basis of support, 58, 89, 96,
   102–08 *passim,* 147–48, 172, 286,
   288, 295, 336;
_____beginnings, 92–93, 147;
_____"Bolshevization" of, 94–96;
_____and T. G. Masaryk, 61, 66–67,
   314;

_____and the national question, 178,
   182, 213–16, 242–50 *passim;*
_____and national traditions, 59–61,
   68, 95, 99–100, 232–36, 250–51,
   278, 284–85, 294;
_____reformist tendencies in (1920s–
   30s), 93–97, 321;
_____reformist and opposition forces
   in (1960s–70s), 155 ff., 244–45, 276,
   281, 331, 355;
_____in Second World War, 103,
   117–18, 323;
_____takeover of power (1948), 58,
   101 ff., 214, 272–74.
Communist Party of Slovakia (KSS),
   98, 102–04, 108, 117, 214, 228,
   242 ff., 248, 349.
Crime, 30, 36–38.
Culture, 4–8;
_____and political culture, 5, 7–8.
_____and behavior, 6, 300–01.
Cvekl, Jiří, 158, 161, 167.
Czechoslovak Republic:
_____First, 54, 62–69 *passim,* 77, 86,
   174, 179–81, 186, 187, 191, 232,
   233, 252, 288, 312, 326; authoritarian subcultures in, 81, 84, 88 ff.;
   Communism in, 92 ff., 244; Czech
   domination of, 85, 87; foreign influence in, 82; political parties in,
   135–37, 146, 147–48, 199, 201; Slovaks in, 199, 204 ff., 216, 225, 227–
   28, 231, 237 ff.;
_____Second, 153, 213;
_____Third, 55, 82, 102, 154, 213.
Czechoslovak Union of Youth
   (ČSM), 22, 93, 158.
Czechoslovak Writers' Union, 155,
   157, 158, 168, 331.
Czechoslovakism, 75, 87, 89, 149,
   178, 183, 185, 191–92, 194 ff., 200 ff.,
   216–17, 239.

"Dacha mania," see Holiday cottages.

————and pluralism, 134–35, 175;
————and political symbols, 284, 288;
————and revolution, 1–2, 287;
————and subcultures, see Subcultures.
Political socialization, 5, 9, 19, 21–23, 35, 41–42, 44, 131.
"Prague Spring" (1968), 22, 25–26, 35–36, 42–43, 50–52, 59, 62, 63, 76–77, 82, 85, 128, 130–31, 136, 155ff., 171ff., 178, 230, 234, 244–48, 274–78 passim, 284, 286, 287, 292, 294, 298, 304;
————and Warsaw-Pact intervention, 25, 43, 50, 54, 63, 173–74, 189, 234, 244–46, 252, 256, 265–68, 275, 291.
Praxis group, 91.
Proletarian internationalism, 60, 126, 178, 250.
Pye, Lucian W., 3, 10, 299, 302.

Rapant, Daniel, 228, 282.
Rázus, Martin, 199, 201, 204, 236, 240.
Religion, 39, 60–62, 70–72, 85–86, 184, 185, 190, 198, 200, 225ff., 312.
Resistance, 253, 254, 277–78;
————during First World War, 253;
————during Second World War, 57, 58, 253–55;
————to invasion of 1968, 267, 274;
————passive, 253, 261, 265–67, 269.
Revolution, 9–10, 101–02, 269, 270, 287;
————Marx and Lenin on, 17;
————in Czechoslovakia, 11, 50, 58, 61, 159, 161–62, 250, 270, 293–94;
————in the USSR, 17–20;
————and nationalism, 226–27;
————of 1848, 144, 255.
Richta, Radovan, 156, 168–69, 335.
Rosenau, James N., 12, 302.

Šafárik (Šafařík), P. J., 193, 201, 239.
Salzmann, Zdeněk, 220, 339.
Sartre, Jean-Paul, 330.
Second World War, 57–58, 97–98, 102–03, 117, 182, 265–68.
Sidor, Karol, 227, 313, 320, 344.
Šik, Ota, 156, 170, 245, 335.
Skilling, H. Gordon, 277, 304, 309, 312, 317, 318, 319, 321, 322, 336, 353.
Slovak National Uprising (1944), 57, 63, 103, 104, 213, 214, 224, 234–36, 242, 253, 255, 277, 294, 349.
Slovak People's Party (HSĽS), 88, 89, 149, 150, 199–201, 206, 224, 227ff., 235, 236ff.
Slovak Republic (1939–45), 57–58, 182, 199, 224–26, 236, 295.
Šmeral, Bohumír, 93.
Smrkovský, Josef, 42, 245, 274, 354.
Social Democratic Party, 67, 89, 92–96 passim, 102–03, 105, 137, 146–50 passim, 154, 155, 172, 200–04 passim, 310, 322, 323, 342.
Social differentiation:
————under capitalism, 133–38, 140 ff.;
————under socialism, 153, 158ff.;
————and political pluralism, 133–35, 144ff., 166–67, 171, 173, 174.
————and political power, 165, 166 ff.;
————and stratification, 159–60, 162–65, 334.
Socialist Union of Youth (SSM), 22.
Solomon, Richard H., 299.
Soviet Army, 103, 105, 106, 268.
Soviet Union, 43–44, 50, 55, 63, 78–82, 94, 98, 115–17, 235, 246, 250, 272–73, 279, 293, 297–98, 309, 354;
————and the East European Empire, 58–59, 83, 85, 99–100, 101, 106–07, 121ff.
Šrobár, Vavro, 152, 194, 200, 201, 206, 211, 233, 240, 330, 348.
Stalin, J. V., 8, 9, 18–20, 78, 79, 83, 100, 106, 107, 181, 228, 273, 287.
Stalinism, 59–61, 84, 155, 159, 178, 187, 277–78, 286;
————and destalinization, 61, 99;
————purges, 98–99, 214, 231, 235, 242.
Štefánik, Milan R., 152, 179–80, 200, 206.
Steiner, Eugen, 207, 338.
Štrougal, Ľubomír, 26–28, 307.
Štúr, Ľudovít, 60, 63, 74, 75, 193, 204, 232–34, 348.
Subcultures, 81, 102, 283;
————as basis of authoritarian politics, 83, 85, 88ff., 175;
————Communists as, 80, 84, 89, 100, 101, 107ff., 119–20, 123, 128, 284, 293;
————Slovak nationalist, 89, 131.
Švejk, Josef, see Hašek, Jaroslav.